THE LAST WARRIOR

THE LAST
WARRIOR

ANDREW MARSHALL AND THE SHAPING
OF MODERN AMERICAN DEFENSE STRATEGY

ANDREW KREPINEVICH AND **BARRY WATTS**

FOREWORD BY ROBERT M. GATES

BASIC BOOKS
A Member of the Perseus Books Group
New York

Published by Basic Books,
A Member of the Perseus Books Group

Books published by Basic Books are available at special discounts for bulk purchases in the United States by corporations, institutions, and other organizations. For more information, please contact the Special Markets Department at the Perseus Books Group, 2300 Chestnut Street, Suite 200, Philadelphia, PA 19103, or call (800) 810-4145, ext. 5000, or e-mail special.markets@perseusbooks.com.

Set in 10.75 point Adobe Caslon Pro

Krepinevich, Andrew F.
    The last warrior : Andrew Marshall and the shaping of modern American defense strategy / Andrew Krepinevich and Barry Watts. — First edition.
        pages   cm.
    Includes bibliographical references and index.
    ISBN 978-0-465-03000-2 (hardcover) — ISBN 978-0-465-08071-7 (e-book)
1. Marshall, Andrew W., 1921– 2. United States—Military policy. 3. United States. Department of Defense. Director of Net Assessment—Biography. 4. United States. Department of Defense—Officials and employees—Biography. 5. Rand Corporation—Biography. 6. Military planning—United States—History—20th century. 7. Military planning—United States—History—21st century. 8. United States—Foreign relations. 9. Strategy. 10. Cold War. I. Watts, Barry. II. Title. III. Title: Andrew Marshall and the shaping of modern American defense strategy.
UA23.K77622 2014
355'.033573—dc23   2014024139

10 9 8 7 6 5 4 3 2 1

To
Andrew W. Marshall
and in Memory of
James R. Schlesinger
The Fathers of Net Assessment

CONTENTS

FIGURES

FOREWORD

This book chronicles the life of a remarkable, but little-known nonagenarian: Andrew Marshall, who has served every defense secretary extending back to James Schlesinger's tenure during the Nixon administration. The book's authors, Andrew Krepinevich and Barry Watts, are well qualified to tell Marshall's story. Both have known and worked for Marshall for some three decades; Krepinevich also served on the Defense Policy Board during my tenure as secretary of defense.

The authors describe the book as Marshall's intellectual biography. It is that, and more. It offers a unique perspective on the history of the Cold War, as well as the quarter century that has passed since the Berlin Wall's fall.

In the course of their book, Krepinevich and Watts introduce us to Marshall's groundbreaking work on organizational theory, which came to have a profound influence on our understanding of the Soviet leadership's decision-making process. His influence was revealed in Roberta Wohlstetter's *Pearl Harbor: Warning and Decision*, and Graham Allison's *Essence of Decision*. Both of these works greatly changed the way in which we viewed the role of intelligence, our ability to achieve early warning of an attack, and our capacity for effective deterrence. Both authors cited Marshall as the inspiration for their work.

In the late 1960s, during his second decade on the staff at the RAND Corporation, Marshall began his effort to address the limitations of systems analysis, while also looking for ways to improve the United States' ability to craft better strategies in what had become a long-term competition with the Soviet Union. The result was his analytic methodology known as "net assessment." It only took a few years before an Office of Net Assessment was established at the Pentagon, with Marshall as its head.

Thanks to its charter to think innovatively on matters of strategic importance, during its forty-one years existence the Office of Net Assessment (which is to say, Marshall himself) has consistently identified emerging challenges and opportunities that required the attention of the Defense Department's senior leadership. For example, in the early 1970s the CIA estimated the burden Soviet defense spending placed on the USSR's economy to be 6 or 7 percent. Marshall's independent assessment of the Soviet defense burden led the CIA to double its estimate. This led to a fundamental rethinking of our long-term competitive position in the Cold War. It convinced a number of key senior leaders that it would be difficult for the Soviets to sustain this level of effort over the long term. Put another way, it suggested that time was on our side. A decade later, Marshall was proved right.

Later, Marshall's development of "competitive" or cost-imposing strategies as a way of imposing disproportionate costs on America's enemies helped offset declining defense budgets toward the latter half of the 1980s. The concept was simple, yet profound. Instead of constantly looking for ways to respond to Soviet threats, Marshall argued, we should also look for opportunities to undermine the value of their military investments. Beginning in the late 1970s, in looking at the Soviet military's heavy investment in submarines, Marshall suggested we exploit our advantages in quieting technology and in undersea sensors to enable our submarines to avoid detection while also enhancing our ability to detect Soviet subs. In the wake of the Carter administration's cancelling of the B-1 bomber, Marshall strongly urged then defense secretary Harold Brown to "stay in the bomber business" even though the Soviets had no effective defense against our nuclear missile forces. Marshall pointed out that, while this was true, we needed to look at the bigger picture. The USSR, he noted, had the world's longest border. As the Berlin Wall and the shooting down of a Korean airliner that wandered into its airspace showed, its regime was determined to control access to its territory. To this end they had deployed a massive air defense system, primarily to defend against the U.S. bomber force. By maintaining that force, Marshall noted, we would incentivize the Soviets to maintain and modernize their advanced air defense system, which cost far more than our B-2 stealth bomber program. By the mid-1980s defense secretary Caspar Weinberger was making competitive strategies like these a centerpiece of his defense strategy.

As the Cold War approached its end, Marshall was already exploring the strategic horizon a decade or two out. As we were negotiating the INF Treaty with the Soviets in 1987, Marshall was informing senior Pentagon officials that the biggest challenge the United States would face in the coming decades was the rise of China to great power status, eclipsing the Soviet Union. The greatest potential opportunity would come, he declared, from the onset of precision warfare, what became known in the 1990s as the "Revolution in Military Affairs." He thereby identified the emerging revolution in precision-strike warfare that has reshaped major components of our military.

More recently, during my tenure as defense secretary, Marshall's Office of Net Assessment brought to the fore the emerging challenge to U.S. power-projection from rivals developing what is now commonly referred to as anti-access/area-denial capabilities. He also demonstrated the need for our military to adopt new concepts of operation, such as Air-Sea Battle, to meet the challenge.

Marshall's story, as presented in these pages, shows that while so much effort in the Pentagon is understandably consumed by the press of day-to-day operations, there is an enduring need for what Marshall has created in this small office, modestly funded, charged to engage in innovative thinking, and reporting directly to the secretary of defense. Those of us who have served with Marshall have been the fortunate beneficiaries of his wisdom and insight, which have repeatedly paid enormous dividends during some of the most challenging periods in our recent history. We are now entering another such period, one in which the contributions of the Office of Net Assessment will be needed by senior defense officials every bit as much as they have been in the past.

Robert M. Gates

AUTHORS' NOTE

Our fundamental aim in writing this book was not to produce a biography of Andrew Marshall, but rather his intellectual history. We hoped to provide a window into how Marshall came to think about and assess long-term military competitions involving the United States. While his development of net assessment initially focused on the Cold War competition between the United States and the Soviet Union, the conceptual framework he developed in the early 1970s has also proved to be a useful way of thinking about areas as diverse as the revolution in warfare that arrived with the advent of precision-guided munitions and battle networks, the rise of China, and the proliferation of nuclear weapons. In all these cases, Marshall's Office of Net Assessment (ONA) sought to provide the Secretary of Defense and other senior US national security decision makers with early warning of emerging strategic problems, as well as opportunities to pursue strategic advantages over the nation's competitors.

We have endeavored to be as unbiased and objective as we could in describing Marshall's long intellectual journey from Detroit during the Great Depression and the Second World War to over four decades as the Pentagon's director of net assessment. Yet neither of us can claim to be disinterested observers. We both have a long history with Marshall. Watts served on his Office of Net Assessment (ONA) staff during 1978–1981 and 1985–1996, and Krepinevich during 1989–1993. Both of us retired from active military service when we left Marshall's staff and went on to have long careers in the security studies field. Yet neither of us fully left Marshall's orbit. Over the years we have both participated in a range of activities sponsored by Marshall covering a multitude of issues. As employees of the Center for Strategic and Budgetary Assessments, which provides consulting support to ONA, both of us have been involved in diverse projects funded by that office. Once a member of Marshall's coterie of trusted former net assessors and outside defense experts—"St. Andrew's Prep"—always a member.

As with all authors, our ability to share our story with the reader is limited by our analytic and literary shortcomings. In this instance we were also constrained by the fact that many of the products of Marshall's intellectual efforts remain classified. Thus Marshall's full intellectual history will not likely be known for decades to come, until the time when these documents have been declassified. That being said, we believe that even with these limitations, Marshall's story is one worth the telling. We leave it to the reader to judge how well we have succeeded.

This book could not have been written without considerable help from a great many people. Principal among them is Marshall himself, who kindly submitted to a series of interviews by the authors, and who promptly and graciously responded to specific questions that emerged when the manuscript was in its final stages. A debt of thanks is also owed to Kurt Guthe, who some twenty years ago conducted a series of taped interviews with Marshall about his life and the practice of net assessment. These interviews provided an invaluable window into Marshall's personal life experiences as well as his intellectual development over seventy years. The interviews themselves were sponsored through the generosity of the Smith Richardson Foundation, with the help of Devon Cross and Marin Strmecki. Our appreciation also extends to the many members of St. Andrew's Prep who kindly shared their experiences of being mentored by Marshall.

Our gratitude extends to our literary agent, Eric Lupfer, who was instrumental in helping us develop the major themes that form the foundation of this book, as well as guiding us through the publication process. Our editors, Alex Littlefield and Tim Bartlett, provided a helpful mix of encouragement and prodding, along with a keen editorial eye for how we might enhance the value of our story. We were also ably supported by Elizabeth Dana, editorial assistant, and Rachael King, our project editor. Their copyediting and fact-checking substantially improved the manuscript. Of course, any remaining errors of fact or grammar are our responsibility, and ours alone.

Since October 1973, when Marshall assumed the directorship of the Office of Net Assessment, over 90 military officers and civilian analysis have served on Marshall's staff. Outside ONA an even larger number of analysts and scholars in the intelligence community, academia, the military services, and various think tanks, have also contributed directly and indirectly to the development and practice of net assessment. In writing this book we realized early on that due to limits on its length it would necessarily constrain who as well as what we could include.

A brief word is in order about our title choice. As the reader will discern, Marshall was never a warrior in the military sense, although he was a "soldier" in America's "Arsenal of Democracy," and a "Cold Warrior" as well. But he is very close to being the last of Tom Brokaw's "greatest generation": men and women who grew up during the Great Depression and experienced the Second World War when they were still young, and who met the challenge of the "long, twilight struggle" with the Soviet Union. A defining characteristic of this generation, in our view, is its determination to meet these challenges, not because they are easy but, as President Kennedy, declared, "because they are hard." As Marshall is likely the last of his generation to serve in a senior government position, our title, *The Last Warrior*, seems appropriate.

Lastly, the greatest sacrifices made in writing this book were not borne by the authors, who accomplished most of their writing and editing on weekends and during evenings, but by their wives. They have shown remarkable understanding as the two of us engaged in what has been first and foremost a labor of love. To our far better halves, Julia Krepinevich and Hope Watts, we owe a large measure of gratitude, along with our love.

INTRODUCTION

On the third floor of the innermost, or "A" ring, of the Pentagon, near where the ninth and tenth corridors come together, sits the sole entrance to the Office of Net Assessment. Labeled "3A932," the nondescript door faces the Pentagon's central courtyard. During the Cold War the courtyard was nicknamed "ground zero," because it was assumed that Soviet nuclear missiles were aimed at the snack bar at its center.

The A ring is one of the five concentric rings of offices in the five-storied, five-sided building. Most senior defense officials' offices, including that of the secretary of defense, are situated on the structure's outermost, or E ring, which is considered prime Pentagon real estate. But despite the separation between the A and E rings, it takes only a few minutes to walk from the defense secretary's E-ring suite down the ninth corridor to 3A932. The proximity is important, for 3A932 houses the defense secretary's own private think tank.

To enter 3A932 visitors must announce their presence by pressing a button next to the office's entry door. Following a buzzing sound indicating that the locks have been disengaged, the heavy door can be opened and the office entered. This security is necessary, even inside the Pentagon, as the office stores highly classified material. In Pentagon parlance, it is a sensitive compartmented information facility—or "SCIF" (pronounced "skiff").

Once inside, any visitor expecting a scene out of a Hollywood movie will be disappointed. There are no electronic displays. People are not scurrying about. Rather, to the left are cramped cubicles for junior staff, along with a few small offices. To the far right sits a conference room. The furnishings are what one might find at a discount warehouse.

Located slightly to the right of the entrance is a larger office, roughly 20 by 30 feet, assigned to the director. Inside is a fully stocked bank of bookshelves to the right, and a rectangular conference table off to the left large enough to seat four or five people comfortably but equipped with only a few chairs. The reason is that the table and most of the other horizontal surfaces in the office serve a different purpose. They are stacked high with scholarly papers and books on subjects as diverse as anthropology, nuclear weapons, demographics, and cognitive science, many of them sent by their authors in the hope the director of net assessment will read and perhaps even comment on them.

There is a desk in the director's office; like the conference table, it sags under the weight of books and papers. Nearby are two worn leather armchairs. One accommodates short stacks of papers on its arms, with the seat hosting a slightly larger pile. On the floor in front of this chair, where a person sitting in it might place his or her feet, rests yet another stack of books and papers.

In the other chair, on most days, sits a nonagenarian who could easily pass for a person twenty years younger. He is a few inches short of six feet, and bald except for an arc of gray hair along the sides and back of his head. A slightly large and hawkish nose and an ever-present pair of slightly out-of-date wire-rimmed eyeglasses dominate his features. Behind the spectacles sparkle a pair of brilliant blue eyes. He speaks softly and sparingly. But when he does speak his often-cryptic comments almost invariably go to the core of the issue at hand.

His name is Andrew Walter Marshall. Since the early days of the Cold War he has been one of America's most influential and enduring strategic thinkers.

Now well into his seventh decade of public service, Marshall has been described as one of the "Wizards of Armageddon"—an intellectual giant comparable to such nuclear strategists as Bernard Brodie, Herman Kahn, Henry Kissinger, James Schlesinger, and Albert Wohlstetter, men whose insights influenced the decisions of US presidents, defense secretaries, and senior military leaders during the Cold War and beyond. His intellectual journey toward becoming one of the nation's most influential behind-the-scenes strategists can be dated to the late 1940s, when he was studying for a master's degree of economics at the University of Chicago. There, among other things, he assisted the legendary physicist Enrico Fermi with a cyclotron and played bridge with Kenneth Arrow, who later won the Nobel Prize in economics. Joining the RAND Corporation in 1949, Marshall was quickly drawn into the unprecedented intellectual challenges confronting US strategists during the early days of the nuclear missile age. From his pathbreaking work at the RAND Corporation in the 1950s and early 1960s to his establishment of a net assessment program in the Pentagon, Marshall emerged as one of the United States' leading strategic thinkers during what proved to be a long, bitter, and dangerous standoff with the Soviet Union. After the Cold War ended, he fathered the debate within the US military over the "revolution in military affairs" and foresaw more clearly than most the emerging changes in America's national-security environment and the challenges they would pose as the United States entered the twenty-first century.

The crowning intellectual achievement of Marshall's twenty-three years at RAND (1949–1972) was arguably his creation of a long-term competition framework for analyzing the US-Soviet rivalry in intercontinental nuclear forces, which he recognized was fundamentally a series of moves and countermoves in peacetime aimed at gaining relative advantage. Subsequently, while working on Henry Kissinger's National Security Council, he drew on this framework to develop a conception of net assessment that remains valid to this day. For Marshall net assessments were careful comparisons of US weapon systems, forces, operational doctrines and practices, training, logistics, design and acquisition approaches, resource allocations, strategies and likely force effectiveness with those of prospective and existing rivals. Net assessments have consistently sought to determine where the United States stood in various areas of military competition relative to rivals and adversaries. Their ultimate aim has been—and remains—to illuminate emerging problems and strategic opportunities far enough in advance for senior leaders to have time to make decisions that will either mitigate the former or exploit the latter. From the USSR's achievement of strategic nuclear parity in the early 1970s to America's wars in Iraq and Afghanistan following al Qaeda's 9/11 (September 11, 2001) attacks on the World Trade Center and the Pentagon, Marshall's net assessments have been remarkably prescient in identifying the "next big thing" for senior national security officials to worry about or capitalize on. Far ahead of most others, he foresaw the consequences of the revolution in warfare brought about by precision weaponry and the rise of China as a major strategic competitor.

Remarkably, although Marshall has continuously refined the practice of net assessment since 1972, his fundamental conception of the enterprise has stood the test of time. Since the end of the Cold War, the international security environment has undergone dramatic transformation. We have witnessed the rise of Islamic terrorism, China's astonishing economic growth and military buildup, the continuing proliferation of nuclear weapons in the developing world, and, most recently, the reemergence of revanchist ambitions in Moscow. Yet net assessment—understood as an analytic framework for comprehending the fundamental character of a competitive situation—remains the necessary first step in the formulation of sound strategies, particularly ones that seek to impose disproportionate costs and difficult challenges on the other side.

Marshall has been influencing American strategic thought since the 1950s. His ability to wield influence over such a protracted period of time stems from a rare combination of intellectual and personal qualities. He is clearly brilliant. During RAND's "golden age" in the 1950s and early 1960s Marshall was described by one colleague as "first among equals." He also possesses an intense and abiding curiosity as to how things really work. Then there is his intellectual honesty: his willingness to reconsider his beliefs when they conflict with the facts, and to challenge the conventional wisdom whenever it becomes apparent that such thinking does not reflect reality.

Marshall's intellectual integrity has won the admiration of senior policy makers across the political spectrum. His reputation is such that despite the growth of partisan politics in recent times, he has served under every defense secretary since James Schlesinger and every president since Richard Nixon. His longevity as a senior government policy official is nothing short of astounding.

Although many of his contemporaries have made lasting contributions to America's security, Marshall is the only one still actively serving in a senior position. He is the last: the last of the generation that grew up during the Great Depression, the worst economic collapse in modern times; the last of the generation that in early adulthood provided the muscle and sweat behind what President Franklin D. Roosevelt termed the "arsenal of democracy"; and the last of the generation that shed its blood fighting and winning the most costly war in human history against some of the darkest forces the world has ever seen. In middle age, some of his contemporaries rose in prominence to help bring about the postwar economic boom, while a handful of others helped guide the country through some of the Cold War's most perilous hours. As they reached seniority, those few who attained the highest positions of responsibility played central roles in ending the forty-year standoff with the most formidable enemy their country had ever confronted, hoping that they had at last witnessed the triumph of liberal democratic order and the "end of history," as political scientist Francis Fukuyama famously described the triumph of Western values over Soviet communism.

It was not to be. As the few remaining members of this cohort—now labeled by some the "greatest" generation—passed from the public scene, new and formidable challenges, some geopolitical, others economic, emerged once again. Yet Marshall remains, still serving his country.

In recent years some members of the strategic studies community have taken to referring to Andrew Marshall as "the most influential man you've never heard of." Other members of the defense cognoscenti have gone so far as to call him "Yoda" as a tribute to his long experience, wisdom, aversion to the spotlight, and the impressive group of scholars and senior officials whom he has mentored over the years. His close protégés, for their part, have been referred to as "Jedi warriors," another reference to the Star Wars series of motion pictures. The "Jedi warriors" themselves adopted a more modest term when referring to themselves: They are all proud graduates of "St. Andrew's Prep." Most would freely admit that the education they received from Marshall's mentoring has had a profound influence on their thinking and their work.

Marshall cringes at even this much attention. He has always preferred to operate behind the scenes. To this day, this is predominately where his influence has been felt. His thinking about such subjects as surprise attack, the role organizations play in decision-making, and competitive strategies, has been the inspiration behind the principal contributions of such well-known scholars as Graham Allison and Roberta Wohlstetter. Marshall himself, more often than not, is discernable only in the background, his presence felt but not always openly acknowledged in the many ideas and thinkers he has influenced. This book, then, is an attempt to bring him out of the wings and onto center stage.

The Last Warrior strives to capture Marshall's intellectual contributions to US defense strategy. Unfortunately, much of what he has written, as well as the products of the Office of Net Assessment, remains classified. Consequently, this book is based on extensive interactions and interviews with the man himself as well as those documents and materials that are publicly available. They offer the most complete picture of his life and work as we are likely to have for a generation or two, until the full extent of his contributions is revealed through the progressive declassification of documents stretching back to the early days of the Cold War. Yet, although necessarily incomplete, much of what is presented in the pages that follow is not widely known, even to those who have known Marshall longest.

In large part this incomplete understanding of Marshall's intellectual legacy stems from his strong aversion to self-promotion; indeed, one of his fondest sayings is, "There is no end to the good a person can do if he does not care about who gets the credit." Another reason for his lack of public fame centers on his belief that others, especially those he has mentored, should be left to travel their own intellectual journeys of discovery, much as he has done himself. Marshall's own contributions are very much the product of self-education and the informal exchange of ideas with colleagues. Rather than impose his intellectual views upon others, he has instead sought to provide them with the guidance and encouragement they need to develop their own views.

Similarly, in his exchanges with several generations of America's most senior government officials, Marshall has steadfastly avoided giving them detailed recommendations as to what course of action they should pursue. Using a medical metaphor, he has been perhaps his country's foremost strategic "diagnostician." He has been very reticent about offering specific "prescriptions." This stems from his realization that an accurate diagnosis is the key to identifying the proper strategic prescription. Or, as Marshall has on occasion put it, "I'd rather have decent answers to the right questions than great answers to irrelevant questions."

This behind-the-scenes approach to exerting influence has suited both Marshall's intellectual preferences and innate modesty. It has also allowed him to avoid the wider recognition his contributions richly merit. Some sense this; hence the "Yoda" references he disdains. Yet the fact remains that Andrew Marshall stands as perhaps one of the most enduring—and insightful—contributors to the evolution of US national security and defense strategy since this nation emerged as a global power seventy years ago. His story, in a sense, is the story of the United States as a superpower—and it is one that anyone wishing to understand the past, present, and future of American foreign policy and defense strategy would do well to study for insights into how this country has made it this far, what dangers lie ahead, and how they might be avoided or overcome.

1

A SELF-EDUCATED MAN
1921–1949

*I'd rather have decent answers to the right question
than great answers to irrelevant questions.*
—ANDREW MARSHALL

A ndrew Walter Marshall arrived in this world on September 13, 1921, in the city of Detroit. His parents named their first son after the infant's seafaring grandfather.

The newborn's father, John Marshall, was born in 1886 in the port city of Liverpool, some 175 miles northwest of London along England's west coast. He was the youngest of four children, with two brothers and a sister. Their father, Andrew Marshall, was the engineer on a ship that ran between Liverpool and Buenos Aires. After he was killed in an accident at sea, his wife took their children, including John, back to Carluke, a small town between Glasgow and Edinburgh, where she had grown up. Not long afterward she passed away as well.

Not much is known about how the four orphaned children were raised. What is known is that John Marshall was less educated than his two elder brothers, perhaps due to their parents' untimely deaths. Upon reaching adulthood they all emigrated from Scotland to either Canada or the United States. Christina, John's sister, chose Canada and eventually married a World War I fighter ace, settling down on a large farm in Saskatchewan. One brother, Arthur, came to the United States and migrated west. Over time the family gradually lost track of him. The other brother, who was also named Andrew, had attended a technical school and became a craftsman-engineer, settling in Dayton, Ohio, where he worked at Wright Field with two of his cousins, Fred and Tom Russell.

Unlike many European immigrants who entered the United States at Ellis Island in New York harbor, John Marshall took an indirect route. He traveled first to South Africa, India, Australia, and then to Canada as he looked for a place to settle down. He arrived in Detroit via Ontario, where he met Katherine Last who, like him, was a British expatriate.

Katherine was born on December 27, 1894, the middle child in a family of thirteen children. She was raised in the small town of Halstead in Essex County, northeast of London. In the late nineteenth century Essex was a manufacturing center and Halstead was known for its weaving. One of Katherine's more enterprising elder sisters, Maude, immigrated to the United States and settled in Detroit. In 1916 Katherine joined her there.

John and Katherine married in 1920. Having met in Detroit, they decided their family would plant its roots in the United States, and they both became American citizens.

The year after their marriage Andrew Marshall was born in his parents' home, a relatively rare event in today's America but quite common in those times. The two-story detached house was modest but comfortable, a reflection of the lower-middle-class blue-collar section of Detroit where the Marshalls lived. A second son, Frederick John Marshall, was born in December 1922. He was named after one of his mother's brothers, but everyone called him Jack.

Unlike the hollowed-out, financially insolvent city of today, the Detroit of Andrew Marshall's youth was a vibrant, growing metropolis. The city was a key part of America's rapidly expanding industrial sector—a kind of early-twentieth-century Silicon Valley. Automobiles were the new sensation. Such innovations as Henry Ford's assembly-line production techniques made cars affordable for the middle class. The United States was becoming a nation on wheels, with Detroit—"Motor City"—its capital.

Andrew Marshall's boyhood years were in many ways typical of that bygone era. He enjoyed sports, playing pickup baseball and football, and, during Michigan's long, cold winters, ice-skating. The family made periodic trips to Dayton to visit his father's brother Andrew. Young Andrew bonded with his uncle, who on one occasion took him to an open house day conducted by the Army Air Corps at Wright Field. The airplanes on display, especially the large bomber aircraft, awed young Andrew, who would develop a lifelong interest in military affairs.

Marshall's father was a kind and generous man, and within the family Andrew naturally gravitated toward him. This was made all the easier as Katherine was the source of order in the family, the principal disciplinarian for Andrew and Jack. She also managed the family finances with intelligence and prudence. Even during the Great Depression, when her husband went through a long stretch during which he had trouble getting work as a stonemason, Katherine's financial acuity enabled the family to weather the country's economic downturn without the severe hardships that were visited upon many of their neighbors. Things were tight but there was no wolf at the door.

Young Andrew possessed an intense curiosity, combined with a love of reading, both of which he inherited from his father, whose interests were diverse. The family's modest library included a multivolume literature collection and a set of encyclopedias. Andrew devoured the books and, in seeking further intellectual stimulation, discovered the main Detroit Public Library. Funded by Andrew Carnegie, the library opened its doors in the same year as Marshall's birth. Andrew started visiting the library at an early age. He also began using his modest allowance to buy his own books, reading widely on topics ranging from chess and mathematics to history, literature, and warfare.

On a trip to one of his mother's relatives in the city, Andrew came upon a set of the 1911 edition of *The Encyclopaedia Britannica*. During subsequent visits the precocious young man would steal away to sit by himself and read entries, many of which were written by some of the leading figures in their respective fields. Having access to some of the best minds in the world in this way so excited Marshall that he started saving money to buy a set of his own, which he did as a teenager—quite an accomplishment, given the considerable cost of *The Encyclopaedia Britannica*, then and now.

Marshall attended Marxhausen Elementary School, about a half-dozen blocks from his home. This was followed by what today would be called middle school at Barbour, a little farther away. In those days children walked to school, irrespective of the weather, and even a few blocks' distance could be a challenge in the Michigan winter. At Barbour, students were separated into homerooms according to academic proficiency. Andrew's homeroom boasted the top students.

Toward the end of his last year at Barbour, Marshall and his classmates were given an exam, a kind of aptitude test. Some days later the principal asked to see Andrew, another boy, and three girls. The principal questioned them about their plans for further education. "Where are you going to go to high school?" she wanted to know. It was quickly apparent to Andrew that she had called them in because he and the others had scored extraordinarily high on the exam. When Andrew told her his parents planned for him to attend Cass Technical High School, she expressed some concern. Cass was a good school, she said, but she emphasized that he should go to college, and a technical high school wouldn't give him the preparation he needed. She seemed to fear that since his father was a stonemason, Andrew would see Cass as the way to acquire a trade or craft and not fulfill his intellectual potential.

Despite the principal's misgivings, Marshall went to Cass, thinking—as did his parents—that it would offer him the best future. Cass was not like many of today's trade schools; it did have aspects of a vocational or trade school, but students had to have good grades to be accepted. In some respects it was like a magnet school. Its curriculum featured more courses in such subjects as mathematics and chemistry than did any other high school in Detroit. The school's "celebrity" teacher was Charles Lindbergh's mother, Evangeline Lodge Land Lindbergh, who taught organic chemistry. Many students and their parents saw attending Cass as an honor.

Cass was also, however, geared toward teaching technical skills in a way not seen in the more academically oriented high schools of the time. Cass had machine and electrical shops and even a foundry. Marshall learned to run lathes and milling machines. His homeroom, on the school's seventh floor, was in the foundry where students learned to cast metal molds. Every few weeks the furnace was lit and the students were able to work with molten metal, pouring it into their molds to make castings. By the time he graduated from Cass, Marshall had acquired considerable skill with machine tools as well as a first-rate education in mathematics and the hard sciences.

Like many young boys of high school age, Marshall enjoyed sports. After setting aside funds for his future book purchases, he went as often as time and money would allow to Briggs Stadium to see the Detroit Tigers baseball club. The team was quite a powerhouse for much of the 1930s and boasted some of the game's biggest stars, including future Hall of Famers such as slugger and first baseman Hank Greenberg, catcher Mickey Cochrane, and second baseman Charlie Gehringer. Admission to the bleacher section was cheap, only fifty cents. In the fall Marshall went to see the

Lions, Detroit's professional football team. John Marshall would often take his sons to the Thanksgiving Day game, which began at eleven a.m. so everyone could get home in time for a big dinner.

Marshall proved to be a better-than-average athlete. In those days the city's leading newspaper, the *Detroit Free Press*, sponsored a kind of decathlon. Participants engaged in events involving sprinting, throwing a javelin, putting the shot, and broad jumping, along with sit-ups, pull-ups, and chin-ups. Marshall's performance was sufficiently notable to earn him several medals.

While at Cass, Marshall's intellectual curiosity could not be contained within the bounds of his father's modest library, or those of his relatives. He continued trooping down frequently to the public library, where he began in earnest what amounted to a lifelong process of self-education. He was especially impressed by Ford Madox Ford's *The March of Literature: From Confucius' Day to Our Own*.[1] Written for general readers rather than scholars and first published in 1938, it presents Ford's views of what is valuable in literature, and why. After reading Ford's favorable accounts of various works, Marshall set off to read them himself, devouring such novels as Dostoyevsky's *Crime and Punishment* and *The Brothers Karamazov*, then on to Tolstoy's *War and Peace* and *Anna Karenina*, and many others besides.

Marshall pursued his curiosity about military affairs, and naval warfare in particular, by heading to the city's main library and poring over books such as *Jane's Fighting Ships*, a ponderous annual publication that provided exquisitely detailed accounts of the vessels of the world's naval powers. Marshall also read histories of the First World War and B. H. Liddell Hart's writings on strategy. As World War II approached, Marshall began following the columns of the military historian S. L. A. Marshall in the *Detroit News* and even heard him speak once at the local library. Marshall's eclectic interests also found him burrowing into books on mathematics, such as Richard Courant and Herbert Robbins's *What Is Mathematics?*[2] Marshall read nearly all of Alfred North Whitehead and George Santayana's works, followed by specialized philosophical works, such as F. H. Bradley's *Ethical Studies*, which criticized utilitarianism.

While browsing through a magazine one day during the 1930s, Marshall came upon a reference to Arnold Toynbee's *A Study of History*. The first three volumes had come out in 1934, and three more were to be released in 1939. Marshall scraped together the money and bought the first three volumes, reading them in rapid succession. When the second set was published, he purchased them as well.[3]

Toynbee's writings were an epiphany for Marshall. Later he would recall that, as he read Toynbee, he was beginning to understand for the first time the broad sweep of history; the various cultures that had emerged over time; how civilizations had changed from one era to the next; and how states acquired power, wielded and preserved it, and eventually lost it. His readings gave young Andrew a sense of how quickly things could change, how fragile human societies could be, and of how different groups of human beings were capable of visiting unspeakable depredations on others.

Marshall's growing understanding of human strengths, weaknesses, and proclivities was reinforced by the dark days of the Great Depression, and by reports of Communist and Fascist states inflicting enormous suffering on their own peoples while pursuing expansionist policies to enslave others. It also led him to conclude that the popular view of the past in any given era can often be very wrong—in some cases dangerously so. Simply put, Marshall realized that the popular, or conventional, wisdom regarding what constitutes "reality" is wrong more often than people care to admit.

In later years the self-education derived from Marshall's intense curiosity would manifest itself in a healthy skepticism when presented with the latest version of the "conventional wisdom" on any given subject. Although he could not have known it at the time, Marshall's eclectic interests would serve him well years later, when he began struggling to understand the dynamics of the complicated and dangerous geopolitical rivalry between the United States and the Soviet Union that emerged after World War II.

In the spring of 1939, toward the end of Marshall's four years at Cass, he and some of his fellow seniors in the city were given an aptitude test, similar to the Scholastic Aptitude Test (SAT) of today but limited to students with high grade point averages. Among the roughly four hundred honor students who took the test, Marshall scored the second highest. Cass, it turned out, would not be the end of his formal education.

Marshall's parents rarely discussed their personal histories, even in front of their two sons. But during the 1930s they often talked about the growing likelihood of another world war. Totalitarian states in Europe and Asia seemed intent on expansion: Japan's emperor, Hirohito, seized Manchuria from China in 1931; his troops invaded China itself in 1937 on the way to creating what the Japanese labeled the "East Asia Co-Prosperity Sphere." In 1932 the Soviet Union's brutal dictator, Joseph Stalin, sanctioned the starvation of millions of his people in Ukraine to liquidate private property and spur industrialization while he looked for opportunities to prey on weak countries along his borders. Three years later Italy's Fascist dictator, Benito Mussolini, invaded Ethiopia as part of his bid to create a new Roman Empire. Speaking of the need for "living space" to create a "Greater Germany," in 1938 Adolf Hitler sent German troops first into Austria and then into Czechoslovakia's Sudetenland. In the spring of 1939 Germany occupied the rest of Czechoslovakia, and began making demands on Poland.

The League of Nations, the international institution created after World War I to ensure there would never be another great war, had proven both feckless and toothless in its attempts to arrest these acts of aggression. The victors of World War I, Great Britain and France, alternately threatened sanctions against Italy and pursued appeasement with Germany, all to no avail.

Like many other parents at that time, John and Katherine Marshall believed that if another war came, the casualties would be enormous and few families would be spared suffering. One of Katherine's brothers had been killed at the Battle of the Somme during the Great War only twenty years before. Another had been made an invalid, and still another came home mutilated. John Marshall was spared only because he fractured his foot during a training exercise and was ruled physically unfit for combat duty.

This somber mood about the future was not limited to Marshall's parents. Shortly before graduation, Marshall's metallurgy class teacher, when describing a type of steel, told the students that it was of the kind used in armor and helmets. He said he feared the students soon would become very familiar with these instruments of war.

Most high school graduations are happy affairs, occasions to recognize years of accomplishment and to anticipate a future of exciting possibilities. This was not the mood at the graduation exercises for Cass Technical School's Class of 1939. Rather than an atmosphere of celebration, a cloud of foreboding hung over the ceremony. Parents sat somberly in their seats. War was in the air, and it appeared to many that, as in the last war, the United States would not be able to avoid involvement. It seemed likely that the conflict would consume many of the young men now awaiting their diplomas. Cass had a junior Reserve Office Training Corps (ROTC) unit, quite normal in high schools at that time. At graduation the ROTC cadets, as was the tradition, wore their uniforms and sat together. The sight of the assembled cadets moved many women, and not a few men, to tears. Marshall would later recall it as the most emotional public experience of his life.

On September 1, 1939, Germany invaded Poland, followed later that same month by Soviet forces, part of an agreement that Hitler and Stalin had reached only days before. Both Britain and France responded by declaring war on Germany, but failed to come to Poland's aid. Abandoned by its Western allies, and with Stalin's armies moving in and occupying the eastern half of the country, Warsaw surrendered after only a few weeks' resistance.

After a long lull in the fighting, in April 1940 the Germans invaded and quickly conquered Denmark and Norway, while Stalin seized control over the Baltic states of Estonia, Latvia, and Lithuania. Then, in May, the world was stunned by a massive German offensive against France and the Low Countries. Germany's revolutionary blitzkrieg form of warfare, combining large concentrations of tanks and aircraft linked by radio, enabled the Wehrmacht—Germany's unified air force, army, and navy—to defeat British and French forces in a six-week lightning campaign that saw France surrender and the British Expeditionary Force evacuated from Dunkirk. This left Great Britain to face Germany—now the master of much of Europe—alone. In the Far East, Japan pressed its advantage in China and, following the defeat of France, moved to occupy French Indochina as well.

Despite the growing threats from Germany and Japan, the United States maintained its neutrality. Marshall, meanwhile, was in kind of limbo as well. Although his high grades and his score on the aptitude test had earned him a scholarship to an engineering school, he decided to delay further education. Instead he spent the next year running a lathe in a factory where the father of one of his friends worked.

Finally, in the fall of 1940, Marshall enrolled at Detroit University. The school required entering students to take a medical exam. Marshall's physical revealed that he had a heart murmur. The condition later precluded him from military service when the United States entered World War II.

Marshall found Detroit University's curriculum disappointing. Many of the courses merely repeated work he had done at Cass. He felt he was wasting his time, and left school after a year to take a job at the Murray Body Company. Named after its cofounder John William Murray, a native of

Ann Arbor, Michigan, the company had been formed in 1913 to manufacture sheet metal parts for the rapidly growing automotive industry. Its customers included Ford, Hudson, Hupmobile, King, and Studebaker. In the 1920s the company merged with others to form the Detroit-based Murray Body Corporation, which boasted over a million square feet of floor space and employed over one thousand men and women. By the time Marshall joined the company it had converted to aircraft production, and Marshall's job was to build machine tools for use in fabricating aircraft parts; most of the work at that time was for planes bound for Great Britain.

On December 7, 1941, a Sunday, Marshall took his usual six-hour shift at Murray, heading home shortly after one o'clock. When he arrived back at his parents' home, he turned on the radio in the living room to get the day's news. After a few moments the program was interrupted by a flash bulletin: Reports were coming in of an attack by Japanese forces on the United States' main Pacific naval base at Pearl Harbor.

Marshall called his parents, who came rushing into the room. There the three of them stood in silence as bulletin after bulletin provided further details. They were surprised at the timing and character of the attack, but not at the fact that the United States would no longer be able to maintain its neutrality. What had long seemed inevitable was now a reality.

Congress declared war on Japan on December 8, and on Germany and Italy three days later, in response to the two European Axis powers' declarations of war upon the United States. Suddenly Marshall found himself on the front lines of the home front. Given its ongoing work on military contracts, Murray was well positioned to support the war effort, and over the next two years the company's workforce expanded to over thirteen thousand workers, most of them women. Murray's sheet presses worked around the clock to fulfill the company's role in America's "Arsenal of Democracy," as FDR had termed it a year earlier. The plant produced wings and other components used in the Boeing B-17 Flying Fortress and B-29 Super Fortress bombers, as well as in Douglas's A-20 Havoc light bomber and Republic Aviation's P-47 Thunderbolt fighter.[4]

Marshall's work at Murray kept him busy for ten hours a day on weekdays, eight hours on Saturdays, and six hours on Sundays. So it is perhaps surprising that, by the autumn of 1943, he was itching to continue his formal education in addition to his heavy workload. He enrolled at Wayne University to take a few courses in the evenings, and continued night school through the spring of 1945. By that time Germany had been defeated and it was clear the war against Japan would end soon. War production would be winding down and Marshall would be free to pursue his education full-time.

One of Marshall's friends at Wayne University had been accepted to the University of Chicago's divinity school and their discussions about the university piqued his interest. Marshall read up on the school and was impressed by its reputation. He applied and took several entrance examinations. Word came back from the university that Marshall had been accepted into Chicago's graduate school, even though he had never received an undergraduate degree.

M arshall arrived on the University of Chicago campus in September 1945, shortly after the Japanese had formally surrendered on the deck of the US battleship *Missouri*. While he would have preferred pursuing studies in mathematics, he decided that economics would offer him a better chance to make a good living. And so he opted for the latter discipline.

In postwar America the University of Chicago was an incubator of cutting-edge economic thought, attracting some of the country's best economists. Marshall's teachers included such scholars as Rudolf Carnap, Milton Friedman, Frank Knight, Jimmy Savage, and W. Allen Wallis. Friedman and Knight were two of the leading lights of what in the 1950s would become known as the Chicago School of Economics, which challenged Keynesian economics in favor of monetarism. Marshall took classes from both Knight and Friedman. Knight made a particularly lasting impression on Marshall by introducing him to broader conceptions of human decision-making than envisioned and recognized by the economic theory of that time.* Although Knight became known as the father of price theory, he also stressed the limits of rationality in economic choice. Knight's arguments resonated strongly with Marshall, given his interest in how the world worked in practice, rather than in abstract theory.

The University of Chicago was also then home to the Cowles Commission for Research in Economics, which Alfred Cowles had founded in 1932. The commission dedicated itself to pursuing the linkages and relationships

---

*Knight made his reputation with his 1921 *Risk, Uncertainty, and Profit*. For Knight, *risk* referred to situations in which the probability of an outcome could be determined, whereas *uncertainty* referred to events whose probabilities could not be known.

between economics, mathematics, and statistics. Its motto was "Theory *and* Measurement." Work at Cowles contributed greatly to the emergence of econometrics and general equilibrium economic theory.*

The commission's emphasis on mathematics and statistics appealed to Marshall and he took some courses in those subjects. At Cowles he spent time with Tjalling Koopmans, who became the commission's director in 1948. Herbert Simon, a former student of Frank Knight's, participated with them in some of the seminars. Marshall also became friends with a young woman, Selma Schweitzer, who was in several of his economics classes. At the time Schweitzer was dating a young scholar at Cowles, Kenneth Arrow. On various occasions Marshall and a fourth would join the Arrows, who married in 1947, to play bridge. Arrow, Friedman, and Koopmans would each go on to win the Nobel Prize in economics, as would Simon.

While Marshall was pursuing his studies he earned a little extra money working a part-time job at the university's Institute for Nuclear Studies, formed shortly after the war ended. Among its distinguished members was Enrico Fermi, who had played a key role during the war in the US effort—known as the Manhattan Project—to develop the atomic bomb.[†] It was a remarkable chance meeting between one of the vanguards of nuclear physics and the young man who would later become a leading American nuclear strategist during the Cold War. The crossing of their paths would soon afford the young Marshall his first experience with nuclear technology.

The machinist skills Marshall had acquired at Cass earned him an assignment in the machine shop located in the basement of Eckhart Hall, the university's mathematics building, where he helped the school upgrade its cyclotron. (Cyclotrons are particle accelerators that dispatch charged particle beams outward from their center along a spiral or cyclical path, enabling nuclear physicists to examine the results of collisions between the accelerated particles and target atoms.) The university physicists often visited the

---

*General equilibrium economic theory seeks to demonstrate that the multiple, interrelated sectors of an economy, when viewed together, rather than individually, bring supply, demand, and prices into a state of total (or general) equilibrium over the long term.

[†]The institute was renamed the Enrico Fermi Institute for Nuclear Studies in 1955, and renamed once again in 1968 as the Enrico Fermi Institute. Aside from Fermi, other notable members of the institute included James Cronin, Yoichiro Nambu, and Harold Urey, all of whom were awarded the Nobel Prize.

machine shop; it was not unusual to see Fermi himself working on some piece of equipment alongside the machinists.

Today, when such scientific marvels as the Large Hadron Collider particle accelerator outside Geneva have taken nuclear physics to a whole new level, it is difficult to imagine how much of the success in this field in the late 1940s required a certain amount of craftsmanship as well as theoretical brilliance. It had been less than five years since Fermi had achieved the first nuclear chain reaction using an "atomic pile" (nuclear reactor) made of uranium and graphite blocks stacked beneath the abandoned stands on a racket court at the school's Alonzo Stagg football stadium.

It was clear to both Fermi and Marshall that the cyclotron they were trying to get back in operation had been very badly designed. Working together they were able to get the device back in working order. Marshall's contribution to the effort was hardly insignificant; he redesigned and fabricated the cyclotron's reflector, which alone enabled an order-of-magnitude improvement in performance.

Marshall's studies fed his growing skepticism regarding the ability of economic theory to describe, let alone predict, how economic systems really work. These doubts emerged in Marshall's master's thesis, which examined the ability of a linear mathematical model to capture the workings of the US economy. His thesis focused on the extent to which the macroeconomic predictions of Lawrence Klein's Model III of the US economy matched the actual data for the postwar years 1946 and 1947. Marshall discovered that whereas four of the model's twelve linear equations "fit very well over the two-year period," and three others fit "as well as could have been expected," three equations "fit very badly" and the remaining two "were rejected for the year 1947."[5] Klein's model, in short, failed to capture economic reality.

Marshall's experiences as a graduate student in economics at the University of Chicago had two far-reaching consequences for his subsequent career and intellectual development. First, it reinforced his inherent reluctance to assume human behavior was rational, and strengthened his appreciation of the limits of abstract models of reality. If he had ever wondered whether any major economy's performance could be reduced to a set of linear equations, his work on his master's thesis had put that question to rest.

Second, the field of economics appeared to Marshall to be headed in the wrong direction, toward a greater emphasis on abstract work. There was, he felt, a corresponding decline in the applied side of the discipline: how economies *really* worked. More broadly, he was also put off by an increasing number of economists who, having lost faith in market capitalism as a consequence of the Great Depression, appeared to assume that other ways of organizing a country's economy, including top-down management by central economic planners along socialist or communist lines, would be more successful.

Marshall saw evidence of this trend for himself during a visit to the University of Chicago by celebrated Austrian economist Friedrich Hayek. Hayek—who later shared the Nobel Prize in economics for his work on monetary theory, economic fluctuations, and the interdependence of economic, social, and institutional phenomena—came to Chicago to speak at a political economics club that Marshall frequented. Hayek's arguments against centralized economic planning were greeted with skepticism even by some of the emerging Chicago School crowd who were decidedly in favor of free-market economics. Not for the last time Marshall saw bright people who were willing, even eager, to ignore Hayek's contention that the extended order created by market economies could call up and utilize "widely dispersed information that no central planning agency, let alone any individual, could know as a whole, possess or control."[6] Years later, Marshall would recall thinking of many of the economists who denigrated Hayek as being "like weathermen who never look out the window."[7]

His faith in market capitalism, and his corresponding aversion to what Hayek termed the "fatal conceit" that central economic planners might possess all the information needed to run an economy efficiently, would shape the course of Marshall's life. He had completed his studies and written his thesis. But although he was graduating with a master's degree in economics from one of the country's most prestigious graduate schools, Marshall had come to the conclusion that he did not want to pursue a PhD in the discipline.

Instead Marshall now sought a new direction for his insatiable interests and curiosity about the world. Among the courses he had taken while at Chicago was one in statistics, conducted by W. Allen Wallis, in which he had done well. Marshall had originally rejected the idea of pursuing a degree in mathematics out of concern that he could not make a decent living in that field. But now he concluded he could, and determined that he would, pursue his doctorate in statistics.

At the time, however, the University of Chicago did not offer a PhD in statistics. So once again Marshall decided to defer his formal education. He would instead look for a job while he made up his mind about where to go for further education. This time, though, he wouldn't need to seek work as a machinist; his performance at the University of Chicago had earned him a growing network of admirers, including the very professor who had interested him in statistics in the first place.

Wallis, who had taken a liking to Marshall, tried to help out. He told Marshall of a US government office in downtown Chicago that might be hiring statisticians. But there was another possibility. A new kind of institute called RAND was being organized out in California. Part of its work involved statistical analysis. An acquaintance of Wallis's, a sociologist named Herbert Goldhamer, was embarking on a project to determine whether the occurrence of psychosis was rising in the US draft-age male population. He had asked Wallis for help in finding someone who could do the necessary statistical analysis.

Marshall expressed interest in the position at RAND, and Wallis arranged for him to interview with Goldhamer, who was in charge of the project. Goldhamer came away from the meeting impressed, and offered Marshall a job at a salary roughly 50 percent higher than what the government position in Chicago paid. It did not take a graduate degree in economics for Marshall to decide to opt for RAND, and he was soon on his way to the new think tank's Washington, DC, office.

2

EARLY RAND YEARS
1949–1960

There's only so much stupidity one man can prevent.
—ANDREW MARSHALL

For most Americans the 1950s were an era of confidence, affluence, and anxiety. The Allies had triumphed over Nazi Germany and Imperial Japan in World War II, and the United States had long since recovered from the Great Depression. After the war many US business and political elites perceived virtually no limits to what American ingenuity, hard work, and leadership could accomplish, either domestically or internationally. The nation was enjoying the greatest economic boom in its history and its citizens unprecedented material prosperity. By 1950 the United States' economic output accounted for over 25 percent of the world's goods and services even though the country held only 6 percent of the world's population.[1]

The citizens of the nation that had successfully met the challenges of World War II were, understandably, less interested in military preparedness than in new homes, new cars, and new technological marvels such as television. But as the postwar era took shape, it became clear that challenges to US national security were by no means over. The United States and its close allies were soon confronted by a new foe, the Union of Soviet Socialist Republics (USSR). In the closing days of World War II Soviet forces had occupied Eastern Europe; and by 1949 the Kremlin had installed puppet governments in Bulgaria, Czechoslovakia, Hungary, Poland, and Romania, and would shortly do the same in its sector of occupied Germany. The growing rivalry between Washington and Moscow was already transforming the post–World War II security environment into a "cold war" that would last over four decades.

In April 1948 the first major crisis between the two emerging super-powers erupted when the Soviets began restricting ground traffic between the city of Berlin and the American, British, and French zones in occupied Germany. Berlin had been divided among the four victors of World War II, yet the city lay some 90 miles inside the Soviet occupation zone. In late June 1948 the Soviets cut off all surface traffic to Berlin.

Seeking to avoid war, the United States responded by organizing and leading an airlift to resupply the three western sectors of the city. This be-nevolent gesture carried as well a tacit yet pointed message to the Soviets regarding Western resolve.[2] Foreshadowing the atomic diplomacy of later US-Soviet crises, in July 1948 the United States deployed ninety B-29 bomb-ers to England. Although none was a Silverplate B-29 modified to carry atomic bombs (and indeed no such bombs were deployed overseas), most observers and historians, then and later, assumed the B-29s' deployment was meant to signal President Harry Truman's willingness to use atomic weap-ons in the event of war.[3]

The airlift's success and the backlash of West European public opinion against the Soviet Union led Joseph Stalin to end the blockade on May 12, 1949. Far from fracturing Western solidarity as he had intended, Stalin's gambit had actually brought the United States, the countries of Western Eu-rope, and other wartime allies closer together. During the airlift pilots from Great Britain, Australia, Canada, New Zealand, and South Africa had flown supply missions into Berlin alongside their American counterparts, who flew three quarters of the sorties. The perception of a common Soviet threat also led the United States to abandon its long-standing peacetime policy of semi-isolation. On April 4, 1949, in Washington, DC, eleven nations, including Great Britain, Canada, France and Italy, joined with the United States in establishing the North Atlantic Treaty Organization (NATO). Crucially, Article 5 of the North Atlantic Treaty stated that its twelve founding mem-bers would consider an armed attack against one or more of them an attack against them all. In ratifying this treaty, the United States finally broke deci-sively with the admonitions of George Washington and Thomas Jefferson a century and a half earlier to avoid "entangling alliances."

The Berlin airlift and the creation of NATO occurred within the broader context of the Truman administration's adoption of policies aimed at containing the threats to US security stemming from the USSR's hostile intentions, formidable power and the very nature of the Soviet system. Only weeks after his victory over Thomas Dewey in the 1948 presidential election, Truman approved National Security Council (NSC) 20/4, "Report by the National Security Council on US Objectives with Respect to the USSR to Counter Soviet Threats to U.S. Security." The State Department's Policy Planning Staff under George Kennan was heavily involved in drafting NSC 20/4.[4] The document reflected Kennan's assessment that, for the foreseeable future, the main element of US policy toward the Soviet Union "must be that of a long-term, patient but firm and vigilant containment of Russian expansionist tendencies."[5] Kennan had first articulated this diagnosis of the nature of the Soviet state in his famous "Long Telegram" from the US embassy in Moscow in February 1946. Although NSC 20/4 did not use the word *containment*, it is considered the initial formulation of the policy that would come to bear this name. Truman approved NSC 20/4 some seven months into the 1948–1949 Berlin crisis.

In September 1949 US concerns about Soviet expansionist tendencies were reinforced when air samples collected by a US reconnaissance aircraft revealed the Soviet Union had successfully tested its first atomic weapon in August, just as Communist forces under Mao Zedong were gaining control of the Chinese mainland. While the defeat of Chiang Kai-shek's Chinese Nationalist forces had been anticipated for some time in Washington, the USSR's breaking of the US atomic monopoly had occurred years earlier than expected, in no small part due to highly successful Soviet espionage. The USSR's first atomic bomb, RDS-1 (code-named "First Lightning" by the Soviets and labeled "Joe-1" by the West), copied the design of the American plutonium implosion bomb dropped on Nagasaki in August 1945.[6] The USSR's crossing the nuclear threshold prompted Truman to initiate the development of a "super," or hydrogen bomb in January 1950. Although Truman did not know it, Stalin had ordered his scientists to do the same a year and a half earlier.[7]

The race was on to develop thermonuclear weapons, whose destructive potential was practically unlimited. These events accelerated US-Soviet competition in nuclear arms. Eventually each superpower would amass a stockpile totaling tens of thousands of nuclear weapons.

NSC 20/4 was followed in April 1950 by NSC 68. Drafted primarily by Paul Nitze, then head of the State Department's Policy Planning Staff, NSC 68 emphasized building up US conventional military capabilities to deter Soviet aggression.[8] But neither Truman nor his defense secretary, Louis

Johnson, was inclined spend the money to do so.[9] They wanted to cut US defense spending, not increase it, in order to bring projected federal budget expenditures into rough balance with projected revenues. However, North Korea's invasion of South Korea in June 1950 and the US-led United Nations' armed response made further cuts impossible. Instead, US defense spending quadrupled by fiscal year 1952. Even so, when the conflict ended in a ceasefire between the Soviet-backed communist forces of North Korea and China, and the US-led United Nations (UN) forces in July 1953 neither side gained appreciable territory. The demilitarized zone established by the armistice ran not far from the 38th parallel that had separated North and South Korea before the war.

These developments inevitably fueled American fears and anxieties. As the Soviet nuclear arsenal grew, Americans built fallout shelters and schoolchildren across the country were drilled to hide under their desks in the event of a Soviet attack. Nevil Shute's 1957 postapocalyptic novel *On the Beach*, in which nuclear war had devastated the Northern Hemisphere and radiation was slowly poisoning the rest of the planet, voiced for many the anxieties of the early nuclear age.

By the late 1950s RAND had become one of the leading sources of nuclear strategy for America's evolving competition with the Soviet Union. RAND, however, had been founded before it became commonplace to refer to the ideological competition between the United States and the Soviet Union as the Cold War—or the "peace that is no peace" to use George Orwell's telling phrase.[10] Over a decade before the publication of Shute's *On the Beach*, several years before the Soviets had the bomb, and while the embers of World War II still smoldered, the US Army Air Forces had established Project RAND—"RAND" being an acronym for "Research ANd Development." RAND's principal purpose was to help America's air arm understand how best to cope with the terrible new instruments of destruction that now confronted mankind, as well as those that might be lurking on the horizon.

The historical impetus for RAND's creation was the US government's unprecedented success in drawing on the talents of scientists and industrialists during World War II to develop new weapons and other military capabilities. World War II was the first war in human history whose outcome was decisively affected by weapons unknown at the outbreak of hostilities.[11] These new weapons were developed under the leadership of Vannevar Bush, an electrical engineer, inventor, and science administrator who headed the country's wartime Office of Scientific Research and Development (OSRD). As head of OSRD, Bush reported directly to President Franklin Roosevelt and had both the funding and authority to initiate research and development contracts to support the war effort. In addition to having held senior administrative positions at the Massachusetts Institute of Technology (MIT), Bush had founded the company now known as Raytheon in 1922, and within five years he developed an analog computer with some digital elements. In 1938 he became president of the Carnegie Institution, and was serving in that position when war came to America. Among OSRD's wartime innovations were the airborne radars developed at MIT's Radiation Laboratory, computerized fire-direction systems, proximity fuzes, and the atomic bomb.[12]

Even before the war was over, visionary leaders, such the US Army Air Forces' wartime chief, General H. H. "Hap" Arnold, understood that if the US military was to keep up technologically it would need to continue the wartime collaboration among university researchers, defense firms, and the military. But how could this done? While OSRD's scientists had willingly supported the war effort, they had also chafed under the military's restrictions and administrative red tape. With the war over, most of them wanted to return to their universities and laboratories.[13] The civil service could neither attract nor hold the kind of talent necessary to continue the research and development needed to keep the United States on the cutting edge of advances in military-related technologies.

This conundrum prompted Arnold, at a September 1945 Pentagon meeting only days after Japan's formal surrender, to initiate steps to institutionalize the wartime collaboration with academia and industry. He directed Douglas Aircraft's Frank Collbohm, who was at the meeting, to drop everything and fly back to Santa Monica to determine, together with Douglas Aircraft's founder, Donald Douglas Sr., what facilities, men, and money would be needed to establish the first-rate "think tank" Arnold desired. A few days later, on October 1, they all met at Hamilton Field in California and set up Project RAND under a special contract to Douglas Aircraft.

Project RAND's mission was to recommend "preferred instrumentalities and techniques" to the US Army Air Forces (after September 1947, the US Air Force).[14] While the organization was to be highly independent, it also reported to the Air Staff—initially to the deputy chief of staff (DCS) for plans, General Lauris Norstad, and subsequently to the deputy chief of staff/research and development (DCS/R&D), Major General Curtis LeMay. In

1943, as commander of the Eighth Air Force's 305th Bomb Group in Europe, LeMay had emerged as the US Army Air Forces' preeminent combat leader in the European Theater. In 1945, as the commander of the Twenty-First Bomber Command in the Pacific, he oversaw the fire raids against Japanese cities and the atomic bombings of Hiroshima and Nagasaki.

Project RAND grew rapidly. In March 1946 the Army Air Forces executed a $10 million contract that put RAND under Frank Collbohm's direction in a separate area within the Douglas Aircraft plant at Santa Monica's municipal airport, Clover Field.[15] Collbolm, an aviation engineer, had helped design and test fly such trailblazing aircraft as the Douglas DC-3. He would head RAND until his retirement in 1967.

In the early years both RAND's divisions and personnel were heavily skewed toward engineering and the physical sciences. The first people hired into Project RAND were primarily engineers and mathematicians recruited from the aircraft industry. By late 1947 RAND's hiring had expanded to include electronic engineers and physicists from the wartime Radiation Laboratory at MIT and such nuclear scientists as Arnold Kramish, who had been involved in the Manhattan Project that produced the atomic bomb.

In May 1946 RAND published its first report, "Preliminary Design of an Experimental World-Circling Spaceship." Requested by LeMay, the report discussed the design, performance, and potential uses of man-made, Earth-circling satellites. This report was followed in 1947 by a comparison of ramjets and rockets, including ballistic missiles, as offensive weapons.[16] These studies presented remarkably prescient ideas at least a decade ahead of their time. But although RAND analysts were offering US Air Force leaders a view of where military technology was headed, the service, dominated by World War II bomber generals, initially showed little inclination to pursue either satellites or ballistic missiles.

By 1947 it was becoming clear that RAND needed more than engineers and hard scientists. That fall, two years before Marshall joined the organization, RAND held a conference in New York to which a number of prominent economists and other social scientists were invited. The event was a first step toward enlisting experts from these disciplines to join the organization. The motivation was a growing realization within RAND's top management that physical scientists were trained to shun making value judgments about the "preferred instrumentalities and techniques" for deterring or waging nuclear war.[17] The conference, it was hoped, would provide an opportunity to elicit from social scientists whether and how they might be able to help RAND address the problems of judging the nontechnical aspects of a new capability's military worth.[18]

The conference succeeded. Frank Collbolm was sufficiently impressed that he decided to organize economics and social science divisions at RAND. In 1948 he brought in Charles Hitch to head the Economics Division and Hans Speier to lead the Social Science Division. Both men had been among the conference's most impressive participants.[19]

By early 1948 RAND had over two hundred staff members and was rapidly outgrowing its Douglas Aircraft facilities at Clover Field. In May Project RAND was incorporated in the state of California as a nonprofit research institution for the US Air Force, which itself was less than a year old. RAND relocated its headquarters (or "main campus," as staffers called it) to facilities at Fourth Street and Broadway in downtown Santa Monica. The organization's future was secured by an interest-free $1 million loan guaranteed by the Ford Foundation. By then RAND's professional staff were mostly physicists, mathematicians, statisticians, aerodynamicists, and chemists but now included a sprinkling of economists and other social scientists.[20] Young Andrew Marshall would soon be among them.

The RAND Corporation may have been young, but by the time Marshall joined the organization's Washington Office in January 1949 it was already entering its golden age as an incubator of US nuclear strategy. The think tank's principal focus in the 1950s was, initially, to explore the profound problem of how the United States should deal with the threat of atomic weapons delivered by long-range bombers and, subsequently, the threat of thermonuclear weapons delivered by ballistic missiles. The destructive power of thermonuclear-tipped ballistic missiles was not only without precedent, it threatened the United States' very existence. In the nuclear missile age, the oceans that had rendered the country beyond the immediate reach of hostile powers in Europe and Asia no longer guaranteed safety.

There were no experts in nuclear strategy when Marshall joined RAND. Nobel Prize winners were not necessarily any better than graduate students when it came to determining how nuclear weapons would change the conduct of war. Consequently RAND meetings and working group sessions accepted no hierarchy.[21] Individuals were only as good as the ideas they brought to the table.

It was this combination of talent and intellectual freedom that enabled RAND to shape how senior American political and military leaders viewed strategy in the nuclear age. As political scientist and military strategist Bernard Brodie later recalled from his days at RAND that virtually "all the basic ideas and philosophies about nuclear weapons and their use" were generated by civilians at such institutions as RAND, working independently of the military.[22] Worth adding is that while RAND strategists had a remarkably extensive impact on American nuclear strategy, "the group of real strategists at RAND probably never numbered more than about 25 people."[23]

Upon his arrival at RAND's Washington office in January 1949 to work in the Social Science Division, the twenty-seven-year-old Andrew Marshall knew very little about the organization he had joined. In fact, his main reason for choosing RAND over the other job offer he had considered in Chicago had been pecuniary.[24] He thought the higher salary he got from RAND would shorten the time it would take him to save enough money to pursue a PhD in statistics.

There was little in Marshall's background or his arrival at RAND to suggest that he would become a leading member of RAND's foremost strategic thinkers. Goldhamer, after all, had hired him simply to do statistical analysis of data on mental illness among the draft-age male cohort. Yet in the course of little more than a decade, that is precisely what happened.

Marshall's development as a strategist was unquestionably influenced by RAND colleagues and mentors such as Goldhamer and Hitch. But how much of his thinking was shaped by these prominent individuals is impossible to say. His early interests in fields as diverse as mathematics, military history, human evolution, and literature; his deep innate intellectual curiosity; and his strong preference for empirical data over abstract models and theories all predated his arrival at RAND. What is indisputable, however, is that once Marshall joined RAND, he was quickly captivated by the real-world problems of the nuclear age. Given his involvement in these issues, it should come as no surprise, then, that he would later recall the RAND of the 1950s as a "fantastic place" with "wonderful people."[25]

The strategic implications of the rapidly evolving long-term competition between the United States and the Soviet Union would occupy Marshall's professional life for the next four decades. Yet, upon arriving at RAND he was set to work on something far more mundane: helping Goldhamer to determine whether the incidence of mental illness or psychosis in the US population had increased during the preceding century. In both world wars, the US military had rejected substantial numbers of individuals for mental or psychological reasons. Was the incidence of mental illness in the US population growing, as many presumed? RAND's formal interest in this question stemmed from the scale of US military manpower mobilization that had been required to defeat Nazi Germany and Imperial Japan in the Second World War. In the four years after the Japanese attack on Pearl Harbor, over 16 million Americans would serve in the US military out of a population of roughly 137 million.[26] In 1945 the number of active duty US military personnel had peaked at just over 12 million; but by 1947 less than 1.6 million remained in uniform.[27] Many senior defense officials believed that another major conflict could not be ruled out and that if it did occur, a European war against Stalin's massive Soviet Army might require the United States to mobilize manpower on a similar scale. If so, then a growing incidence of mental illness could significantly constrain the country's military potential.

The prevailing wisdom at the time held that the rate of mental illness in the US population had been growing since the 1840s due to the increasing urbanization of the nation's population combined with the "killing" pace, insecurity, and intense individualism associated with life in American cities. Goldhamer, with Marshall's help, aimed to discover whether data would confirm this view, and, if this hypothesis was confirmed, whether the trend had been accelerating in the first half of the twentieth century. If the conventional wisdom proved correct, the growing incidence of mental illness among draft-age men could significantly undermine American national defense in the event of a major-power conflict on the scale of World War II.

The Goldhamer-Marshall collaboration produced two RAND papers in 1949. Marshall's contribution was a statistical analysis of the available data. Both papers were subsequently published together under the title *Psychosis and Civilization*.[28] The first paper overturned the conventional wisdom, conclusively demonstrating that there had been no increase in the frequency of mental illness in the United States over the previous one hundred years. This was the good news. But there was also some bad news. The second paper estimated that individuals who survived to age forty-five would have one chance in twenty of being stricken by a serious mental illness, and one chance in ten if they lived to age sixty-five. The greater incidence of psychosis was not driven by urban living but by the growing number (and percentage) of Americans living well into old age. Mental health in the United States remained no better—and no worse—in the 1940s than it had been during the previous century; there were simply more mentally ill people now than there had been before.

Through the course of their initial collaboration, Marshall and Gold-hamer became close friends. The young Marshall found Goldhamer, who had once been the junior chess champion of Canada, both bright and intellectually stimulating. When the two men spent most of September and October 1949 in Santa Monica monitoring the statistical analyses and data processing for their mental illness studies, Goldhamer introduced Marshall to a variation of chess known as *Kriegspiel* (literally German for "war play"), which had become a popular recreational activity among RAND staffers. *Kriegspiel* is chess with incomplete information: each player can see the positions of his own pieces on the board, but not those of his opponent. A referee with complete information adjudicates each move as "legal" (that is to say, within the rules) or not and provides information on checks or captures. In the late 1940s John Williams, who headed RAND's mathematics division, was the center of a lively *Kriegspiel* activity at lunchtime and in the evenings. During his fall 1949 trip to Santa Monica, Marshall spent many evenings playing *Kriegspiel* at Williams's Pacific Palisades house just north of Santa Monica.

Not long after joining RAND Marshall was granted a Top Secret security clearance. Granting such clearances to RAND employees was commonplace at the time. LeMay had been emphatic that members of RAND's staff were to be kept current on both the Air Force's plans and its intelligence information—requirements that necessitated high security clearances. Since Project RAND's aim was to provide the Air Staff with unbiased advice, LeMay also specified that no one on the Air Staff would tell RAND researchers what to do or—just as important—what not to do.[29] Even more remarkable, the Air Staff was instructed to provide Project RAND with information on its other contract programs to avoid unnecessary duplication. These policies continued into the 1960s and made Project RAND an unusual enterprise from the outset. Finally, as Marshall could attest, RAND's top managers were both willing and able to pay top dollar to attract the best talent. When it came to intellectual horsepower, they preferred quality over quantity, hiring some very bright and unusual minds to address specific problems. Decades later, after being appointed the Pentagon's director of net assessment, Marshall would apply much the same approach to his outside research program.

While in Washington Marshall took advantage of the region's universities to continue his education in statistics. He began taking courses from

Solomon Kullback at George Washington University. Kullback, an American cryptanalyst and mathematician, had been one of the first three employees hired by the US Army's Signal Intelligence Service in the 1930s. Before and during World War II he had worked on deciphering both Japanese and German codes, including Japan's RED cipher machine messages. When Marshall arrived in Washington, Kullback was teaching evening classes in advanced statistics. Marshall availed himself of the opportunity, earning "As" in Kullback's classes.

A year before Marshall joined RAND, an economics division had been established under Charles Hitch. Hitch had come to RAND with an impressive résumé. Nearly two decades earlier he had entered Oxford as a Rhodes scholar. Three years later, in 1935, when he sat for his oral examination for a master's degree in economics, the Oxford faculty members on his committee, rather than questioning him, just tipped their academic caps to him in a show of respect and awarded him his degree. Shortly thereafter Hitch became the first American Rhodes scholar to be appointed an Oxford don. He also became general editor of the *Oxford Economic Papers*, which still publishes refereed papers in economic theory, applied economics, econometrics, economic development, economic history, and the history of economic thought.

During World War II Hitch gained practical experience in economic matters. While on leave from Oxford he served on the first Lend-Lease mission in London; the War Production Board; and in the Office of Strategic Services, where he helped evaluate the effects of strategic bombing on Germany. He ended his wartime service as chief of the Stabilization Controls Division of the Office of War Mobilization and Reconversion. When he joined RAND in 1948 Hitch was a visiting professor at Yale, the University of California–Los Angeles (UCLA), and the University of São Paulo in Brazil. He traveled frequently to speak before audiences throughout continental Europe and England.

In 1949 Russell Nichols, Hitch's only representative in RAND's Washington office, had become impressed by Marshall and approached him to point out the opportunities that the new department might hold for a young man of his talents. Then, in the spring of 1950, Hitch invited Marshall to spend the summer in Santa Monica with a team of RAND staff members that was exploring how the Air Force might best use atomic weapons to target the Soviet economy in the event of war. When Marshall arrived in California in late May 1949, he was still working with Goldhamer on the mental illness project, so he agreed to split his time between the social science and economics divisions. But he soon became immersed in the targeting project. In the end he concluded that destroying the Soviet economy with the Strategic Air Command's then modest stockpile of a few hundred atomic bombs would be difficult given that the Soviet Union was an enormous country with widely dispersed industrial facilities.

His brief introduction to RAND's main campus in California convinced him to relocate to Santa Monica in November 1950 to work full-time for Hitch, who would become one of Marshall's most influential mentors. Hitch's brilliance, combined with his willingness to challenge the conventional wisdom, predilection for multidisciplinary research, and respect for empirical facts strongly resonated with the young Marshall's own intellectual inclinations.

Hitch and Marshall also became close outside their professional interactions. Although most of the division heads at RAND during the 1950s were not inclined to do a great deal of entertaining, Hitch was a notable exception, regularly hosting parties and dinners at his home. After Marshall's marriage, he and his wife Mary became regular guests at the Hitches' social events. The close friendship between the two couples did not end with Hitch's move to the Pentagon in 1961 to be Defense Secretary Robert McNamara's comptroller. Even after Hitch had left the Pentagon in 1965 to head the University of California, the Hitches and the Marshalls often spent the Christmas holidays together in such places as Yosemite Valley in the Sierras.

Another RAND colleague Marshall became very close to during the 1950s was a young physicist by the name of Herman Kahn. Like Marshall, Kahn had bounced around the academic world. After World War II, he had begun a PhD program at the California Institute of Technology (Caltech). He eventually dropped out, settling for a master of science degree. Kahn then briefly sold real estate until recruited into RAND's Physics Division by a friend, Samuel Cohen.* Although he never acquired a doctorate, Kahn subsequently worked closely with three titans of science—nuclear physicists

---

*Cohen is generally credited with inventing the neutron bomb, a fission-fusion weapon designed to kill primarily with radiation rather than heat and blast.

Edward Teller and Hans Bethe, and mathematician and polymath John von Neumann—on the hydrogen bomb. Later Kahn's outspoken views on nuclear war would earn him a reputation as RAND's *l'enfant terrible*, and he would gain fame as a strategist from his books on nuclear strategy, which included *On Thermonuclear War* and *Thinking the Unthinkable*.

Kahn shared Marshall's intense curiosity about how the world actually works. Both men had started self-educating themselves at an early age in fields other than those in which they later earned formal degrees. Given their wide range of interests, intelligence, and skepticism regarding what others accepted as "conventional wisdom," the two men soon became close friends. During the early 1950s, they were inseparable whenever both of them were in Santa Monica. Marshall shared his thinking about economics and anthropology with Kahn, and Kahn reciprocated with insights into nuclear bomb design. By 1951 Kahn was regularly commuting to the Lawrence Livermore National Laboratory to work on the hydrogen bomb. Toward the end of the year, he began telling Marshall about the design breakthrough based on the concept of a two-stage device in which radiation confinement from the first-stage (or "primary") fission "trigger" would compress the fuel in the second stage (or "secondary") to produce a fusion reaction similar to what occurs in the sun. Turning the concept into a working thermonuclear device required extensive calculations of such things as the width of the channel through which radiation would flow from the primary to the secondary. During this period Kahn and Marshall were also collaborating on Monte Carlo statistical methods, which relied on random sampling of a large number of cases. Given their efforts to improve these methods, it was only natural that Kahn and Marshall ended up spending late nights at UCLA running Monte Carlo calculations on a new computer estimating H-bomb radiation flows.[30]

Their work paid off. On October 31, 1952, the United States set off the world's first thermonuclear explosion on the Pacific atoll of Enewetok. The experimental shot, nicknamed "Mike," had a yield equivalent to 10.4 million tons (or 10.4 megatons) of TNT—roughly a *thousand times* the yield of the atomic bomb dropped on Hiroshima.[31] The Soviets followed suit in April 1954 with RDS-37, a two-stage, radiation implosion thermonuclear bomb. Air dropped from a Tu-16 Badger bomber, the device produced a yield of 1.6 megatons.[32] Significantly the physics underlying Mike and RDS-37 did not appear to impose any obvious upper limit to the yield possible from thermonuclear weapons.* Thus was born the thermonuclear age in which both Washington and Moscow began fielding ever larger numbers of megaton-class nuclear weapons.

Although the United States was the first of the two superpowers to test a thermonuclear device, Mike was an 82-ton experimental behemoth, not an operational weapon. Much progress in both physics and engineering had to be made before megaton-class thermonuclear warheads could be built both small and light enough to be delivered by either aircraft or intercontinental ballistic missiles (ICBMs). Nevertheless, even at this early stage it was clear that thermonuclear weapons would fundamentally change the strategic outlooks of both the United States and the Soviet Union. In their 1952 paper on the implications of large-yield nuclear weapons, Brodie, Hitch, and Ernst Plesset argued that over time the nuclear balance between the two nations would almost certainly evolve from the current period of near American monopoly and atomic scarcity to one of strategic parity and thermonuclear plenty.[33] They accurately foresaw that nuclear weapons with yields of 1 to 25 megatons—or more—would eventually be available to both the United States and the Soviet Union in relatively large numbers. Once that shift in the US-Soviet nuclear balance had occurred, they warned, any large-scale thermonuclear exchange between Washington and Moscow would be an act of mutual suicide.

While obvious in retrospect, at the time these findings were both stunning and sobering. They quickly gave rise to efforts by RAND to develop concepts and strategies to cope with the growing threat. Marshall found himself on the ground floor of these developments. After witnessing a low-yield atomic test at the Nevada Test Site with Arnold Kramish in the spring of 1952, Marshall came way awed by the sheer power of even a 10–15 kiloton atomic device.

He and Kramish had driven from Santa Monica to Las Vegas the day before the test. After an early dinner in Las Vegas they drove out to the Nevada Test Site, checked in, and spent the night on army cots before being

---

*Later, in October 1961, the Soviets successfully tested a hydrogen bomb dropped from a Tu-95 Bear bomber that yielded some 50 megatons. This weapon, RDS-220, also known as Tsar Bomba, was actually a 100-megaton design. Like RDS-37, RDS-220 was intentionally derated for the test on Novaya Zemlya Island. Even so, the blast caused damage as far as 1,000 kilometers away, breaking windows in Finland and Sweden.

aroused hours before daybreak to drive to the location from which they were to observe the test. They were not even provided with protective goggles, and when the device detonated Marshall, who had covered his eyes with his hands, was able to see the bones in the thickest part of his palms from the explosion's initial flash of light. Reflecting on this experience decades later, Marshall suggested that it would behoove the leaders of nuclear states to witness such detonations at least once in their lives to gain a firsthand appreciation of the enormous destructive power inherent in these weapons.

Following his visit to the Nevada Test Site, Marshall was sent to assist the head of RAND's Washington office, Larry Henderson, in briefing the Brodie-Hitch-Plesset study to the Bureau of the Budget. While in Washington Marshall took on another project, this one with RAND analyst James Digby. He and Digby were directed to spend four months conducting an on-site assessment in Wiesbaden, West Germany. The objective: to help the US Air Forces in Europe's (USAFE) intelligence directorate analyze the growing problem of securing reliable strategic warning of a Soviet nuclear attack.

During Marshall's early years at Project RAND, which is to say before both the United States and the Soviet Union had large numbers of nuclear weapons, it was still possible to believe that a future war between the two nations would, in many respects, resemble World War II. In planning for such a war in the late 1940s the Air Force's initial inclination was to emphasize strategic bombing, only this time employing all available atomic weapons at the outset. The aim was the same as that which the Army Air Forces had pursued against Germany from 1943 through 1945: to destroy or otherwise neutralize the Soviet Union's "industrial web"—the raw materials, factories, weapons and munitions, and transportation infrastructure that fueled a country's ability to make war.[34] As Marshall had discovered in 1949, the United States' inventory of atomic weapons then consisted of only about two hundred Mark-3 and Mark-4 atomic bombs with maximum yields of 49 and 31 kilotons, respectively.[35] After this small inventory of atomic bombs had been expended in an initial "atomic blitz" against the USSR's industrial infrastructure the bombing campaign would have to fall back on attacks with conventional weapons similar to those employed during the 1943–1945 Combined Bomber Offensive against Germany in attempting to finish the job of destroying the Soviet war machine.

As one would expect, RAND researchers in the late 1940s looked for alternative ways of using America's small but growing atomic arsenal more effectively. One possibility was to make just a few atomic strikes on the Soviet Union and then drop leaflets encouraging the Soviet people to evacuate their cities. Such a strategy, some thought, might force the Soviet government to surrender, fearing that additional attacks by US atomic weapons held in reserve could destroy the USSR's economic infrastructure. This and other options were explored in RAND's "Warning and Bombing" (WARBO) study of 1949–1950.[36] The study's main idea was to find ways to control the level of violence so that it might be possible to achieve meaningful political objectives even in a nuclear war. For Bernard Brodie in particular this suggestion from WARBO appeared to offer a more rational alternative to the Air Force's all-out "atomic blitz."[37]

Another option that surfaced within RAND during the early 1950s involved mounting a preventive war against the Soviet Union before its leaders could create an atomic arsenal of their own. The head of RAND's mathematics division, John Williams, was a strong advocate of this view on the grounds that all-out war between the United States and the USSR was only a matter of time. If so, he argued, then it made sense to "throw the first [atomic] spear" should the Soviets refuse to relinquish their nuclear arms to international control.[38] Others who advocated preventive war included Plesset, who headed RAND's physics division, and John von Neumann, who had become an influential adviser to Project RAND due, among other things, to his help in developing the implosion (plutonium) version of the atomic bomb and his numerous contributions to theoretical and applied mathematics.[39] But as Brodie pointed out during his acerbic disagreement with Williams over the preventive-war option, President Dwight Eisenhower had emphatically rejected it on the grounds that no moment could be propitious for initiating general war with the Soviet Union.[40]

At this early stage in the Cold War another contingency worrying US war planners and RAND strategists alike was that, since the conventional military balance in Europe greatly favored the Soviets, the Kremlin might attempt to overrun Western Europe with conventional forces even in the face of a nuclear-armed United States. At the time of the Berlin blockade, for example, the Soviets had one and a half million troops in the sector surrounding Berlin, including the combat-experienced Third Shock and Eighth Guards armies.[41] By comparison, in July 1948 there were less than 91,000 American troops in all of West Germany. Operational US forces consisted of the 12,180 men of the First Infantry Division plus two infantry and two field artillery battalions.[42] During the brief period of the United States' atomic monopoly, the prevailing wisdom among US military analysts was that a Soviet conventional assault on Western Europe would quickly overwhelm NATO's conventional forces. Although West Germany, the Low Countries, and France would likely be lost, it was believed that NATO forces would be able to stop the Warsaw Pact's advance at the Pyrenees Mountains along the Franco-Spanish border. As NATO ground forces retreated, the US Air Force would unleash its atomic blitz against the USSR's industrial centers,[43] while the United States would mobilize its own conventional forces as it had in World War II, eventually retaking Western Europe and advancing on Moscow to depose the Bolshevik regime.

Importantly, this early vision of a future European conflict assumed that the United States had atomic weapons and the Soviets did not. As the latter began to field atomic weapons and delivery systems able to reach the United States itself, it became less and less realistic to think that one side could use nuclear weapons against the adversary's homeland while remaining unscathed itself. To be sure, the US atomic monopoly did not end in August 1949 when the Soviets exploded Joe-1; not until the mid-1950s did Soviet Long Range Aviation begin fielding heavy bombers with sufficient range to deliver nuclear weapons against targets in the continental United States and return to Soviet bases.

But once the Soviet Union had the bomb the handwriting was on the wall. It was increasingly evident that the strategic relationship between the USSR and the United States was rapidly evolving, and not in the United States' favor. The 1952 Brodie-Hitch-Plesset RAND study of high-yield nuclear weapons had accurately foreseen both nations' building up large arsenals of thermonuclear weapons. In May 1953 von Neumann assured Colonel Bernard Schriever, who went on to develop the Air Force's first ICBMs, that by 1960 it would be possible to reduce the weight of a 1-megaton hydrogen bomb to less than a ton.[44] This meant that thermonuclear warheads could be delivered by ballistic missiles against which there were no effective defenses. It was a terrifying possibility—and one that, as it emerged, would demand the intellectual talents of Marshall and other RAND strategists to address.

By the mid-1950s Marshall had demonstrated his impressive analytic abilities across a range of subjects bearing on nuclear strategy. This led to his time being split among more projects than ever before. His insights on the limits of a nuclear bombing campaign targeting the Soviet economy, for instance, led both Air Force intelligence and the Central Intelligence Agency (CIA) to bring him onboard as an adviser to help with their projections of future Soviet nuclear forces. Marshall and Herman Kahn were also asked to continue exploring aspects of nuclear strategy, as well as more efficient approaches to Monte Carlo statistical methods, even after their work on the hydrogen bomb effort was complete. Their efforts on ways to streamline Monte Carlo computations led to a joint paper that was published in late 1953 by the *Journal of Operations Research Society of America*. In it the two authors offered ways of greatly reducing the large sample sizes such calculations had previously required.[45]

Still yet another project found Marshall working with his RAND colleague Marc Peter to reexamine the data from the atomic attacks on Hiroshima and Nagasaki. In doing so they concluded that the vulnerability of steel-frame structures in the two cities had been overstated.[46] This led the Air Force to rethink what it could expect to accomplish with its small inventory of a few hundred relatively low-yield fission bombs.*

Marshall and Kahn also identified several other problems with RAND's overall approach to analysis. They found RAND tended to rely too heavily on models whose abilities to provide "good-enough" approximations to reality were often suspect. Many RAND analysts also viewed the Soviets as being supremely rational in their decisions on strategic nuclear forces despite growing evidence to the contrary. And the two men agreed that RAND's analysis was often woefully inadequate regarding the treatment of uncertainty.[47]

Over time Marshall discovered that these issues were not unique to RAND, but were endemic in most individuals and organizations devoted to security studies. Whenever he encountered them, Marshall would challenge analyses that had fallen into these traps, especially the "rational-actor model" that assumed individuals and organizations made optimal strategic choices. And when at last he was put in charge of an analytic organization of his own, he would seek to purge it of these shortcomings, despite eventually admitting that "there is only so much stupidity one man can prevent." Such limitations, however, did not prevent Marshall from trying.

---

*The first operational US Air Force H-bomb was the MK-17. This weapon weighed over 41,000 pounds and was soon succeeded by the "lightweight" MK-15, which weighed less than 8,000 pounds.

As Marshall's reputation at RAND steadily grew, his personal life was undergoing major changes as well. In 1952 he had become engaged to be married. But when he met his bride-to-be in Paris at the end of November, she called off the wedding, instead marrying William Kaufmann, one of Marshall's RAND colleagues. Returning to California, Marshall eventually recovered from the shock and developed a new romantic interest: an attractive young RAND employee named Mary Speer, who also happened to be Hitch's secretary. Although there was no formal rule against dating other RAND staff members, Marshall was initially reluctant to approach Mary as they both worked in the same division. Eventually, however, he asked Mary whether she knew a Marjorie Speer, whose acquaintance he had made during his time in Chicago. Marjorie had recently moved to Los Angeles with her husband, Walter Richmond. It turned out that Mary and Marjorie were sisters. Marjorie was invited to attend an early 1953 open house RAND held to inaugurate the think tank's new facility on Main Avenue in Santa Monica. At the inauguration it was agreed that Andrew and Mary would come to dinner at the Richmonds' house in the San Fernando Valley, which they did. Shortly thereafter Marshall asked Mary out on a first date.

From there things moved quickly. Marshall's marriage to Mary Speer took place on September 12, 1953, with Herman Kahn as best man. Although neither Marshall nor his new bride could have known it at the time, their union would last for over half a century.

Shortly after he and Mary tied the knot, Marshall took a leave of absence from RAND to return to the University of Chicago. The university now offered a PhD in statistics, and his former mentor, W. Allen Wallis, was still teaching statistics there. But much to his surprise, upon arriving in Chicago Marshall discovered that Wallis had been asked to head a Ford Foundation study to determine how best to allocate its grant-funding support to universities. As this required Wallis's full attention, he would not be able to teach in the 1953–1954 academic year. Wallis asked Marshall to take on the classes in his absence, and he agreed.

During two semesters at Chicago Marshall discovered two things. First, in taking over his mentor's classes he came to understand that his knowledge of statistics was already at such an advanced level that he perhaps did not need to pursue the PhD after all. Second, Marshall found he missed both the intellectual stimulation and the sense of purpose that he had experienced at RAND. In Santa Monica he had been working on projects of great importance to his country—something that, he now realized, gave greater meaning and satisfaction to his work.

As a result, Marshall chose not to remain in Chicago. By the spring of 1954 he had decided that tackling the real-world problems of nuclear strategy at the dawn of the thermonuclear missile age was far more interesting and rewarding than continuing his academic education. He and Mary returned to Santa Monica in April, eventually settling in a house on Kenter Avenue in the Brentwood Hills section of Los Angeles.

No sooner had Marshall returned to Santa Monica than Hitch recruited him to join a small group of RAND's top strategists known as the Strategic Objectives Committee (SOC). The dawning of the thermonuclear age had convinced Hitch that diagnosing its defining characteristics and strategic implications should be given high priority. Hitch formed the SOC to identify the major issues the think tank's research on nuclear strategy and forces should pursue over the next ten years.

One of the members of the SOC, Bernard Brodie, had argued only months after the atomic bombings of Hiroshima and Nagasaki that the sheer destructiveness of atomic weapons meant that the main purpose of the US military was no longer to win the nation's wars but to deter them.[48] Recognition that both the United States and the USSR would eventually be able to field large stockpiles of thermonuclear weapons only reinforced this view. Once the United States could no longer strike first and expect to escape Soviet nuclear retaliation, Brodie concluded, unrestricted nuclear war would be suicidal for both sides.[49] Yet deterrence of nuclear war hinged on being ready and able to inflict nuclear retaliation on the opponent. Given this dilemma, what new ideas and strategies should the think tank pursue in the years ahead to help the Air Force and the nation deal with the looming thermonuclear missile age?

The committee members were a veritable who's who of RAND's leading thinkers. Besides Marshall, Brodie, and Hitch (the SOC's first chairman), the group included Arnold Kramish; electrical engineer James Digby; Victor Hunt, a social scientist; James Lipp, an aeronautical engineer (the SOC's second chairman); Alex Mood, a statistician; and John Williams (the SOC's third chairman). Over time the group would also draw in Herman Kahn and economist Malcolm Hoag to support its efforts.

The various roles Marshall played in the Strategic Objectives Committee are a good example of the collaborative, multidisciplinary teamwork of many of RAND's projects during the 1950s. John Williams was fascinated with the idea that game theory could help RAND analysts to anticipate possible Soviet responses in the event of a nuclear conflict. Toward this end, Alex Mood developed a Strategic Air Warfare game that allowed opposing teams of RAND researchers to play out US-Soviet conflicts that escalated to large-scale nuclear exchanges. Because of the natural desire of players on both sides to "win" in some sense, the teams began to judge their success based on where the front lines between NATO and Soviet forces in Europe ended up at the game's end. Given this criterion for measuring success, opposing players tended to resort to nuclear weapons early and pay little or no attention to the damage their decisions wreaked on their respective homelands. Players on the US side found themselves sacrificing half of the American economy to Soviet nuclear attacks in order to prevent the Soviets from advancing a few more miles into West Germany and the Low Countries.

Marshall found the game neither realistic nor sensible because of the measure of military worth the players were using.[50] Concentrating on where the front lines ended up in Europe ignored the damage each side's nuclear weapons could inflict on the other's homeland. Moreover, since 1945 American leaders had shown little inclination to resort to nuclear weapons in response to such aggressive acts as the Berlin Blockade and the invasion of South Korea. And Eisenhower had categorically rejected the option of using nuclear weapons in a preventive war to block the Soviets from fielding their own intercontinental nuclear arsenal.[51]

In an effort to address these problems Marshall and a colleague, Jack Hirschleifer, developed more complex measures of merit for game outcomes that included limiting the damage nuclear exchanges would inflict on either nation's economy. This greatly improved the game's realism, and thus its value. Despite the initial problems with Mood's war game, Marshall felt that by playing games the researchers tended to develop good strategies so long as the games were well designed and played often enough. His conclusion was not to reject war games, but to insist that they be more carefully designed.

Another SOC project that Marshall became involved in during the second half of 1954 involved estimating the growth of the US nuclear stockpile over time based on public documents and congressional testimony. The true size of the stockpile was a closely guarded secret—or at least it was supposed to be. Kramish, who was a SOC member, knew what the actual stockpile numbers were. He insisted that someone like Marshall could develop good estimates based on open sources. In the end, Kramish proved right. Marshall took on the challenge and crafted a close estimate without any use of classified data. This would not be the last time that he was able to reach accurate conclusions with incomplete or even anecdotal data. Indeed, being able to reach sound conclusion on matters relating to national security based in minimal evidence has been one of Marshall's main intellectual strengths, no doubt enabled at least in part by the breadth and depth of his knowledge on a wide range of issues bearing on the problem at hand.

The SOC's final product, published at the end of December, was an internal RAND paper, "The Next Ten Years," cowritten by Brodie, Hitch, and Marshall. In considering the lines of research on nuclear forces that RAND should emphasize through the mid-1960s, the authors began by focusing on the broad trends in weapons technology and delivery systems that would shape the US-Soviet competition in nuclear arms over the coming decade. First, they concluded that the rivals' stockpiles would most likely grow to several thousand weapons apiece by the mid-1960s; second, that H-bombs with yields of up to 3 megatons would become light enough to be delivered by tactical aircraft and ballistic missiles; and third, barring unforeseen advances in missile defenses, within five to ten years both sides would begin fielding thermonuclear-tipped ICBMs, establishing the absolute superiority of the offense over the defense.[52] In light of the anticipated Soviet nuclear buildup, the superiority the United States then enjoyed due to its virtual monopoly in long-range, or "strategic," nuclear bombers would fade.[53] Years later the value of identifying broad trends that could produce disruptive shifts in military competitions would emerge as a staple feature in the net assessments that Marshall's Pentagon office would undertake. In light of the trends Brodie, Hitch, and Marshall saw in nuclear weaponry, "The Next Ten Years" concluded that deterring a surprise attack by the USSR would quickly become the essential, primary component of US strategic policy. In that case, a Strategic Air Command (SAC) impervious to a Soviet nuclear "Pearl Harbor" would be the keystone of the United States' deterrence strategy.[54]

This finding triggered alarm bells in Santa Monica and beyond. Only a few months earlier another RAND analysis had concluded that the SAC bomber force was not, in fact, likely to be invulnerable to a surprise nuclear attack. In April 1954 Albert Wohlstetter, along with Robert Lutz, Henry Rowen, and Fred Hoffman, completed a study of SAC basing options. At the time the bulk of SAC's bomber force was composed of approximately

1,600 medium-range B-47s and RB-47s. In addition, the Strategic Air Command had some 300 long-range B-36s and RB-36s, about a wing of B-52s, and over 700 KC-97 tankers.[55] The basing scheme SAC had settled on for the period from 1956 to 1961 called for its bombers to be based in the continental United States (CONUS) in peacetime. In the event of nuclear attack, the bombers would deploy to preselected overseas bases. Wohlstetter's *Selection and Use of Strategic Air Bases* (RAND report "R-266") demonstrated that SAC's bases in CONUS were growing increasingly vulnerable to atomic attack by Soviet bombers. The picture was even worse at SAC's overseas operating bases, which were much closer to the Soviet Union.[56] To minimize the risk to US bombers operating from forward bases, Wohlstetter recommended using these bases strictly for ground-based refueling of SAC bombers en route to their targets in the USSR.[57] Unfortunately, the cost of pursuing this option for a force dominated by medium-range bombers was judged so high that it would drastically reduce SAC's total striking power against an expanding Soviet target base.[58] Fortunately, long-range B-52 bombers were entering the force. Over time they would displace the older bombers and Wohlstetter's preferred option would become a reality.

Wohlstetter's *Selection and Use of Strategic Air Bases* was one of RAND's most influential analyses. Long before the study was completed Wohlstetter began sharing its preliminary findings with RAND's Air Force sponsors. Starting in 1952, versions of R-266 were briefed over ninety times to SAC and the Air Staff.[59] As a result, the study had an important influence on the Air Force's strategic planning even before it was finished. By 1954 SAC was already moving away from its original plans to depend on overseas basing. Later, in 1959, the Air Force estimated that Wohlstetter's assessment had saved the United States a billion dollars while enabling it to adopt a more secure retaliatory posture for SAC's bomber fleet.[60] In addition to Wohlstetter being an enormous asset to RAND and the US government, it would soon become clear just how crucial he was to Marshall as well.

In Wohlstetter Marshall found a mentor and friend comparable to Hitch and Kahn. Educated in mathematical logic and economics, Wohlstetter had joined RAND in 1951 as a consultant. His love of fine food, fine wine, classical music, and ballet made him one of the social pillars of the organization in the early 1950s. He and his wife, Roberta, also a member of RAND's analytic staff, regularly hosted small groups of RAND strategists at their house in Laurel Canyon, and the Marshalls were regular guests at the Wohlstetters' social gatherings.[61]

One of the enduring insights that Marshall gleaned from Wohlstetter's work was the importance of choosing the right performance metrics, or analytic measures, to gauge the effectiveness of various courses of action. Choosing performance metrics can be exceedingly difficult, since at the outset of a study the analysts may not understand the problem well enough to separate what is important from what is not. Wohlstetter's great "invention," as Marshall later called it, was to remain open to the possibility that an analyst's initial intuitions about the critical factors in addressing a problem might be wrong and need revision as the problem became better understood.[62] Prior to the basing study, most of RAND's major analyses had focused on the composition of SAC's bomber force. Edwin Paxson's massive systems analysis, *Strategic Bombing Systems Analysis* (R-173), completed in March 1950, examined no fewer than 400,000 different bomb-bomber combinations, and calculated the effects of dozens of different variables, many of which were interdependent.[63] The key metric of that study was to pick the most cost-effective bomber force. In contrast, Wohlstetter and his colleagues eventually realized during the course of their bomber basing study that the appropriate measures of effectiveness were not the composition or cost of SAC's bomber force. Instead they turned out to be the distances from SAC bases to Soviet targets, the most favorable entry points for penetrating Soviet air defenses, the sources of supplies for SAC bases, and the locations from which the Soviets could attack US bases.[64]

Selecting the right metrics was a manifestation of what became known within RAND as the criterion problem. Marshall had already encountered this issue in Alex Mood's Strategic Air Warfare game, in which the players' initial metric of limiting the advance of Soviet forces into Western Europe had undermined the value of the game's results. A more sensible metric was limiting the destruction visited on the United States by Soviet nuclear weapons. In the end, the criterion problem proved so central to RAND's analyses that Hitch and his coauthor, the economist Roland McKean, later devoted over twenty pages to it in their influential 1960 book *The Economics of Defense in the Nuclear Age*.

As vital as the selection of appropriate decision criteria was in systems analysis, it had little to offer in helping Brodie, Hitch, and Marshall decide what directions RAND's strategic research should take over the next ten years. After considering some of the requirements of containment and the central role of deterrence in US nuclear strategy, "The Next Ten Years" turned to the vexing questions of American options under the assumption that the Cold War would be an "essentially permanent" feature of America's security environment. If, as some believed, all-out war with the Soviet Union was practically inevitable within a generation, should the United States consider a preventive war before the Soviets could field intercontinental nuclear systems? If not, then what policies should or could the United States adopt to compete more effectively and efficiently against the Soviet Union? What might US objectives be in the context of a nuclear competition based on deterrence? How might the United States prepare for the possibility of limited and peripheral wars while exploiting its own economic and technological advantages? Could the United States hold the NATO alliance together in the face of persistent Soviet efforts to fragment it?

Suggesting even tentative answers to these questions might have provided some direction for RAND's future research on the US-Soviet competition in intercontinental nuclear forces. But Brodie, Hitch, and Marshall instead emphasized the substantial uncertainties involved in trying to answer them. Their emphasis on asking the right questions, even if good answers were not immediately apparent, would prove to be vintage Marshall. In his eyes, whether in 1954 or today, identifying the right questions—those that matter most in determining strategic advantage—is an essential first step in any comparative analysis, including net assessment.

Nevertheless, "The Next Ten Years" did offer some advice for RAND's leadership. Contrary to much of the prevailing wisdom at RAND about Soviet decision-making, the paper emphasized that Soviet leaders were not necessarily the all-seeing, all-knowing, fearless adversaries that senior US civilian and military decision makers generally imagined them to be. "The Next Ten Years" also concluded that it was important to identify Soviet weaknesses and exploit them.[65] Both were insights that Marshall would continue to develop and expand upon in the decades that followed, starting with his collaboration over the next several years with Joseph Loftus on Soviet organizational behavior.

In the end, however, "The Next Ten Years" concluded that in "policy matters even current strategies are not always easy to discover and describe; and while future strategies will somehow emerge out of present ones (and thus be affected by present habits), they will very likely do so in quite erratic fashion."[66] The best Brodie, Hitch, and Marshall could offer concerning the course RAND's strategic analysis should pursue over the next decade was to hope that RAND's best analysts could help shape American nuclear strategy by making "policy makers aware of the facts and implications of weapons developments and by undertaking research projects designed to throw light on strategic choices."[67] In other words, good diagnoses based on asking the right questions were key to gaining competitive advantage and helping US leaders make better strategic choices.

Marshall and his two coauthors appear to have been satisfied with the results of their efforts. John Williams, however, was not. Williams wanted more than an identification of the most important questions bearing on RAND's future research on nuclear strategy. He wanted detailed, action-able answers. Williams saw three of the brightest, best-informed strategists in America devoting their efforts to identifying issues and questions rather than addressing and answering them.[68] As he wrote in a September 1954 memo to Brodie, Hitch, and Marshall, "Chums, it seems to me that you have laid an egg—an elegant, ellipsoidal, academic egg to be sure, but nev-ertheless one which can serve henceforth as the model for the cipher."[69]

An increasingly acerbic exchange between Williams and Brodie fol-lowed Williams's initial criticism of "The Next Ten Years." In the ensuing flurry of memos Brodie adamantly rejected Williams's attraction to mount-ing a preventative war again the USSR. Marshall came away from the expe-rience feeling that Williams had missed the point. The object of the exercise was not to provide answers to the US defense establishment, but rather to identify the key issues upon which RAND should focus its efforts over the coming decade. Clearly evident in "The Next Ten Years" was Marshall's growing sense that the first priority should be identifying the right ques-tions rather than elaborating precise or elegant answers.

For Marshall, the 1950s at RAND were a period of tremendous intellectual development, most of which came from a combination of self-education and the good counsel and encouragement he received from such men as Hitch, Goldhamer, and Wohlstetter—as well as his interactions with peers such as Herman Kahn and, later, Joseph Loftus. But as he grew intellectu-ally Marshall also began mentoring others. Some of this occurred naturally, as colleagues began to approach him for guidance. Yet it was his remarkable generosity with his time and patience with those individuals in whom he saw promise that encouraged them to produce some of the more insightful works that emerged from the US strategic studies community during the second half of the twentieth century.

Over time the effects of Marshall's "hidden hand" mentoring would become so pronounced that they were impossible to ignore. But in the 1950s
his influence was more subtle and limited—although he did have a lasting
effect on some of the people whose lives he touched during this time. One of
the first to benefit from Marshall's good counsel was Roberta Wohlstetter.

Because Marshall and the Wohlstetters were close socially as well as
professionally, it was only natural that in 1957, when Roberta was searching
for ideas as to what might constitute promising topics for new research, she
approached Marshall for advice. The result was *Pearl Harbor: Warning and
Decision,* which explored and assessed the causes of the US intelligence failures that enabled Japan's successful surprise attack on Pearl Harbor in 1941.
In her introduction Wohlstetter wrote: "The initial stimulus for the book
came from my friend, Andrew W. Marshall." She went on to say that she
was "deeply grateful to him" for his "constant encouragement and advice
through five years of research."[70] The book was published to great acclaim.
In adding *Pearl Harbor* to its professional reading list at the time of its publication, the US National Security Agency declared it "the clearest exposi-
tion of the subject that has yet been published" while concluding that it "is
one of the most thorough analytical studies of the events leading up to any
war and will probably become *the* book on the controversial question of the
surprise attack on Pearl Harbor."[71]

One of the many insights that emerged from the book concerned
MAGIC, the process by which US code breakers were able to decode Japan's secret diplomatic messages. Wohlstetter showed how the necessity for
preserving the extreme secrecy associated with MAGIC undermined efforts
to share the intelligence it produced on the possibility of a Japanese attack.
She explored, in all, fifteen different intelligence signals that in retrospect
clearly seemed to indicate an attack on Pearl Harbor was forthcoming. Yet
the attack came as both a strategic and tactical surprise. In explaining why,
Wohlstetter concluded that some intelligence failures are inevitable because
of the difficulty in distinguishing the accurate intelligence "signals" from
the background "noise" of many intelligence inputs.

In part Marshall had suggested strategic warning as a topic for Wohlstetter because he had done a similar study in 1952 on the strategic warning
problem facing NATO in Central Europe. He later recalled that in itself
Pearl Harbor didn't influence his "own subsequent thinking very much, because the main conceptual ideas were pretty clear [to me] much earlier."[72]

In fact, Wohlstetter's book brought into the public eye Marshall's growing concerns over the role that organizations play in decision-making as well as the need to avoid making analytically convenient but unwarranted assumptions that ignore the factor of uncertainty. As Wohlstetter wrote, "If the study of Pearl Harbor has anything to offer for the future, it is this: We have to accept the fact of uncertainty and live with it."[73]

In his foreword to Wohlstetter's book, Nobel laureate Thomas Schelling echoed her concerns about the tendency "to focus on a few vivid and over-simplified dangers." Rather, wrote Schelling, "The planner should think in subtler and more variegated terms and allow for a wider range of contingencies." The consequences for policy makers who fail to do so, he pointed out, "are mercilessly displayed in this superb book."[74]

Schelling predicted the book would become a classic in the field, and it did. For senior US policy makers who had lived through the trauma of Pearl Harbor and who later confronted the prospect of a Soviet nuclear surprise attack, Wohlstetter's book had a profound effect. *Pearl Harbor* was awarded the Bancroft Prize, and Wohlstetter would later be awarded the Medal of Freedom—the nation's highest civilian honor—for her "great contribution to the security of the United States."[75]

Wohlstetter's book was an early instance of how Marshall's mentoring led to seminal work in the field of security studies. Given his innate modesty and inclination to avoid the limelight, this "hidden hand" approach suited Marshall. Over time other leading scholars and senior policy makers would benefit from his wise counsel, and acknowledge their intellectual debts to him.

While Marshall was heavily occupied in the SOC, a new analyst arrived at RAND: Joseph Loftus. Although Marshall's development as an analyst and strategist was certainly influenced by Goldhamer, Hitch, Kahn, Wohlstetter, Digby, and others at RAND during the 1950s, Loftus unquestionably had the greatest impact on the young strategist's thinking about Soviet decision-making and the evolution of their nuclear forces. Perhaps even more important, Loftus indirectly contributed to Marshall's growing conviction that a fundamental assumption of much contemporary analysis—that rivals could be counted on to behave "rationally"—was seriously at odds with their actual behavior.

Prior to Pearl Harbor, Loftus had completed the course work and research for a doctoral dissertation on bank capitalization at Johns Hopkins

University. But he never wrote his dissertation. A few months after the Japanese attack Loftus joined the US Navy, serving in Panama, the Aleutian Islands, and the Ryukyu Islands. After the war, he took a job as an assistant economics professor at American University, where he taught and conducted research until mid-1950. With grant money for his research running out, he then joined the Air Target Division of Air Force intelligence as a civilian, and spent the next four years tracking the USSR's emerging nuclear program.

Soon after Loftus joined RAND he and Marshall found themselves spending long hours together discussing "The Next Ten Years," Soviet nuclear developments, and the Air Force's strategic warning problem. Their talks quickly evolved into an effort to understand Soviet organizational behavior. Their collaboration lasted until the early 1960s when Loftus was forced to retire for medical reasons.

In early 1955 Loftus, Marshall, and a RAND colleague, Robert Belzer, were asked to help the Air Force establish a worldwide network of centers to provide early warning of a Soviet nuclear surprise attack on the United States. With preventive war off the table the United States had little choice but to try to achieve strategic warning and avoid a "nuclear Pearl Harbor." Some three years earlier, Marshall and Digby had gone to Wiesbaden to work on this problem, but the Air Force had been unwilling to grant them access to highly sensitive communications intelligence (COMINT) that could have provided critical insights regarding Soviet plans and decisions. This time Marshall, Loftus, and Belzer all received COMINT clearances, enabling Loftus to share with Marshall the detailed knowledge about the USSR's nuclear program he had gained during his four years in Air Force intelligence. Once back in Santa Monica they were also able to keep abreast of ongoing Soviet developments by visiting the COMINT facility at March Air Force Base in nearby Riverside, California. At the time, only a handful of RAND staffers had access to this rich source of intelligence on Soviet nuclear developments. COMINT clearances gave Loftus and Marshall far greater insight into this area than nearly all of their RAND colleagues.*

As their collaboration deepened, Loftus and Marshall began to realize how wide of the mark some of RAND's forecasts about the USSR's future

---

*COMINT remained a rich intelligence source through the late 1950s, but declined rapidly after the 1960 defection to the USSR of two National Security Agency cryptologists, Bernon Mitchell and William Hamilton Martin.

strategic forces were. In one instance in 1954, a RAND research project attempted to predict where Soviet Long Range Aviation (LRA) bomber bases would be located. At that time US intelligence projections of Soviet nuclear forces were not yet being made on any consistent or regular basis. Forecasts might look out three years, or ten, or some number of years in between. In the absence of consistent projections of Soviet nuclear forces, RAND analysts had to make their own. Doing so required them to put themselves in the Soviet's position. RAND researchers had to decide how they would position LRA's bomber forces if they were responsible for them.

Many RAND analysts assumed that the Soviets were supremely rational planners—that their major decisions about military forces were carefully calculated to pose the greatest threat to the United States in general, and to SAC in particular. This construct had great appeal at RAND and elsewhere in the US national security establishment because it allowed analysts to simplify their assumptions about Soviet behavior. By assuming the Soviets would behave rationally (at least as viewed from a US perspective), one could forecast future Soviet strategic forces without having to delve into the history, propensities, strengths and weaknesses, rigidities, military doctrines, operational methods, and organizational complexities of the Soviet state.

Adopting this approach, the research on the LRA-basing issue concluded that the Soviets would locate their bomber bases in western Siberia along the Trans-Siberian Railway on a path from Omsk in the west to Krasnoyarsk in the east.[76] This conclusion was intended to reflect how the Soviets would address the basing problem. It was based on the theory that "rational" Soviet decision makers would choose to make LRA's bases as difficult as possible for SAC bombers to attack by locating them deep in the USSR's interior.

Loftus and Marshall knew from COMINT that this forecast was dead wrong. Soviet bomber bases were mostly dotted along the USSR's periphery, their locations having been chosen during the early days of military aviation. At that time aircraft ranges were modest compared to what they later became, and basing LRA on the USSR northern periphery shortened the distances to US targets. The dilemma for Loftus and Marshall was that they could not share what they knew about LRA and Soviet nuclear programs with RAND colleagues who lacked COMINT clearances. The best they could do was to suggest alternative—or "nonrational"—ways of looking at the LRA-basing issue. Marshall and Loftus pointed out that most of the SAC bomber bases were on the periphery of the United States, where they had been since the early days of US military aviation. Might not this be the case with the Soviet Union's? And if LRA's mission was the atomic attack of the US homeland, then wouldn't the limited ranges of early LRA bombers also argue for basing them on the USSR's periphery? RAND analysts largely rejected these arguments as not fitting their rational-actor model of Soviet decision-making.

There was, however, a larger strategic planning issue beyond this single RAND study. Early in their collaboration the more Loftus and Marshall looked into what the Soviets were actually doing as compared to what RAND and US intelligence analysts were forecasting, the more they began to realize that the forecasts relying on the rational-actor model often did not fit the facts. This realization led the pair to begin not only questioning the validity of the rational-actor model of Soviet decision-making, but to start looking for better models. The question they ultimately asked themselves was: Whose behavior and decisions are US analysts trying to forecast? After reviewing the evolution of the Soviet Union's strategic posture they concluded that it was "more plausible that the Soviet posture evolved as the result of decisions taken within a large bureaucratic structure than as the output of a small set of individuals working in a highly consistent manner."[77]

The clear implication was that RAND's efforts to forecast the evolution of Soviet nuclear forces needed to incorporate the effects of actual Soviet organizational behavior—how they really functioned, as opposed to what abstract theory posited. Marshall and Loftus decided to try to build on this insight to improve RAND's forecasts. In late 1956 or early 1957 they initiated an internal consulting effort. Loftus coined the endeavor Project SOVOY, an acronym he drew from the Russian for "Soviet military" (Советские воиска). The project's specific objective was to help RAND researchers improve their forecasts of Soviet nuclear forces.

In the end, SOVOY was less a project than a series of "help memos" to RAND researchers. Nor did the effort prove as successful as Loftus and Marshall had hoped. For many analysts, then and later, the simplicity and attractiveness of the rational-actor model offered a relatively quick and simple analytic path toward a conclusion. Embracing the advice proffered by Marshall and Loftus would not make their work easier, but more difficult. To these objections Marshall would have no doubt responded by noting that estimating military power was not easy, but hard.

Despite the generally poor reception to their efforts, SOVOY did convince Marshall, Loftus, and some others to begin developing an alternative

view of Soviet decision-making, taking explicitly into account the bureaucratic behavior of the various Soviet organizations involved in developing
the USSR's nuclear forces. Whose decisions RAND and US intelligence
analysts wanted to predict ranged from those of the Politburo and the Soviet General Staff to the USSR's military services and their weapons design and production bureaus.* From SOVOY an enduring insight emerged:
all of these Soviet organizations, as well as key bureaucrats within them,
were competing to have their views and agendas prevail. The notion that
one could explain (let alone predict) the behavior of the USSR as the sole
product of rational action by a single entity was a mirage, and a potentially
dangerous one at that.

Marshall's interest in organizational behavior persisted long after his collaboration with Loftus. During the early 1960s he would begin to seek out
academics whose scholarship focused on understanding decision-making
in large organizations such as major American business firms. He found
the work being done by Richard Cyert, James March, and Herbert Simon,
along with a small group of scholars at the Harvard Business School, including Joseph Bower, particularly valuable. Their findings reinforced Marshall's conviction that studying how Soviet organizations made decisions,
including the resource shortages and other constraints that affected their
force posture choices, was the most fruitful way to begin trying to forecast
the USSR's likely force posture eight or ten years in the future.

By 1956 Loftus and Marshall were both consultants to the CIA. This not
only expanded the sources of intelligence available to both men, but also
enabled them to serve as a conduit for some CIA reports that otherwise
would not have made it to RAND. In the decade ahead, Marshall's continuing involvement with the CIA on intelligence issues would bring him
other assignments involving nuclear strategy and sensitive intelligence. One
of the earliest was the commission headed by H. Rowan Gaither Jr., a San
Francisco attorney who in 1957 also sat on the boards of the Ford Foundation and the RAND Corporation. Gaither had been one of RAND's
founding fathers as well as the first chairman of its board.

---

*A difference between the US and Soviet acquisition systems was that in the
USSR design and production were carried out by different organizations, whereas
in the United States both were usually done by the same defense contractor.

Known as the Gaither Commission, the panel got under way in April 1957 when Eisenhower established a Security Resources Panel under his Scientific Advisory Committee. The panel's assignment was to assess "the relative value of various active and passive measures to protect the [US] civil population in the case of nuclear attack"; in addition, it was asked to study "the deterrent value" of US retaliatory nuclear forces and "the economic and political consequences of any significant shift of emphasis or direction in defense programs."[78]

Marshall was tapped to serve on the Gaither Commission's staff. Starting in August 1957, he spent five months in Washington working on the Security Resources Panel's analysis group headed by Robert Prim of Bell Telephone Laboratories and Stanley Lawwill from the Strategic Air Command. Marshall also became involved in an intelligence subgroup that looked at strategic reconnaissance issues. In addition to Marshall, the subgroup included Spurgeon Keeny, who had succeeded Loftus in Air Force intelligence, and Jim Perkins from the Carnegie Corporation. The subgroup's aim was to explore ways of masking the highly classified or "black" Corona spy satellite program then being developed with "white world," or unclassified, information.

The Gaither panel submitted its report, "Deterrence and Survival in the Nuclear Age," to Eisenhower in November 1957. Scholars have debated how influential it was, especially in affecting US nuclear strategy. What is clear in hindsight, though, is that the report considerably overstated Soviet capabilities. It also portrayed the Soviet economy as expanding much more rapidly than that of the United States, having grown from one-third to one-half the size of US gross national product.

Working on the Gaither Commission heightened Marshall's awareness of the fundamental importance of developing an accurate assessment of the Soviet economy's size, and the portion of it devoted to military programs. Marshall also developed a healthy skepticism as to the way in which these estimates were derived. Over time this skepticism would lead Marshall to engage in a long-running dispute with the CIA over the matter, which he viewed as of fundamental importance to understanding the United States' competitive position relative to the Soviet Union.

The main authors of the Gaither report were Colonel George Lincoln, head of West Point's Social Sciences Department, who had served on Eisenhower's Project Solarium strategic exercise in 1953, and Paul Nitze, who had also been the principal author of President Truman's NSC 68, a top secret policy paper outlining US policy for the Cold War. The commission's report came only a month after the Soviets succeeded in launching Sputnik, the world's first man-made earth-orbiting satellite. This remarkable scientific feat brought home even to average Americans the vulnerability of their country to nuclear attack: if the USSR could boost a satellite into space, it had the means to launch a nuclear warhead at any location in the United States. News of Sputnik spawned demands in Congress to meet the challenge by, among other things, augmenting US civil defenses, boosting the military budget, and promoting greater education in mathematics and the hard sciences in public schools.

Moreover, not being privy—as Marshall was—to the intelligence being provided by US U-2 covert reconnaissance flights over the Soviet Union, the Gaither Commission had no way of knowing how far behind the United States the USSR was in terms of intercontinental nuclear forces. In the wake of Sputnik's success, the Gaither commissioners assumed the worst, portraying the Soviets as having made "spectacular progress" in producing fissile material and jet bombers, and asserting that the USSR had probably surpassed the United States in developing ICBMs.[79]

In reality, the first heavy Soviet jet bomber, the Myasishchev M-4, which so worried the commission, proved incapable of flying a two-way mission against the United States. Only 116 of these aircraft were produced by 1960, and most of those were converted to aerial tankers. By comparison, from 1955 to 1962 the United States produced 739 B-52 long-range bombers. As for Soviet ICBM developments, the USSR's first ICBM, the R-7/7A (designated the SS-6 by NATO), became operational in 1960 or 1961. However, it proved to be an enormous, cumbersome missile. It took twenty hours to prepare for launch and its cryogenic fuel meant that it could not be kept ready to launch for more than a day. No more than six of these missiles were ever deployed.[80]

To shore up the US military posture, the commission recommended spending an additional $19.09 billion over 1959–1963 on high-priority military capabilities, plus another $25.13 billion on improvements to active and passive defenses.[81] To put these fiscal recommendations in perspective, the proposed five-year total of $44.22 billion exceeded the Defense Department's total outlays of $41.47 billion in fiscal year 1959.

Marshall's work on the Gaither Commission led him to think more deeply about ways of mediating the apparent disconnect between the requirements of nuclear deterrence and those of nuclear war fighting. On the one hand, the more horrific the nuclear devastation US strategic forces could inflict on the USSR, the more likely the Soviets might be deterred from starting a nuclear war. On the other hand, deterrence might fail. If it did, would the United States be doomed? Would it be destroyed as a functioning entity, or could strategic forces be designed and employed to enable outcomes short of mutual societal destruction without weakening nuclear deterrence?

Once back in Santa Monica, Marshall began talking to Goldhamer about this dilemma. They decided to approach it through game-theoretic methods. They constructed payoff, or utility, matrices using largely hypothetical numbers for both the United States and the USSR, the US goal being neither to maximize deterrence nor achieve the best (or least worst) outcome of a nuclear war. Instead they wanted to get the best expected value for both elements combined.[82] The values used in the model included the proportion of SAC's bombers surviving the first Soviet attack, Soviet estimates of SAC's surviving bombers, US choices of strategy, and both sides' outcome utilities. To illustrate the methodology, they tested it against a single case—a Soviet surprise counterforce attack against US nuclear forces in CONUS and overseas. Reflecting Marshall and Goldhamer's interest in organizational behavior, the analysis specifically highlighted differences in US versus Soviet perspectives and strategies. To assist them with the Soviet side of the analysis they brought in Nathan Leites, a RAND colleague who had focused on these issues in a classic analysis of what he termed the "operational code" of the Politburo.

Some intriguing, if tentative, findings emerged from this effort. Marshall and Goldhamer concluded that if the Soviets attacked first, the best US strategy (and the one the Soviets feared most) would be a mixed targeting strategy in which the United States attacked counterforce targets "using high yield weapons with ground bursts so as to produce extensive fallout" inside the USSR, thereby inflicting heavy civilian casualties as a "bonus."[83] In addition, they found that although tensions between deterrence and nuclear war fighting strategies did exist, they were less numerous, less critical, and more easily addressed than Marshall and Goldhamer had originally supposed.[84]

It is hard to say whether Goldhamer and Marshall's "The Deterrence and Strategy of Total War, 1959–1961" (RM-2301), assuaged concerns within the American national security community about the seeming contradiction between nuclear deterrence and nuclear war fighting if deterrence failed. At the time, US deterrence of a nuclear war with the USSR was predicated on the threat of massive nuclear retaliation. But the threat had to be credible and, as Eisenhower recognized as early as 1953, carrying it out was tantamount to national suicide. From Marshall's perspective, however, the enduring value of RM-2301 was that it represented the beginning of his search for better analytic methods for evaluating military competitions.

In the early 1970s during the second Nixon administration, both Marshall and his close friend, James Schlesinger, would return to the dilemma between nuclear deterrence and nuclear war-fighting—Schlesinger as secretary of defense and Marshall as the director of net assessment. In January 1974 Nixon would approve National Security Decision Memorandum 242 (NSDM-242), which directed the development of a wide range of limited, selective, and regional nuclear options that could achieve early "war termination, on terms acceptable to the United States and its allies, at the lowest level of conflict feasible."[85] The aim was give the president other options than a stark choice between surrendering to Soviet aggression or executing the Single Integrated Operational Plan, the American war plan for all-out nuclear war. Although Marshall, Schlesinger, and many others sought plausible options between these extremes from the mid-1970s on, the problem proved insolvable even for the very best strategists. At the time of RM-2301, though, this reality was far less obvious than it would later become. In the meantime Marshall and Goldhamer's investigation of the tension between nuclear deterrence and war-fighting also foreshadowed the pessimistic conclusions Marshall would draw in the mid-1960s about the ability of analysts to estimate the relative military power between nations.

3

THE QUEST FOR BETTER ANALYTIC METHODS 1961–1969

*If you think you are in the business of giving answers, you
will get the diagnosis wrong, because your people are going
to have preconceptions about what the answer is.*
—ANDREW MARSHALL

During the 1960s Marshall's intellectual outlook matured on a number
of issues. He became ever more convinced that RAND needed to look
beyond systems analysis and undertake basic research on the behavior of
large organizations such as the US Air Force and private-sector business
firms. He also articulated the general problems of measuring relative military power between nations. These problems, which have not been fully
solved to this day, have continued to fuel Marshall's enduring interest in
developing better analytic methods. And, most important, by the end of
the decade he had developed a framework for thinking about the United
States' long-term peacetime military competition with the USSR that no
longer focused, as most prior Cold War analyses had done, on the possible
outcomes of an all-out nuclear exchange between the two nations.

Marshall's views on these matters were not always embraced by many
of his RAND colleagues, especially those outside the economics department. By the late 1960s many of his fellow researchers had become increasingly caught up in debates over how best to wage the Vietnam War,
but Marshall's focus remained primarily on the challenges of helping the
United States be a more effective competitor vis-à-vis the USSR in what
had become a protracted rivalry. This, for him, was the overriding strategic
challenge facing the United States. The 1960s were a decade in which he

followed his own instincts and went his own way to develop the basic elements of what would become known as net assessment.

Before turning to the main intellectual paths Marshall pursued during the
1960s, a few words are in order about RAND's involvement in bringing program budgeting and systems analysis to the Pentagon. This analytic
revolution was led by President John Kennedy's defense secretary, Robert
McNamara. McNamara had been enamored with the use of statistics and
quantitative analysis to manage large organizations since earning a master's
degree from the Harvard Business School in 1939. He began teaching business administration there in 1940, and was soon drawn into the efforts of
the Army Air Forces (AAF) to use statistical controls to manage the United
States' air arm during World War II.

Within months of the Japanese attack on Pearl Harbor Robert Lovett,
Henry Stimson's assistant secretary of war for air, realized that "there was
no centralized administrative control over statistical reporting and analysis
in the Army's air arm."[1] In March 1942 Lovett established the Directorate
of Statistical Control within the Air Staff and put Charles "Tex" Thornton
in charge. Thornton had impressed Lovett with his ability to draw essential
information from a mass of statistics and to present it clearly, as demonstrated in a report on federal housing that he had written in the late 1930s
while working at the Interior Department. Lovett gave Thornton carte
blanche to build a statistical control organization. The underlying idea behind the directorate was that the war should be conducted as if it were a
form of "big business" with a strict accounting of gain and loss.[2] By the
war's end Thornton's empire had grown to over fifteen thousand employees,
including more than three thousand who served with AAF commanders in
the field.

At the outset in 1942, though, Thornton's first task was to assemble a
staff of officers skilled in quantitative methods. He promptly struck a deal
with Wallace Dunham, dean of the Harvard Business School, to set up a
course to do the training.[3] The initial cadre of some one hundred "citizen-
soldiers," all of whom were personally recruited by Thornton for their experience in business, banking, and data processing, reported to Soldiers Field
in Cambridge, Massachusetts, in June 1942.[4] McNamara became one of
the initial instructors in the AAF's statistical school, but in 1943 he took
unpaid leave from Harvard to go on active duty—and quickly found himself
serving in Thornton's directorate.[5] Later McNamara also served in General

LeMay's bomber commands in China and the Marianas. There he established a statistical control unit for LeMay's B-29 operations and played a supporting role in LeMay's development of firebombing tactics against Japanese cities.[6]

McNamara's hands-on experience in the use of statistics and analysis to manage large organizations expanded after World War II when he was hired by the Ford Motor Company along with Thornton and other veterans of the Statistical Control Division. In late 1945 Thornton formed a management group with nine former officers from his wartime organization. With support from Lovett he quickly sold the entire group to Henry Ford's grandson, Henry Ford II.[7] At the time, the iconic Ford Motor Company was in dire need of financial management. After production of Ford's highly successful Model T had ended in 1927, the company had been slow to bring out new and different models. By the beginning of World War II Ford's market share had fallen to less than 20 percent and losses had offset all its profits from 1927 to 1941.[8] Henry Ford's grandson was understandably eager to make his mark by reinvigorating the company, and Thornton's group promised to restore the company to its leadership position. To give a sense of the task Thornton faced, when he arrived at Ford he was shocked to find that the only financial data available on Ford's operations consisted of the cash statement provided by the company's bank.

The former AAF officers who arrived at Ford in January 1946 were all very young and very bright compared to most of the company's employees. Knowing nothing about the auto industry, the newcomers asked so many questions that the staff initially dubbed them the "Quiz Kids."[9] By 1959 the seven of Thornton's original group still at Ford, including McNamara, were "largely in control of the corporation."[10] The "Quiz Kids" had become the "Whiz Kids," the sobriquet now an accolade for their success in bringing order out of the chaos that had existed at Ford before their arrival.[11]

Ironically Thornton himself did not last long at Ford. In 1948 Henry Ford II fired him due to his clashes with Ford executive Lewis Crusoe.[12] But the seven Whiz Kids who stayed the course achieved such success in reinvigorating Ford's fortunes, using statistical controls—"management by the numbers," as it would come to be known—that McNamara was named president of the Ford Motor Company on November 9, 1960, the day after John Kennedy won the presidency.

Following the election, the president-elect first offered the job of defense secretary to Lovett. During World War II Lovett had distinguished himself as assistant secretary of war for air. After the war, he had served as deputy defense secretary under George Marshall from October 1950 until September 1951. Then, as secretary of defense himself, he headed the Pentagon until the end of the Truman administration in January 1953.

Lovett declined Kennedy's offer to return to the Pentagon for a second tour. Instead he suggested McNamara for the post. Kennedy offered McNamara his choice of two positions: either secretary of the treasury or secretary of defense. McNamara initially declined the offers, but finally agreed to think about them and meet later with the president-elect. By the end of McNamara's second meeting with Kennedy, he was so impressed with the new commander in chief that he agreed to take the post at defense.[13]

Kennedy was convinced that the Pentagon's strategic planning was not appropriately reflected in its budget priorities. So when McNamara arrived at the Pentagon he had a clear charter to implement the changes necessary to bring this about.[14] While he had the authority and responsibility to make sound decisions on the crucial issues of national security, such as defense strategy and service acquisition programs, McNamara lacked the management tools that would enable him to do so.[15] To help him wrest control of the budget from the military services he hired Marshall's mentor and friend, Charles Hitch, as the Pentagon's comptroller.

By the early 1960s Hitch was one of the nation's leading authorities on program budgeting and the use of quantitative systems analysis to choose the most cost-effective weapon systems and force postures. His initial tasking from McNamara was to develop the statistical information and management systems McNamara needed to gain greater control over the military services and the Joint Chiefs of Staff. McNamara was further aided by other RAND staff members brought in to serve in the Office of the Secretary of Defense (OSD) to help bring about the desired reforms.

RAND's development of systems analysis had its origins in the successes of operations research (OR) during World War II. The British experimental physicist Patrick M. S. ("PMS") Blackett is considered the father of OR, which draws on statistical methods to aid ongoing military operations. For example, in early 1943, during the Battle of the Atlantic in which German U-boats threatened to sever Britain's logistic lifeline across the Atlantic, the use of OR tools and techniques by Blackett's team at the Royal Navy's Coastal Command led to the adoption of convoys larger than the British Admiralty's limit of sixty merchantmen.[16] The larger convoys, in turn, helped reduce shipping losses when the U-boats did intercept them.

World War II OR used mathematical analysis to improve current operations. Efficient search patterns, for instance, were amenable to mathematical analysis. In the late 1940s and throughout the 1950s RAND's staff built on wartime OR to help the Air Force make better, more cost-effective choices regarding its force posture, particularly with respect to the numbers and types of bombers it should field.[17] Ed Paxson organized RAND's first major analysis of a prospective air campaign against the Soviet Union and coined the term *systems analysis* to distinguish this broader kind of study from wartime operations research.[18]

Once in the Pentagon the first order of business for McNamara and Hitch was to centralize control over the Pentagon's budget. The existing system had no programming function to bridge the gap between service budgets and military planning, nor could it provide the information McNamara needed to link missions to costs.[19] To remedy these problems Hitch and his staff created what became known as the Planning, Programming, and Budgeting System (PPBS), which introduced a programming function to relate plans to budgets. Given six months by McNamara to implement PPBS rather than the eighteen months Hitch initially proposed, the new comptroller and his staff managed to prepare the Fiscal Year 1963 defense budget using the new system and submit it to Congress in January 1962.[20] Its limitations notwithstanding, PPBS has proved to be a major management innovation, and is used by the Defense Department to this day.

To provide the underlying cost-effectiveness analyses PPBS required to inform major decisions on forces and weapons programs, McNamara and Hitch introduced systems analysis. Hitch asked Alain Enthoven, who had left RAND for the Pentagon in 1960, to set up an Office of Systems Analysis (OSA) within Hitch's office. OSA's purpose was to conduct cost-effectiveness studies aimed at quantifying alternative ways of accomplishing various national security objectives so that senior decision makers could understand which of them contributed the most to a given objective for the least cost; that is to say, those that were the most cost-effective.[21] This innovation, too, has endured the test of time, although the office responsible for the function itself has undergone several name changes.[22]

By 1965 Hitch concluded that the programming function in PPBS had been generally well received within the Pentagon. The reaction to OSA's cost-effectiveness studies was another matter. Systems analysis was controversial then and remains so to this day. As an economist, Hitch found the resentment of the uniformed military over cost-effectiveness studies deeply puzzling. After all, as he and Roland McKean had noted in 1960, "Resources are always limited in comparison with our wants, always constraining our action. (If they did not, we could do everything and there would be no problem of choosing preferred courses of action.)"[23] Thus there was, in Hitch's mind, a clear need to determine how military tasks could be accomplished at the required level of effectiveness for the lowest possible cost.

Hitch attributed the controversy over systems analysis studies to a belief among military officers that the analysts would favor the least costly weapons rather than those that offered the greatest effectiveness on the battlefield.[24] He was wrong. The services' problems with systems analysis ran much deeper. The fact of the matter was that McNamara, Enthoven, and other Pentagon Whiz Kids used systems analysis to justify choices that often went against the vested interests and professional judgments of senior military leaders. In effect systems analysis transferred decision-making on key investment choices from the military services to the Office of the Secretary of Defense.

Marshall was not directly involved in the controversies inside the Pentagon over systems analysis during the 1960s. However, he was concerned about what he considered to be the excessive reliance on systems analysis, especially within RAND's strategic studies program. While he was willing to employ quantitative methods himself to explore such issues as countervalue versus counterforce targeting, he could see the detrimental effects that overly narrow cost-effectiveness studies were having on RAND's efforts to assess the US-Soviet competition in strategic (or intercontinental-range) nuclear forces.

At the heart of Marshall's misgivings about systems analysis was his growing awareness that decisions about nuclear forces, whether made in Washington or in Moscow, could be influenced by the vested interests of various decision makers and the various bureaucratic power centers. In the late 1950s he and James Loftus began paying attention to the influence that Soviet organizations from the Politburo down to design centers had on the choices the USSR made about its nuclear forces. They had started Project SOVOY to encourage RAND analysts to begin taking these sorts of organizational considerations into account. By the early 1960s this line of thought led Marshall and a few others at RAND to begin advocating an explicit effort to develop analytic methods beyond systems analysis. One of Marshall's strongest supporters for moving strategic analysis in this direction proved to be a young economics professor from the University of Virginia by the name of James Schlesinger.

From RAND's earliest days a recurring concern of the organization's management had been recruiting top talent, the best people in the entire country to work on any given problem. One of the ways in which this was accomplished was by inviting promising individuals to spend a summer at RAND working with members of the think tank's staff. In 1962 one of the summer invitees was Schlesinger, who had come to RAND's attention as a result of his 1960 book *The Political Economy of National Security*.[25] It included a chapter comparing Soviet economic growth to that of the United States, a subject that was of interest to Marshall.

When Schlesinger arrived in Santa Monica he was assigned to Marshall. Schlesinger found RAND to be a "revelation," and working with Marshall a "delight."[26] That summer, the two men spent many long hours discussing all manner of issues. In 1963 Schlesinger joined RAND, abandoning academia. Over time he and Marshall became intimate friends, both socially and intellectually. By the early 1970s both men would migrate to Washington, DC, and their friendship would continue until Schlesinger's death in 2014.

Once at RAND, Schlesinger quickly became engaged in the efforts of Marshall and others to develop analytic methods that transcended the limitations of systems analysis. In September 1963 Schlesinger and Richard Nelson, who with Sidney Winter later became leading figures in the revival of evolutionary economics, proposed a new long-range research program for RAND's economics department centered on the theory of organizations.[27] They acknowledged the important advances that RAND's development of quantitative methods had achieved during the 1950s. In the case of the Defense Department, they observed, the battle for quantitative research had largely been won due to the "McNamara revolution."[28]

In a 1967 RAND paper Schlesinger reiterated the importance of quantitative methods by stating unequivocally that the "usefulness of systems analysis has been amply demonstrated."[29] Yet Schlesinger argued that it also remained true that such studies "inevitably incorporate a number of non-technical assumptions" in setting the scope of the problem, selecting the alternatives to be examined, and choosing criteria for measuring the alternatives' effectiveness.[30] Simply put, one must exercise diligence in selecting the assumptions that underlie any analysis. Recurring questions for Marshall and Schlesinger were, "What are the proper metrics to apply in this case? Have we framed the analysis to address the right questions?" To be sure, the costs of each alternative could be reduced to dollars. But what about the effectiveness of the alternatives measured against such goals as deterring a Soviet nuclear attack on the United States or its allies? "For higher-order problems," Schlesinger observed, "the measures of effectiveness must be based on some broad strategic criteria, in which political or psychological assessments inevitably play a role, whether this be admitted or not."[31] For Schlesinger and Marshall, the framing of any systems analysis would always elude attempts at rigorous quantification and necessarily involve human judgment.

Schlesinger, then, was "an unabashed, if qualified, defender of the value of [systems] analysis in policy formulation." He was willing, he said, to give systems analysis two-and-a-half cheers but not three.[32] By the late 1960s the limitations and distortions of systems analysis within the Pentagon were evident to others at RAND beyond Marshall and Schlesinger. Later, OSA veterans Alain Enthoven and Wayne Smith would acknowledge that systems analysis under McNamara could not claim total objectivity or infallibility and had made its share of mistakes.[33] In Marshall's opinion, if the Office of Systems Analysis had committed an original sin in the 1960s, it was in trying to extend systems analysis to decide issues that ultimately involved qualitative factors—the higher-level political and military professional judgments that are inevitably involved in strategy formulation and implementation. Indeed, Wohlstetter's adoption of an iterative approach to his bomber-basing study, one that explicitly sought to limit and mitigate the effects of uncertainty about the future, was in Marshall's view an example of good strategic analysis: it took into account such nonquantitative factors as the distinctive goals, resources, cultures, and strategies of the competitors; contextual elements, such as technology or climate beyond the control of the competitors; long-term trends in many of these variables; enduring asymmetries between the participants that provided the basis for identifying, developing and exploiting areas of competitive advantage; and the risks that uncertainties about the future posed, particularly in peacetime. But Marshall wanted to do more than simply catalog the limitations of systems analysis. He wanted to develop analytic tools that could better take into account the higher-level aspects of strategic choice.

By the time that Nelson and Schlesinger proposed that RAND's economics department initiate a program on organizational theory, Marshall had begun exploring the emerging literature on the behavior of formal organizations such as commercial business firms. Here he was struck by the seminal work of James March and Herbert Simon. The unifying construct in their 1958 classic, *Organizations*, was "not hierarchy but decision making, and the flow of information within organizations that instructs, informs, and supports decision making processes."[34] While it was natural to assume that an organization's decisions generally were made at the top and flowed down its formal chain of command, in reality informal bureaucratic structures also served to process information that influenced the organization's strategic choices.[35] Such findings confirmed Marshall and Loftus's growing doubts about the ability of any large organization to act as a unitary, rational actor.

March collaborated with Richard Cyert in another classic work that influenced Marshall: *A Behavioral Theory of the Firm*, which was first published in 1963. In it the authors concluded that the decisions of senior executives often were based on relatively simple rules, rather than the product of detailed analysis.[36] Moreover, they discovered that firms were composed of individuals and suborganizations whose priorities often varied, leading to competition and negotiation among them in the course of generating information and options on which decisions would be based. They also found that, in part because of these factors, firms typically engaged in "satisficing"—making decisions that were "good enough" rather than optimal.

Simon had been pursuing the notion of bounded (limited) rationality since the early 1950s when he was a RAND consultant.[37] Looking to apply this kind of thinking to the US competition with the Soviet Union, Marshall approached Simon in 1963 to undertake the kind of research into organizational behavior that Schlesinger, Nelson, and others advocated. Simon, however, declined. Marshall wanted to continue pursuing this line of research with others, but he was diverted by another RAND project.

McNamara had requested RAND's help in preparing for a ten-year review of NATO's defense posture. The defense secretary's request arose from an agreement he reached with NATO's secretary general, Dirk Stikker. They had decided that RAND would supply analytic support for the review over an eighteen-month period stretching from late 1963 to early 1965.[38] The team would be based at NATO headquarters in France.

The small group deployed to NATO in response to McNamara's request included Marshall, Fred Hoffman, and Oleg Hoeffding from RAND along with Peter Szanton from the Pentagon's policy planning staff for International Security Affairs (ISA).[39] Burton Klein, who had succeeded Hitch as head of RAND's economics department in 1961, was asked to lead the group. Klein had worked on the US Strategic Bombing Survey for John Kenneth Galbraith and in 1959 had published the widely cited book *Germany's Economic Preparations for War*, which dispassionately debunked the myth that Germany had prepared for total war prior to invading Poland in 1939, or even immediately thereafter.[40] For the NATO mission, Klein left RAND to serve as a special assistant to McNamara.[41]

Participation in the NATO mission precluded Marshall from launching a RAND research program aimed at informing forecasts of the USSR's future nuclear posture with the observed patterns of past Soviet organizational behavior. Before he left for Paris in August 1963, however, Marshall was able to secure Collbohm's agreement that following his return to the United States, he would be able to continue that research. In the meantime he and Mary embarked on an extended stay in France.

The Marshalls had spent several months in the fall of 1960 touring France with the Hitches, an experience they had greatly enjoyed. Mary Marshall readily accompanied her husband back to France in 1963. They rented an apartment close enough to NATO headquarters at Rocquencourt, outside Paris, that Marshall could walk to work. Their life in France during these two years was filled with good food, good wine, and pleasant living. As Marshall later recalled, this time may well have been the happiest of their married lives.[42]

Marshall's work at the Supreme Headquarters Allied Powers Europe (SHAPE) proved less satisfying. The RAND contingent was asked to perform three studies, one of which Marshall ended up leading in collaboration with a succession of French colonels. Its purpose was to determine whether the United States' NATO allies were fulfilling their military commitments to the alliance. More specifically, did they have the agreed-upon numbers of tanks and ammunition stocks? Marshall was astonished to discover that the West Germans, for example, only had three days' worth of ammunition despite a requirement to maintain at least forty days' worth.[43] Marshall was appalled that NATO could support a large, well-paid bureaucracy and yet permit its members to essentially ignore their military obligations. He took this discovery as yet another piece of evidence that organizations more often than not fell far short of the utility-optimizing choices associated with the rational-actor model of decision-making.

Marshall returned to Santa Monica in the spring of 1965 and renewed his efforts to apply advances in organization theory to security studies. Besides digging into the emerging literature he began looking into business strategy, thinking it could be applicable to military strategy. Good business leaders, he knew, try to exploit the strengths of their firms so as to capture markets and drive competitors out of specific product lines and businesses.

Marshall also began reaching out to some of the leading lights at the Harvard Business School. Among his earliest contacts were the business strategists Joseph Bower and C. Roland Christensen. He had first met Bower in the summer of 1963 while he was visiting RAND.[44] During 1966 and 1967 Bower would become involved with Marshall in RAND projects that dealt with organizational and bureaucratic behavior. In 1967 Marshall recruited both Bower and Christensen to participate in an effort for the Office of Systems Analysis to improve intelligence forecasts of Soviet forces based on the organizational behavior of USSR's bureaucracy.

Once back in Santa Monica Marshall's discussions with Schlesinger on organizational behavior and decision-making resumed. Their conversations focused on recent research into the cognitive limits of rationality, conflicts within organizations, motivational constraints to participation in decision-making, innovation, and comparative advantage. They also became interested in ethology, the study of animal behavior under natural conditions. Among other works in this area they read and discussed were Robert Ardrey's 1966 *The Territorial Imperative: A Personal Inquiry into the Animal Origins of Property and Nations*, and Konrad Lozenz's 1963 *On Aggression*, which first appeared in English translation in 1966.[45] One of the central themes in *The Territorial Imperative* was that the propensity to acquire and possess territory, which was manifest in the behavior of many animals, was also manifest in man and very likely played a role in warfare.[46] Similarly, Lorenz argued that in both beast and man, aggression directed against members of the same species must be considered a part and consequence of natural selection, especially when individuals compete over resources.[47]

Marshall came to view ethology as offering a more fruitful way of thinking about what drove human behavior than the utility-maximizing, rational-actor construct—*homo economicus*—so beloved by many economists. The nonrational aspects of human behavior, he concluded, could not be ignored in defense studies and strategy formulation. They had implications for the deterrence of nuclear war with the Soviet Union as well as for the continuing peacetime competition between the two superpowers.

Not long after Marshall's return from Paris, Henry Rowen approached him and suggested he meet with Richard Neustadt, a political historian who specialized in the US presidency. Neustadt was engaged in researching the way that presidents persuade and bargain with other power centers in the federal government to influence policy formulation and, especially, its implementation. He concluded that presidents must bargain to influence not only other branches of government (particularly Congress), but also various power centers within the executive branch itself. For Neustadt, "Presidential power is the power to persuade."[48]

Marshall's meeting with Neustadt in 1965 led to creation of a group chaired by Harvard's Ernest May, a historian specializing in US foreign policy. The May Group, as it came to be known, began meeting in the spring of 1966 to discuss the influence of organizations and bureaucracies on policy. The participants were especially interested in the gap between the intentions of government decision makers and the results of governmental actions. The May Group held a series of seminars examining the rational actor, organizational process, and governmental politics models of decision-making (Models I, II, and III respectively). In addition to Marshall, May, and Neustadt, the group included such luminaries as Morton Halperin, Fred Iklé, William Kaufmann, Don Prince, and Rowen. It also included a young student, Graham Allison, as rapporteur. Allison was searching for a dissertation topic and quickly became "hooked" on the problem of closing the gap between what policy makers desired to achieve by their decisions and how their intended goals tended to be distorted in the course of implementation. Supplied "with more ideas than I could assimilate" from the May Group seminars, Allison completed his doctoral dissertation in 1968, and began transforming it into the influential book *Essence of Decision*, published in 1971. In it Allison employed the 1962 Cuban missile crisis as a case study to explain how governments both make and execute decisions in ways often at odds with what, after the fact, appears to be rational behavior, both to their rivals and, in many cases, to their own leaders.

In *Essence of Decision* Allison contended that many international relations studies assumed states and policy makers' actions are based on their evaluation of all available options. He argued that this rational-actor approach (Model I) is flawed—that one must also examine the effect of organizational (Model II) and bureaucratic actors (Model III) on how decisions are made and executed. Model II—what Allison termed the "Organizational Process" view of decision-making—derives from the fact that "governments perceive problems through organizational sensors. Governments define alternatives and estimate consequences as their component organizations process information." Allison concluded that "few important issues fall exclusively within the domain of a single organization. Thus government behavior relevant to any important problems reflects the independent output of several organizations, partially coordinated by government leaders."[49] Consequently the rational-actor model alone could not adequately explain the decisions in Washington and Moscow during the Cuban missile crisis.

Allison cited Roberta Wohlstetter's analysis in *Pearl Harbor: Warning and Decision* as an example of organizational process (Model II) at work.[50] Prior to the attack on Pearl Harbor, he noted, Japan's senior military and civilian leaders responsible for making the decision to go to war knew their country lacked the industrial capacity and military might to prevail in a protracted conflict with the United States. Yet they proceeded to attack anyway. Again referencing Wohlstetter, Allison commented that US leaders had sufficient intelligence to indicate that Japan was about to attack Pearl Harbor, but failed to understand what they had and respond accordingly. When, for instance, the War Department warned Lieutenant General Walter Short, the Army's senior commander in Hawaii, to be prepared for "hostile activities," Short interpreted the warning to mean acts of sabotage, and not an attack by Japan's main forces.[51]

Like most groundbreaking works *Essence of Decision* was far from immune from criticism. Some noted that the information required to make and execute good decisions required by Allison's Models II and III would be so large as to be impractical during a crisis. Allison conceded as much, but also pointed out that this is hardly an argument for relying solely on the rational-actor model. In this regard he restated Wohlstetter's (and Marshall's) warning that one cannot simply discount key aspects of analysis simply because they cannot be easily quantified or explained.

Essence of Decision also seconded Roberta Wohlstetter's concerns that the concept of mutually assured destruction might not serve as a barrier to nuclear war, and that intelligence failures similar to those that led to the surprise at Pearl Harbor might also occur in the nuclear age, "with possible consequences of an ever greater and perhaps more fatal magnitude."[52] Similarly, Allison argued that the organizational and bureaucratic models of decision-making could lead to states making irrational decisions or executing decisions in unintended ways, thereby undermining the fundamental assumption that a rational decision maker would never order a nuclear attack that would result in his or her own country's destruction. Simply put: despite the efforts of a state's leaders to act rationally, one could not discount the prospect that, like Imperial Japan in December 1941, they could could choose the path of nuclear war even though it would be tantamount to "committing suicide."

Allison cited Marshall as one of four individuals who "deserve special note for the intellectual and personal debt" he had incurred in writing *Essence of Decision*. He went on to state, "The impact of ideas that Andrew W. Marshall has been propagating for a decade is marked, especially in my chapter on Model II." That said, Allison's thinking in *Essence of Decision* had a somewhat different focus from Marshall's. Whereas Allison concentrated on alternative models of decision-making in crises potentially leading to war, Marshall's main concern was with decision-making in protracted peacetime competitions. As he stressed to RAND's board of trustees in April 1968, a principal objective of RAND's studies on organizational behavior was aimed at improving the United States' ability to enhance its estimates of the USSR's future military posture, thereby providing a firmer basis for choosing weapons and force postures to deter conflict.[53] As we will see, Marshall's emphasis on decision-making in peacetime would lead him to develop a new perspective on the competition between Washington and Moscow.

By the mid-1960s it was becoming clear to Marshall that RAND's core mission of advising the Air Force on the "preferred instrumentalities and techniques" for intercontinental strategic warfare required an in-depth assessment of the relative military power of the two competitors. For nearly two decades Marshall had thought increasingly about the problem of measuring military power. But it was William Kaufmann who persuaded him to set down his thoughts on this issue.

Kaufmann had left RAND in 1961 and joined the political science department of the Massachusetts Institute of Technology. In 1966 Kaufmann was asked to run a panel at the September meeting of the American Political Science Association. This opportunity prompted him to ask Marshall to present his views on estimating military power. The result was Marshall's classic "Problems of Estimating Military Power" (P-3417). The paper detailed the profound conceptual problems and practical difficulties confronting all attempts to define appropriate measures of the capability of one country's military forces to deal with those of another across a range of relevant contingencies.

Marshall's skepticism about reliance on quantitative metrics was evident in his observation in the paper's introduction where he declared that any attempt to estimate the military power of the United States, or of any other nation, contained so many conceptual and practical challenges that "there seem to be only problems and very few, well-accepted adequate methods of making such estimates."[54] The most common approach to estimating one nation's military power relative to another's, he elaborated, was to count up the personnel under arms, the weapons of various types, and the major formations (divisions, fleets, air wings, etc.) on each side and compare the numbers. But such tabulations, Marshall argued, were "an evasion of the problem" because they said "nothing about the actual capabilities of the forces of one country to deal with another."[55] They ignored the influence of geography and logistics on combat outcomes as well as the effects of human error, misguided doctrine, stodgy planning, and the unpredictable behavior of governments and military organizations under the stresses of wartime.

At a practical level, a simple compilation and comparison of opponents' forces implicitly assumed that quantitatively equal forces would give rise to equal military power. But in Marshall's judgment the whole history of military conflict indicated that actual outcomes could diverge dramatically from comparisons of the numbers of personnel, weapons, and military formations. For example, in World War II the German attack through the Ardennes in May 1940 quickly defeated the forces of France and Low Countries and ejected the British from the continent at Dunkirk, even though the Allies had more men, divisions, and tanks than did the Germans.

In light of such disconnects between the usual quantitative comparisons of military forces and combat outcomes, Marshall concluded that the conceptual problems of constructing adequate or useful measures of military power had yet to be squarely and honestly faced. Defining adequate measures, he wrote, "looks hard, and making estimates in real situations looks even harder."[56] These conclusions reflected Marshall's long-standing interest in military history and preference for empirical data on a diverse range of factors over simple "bean counts" of forces and weapons, or abstract theory. His reservations concerning anyone's ability to predict probable war outcomes would receive dramatic confirmation in the ease with which US-led coalition forces ejected the Iraqis from Kuwait in 1991 despite the belief of many that coalition forces would suffer high casualties in attempting to do so.

In the second half of his paper, Marshall returned to the problem of estimating the future military forces of potential opponents. Based on his earlier collaboration with Loftus he identified the key challenge as the generation and documentation of useful hypotheses concerning the behavior of large governmental institutions and military bureaucracies.[57] Rational-actor explanations of the slow, complicated process of Soviet military force developments since World War II, he wrote, "were substantially in error."[58] He warned that until it was possible to arrive at a far better understanding of the decision-making processes within typical military bureaucracies, it was doubtful that US analysts could produce even rough projections of the USSR's military posture—or that of any other nation—more than four or five years into the future.[59]

As with the problems of estimating military power, those relating to estimating the future military postures of potential adversaries have not been definitively resolved in the decades since Marshall's 1966 paper. Estimating likely combat outcomes in actual situations appears to remain beyond our powers of prediction. War continues to be an incredibly complex phenomenon characterized by massive uncertainty. Strategy, tactics, decision-making in times of immense stress, and other human factors matter greatly. Even in the short-term, combat outcomes are highly sensitive to scores of such factors, and small changes in any of them can mean the difference between victory and defeat.

Long-term estimates of the future force postures and strategies of opponents face similar difficulties. Unless one has considerable insight into the histories, preferences, and incentives of the various actors able to influence a nation's choices in preparing for or conducting war, such estimates are unlikely to be accurate. The USSR's continued buildup of nuclear forces after the Kremlin achieved rough parity with the United States in the early 1970s remains a classic example of the difficulties of estimating adversary behavior. Marshall's solution to these problems in the 1960s was to redouble his efforts to understand the actual behavior of Soviet organizations. Here he found an ally in the Pentagon in his former RAND colleague Ivan Selin.

From 1960 to 1965 Ivan Selin had been a research engineer at RAND. In 1963 he left RAND and joined Enthoven's Office of Systems Analysis. There he began working on how the United States could most efficiently address the growth in Soviet strategic nuclear forces, especially in intercontinental ballistic missiles. By 1967 he realized that he needed better forecasts of future Soviet nuclear forces and how the Russians might react to improvements in US nuclear forces.[60] Aware of Marshall's continuing efforts to use insights into Soviet organizational behavior to improve such estimates, Selin asked Marshall to put together a group of specialists in management and organizational theory to see whether their perspectives could help generate better projections.[61] Besides Marshall, the main participants in this exercise were James March from the University of California–Irvine; Joseph Bower and Roland Christensen from the Harvard Business School; Andris Trapans, a RAND Soviet specialist; and Graham Allison.

It took some doing to get this project under way. Selin and Marshall had agreed that the group would need access to the best available intelligence on those elements of the Soviet bureaucracy most able to influence decisions about the USSR's nuclear forces. Obtaining the requisite security clearances proved easier said than done. In the end, the deputy defense secretary, Paul Nitze, had to prevail upon Richard Helms, the director of the Central Intelligence Agency, to grant everyone involved the access needed for the project.

During 1968 the group met four times, and in August of that year it produced a report for Selin. The document rejected the use of simple models of Soviet behavior that assumed effective central direction, complete information, and consistent goals, none of which are usually found in business firms, corporations, or other large organizations. Instead, the group characterized the decision processes of the Soviet military-industrial complex as a loosely coupled collection of intermittently disrupted problem-solving clusters, and noted that some major Soviet decisions were actually made by organizations far below the Politburo, the Main Military Council, or the Soviet General Staff. A preeminent fact about all large organizations, the report argued, is that their sheer size precludes any single central authority having either the time or the information to make all the important decisions. Overall, the Soviet military establishment's decision-making exhibited the "bounded" rationality characteristic of any large organization, including military services.

None of these conclusions should have been surprising. They certainly were not to Marshall. They reflected lines of thought that he had pursued since his collaboration with Loftus, if not earlier, as well as March's findings from his work with Cyert and Simon. But by 1968 Marshall had compiled considerably more empirical evidence for these judgments than he had possessed when he and Loftus started SOVOY. As a result, a much stronger case could be made for embracing an organizational behavior approach to

RAND's research on both Soviet and US military decision-making, especially in the areas of resource allocation and force posture choices.

Instituting this approach within RAND is precisely what Marshall and Sidney Winter proposed to the Air Force in March 1967[62] and to RAND's new president, Henry Rowen, in December of that year. In their memo to Rowen (M-8668), Marshall and Winter began by observing that the field they termed "Organizational and Management Studies" did not exist. The efficient-resource-allocation models used in game theory and employed less formally in strategic analyses, they argued, tended "to abstract completely" the constraints imposed on top-level decision makers by the "cumbersome and contrary organizations below them." It was therefore "time to attempt the development of some intellectual tools powerful enough to close at least some of the gap between the models of systems analysis and the realities of policy making."[63] The potential benefits, they argued, included more effective policy analysis and implementation by RAND for its clients, better assistance to the Air Force in dealing with its force management problems, better theory development to clarify the relationships between rational choice and actual decision processes, and improved predictions of the behavior of governments and military organizations. This, then, was their case for establishing a RAND Department of Management Sciences.

Rowen, however, was not sufficiently convinced to create a new department to develop organizational theory. Although Marshall and Schlesinger devoted considerable time to explaining to Rowen their concerns about the overly quantitative focus of RAND's strategic research and the need to develop new analytic methods to address the limitations of systems analysis, the new RAND president chose a different path. In 1968 he created a new position, director of strategic studies, and appointed Schlesinger to it. In this role Schlesinger was to consolidate and sharpen RAND's continuing research on US and Soviet intercontinental nuclear forces.

One result of Schlesinger's appointment seems to have been that Marshall was able to spend more of his time working on Soviet organizational behavior. In July 1968 he produced a short piece for Selin on the problems posed by the discrepancies between the observed aspects of Soviet military programs and the behavior suggested by the rational-actor model. As an alternative he offered the hypothesis that the design of Soviet weapons mainly took place several levels down within the USSR's political and military hierarchy,[64] and that the top people only decided on the major outlines of Soviet nuclear forces through their control of budgets.

Marshall stayed busy during this time in other ways as well. Starting in 1967, he and Schlesinger had begun serving as consultants to the Bureau of the Budget (renamed the Office of Management and Budget in 1970). Marshall continued to advise the CIA on its national intelligence programs. Reflecting the high demand for his talents, Marshall also undertook a comparison of US and Soviet research and development programs, systems, and technologies for N. F. "Fred" Wikner, who at the time was the special assistant for threat assessment to John Foster, director of the Pentagon's Office of Defense Research and Engineering (DDR&E).

Although the study for Wikner (WN-7630-DDRE) was not published until 1971, it merits mention because of its call for broad net assessments to inform US decision makers on where the United States stood relative to the Soviets in key areas of US-Soviet military competition. Only such detailed analyses, Marshall suggested, would enable the Defense Department's senior managers to do a better job of balancing risks and identifying areas of comparative advantage that the US military could exploit through the development of specific technologies and capabilities.[65] It was a position he would have a much greater ability to advance during the next stage of his career.

After Richard Nixon won the November 1968 presidential election Schlesinger took a leave of absence to work on the new administration's transition team. In January 1969 he left RAND permanently to be Nixon's assistant director of the Bureau of the Budget, with primary responsibility for the defense portfolio. His departure left RAND's director of strategic studies position vacant. At Rowen's urging Marshall accepted the job.

In his new position Marshall began reviewing all the research being conducted throughout RAND on US and Soviet strategic nuclear forces. He soon concluded that they lacked coherence. While the studies addressed all sorts of nuclear and related issues, they rarely focused on the central task of finding ways in which the United States could be more effective in its nuclear competition with the USSR.

Reflecting on his two decades at RAND, Marshall was struck by the fact that there had been no US-Soviet general nuclear war during those years. Yet most analyses of the nuclear competition, at RAND and elsewhere, had focused on exploring the consequences of the so-called arsenal exchanges in the event that deterrence failed. The dominant US scenarios were either a nuclear war that began with an all-out Soviet nuclear attack on the United States or a NATO–Warsaw Pact conflict in Europe that escalated to general nuclear war. But with the Cold War entering its third decade, Marshall realized that nuclear deterrence had not failed. True, the United States and the Soviet Union had come perilously close to the nuclear abyss during the Cuban missile crisis in October 1962. But they had stepped back from the brink. Marshall also suspected that the United States' possession of a superior nuclear posture early in the Cold War had produced strategic effects and payoffs that went beyond deterring a Soviet nuclear attack.

Looking ahead, Marshall was convinced that the military competition with the Soviets would be an extended one that would continue for the foreseeable future. Consequently, any and all future choices that the United States made regarding its nuclear posture and capabilities should be seen as a series of moves aimed at improving the US position vis-à-vis that of the USSR. How was this to be accomplished? Marshall's answer: by emphasizing areas of US competitive advantage, such as advanced technology; by exploiting known Soviet weaknesses and propensities; and by making strategic choices that posed major difficulties for Soviet decision makers. Of course, to achieve these goals required a coherent strategy. That strategy, in turn, had to meet two requirements: (1) careful net assessments to monitor how the United States was doing in the key areas of the protracted *peacetime* competition with the Soviet Union; and (2) greater understanding of Soviet organizational behavior, particularly of the enduring organizational and resource constraints on Soviet decision-making. Looking back after the Cold War had ended, Marshall would recall thinking that this approach represented a "terrific new way" of looking at the United States' rivalry with the USSR.

In 1970 Marshall spelled out this new perspective in a paper he titled the "Long-Term Competition with the Soviets: A Framework for Strategic Analysis" (R-862-PR). Although RAND did not publish R-862-PR until 1972, Marshall finished drafting it in 1970, around the same time he was being drawn into addressing Richard Nixon and Henry Kissinger's concerns over the flow and quality of the foreign intelligence coming into the White House. R-862-PR echoed the data-driven understanding of Soviet nuclear force development that he and Loftus had pursued from the mid-1950s to the early 1960s, when they began trying to understand the behavior of Soviet organizations. More important, however, Marshall's long-term-competition framework contained the seeds of major themes that he would later stress as the director of net assessment. During every annual Pentagon budget cycle, the military services competed for shares of the defense budget and sought to fund the forces, acquisition programs, and capabilities they considered most vital. This practice inevitably led the services to down-play US strengths and exaggerate Soviet capabilities. Marshall's paper on the long-term competition with the Soviets argued instead for identifying strategic choices that capitalized on areas of US comparative advantage and exploited Soviet weaknesses and behavioral propensities so as to impose disproportionate costs on the USSR.

Marshall's long-term competition framework was even more of a water-shed in influencing US Cold War strategy than was his seminal paper on the problems of estimating military power. He was—and remains—a pragmatic strategist who has consistently looked further into the future and focused more on the first-order problems of long-term competition in peacetime than those around him. And starting with a phone call in the fall of 1969 from President Nixon's national security adviser, Henry Kissinger, Marshall would soon bring his strategic acumen and insight to Washington, DC.

4

THE BIRTH OF NET ASSESSMENT
1969–1973

We're here to inform, not to please.
—ANDREW MARSHALL

From 1953 to 1965 the National Security Council had a secretive subcommittee that conducted annual "net evaluations" of the impact of a Soviet nuclear attack on the United States. This subcommittee was disestablished in 1965. Within a few years, however, calls began to surface for reestablishing a net assessment function within the NSC. By 1969 the need for better, more precise comparisons of where the United States stood relative to the USSR in various areas of competition was becoming increasingly apparent and ultimately resulted in Andrew Marshall's establishing a net assessment capability in the Pentagon.

This piece of Cold War history began in January 1953. On his last day in office, President Truman established the Special Evaluation Subcommittee (SESC), which was renamed the Net Evaluation Subcommittee, or NESC, in 1955.[1] The SESC's purpose was to prepare annual reports on the net effects—overall damage, human losses, and politico-military outcomes—of a Soviet nuclear attack on the United States. The SESC's first report in June 1953, for example, assumed that if Soviet leaders decided to initiate a nuclear attack, it would start with strikes by Soviet Long Range Aviation on US bomber bases in the United States, Europe, and the Far East along with the "heaviest possible attack" on major population, industrial, and control centers in the continental United States.[2] The report estimated that, in the period from 1953 to mid-1955, 24 to 30 percent of US nuclear-capable bombers would be lost in the opening Soviet attack, the US population would suffer over 10 million casualties (50 percent of which might be fatal), and there would be initial paralysis of all industry within the areas attacked.[3] Nonetheless, the SESC also concluded that even after such a Soviet attack the United States would be capable of mounting a "powerful initial retaliatory atomic air attack, continuation of [the] air offensive, and [the] *successful prosecution of the war* [emphasis in the original]."[4]

For over a decade the SESC/NESC continued to provide annual studies of the net capabilities of the USSR " . . . to inflict direct damage upon the United States and to provide a continual watch for changes that would significantly alter those net capabilities."[5] However, in December 1964 Defense Secretary McNamara advised President Lyndon Johnson that these studies had outlived their usefulness because they did not, in his opinion, provide "a basis for planning guidance."[6] In March 1965 the NESC was judged to have served its purpose and disbanded.[7]

Within three years recommendations began to surface advocating the creation of a replacement for the NESC.[8] In 1968 Lieutenant General (Ret.) Leon Johnson, who had directed the NESC from 1961 to 1964, recommended that an organization be established to provide the president with "across-the-Government analysis of our relative nuclear strategic strength with the Russians." His proposal, however, fell on deaf ears.

By this time there were two major incentives for reestablishing a government-wide net assessment capability. First, the USSR was approaching rough nuclear parity with the United States. Second, discounting US spending on operations associated with the Vietnam War, the Soviet military was beginning to outspend the Department of Defense. Hence the United States could no longer solve strategic problems in its military competition with the Soviet Union by simply throwing money at them as it had done in the past. Instead, careful net assessments were needed to understand exactly where the United States stood in various areas of the competition, including whether the USSR was not only outspending the Pentagon but also more efficient in converting resources into military capability.

By the fall of 1969 Andrew Marshall was in his twenty-first year at RAND and the United States was entering the fifth year of major combat operations in Vietnam. American forces in South Vietnam now numbered over 500,000. The previous year's Tet offensive, launched by the Communists, had proven a military failure but a strategic success. While

FIGURE 4.1A. US–USSR Strategic-Nuclear Force Ratios.

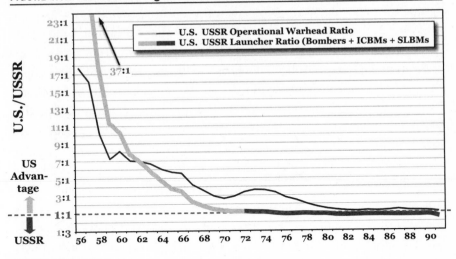

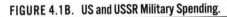

SOURCE: Natural Resources Defense Council (NRDC), "Archive of Nuclear Data from NRDC's Nuclear Program," http://www.nrdc.org/nuclear/nudb/datainx.asp

FIGURE 4.1B. US and USSR Military Spending.

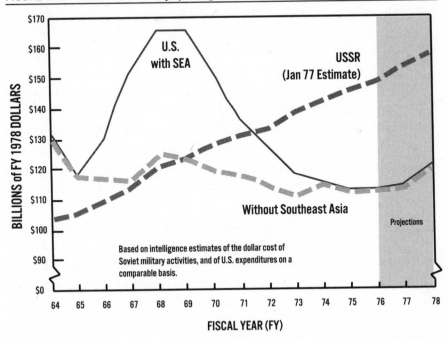

SOURCE: Donald H. Rumsfeld, "Annual Defense Department Report FY 1978," January 17, 1977, p. 3.

the offensive had decimated communist forces in South Vietnam, it had
turned US public opinion against the war.

Nor was the situation in Europe, the Cold War's front line, all that encouraging. The previous year had seen the fragile blossoms of political lib-
eralization in Czechoslovakia known as the Prague Spring brutally stamped
out by an invasion spearheaded by Soviet Army troops. Only months later
West Germany's chancellor, Willie Brandt, increased US anxieties further
when he advocated a *Neue Ostpolitik* (new eastern policy) that sought a rap-
prochement with the Soviet Union and its Warsaw Pact allies.

In the Middle East Egypt and Israel were engaged in a low-level conflict following the latter's spectacular victory in the June 1967 Six-Day War.
The subsequent period of hostilities between Israel and Egypt, known as
the War of Attrition, had been proclaimed by Egyptian leader Gamal Ab-
del Nasser two months after Nixon's inauguration. Periodic artillery duels,
commando raids, air strikes, and brief small-scale incursions became common as both sides faced off along the Suez Canal. Meanwhile Egypt and
Syria were being rearmed by the Soviet Union, which also sent military
personnel to fly combat missions, man surface-to-air antiaircraft missile
batteries, and engage in other military activities.

As the United States began searching for ways to end the Vietnam
War the Soviet Union continued its broad military buildup. At home the
American public evinced growing skepticism and in some quarters open
hostility to pursuing the activist role in the world advocated by President
Kennedy when he had declared in 1961 that the United States would "pay
any price, bear any burden, meet any hardship, support any friend, oppose
any foe, to assure the survival and the success of liberty."[9] Richard Nixon
had been elected president in November 1968 due in part to his assurance
that he had a plan to end the Vietnam War on terms acceptable to the
United States.

Confronted with an array of security challenges, President Nixon saw the
need for a shift in US strategy. As was the case with President Eisenhower,
under whom Nixon had served as vice president, he was prepared to be personally and persistently involved in crafting a new strategy. Among other
things this would require good intelligence regarding adversaries' intentions
and capabilities—most of all those of the Soviet Union. In his first months
in office, however, the new president found the products provided by the
US foreign intelligence community sorely lacking. Henry Kissinger, a Harvard professor Nixon had selected as his national security adviser, shared his

views on the shortcomings of US intelligence products. Both agreed something needed to be done to address the problem, and soon.

In September 1969 Marshall and his wife, Mary, were preparing to set off on an extended vacation in Europe. Since their time in France during the mid-1960s when Marshall was at NATO headquarters, they had periodically returned, spending a month or so touring the country, sampling the French cuisine, and enjoying a break from day-to-day life back home. The couple's planning was abruptly interrupted by a call from Kissinger. Could Marshall stop in Washington and meet with him on his way to Europe? He agreed.

When Marshall arrived for their meeting, Kissinger told him of Nixon's frustration with the intelligence reports coming into the White House, recounting how Nixon's attorney general, John Mitchell, had read some of the National Intelligence Estimates (NIEs) provided by the Central Intelligence Agency and thought them lacking in logic, substance, and even in grammar and composition. Kissinger had his own complaints. One area of analysis that he personally valued was personality profiles of foreign leaders and key officials that could help him develop his negotiating tactics with the Soviets over strategic nuclear arms. But the CIA was proving little in the way of this sort of intelligence. Kissinger also judged the intelligence products being sent to the White House to be even worse than what one could find in the national press, describing them to Marshall as "lousy."[10]

Having summarized the new administration's collective dissatisfaction with US foreign intelligence, Kissinger asked Marshall whether he would be willing to come to Washington to address the issue. Marshall told Kissinger he would get back to him with an answer shortly. He wanted to broach the subject of spending time in Washington with Mary. She was not keen on the idea of leaving their friends and home in California. Mary finally relented, however; a few months in Washington were something she could endure. So Marshall accepted Kissinger's offer with the proviso that he would begin working on the intelligence issues after he and Mary returned from their planned vacation. Kissinger agreed.

Despite this arrangement with Kissinger, the Marshalls' time in France was soon punctuated by phone calls from Kissinger's military assistant, an Army brigadier general named Alexander Haig, asking why Marshall had not arrived at the NSC. Marshall took Haig's hectoring in stride and, after returning to the United States, calmly went about wrapping up some obligations at RAND. At last, in early December 1969, he appeared at the NSC. Marshall's first task was to provide Kissinger with an assessment of the flow and quality of intelligence coming into the White House, a project the two men agreed would take only a couple of months.

Marshall began his assessment by going over to the White House Situation Room, the focal point for the intelligence coming in for the president and Kissinger. There he interviewed people representing the various US intelligence organizations, including the CIA, NSA, the Defense Intelligence Agency (DIA), and the intelligence arms of the military services. Where did their intelligence come from, Marshall wanted to know, and how did intelligence officials decide what was important enough to send to the White House?

Marshall found that there was no uniform approach. Among the agencies, only the NSA seemed to have a logical method for deciding what to send to the president. Every few months the NSA leadership would meet with its representative in the Situation Room to review current intelligence priorities, adjusting the topics as they deemed appropriate to changing world conditions and whatever seemed of interest to the president and Kissinger at the time. The NSA leadership would then inform its staff to prioritize their efforts to obtain intelligence regarding these topics.

The CIA presented a startling contrast to the NSA. The Agency (as it was often called) made little effort to ascertain what topics might be of most interest to the president. Marshall was told that the CIA tracked issues by using stories run in the *New York Times* as the gauge for what was important and what was not. Given this sophomoric approach, and his discussions with the CIA representatives, Marshall concluded that the Agency's senior managers made little or no effort to ensure that their products addressed Nixon's interests and needs. Indeed, they seemed almost hostile toward the president.

Marshall next began examining the CIA's premier intelligence product, the President's Daily Report. As the name suggests, it was dispatched to the White House the first thing every morning. He gathered up the reports that had been provided during Nixon's first six months in office, sat down, and began reading through them. He knew that the president had a strong habit of making marginal notes on everything he read. As Marshall worked his way through the reports he noticed that the president's notes became fewer and fewer until, finally, there were none. Nixon, Marshall realized, had stopped reading the reports.

Marshall discovered that Nixon's disinterest coincided with the introduction of a competing daily analysis generated by the National Security Council. These analyses were drawn from multiple intelligence sources, and there was only about a 60 percent overlap between what the CIA was providing and what the NSC staff was ginning up on its own. The NSC staff also provided the president with intelligence on a wider array of issues. Most important, Marshall found these reports bore Nixon's margin notes.

Marshall went back to the CIA. Why, he asked, did the Agency persist in sending Nixon reports he clearly did not read? Why did the Agency not even attempt to adapt its reports to fit the president's needs? His queries ran into a bureaucratic stone wall. Marshall came away with the impression that the Agency's managers believed their expertise should dictate what Nixon needed to know; hence, they were providing him with only the intelligence they thought he should be interested in. And despite the clear evidence that Nixon was not reading the President's Daily Reports, the Agency continued sending them. The report was the CIA's premier product. It would be developed as the Agency saw fit.[11]

Marshall also took a look at another key Agency product, the National Intelligence Estimates. The NIEs provided intelligence on particular issues and were the product of research and analysis by the National Intelligence Council (NIC). Prior to 1973 the Office of National Estimates (ONE), formed in 1950, had produced these estimates. The office originally drew upon a wide range of talent, to include intelligence officers but also "outsiders" such as former military personnel, ambassadors, and members of the business world and academia. By 1969, however, the CIA's institutional antibodies had progressively reduced the number of outsiders in favor of the Agency's career intelligence officers. Moreover, the NIC had become a career dead end, populated mostly by people awaiting retirement. The office had lost the objectivity and responsiveness that it had had in 1950s and early 1960s, and Marshall discovered the quality of its analyses had declined as well, just as Mitchell had said.[12]

As his review continued, Marshall sensed an enormous gulf separating the CIA from the administration's senior policy makers.[13] Apart from the bureaucratic and institutional priorities undermining the intelligence community's ability to provide the White House with valued information, the Agency seemed to have a very different view of the world and of the major forces shaping that world than did the senior policy makers it was supporting. Nixon and Kissinger thought strategically, on a global scale, with both the near- and (especially) longer-term consequences of their decisions in mind. Marshall felt that Nixon could see both the dangers and, just as important, the opportunities residing in crises and their relationships to America's long-term security. He found, however, that members of the intelligence community typically focused only on the prospective dangers arising out of a crisis. They also seemed to infuse personal beliefs into what was supposed to be a rigorous analysis. Marshall's research suggested that if a situation arose in which Americans were being killed, the Agency's analyses tended to argue the crisis needed to be resolved as soon as possible, even at the expense of sacrificing longer-term US vital interests. Whereas people like Nixon and Kissinger emphasized the long-term consequences that would flow from their decisions, the Agency appeared to conduct its analyses as though there were no long-term consequences.

As Marshall reflected on the situation, he recalled his experience in chess. The situation was a little bit like the game of *Kriegspiel* he had played during his early days at RAND, only with a major variation. In lieu of the referee in *Kriegspiel* who alone has knowledge of the location of both players' pieces, Nixon and Kissinger had to rely on the CIA for information regarding their opponent's position and activities. But the Agency was failing to provide the information on the Soviets that Nixon and Kissinger most valued and needed to know. The Agency didn't seem to understand the rules as Nixon and Kissinger saw them, or understand what the president and his security adviser were trying to accomplish.[14]

After assessing the quality and flow of intelligence into the White House for six months, in May 1970 Marshall submitted his report to Kissinger. Consistent with his work at RAND, his paper was long on descriptions of the problems in the intelligence community and short on recommendations. On the positive side of the ledger, as far as Marshall could tell the CIA was not actually withholding information from the White House. He also found that its analysis of hard data and factual reporting on Soviet forces—their numbers, general locations, and types of equipment—was good. Where he judged the intelligence forwarded to the White House to be poor was in the Agency's use of overly simplified assumptions about Soviet behavior, including frequent reliance on a "model of the Soviet government as a single unified actor pursuing an easily stated strategy."[15] This criticism echoed

Marshall and Loftus's earlier concerns about the tendency of most RAND analysts to assume Soviet behavior could be understood as stemming from the actions of a unitary rational actor. Overreliance on this model of Soviet decision-making undermined the intelligence community's ability to understand the motives behind past and recent Soviet decisions and use that understanding to better estimate the USSR's future strategy and overall military posture.

Marshall's report did offer a few modest suggestions, including the need for clearer communication of White House needs to the intelligence community, and the desirability of encouraging the CIA to generate different intelligence products to address those needs, particularly as they related to decisions with long-term consequences.[16] Yet Marshall noted that the problems were so fundamental—and the political and bureaucratic resistance to taking them on so formidable—that the odds of effecting the necessary reforms were low.[17]

Although Marshall had completed the main task that had brought him to Washington, leaving the NSC and returning to California proved more difficult than he anticipated. Kissinger now wanted him to conduct a follow-on study on the USSR's growing ICBM forces. They settled on doing an in-depth analysis of the Soviet Union's new heavy R-36 ICBM (NATO code name the SS-9 Scarp) to illustrate the sort of intelligence assessments that the president and his security adviser desired from the Agency. Kissinger's underlying motivation for choosing this topic stemmed from his and Nixon's hopes of reaching arms-control agreements that would constrain the USSR's buildup of its strategic nuclear forces. So for the rest of 1970 and well into the following year Marshall found himself in Washington, supervising a CIA effort to lay out the design and bureaucratic history of the SS-9 and its antecedents.

US efforts to negotiate an arms agreement on nuclear forces between Washington and Moscow had begun over two years before Marshall arrived at the NSC. In 1967 President Lyndon Johnson had suggested the two superpowers engage in negotiations to limit their nuclear forces. Although both sides had agreed to talks in the summer of 1968, full-scale negotiations did not begin until November 1969, after Johnson had left office. President Nixon's point men for the negotiations, called the Strategic Arms Limitation Talks (SALT), were Kissinger, based in Washington, and the head of the Arms Control and Disarmament Agency (ACDA), Gerard Smith, who met with Soviet negotiators in Helsinki, Finland. Progress was slow, so slow that by the fall of 1970 Nixon and Kissinger had become concerned that the Soviets might be using the talks primarily as a way of providing cover for the USSR's continued nuclear buildup while giving ammunition to US critics of the Nixon administration's efforts to modernize America's nuclear forces. ·

In part to address these concerns Kissinger convened a Special Defense Panel at the NSC, headed by K. Wayne Smith, to come up with options the president might exercise to pressure the Soviets in the event the SALT talks remained stalled. Marshall was one of the principal members of this special panel, along with some of the country's best and brightest minds on national security affairs, including General Andrew Goodpaster, then serving as the supreme allied commander in Europe (SACEUR), arguably the US military's most important command; Charles Herzfeld, a physicist who had recently headed the Defense Advanced Research Projects Agency (DARPA); William Kaufmann; and Jim Schlesinger.

Early on, to provide context for the panel's eventual recommendations in specific areas of military competition, Herzfeld suggested that they needed a sense of "the general, broad background" of the security challenges confronting the country, in particular an understanding of where the United States stood in its military competition with the Soviet Union, to include an analysis of key military balances and long-term trends. The others agreed that such a national-level assessment was needed. In the past, when the US military was far ahead of the Soviets, particularly in offensive strategic nuclear arms, naval forces, and military research and development (R&D), careful comparative assessments of the sort proposed by Herzfeld had not been as important. But now the competition was close. The United States had far less margin for error. In fact, the Soviets appeared to have caught up with the United States and to be positioning themselves to move ahead in at least some areas that the United States deemed important.[18]

Looking back years later, Marshall concluded that Herzfeld was advocating they do "what was, in effect, a first net assessment."[19] He and Schlesinger agreed to take on Herzfeld's proposal. It soon became clear, however, that Schlesinger's OMB workload would not permit him to devote the level of effort required to perform such a formidable task. So it fell upon Marshall to write the assessment.[20]

The experience confirmed Marshall's conclusions, as expressed in his 1966 paper for Kaufmann, regarding the difficulties of measuring the relative military power of states. His assessment for the Special Defense Panel contained brief and generally unsatisfying discussions of where the United States stood relative to the USSR in ground forces, naval forces, tactical air forces, air defenses, and strategic offensive forces. Strikingly, the document lacked even basic comparative data on US and Soviet force levels (such as the numbers of military personnel, tanks, divisions, ICBMs, tactical aircraft, etc.). Instead it presented Marshall's best judgments as to the state of the US-Soviet military balance in light of existing trends. All he was really able to do was to make "a start on what would have to be a much more systematic and elaborate effort."[21]

In a three-page summary of the full assessment, Marshall began by stating, "Currently, it is difficult to come to clear cut conclusions" about the US and Soviet force postures.[22] One reason stemmed from the differences or asymmetries in the two sides' force postures. In the case of offensive nuclear forces, for example, the USSR appeared to rely far more on ICBMs than on bombers, build less expensive missiles, and operate its nuclear forces differently than did the United States. In addition, there existed no analytic means to assess the capabilities of US forces to deal with Soviet forces in specific contingencies. Yet another reason Marshall cited for not being able to reach clear-cut conclusions was the lack of data in such areas as logistics and readiness, even though military history demonstrated that such factors could greatly affect combat performance.

Nevertheless, this first net assessment did suggest one broad conclusion. Across the board, US weapon systems appeared to be more costly than their Soviet counterparts. The American F-4 fighter, for example, cost $4 million, whereas the CIA estimated its equivalent, the Soviet MiG-21, to cost only $1 million.[23] This led to concerns as to whether the United States was "on the way to pricing itself out of the military competition with the Soviets, or at lease severely handicapping itself through a defective weapons acquisition process, high cost day-to-day operating practices, etc."[24]

Lacking detailed data, all Marshall could do was note that the US military was pursuing a strategy that emphasized the quality of its equipment and personnel rather than trying to match the Soviets in the numbers of their major weapons and forces. Yet the US service chiefs regularly downplayed the value of their own chosen strategy when undertaking assessments of the Soviet threat or when arguing for more resources. Later, as the Pentagon's director of net assessment, Marshall would devote much of his office's resources and energies to trying to answer the main question raised in this first net assessment: Was the United States pricing itself out of the competition?

What he did not know in 1970—although he and Schlesinger already suspected as much—was that the CIA was greatly underestimating the burden Soviet military spending was placing on the USSR economy. The passage of time—and Marshall's persistence—would show that the higher costs of US forces in fact produced military capabilities superior to those of their Soviet counterparts, and that the USSR's command economy was far more prone to inefficiencies than the conventional wisdom of the day allowed.* What was crystal clear in 1970 was that neither the data on US and Soviet forces nor the requisite analytic methods were at hand to conduct the kind of careful net assessments needed to understand where the United States stood in its overall military competition with the USSR.

In July 1969, not long after taking office, President Nixon appointed a "Blue Ribbon" defense panel (also known as the Fitzhugh Commission, after its chairman, Gilbert Fitzhugh) to study the organization and operations of the Defense Department. At the time Fitzhugh was the chairman and chief operating officer (CEO) of the Metropolitan Life insurance Company. The commission was instructed to present its recommendations to both Nixon and Defense Secretary Melvin Laird, a former Wisconsin congressman who had established a reputation as a defense hawk and a critic of McNamara's approach to managing the Pentagon.

In July 1970 the Fitzhugh Commission delivered its report, *Defense for Peace*. Among its 113 recommendations to President Nixon and Defense Secretary Laird, the report called for creating a net assessment group, reporting directly to the secretary of defense, which would undertake "net assessments of the United States and foreign military capabilities and potentials." A related recommendation called for establishing a long-range planning group that would integrate "net assessments, technological projections, fiscal planning, etc." and focus on the longer-term future, beyond the day-to-day activities that often overwhelm senior policy makers.[25] This group, too, would report directly to the defense secretary.

---

*The CIA's consistent tendency to underestimate the magnitude of Soviet defense spending, while overestimating the size of the USSR's economy relative to US GNP, is an important reason that Marshall, Schlesinger, and many others initially mistakenly judged the Soviets to be more cost-effective.

Later, after Marshall had moved to the Pentagon, he became curious about which panel members had pushed for the formation of a net assessment group and what the underlying motivation had been. It turned out that the panel member who had pushed the hardest for a net assessment group was Ruben Mettler, who at the time was president and CEO of TRW, Inc. Mettler believed that the secretary of defense needed a comprehensive picture of the state of the US-Soviet competition, where the competition was headed, and what the most important issues were.[26]

In December 1970 Nixon met with Kissinger and George Shultz, who then headed the Office of Management and Budget. Frustrated with the lack of useful intelligence reaching his desk, Nixon directed them to undertake a study aimed at reorganizing the foreign intelligence community. Nixon anticipated that they could cut the intelligence budget by 25 percent.[27] Kissinger appointed Marshall to represent him on the effort to develop the reforms the president wanted.

Although he was soon to leave RAND and formally become a government employee, Marshall was still alternating between Santa Monica and Washington while the report was being prepared, and did not have the time to take the lead. Shultz asked Schlesinger to lead the study, but Schlesinger was himself busy. Consequently Marshall's old RAND colleague, William Kaufmann, did the actual drafting.[28]

Schlesinger submitted the report in March 1971. To no one's surprise it found that the recent substantial growth in the size and cost of the US intelligence community had not resulted in a commensurate improvement in the scope and quality of its products.[29] Among the reasons cited for this "disturbing" situation were the increasingly fragmented and disorganized distribution of intelligence functions; the community's growing duplicative competition in collection; unplanned and unfocused growth; and the high costs associated with the rapidly expanding reliance on technical collection systems, such as reconnaissance satellites.[30]

To address these problems, Schlesinger recommended that the intelligence community be reorganized, and provided three options for doing so. Looking to avoid reforms that would require congressional action, Nixon cherry-picked from among the options.[31] From the second option the president approved the recommendation that the director of central intelligence (DCI) assume greater responsibility for leading the intelligence community, thereby giving better focus to its efforts while reducing redundancy and attention on areas of marginal value. Henceforth the DCI would be responsible for planning, reviewing, coordinating, evaluating, and producing national intelligence.[32] From the third option he adopted the idea of establishing a National Security Council Intelligence Committee (NSCIC), to be chaired by Kissinger, to represent the concerns and needs of senior policy-level intelligence consumers.[33]

Kissinger asked Wayne Smith take the lead in implementing these changes. Once the main changes had been decided upon, in September 1971 Marshall was asked to draft the final decision memorandum for Nixon along with letters on the reorganization to DCI Richard Helms at the CIA and Secretary Laird at the Department of Defense (DoD).[34] Once Marshall had finished the drafting, Alexander Haig and Wayne Smith began circulating the decision memorandum to the principals to get their general acceptance. During the review process they resurrected a Fitzhugh Commission recommendation, which had not been included among Schlesinger's three options, to establish a net assessment group (NAG) within the NSC. Marshall's recollection is that he was unaware of this suggestion when he began fleshing out what Nixon wanted and drafting implementation memoranda. Nor did he include any such recommendation when drafting the implementation directives. But as soon as the NAG had been added, Haig and Smith started lobbying Marshall to take the new position.[35]

Nixon signed off on the reforms on November 5, 1971. Regarding the NAG, Nixon's directive stated: "As a related matter, I am directing that a Net Assessment Group be created within the National Security Council Staff. The group will be headed by a senior staff member and will be responsible for reviewing and evaluating all intelligence products and for producing net assessments of the US capabilities vis-à-vis those of foreign governments constituting a threat to US security."[36] However, the NAG's initial focus was on the intelligence reorganization rather than net assessments.

Kissinger, already swamped with myriad other responsibilities, joined Haig and Smith in asking Marshall to head the NAG, and in December he agreed to take over the new position and transition to government service as soon as the paperwork could be completed and processed. Marshall began work as the NAG director in January 1972, while still a RAND consultant. Three months later he was officially brought on board as a US government employee.[37]

Kissinger did not immediately pursue the net assessment aspect of Marshall's new position. His reason: Melvin Laird, who considered himself the "strategist in chief" insofar as defense strategy was concerned. Even though he had ignored the Fitzhugh Commission's recommendation to establish a net assessment group, barely a month after Nixon's intelligence reorganization established the NAG Laird signed a directive establishing the position of director of net assessment in the Office of the Secretary of Defense.[38] Laird's move was purely bureaucratic. He was not enthusiastic about the prospect of national net assessments being done by NSC staff outside of his control. So although he created the position in OSD, Laird did not appoint anyone to it. Instead, his special assistant, William Baroody, assigned responsibility for net assessment to an existing long-range planning unit in Laird's Executive Secretariat under retired Army colonel Donald Marshall.

Laird's maneuvers served his aim of keeping the NSC out of the net assessment business. Kissinger backed off. He was disinclined to contest whether the NSC or the DoD should oversee net assessments with a defense secretary as politically powerful as Laird. Instead he delayed initiating the first national net assessment, which called for a comparison of US and Soviet ground forces, until the fall of 1973, after Laird had left office.

In the meantime, Laird's resistance to allowing the NSC to undertake national net assessments had at least one positive, if unintended, consequence. The delay gave Marshall time to think about the nature and scope of net assessment. During the time between taking over as NAG director and the beginning of the first national net assessment in the fall of 1973, Marshall developed a robust conceptual framework for net assessment.

In standing up the NAG Marshall decided one of the first things he would do would be to talk with people who had some understanding of what a net assessment group might do, and to recruit the kind of people who could support him in his efforts.[39] He reached out to two old friends at the Harvard Business School, professors Joe Bower and Roland Christensen. Marshall had met Bower and then, through him, Christensen, while at RAND. He had been impressed with their work on both economic issues and organizational behavior. Bower's dissertation on financial analysis and capital investment in certain industries closely mirrored Marshall's views on the important role organizational processes play in decisions. Bower found that oftentimes a firm's bureaucratic imperatives offered a better explanation of its decisions than what an analysis based strictly on financial factors would produce. And both Bower and Christensen had participated in the meetings on Soviet institutional behavior Marshall had conducted for Ivan

Selin during 1968. Marshall also contacted a third colleague, James March, who had helped to found the field of organizational theory.

Bower mentioned that he had a possible candidate for the NAG in one of his courses at the Harvard Business School, George "Chip" Pickett. Pickett was then on active duty in the Army and getting ready to graduate. The very fact that the Army had sent Pickett to such a demanding institution as the Harvard Business School suggested he was among the best and brightest young officers in the US military. In addition there was Pickett's background in Army intelligence, which suggested he was well prepared to help Kissinger monitor the reorganization of the intelligence community.

One evening shortly thereafter Bower phoned Pickett at his home: Would he be interested in going to work for a fellow named Andy Marshall on the NSC staff? Although Pickett knew nothing of Marshall, he did know that being on the NSC staff was a rare opportunity for an officer of any rank. Pickett said he would be delighted to serve. Marshall interviewed him in Kaufmann's office at MIT,* whereupon Pickett became Marshall's first hire. He would prove to be one of his best.

Next Marshall approached Robin Pirie, a naval officer who had served in the Pentagon's Office of Systems Analysis. Pirie was a submariner. Like all submarine officers, he had served under the demanding and often capricious eye of Admiral Hyman Rickover, who ran the Navy's nuclear propulsion program and who was a power unto himself. Pirie had somehow run afoul of Rickover, but the submariner had impressed Pat Parker, who had served with Pirie in OSA. Parker, who at the time was the deputy assistance defense secretary for intelligence, was yet another one of the many people in Marshall's extensive circle of professional acquaintances that he consulted in looking for good people to bring into the NAG.

Pirie's interview with Marshall went well and he was hired in anticipation that he would spend most of his time getting started on assessment work. He joined the NAG in mid-1972, a few months after Pickett but, thanks to Kissinger's reluctance to begin a national net assessment while Laird remained in the Pentagon, for more than a year Pirie could not do much more than discuss with Marshall how one might conduct a net assessment.

------

*In addition to his other activities, Kaufmann also taught graduate-level security studies courses at MIT. One of this book's authors (Krepinevich) took several of Kaufmann's courses when a student at Harvard in the late 1970s.

Marshall and his tiny staff were assigned an office on the third floor of the Old Executive Office Building adjacent to the White House, next to that of the chairman of the President's Foreign Intelligence Advisory Board (PFIAB). While bureaucratic friction between Kissinger and Laird delayed the start of the first national net assessment, there was nothing to stop Marshall from thinking about the nature of such assessments. Shortly before Marshall was formally installed as the NAG director, he produced a twelve-page draft memorandum aimed at articulating a national net assessment process. With the US involvement in the Vietnam War coming to an end, Marshall recognized that the United States had an opportunity to reorient its defense strategy and policy and military posture. Net assessments, he suggested, could provide needed insights into the roles US military forces should play and the problems and opportunities confronting the US defense establishment.[40] By August Marshall had further distilled his March draft into a two-and-a-half-page memo, "The Nature and Scope of Net Assessments."

The August memo fused Marshall's diverse knowledge and understanding of strategy—and of how the world really works—into a framework for analysis that has stood the test of time. Over forty years later, "The Nature and Scope of Net Assessments" remains the definitive, enduring vision of net assessment. The memo does not offer a by-the-numbers methodology or a formula that one can mechanically follow, but rather a clear statement of the aims of the enterprise and the reasons for net assessment's enduring value.

Marshall began the August memo by explaining the need for careful, net assessments, noting that "National policymakers want to know how the U.S. stands in various types of international competition. They are interested in our relative position and any trends that may affect it. Further, it is most important to know what causes the trends." He continued,

> In the past the U.S. held a clear edge in nearly every aspect of international competition; certainly we did so in military forces and military R&D. Where and when we were challenged we were always able to divert enough resources to the problem area to restore our superiority. That is, we were able to buy solutions to our problems. This is no longer the case. There is severe pressure to reduce military expenditures, and this pressure is likely to continue. Thus there is a high premium on thoughtful and inventive approaches to defense problem solution[s], and on carefully calculated risk taking.[41]

Such assessments were particularly important, Marshall contended, given claims that there were areas of military competition in which the USSR had or was moving toward superiority. There was a belief within the government and among US political elites that the Soviet Union was approaching parity in nuclear arms, while possibly enjoying an advantage in conventional forms of military power.[42] The trends at that time suggested the situation would only worsen over time. The United States had poured enormous resources in men and materiel into a seemingly endless war in Southeast Asia, and the American people's growing opposition to the war had metastasized into opposition to national defense in general. The Soviet Union, it seemed, was not only beginning to outspend the United States militarily but was also catching up technologically with Western weaponry in a number of areas. These circumstances argued, in Marshall's judgment, for undertaking net assessments to devise strategies for competing more effectively with the Soviets. If the US military could no longer prevail by outspending the Soviets, it would have to outthink them.

Marshall's life had been a journey in self-education: there was always something new to learn, always a way to arrive at a better understanding of how the world really works. So it is perhaps not surprising that, in "The Nature and Scope of Net Assessments," he exhibited a reluctance—which he would demonstrate time and again over the next four decades—to produce anything approaching a methodology that could be mechanistically applied to produce net assessments. Instead he was content to describe what he sought to do rather than suggest how: "Our *notion* of a net assessment is that *it is a careful comparison of US weapon systems, forces, and policies in relation to those of other countries* [emphasis added]."[43] But simple as that statement seems, these comparisons had to be comprehensive, encompassing, among other factors, operational doctrines and practices, training regimes, logistics, known or conjectured effectiveness in various environments, design practices and their effect on equipment costs and performance, procurement practices and their influence on cost and lead times, and the political and economic aspects of the competition. "They should evaluate the status of the competition in terms of outcomes of potential conflicts and confrontations. They should compare the efficiency with which the various powers, including the U.S., are conducting the competition."[44]

In insisting that net assessments had to be "comprehensive" Marshall clearly wanted to separate them from systems analysis, which had dominated the Pentagon's decision making since Defense Secretary McNamara had introduced this methodology in 1961. Marshall knew full well that there were problems with the standard systems analysis studies. "For various reasons," he wrote, "systems analysis tends to focus on weapons systems choices in a simplified context. The results of these studies were often expressed in terms of outputs of various force levels and structures, such as submarines sunk, warheads delivered, fatalities caused, etc. The assumptions which are made in achieving the needed simplification may bias assessment outcomes. . . . "[45] Here Marshall was arguing for a holistic approach to comparing US and foreign militaries, not the reductionist kind of thinking typically found in systems analyses. To emphasize the point, he wrote that rather than being prescriptive in their character (as systems analyses typically are), "The use of net assessment is intended to be diagnostic. It will highlight efficiency and inefficiency in the way we and others do things, and areas of comparative advantage with respect to our rivals. It is not intended to provide recommendations as to force levels or force structures as an output."[46] His reason for stopping short of recommendations is compelling. To use a medical analogy, a physician can only prescribe the proper treatment for a malady when he or she has an accurate diagnosis. Without that, the patient might end up with a "cure" that does more harm than the disease. Marshall intended to focus on the former—the diagnosis—as the best way of informing, albeit indirectly, the strategic prescription.

Finally, the August 1972 memo acknowledged the difficulties involved in crafting net assessments, difficulties that he had broached as far back as his 1966 paper on the problems of estimating military power. "Net assessment in the sense we propose is not an easy task. The single most productive resource that can be brought to bear in making net assessments is *sustained hard intellectual effort* [emphasis added]."[47] The parallel between crafting good net assessments and crafting good strategy is revealing. President Eisenhower's view was that while the basic principles of strategy "are so simple that a child may understand them," determining "their proper application to a given situation requires the hardest kind of work. . . . "[48] Years later one of the private sector's foremost business strategists, Richard Rumelt, came to the same conclusion, declaring, "Good strategy is very hard work."[49] From the outset Marshall recognized that the same was true of net assessment.

Marshall's observations regarding the difficulties of crafting good net assessments may appear obvious. Yet in an environment like the Pentagon where the bulk of the activity, then and now, concerns *process*—how something is to be done (or, more often the case, how to *prevent* something from being done)—the need for sustained intellectual effort to get to the truly important problems and opportunities in a competitive situation often goes unappreciated, if not ignored entirely. Perhaps just as sobering, Marshall warned, "The methodologies for doing net assessments are virtually non-existent."[50] They would have to be developed as the new enterprise unfolded. At the same time data problems abounded, as he had realized during his assessment for Kissinger's Special Defense Panel: "Some aspects of Soviet forces important to net assessments have not had high priority in current intelligence efforts, in particular logistics and operational practices. Data on U.S. allies is incomplete and inaccurate. Data on our own forces and programs is frequently not available in a form which permits ready comparison with that available on the Soviets."[51] Consequently, he cautioned, "The initial assessments are bound to be crude, tentative, and controversial." It would take time, the right people, new methods, much in the way of data collection, and sustained hard thinking to accomplish the task before them. Yet Marshall concluded, "Whether difficult or not, the need for net assessments is clear."[52]

The year 1972 ended with Nixon's landslide victory in the November presidential election, whereupon he decided to reshuffle his cabinet. Melvin Laird stepped down as defense secretary. He was succeeded by Elliot Richardson, who had been the secretary of the Department of Health, Education and Welfare (HEW). Jim Schlesinger was informed that he would be leaving his position as head of the Atomic Energy Agency (where he had gone following his stint at OMB) to become the director of central intelligence. Soon after Schlesinger moved to the CIA in January 1973, Marshall started sending him papers on intelligence issues. The two began spending Saturdays together discussing how to stimulate the Agency to be more productive.[53]

Kissinger, for his part, was nominated to serve as secretary of state in addition to his role at the NSC. With Laird out of the picture he moved to put Marshall and his small staff to work conducting actual assessments. On March 29, 1973 he signed National Security Study Memorandum (NSSM) 178, "Program for National Net Assessment." It directed an ad hoc group, chaired by Marshall, to prepare a paper defining the national net assessment process, suggesting appropriate methodologies for a range of topics, and establishing reporting and coordination procedures.[54] Marshall convened the group on April 13, 1973, and it was soon working on guidelines and procedures for conducting national net assessments.[55] Kissinger approved the group's recommendations on June 28, 1973, in National Security Decision Memorandum (NSDM) 224, "National Net Assessment Process, NSSM 178."

Finally, on September 1, 1973, Kissinger signed NSSM 186, which initiated the first national net assessment. Its objective was to compare the costs, capabilities, and performance of US and Soviet ground forces. Given Marshall's paucity of resources, the assessment would be prepared by the Department of Defense in consultation with the NAG, with the assistance of the Department of State and Schlesinger at CIA.[56] Rather than performing the net assessment itself, the NAG had the far more modest role of overseeing an interagency process.

Events then took an unexpected and, from Marshall's perspective, fortuitous turn insofar as the future of net assessment within the US government was concerned. Beset by the growing scandal over the break-in at the Democratic Party's national headquarters in the Watergate Hotel in June 1972, Nixon nominated Elliot Richardson, his new defense secretary, to the position of attorney general as part of a general shakeup.* The president then gave Richardson's vacated post to Schlesinger.

During Schlesinger's transition to the Defense Department he and Kissinger discussed the fledgling net assessment effort. With his confirmation as secretary of state in addition to being the national security adviser, Kissinger found his responsibilities expanding substantially.[57] Schlesinger wanted to bring Marshall to the Pentagon to establish a net assessment function there. In early July Schlesinger began urging Marshall to join him at the Defense Department. The Marshalls had long planned to return to California, and accepting the Pentagon post would extend their time in Washington. In the end, however, Schlesinger prevailed upon Marshall to become his director of net assessment. Schlesinger then engaged Kissinger, who agreed to allow the national net assessment function to be transferred to the Pentagon.[58]

Schlesinger had several motives for acquiring the net assessment portfolio and securing Marshall's services. He wanted a trusted colleague, one with whom he shared a strong intellectual bond, to help him with the

---

*Richardson succeeded Richard Kleindienst, who resigned on April 30, 1973, the same day that the president's counsel, John Dean, was fired and his chief of staff, H. R. Haldeman, and his assistant for domestic affairs, John Ehrlichman, quit.

formidable task of charting a course to sustain the nation's defenses in a difficult time. To accomplish this he needed the kind of comparative analysis Marshall had been advocating and in which he, Schlesinger, was a strong believer. While understanding and appreciating the value of the systems analysis approach that RAND's Whiz Kids had brought to the Pentagon under McNamara, he and Marshall were also intimately familiar with the limitations of this approach. Both saw the potential of net assessment, with its comprehensive and diagnostic approach, as a distinctly different form of analysis—one with more of a strategic as opposed to a programmatic focus.

Marshall would later come to see Schlesinger as the "Father of Net Assessment." It was Schlesinger who persuaded Kissinger to transfer net assessment from the NSC to the Department of Defense; Schlesinger who understood net assessment's potential value; Schlesinger who knew that Marshall was the only person (other than Schlesinger himself) who knew enough about this sort of analysis to give it life. Had it remained at the NSC, Marshall concluded, it would have "degenerated into the kind of process that dominates so much in our government—common-denominator, bland bunkum, in terms of analysis" rather than he and his staff acquiring "the freedom that we've had to kind of tell the truth as we saw it."[59]

The fact that he would be working for a close friend and intellectual colleague undoubtedly influenced Marshall's decision to move to the Pentagon. He certainly had not planned for his "temporary" move to Washington to turn out to be as permanent as it eventually proved to be. The Marshalls had rented a modest apartment in Washington on Virginia Avenue near the Watergate in the belief that their time in the nation's capital would be relatively brief, a few years at most. Mary Marshall only began to stay full-time at the Washington apartment in January 1973.

For years afterward, when asked how long he intended to remain as director of the Office of Net Assessment, Andrew Marshall's stock answer was, "Maybe a year so." But the Marshalls never returned to their home in California. When Mary Marshall passed away at the age of eighty-five in December 2004, she and her husband were still living in their small Virginia Avenue apartment, a home-away-from-home still furnished with rental furniture.

5

MOVING TO THE PENTAGON
1973–1975

I need data!
    —ANDREW MARSHALL

On the morning of October 2, 1973, Marshall met with Defense Secretary
Schlesinger and formally agreed to leave the National Security Council
staff and move to the Pentagon to establish a net assessment program there.[1]
Eleven days later Schlesinger signed a memorandum formally appointing
Marshall as the Pentagon's director of net assessment effective October 15.
In that moment, the Office of Net Assessment (ONA) was born.

The mandate for Marshall's new office was broad. The memorandum
stated that Marshall would formulate and recommend the topics for assessments, supervise the conduct of the assessments and, where appropriate,
obtain the participation and inputs of other government staff elements to
support the effort. Marshall would also represent the Defense Department
on interagency committees dealing with national net assessments.[2]

Marshall's status was codified on November 27, when Kissinger signed
National Security Decision Memorandum (NSDM) 239, "National Net
Assessment Process."[3] NSDM 239 formally transferred responsibility for
the national net assessment program to the Defense Department.* It also
specified that the study of US and Soviet ground forces required by NSSM
186 would be completed under Schlesinger.

NSDM 239 did more than transfer a function—net assessment—from
one part of the government to another. It also enabled Marshall to begin

---

*NSDM 239 rescinded NSSM 186 and NSDM 224.

developing an approach to net assessment that was very different than that envisioned for the NSC's Net Assessment Group. NSSM 186 limited the NAG's role to simply overseeing the work of the DoD-led interagency working group tasked to conduct the assessment of US and Soviet ground forces. Under Schlesinger, Marshall and his staff would do the net assessments themselves.

This change was important because, despite their undeniable brilliance, Kissinger and Schlesinger held very different views regarding the state of the world, America's future in it and, by extension, how best to undertake net assessments. Since Marshall's views were far more closely aligned with Schlesinger's than with Kissinger's, he could count on a powerful ally as he began to establish the new organization and determine the assessment topics of greatest interest to Schlesinger. He and Schlesinger were already of one mind in thinking that the US-Soviet competition in strategic nuclear arms was the most important balance to assess.

The more profound difference in outlook between Kissinger and Schlesinger concerned the possibilities of the United States' winning the Cold War. As President Nixon's national security adviser, Kissinger had been confronted daily for over four years with the image of a United States whose power appeared to be waning, whose domestic environment was punctuated by growing economic uncertainty, antiwar demonstrations, and the erosion of traditional social and moral values.[4] It was, simply, a country whose people—and leaders—appeared determined to avoid foreign adventures and were anxious to pursue a less active role in the world.

This semi-isolationist mood was reflected in American politics. In 1968 Richard Nixon had campaigned successfully on a platform of ending the war in Vietnam. His opponent in the 1972 election, Senator George McGovern, had gone further, brandishing the slogan "Come Home America!" advocating a major retrenchment in US engagement, not only in Southeast Asia but around the world. In that environment, Kissinger sought to create breathing space for the United States to reduce the geopolitical and military competition with the Soviet Union through détente (a reduction of tensions) and arms control. To many observers, Kissinger's approach not only made sense but was also achieving results.

In May 1972, after over two years of negotiations, the United States and Soviet Union signed the Strategic Arms Limitation Treaty (SALT, or SALT I) and the Anti-Ballistic Missile (ABM) Treaty in Moscow. While to some the treaties ushered in a hopeful period of détente between the two superpowers, others saw it as the means by which the Soviets would encourage US restraint while continuing to build up their armaments. Kissinger's critics proved right. As President Jimmy Carter's secretary of defense, Harold Brown, later observed regarding offensive nuclear forces, "Soviet spending . . . has shown no response to U.S. restraint—when we build, they build; when we cut, they build."[5]

Kissinger also served as point man for the Nixon administration's negotiations with the Vietnamese Communists to achieve a US withdrawal from the war in a manner that would ensure, in the president's words, "peace with honor."[6] In January 1973, following a series of negotiations involving Kissinger and the North Vietnamese politburo member, Le Duc Tho, punctuated by a brief but massive US bombing campaign against North Vietnam in December 1972 (known as Operation Linebacker II), an agreement was reached enabling the United States to extricate itself from the war while also securing the release of US prisoners of war held captive by the North Vietnamese. Although the agreement won Kissinger the Nobel Peace Prize, critics nonetheless viewed it as abandoning America's Southeast Asian ally, particularly as the peace settlement enabled North Vietnamese forces to remain in South Vietnam while all US forces were withdrawn. Equally ominous, the communist regime in Hanoi would continue receiving aid from Moscow and Beijing to support its efforts to conquer South Vietnam, whereas the US Congress would prove increasingly unwilling to provide military assistance to protect the beleaguered nation.

Moreover, despite his landslide victory in November 1972, Nixon was rapidly losing political power as the growing Watergate scandal began to command the headlines. The precipitating event was the arrest in July 1972 of five men, later linked by the FBI to Nixon's reelection campaign, for breaking into the Democratic National Committee Headquarters in the Watergate complex, which was just a short walk down Virginia Avenue from the Marshalls' apartment. The subsequent cover-up of the Watergate break-in that would culminate in the president's resignation was not the only domestic political scandal during his truncated second term. On October 10, 1973, Vice President Spiro Agnew resigned after pleading no contest to having failed to report $29,500 of income received in 1967 while governor of Maryland.

The US economy, addicted to cheap oil, also sputtered following the so-called Yom Kippur War* that began with Egypt and Syria attacking Israel in October 1973. Washington's support of Israel triggered a boycott by the Arab oil-producing nations that caused oil prices to skyrocket from roughly $3 to $12 a barrel.† The resulting energy crisis, along with the collapse of the UN's Bretton Woods monetary management system two years earlier,‡ threw the US economy into recession, further eroding the president's popular support.

Under the threat of impeachment, Nixon resigned in August 1974. He was succeeded by Gerald Ford, who had been appointed vice president following Agnew's resignation. When Ford pardoned Nixon for any crimes committed while in office, it triggered a surge of outrage among many Americans. These events combined to produce a rousing victory for the Democratic Party in the November 1974 congressional elections, reflecting not only the American public's anger over the Watergate scandal but also its growing desire to scale back US security commitments. Thus when North Vietnam initiated a major offensive against South Vietnam in March 1975, Congress denied military assistance funding to the Saigon government. Bereft of the kind of US support that had enabled its successful defense against North Vietnam's 1972 Easter Offensive, South Vietnam collapsed within two months. This combination of war-weariness, a sluggish economy, political scandal, and the promise of détente continued to propel the United States toward a period of retrenchment. Viewed from this perspective, Kissinger felt he was playing a weak hand as best he could.

Was America's hand that weak? To Schlesinger and Marshall, Kissinger's pessimism was unwarranted. In Schlesinger's view there was still cause for optimism about the United States' prospects. He went so far as to call himself a "revivalist." He believed that the United States could recover its footing and compete effectively against the Soviet Union in the battle for

---

* Also known as the October War and the Ramadan War.
† The price spike was also due in large part to the peaking of US domestic oil production in 1970, leaving the country with no spare production capacity.
‡ In 1944 delegates from over forty nations, including the major Western allies, met in Bretton Woods, New Hampshire, to establish a postwar economic order. In August 1971, when various factors led to the US dollar's becoming overvalued, President Nixon suspended unilaterally the convertibility of the US dollar to gold at Bretton Wood's set rate of $35 per ounce.

geostrategic advantage.[7] This difference of opinion manifested itself in a growing competition between Kissinger and Schlesinger for the ear of President Ford in formulating national security policy.

As a close observer of both men, Marshall concluded that the conflict between Kissinger and Schlesinger had much to do with their very different views of the relative long-term strengths and weaknesses of the two rival superpowers, an issue to which he would accord great importance in his office's net assessments. Marshall suspected that Kissinger might have been swayed, in a way that he and Schlesinger were not, by the CIA's somber estimates of how small a burden the Soviet military buildup was placing on its economy. As DCI Schlesinger had questioned the CIA's estimate of Soviet military spending as a percentage of the USSR's economic output. He could not understand how an economy half the size of the United States could be fielding and modernizing a much larger military than the United States and still have roughly the same burden, about 6 percent of gross national product. Once in the Pentagon, one of Schlesinger's first tasks for Marshall was to push the CIA to reconsider this estimate.

While Marshall officially oversaw the NSSM 186 assessment of US and Soviet ground forces, the analysis was done by neither him nor his two-man staff. Instead it was conducted by an interagency working group in the Pentagon. Patrick Parker, the deputy assistant secretary of defense for intelligence assessment, was assigned by the Defense Department to head a steering group to guide the analysis. The group included the Army and Navy secretaries,* the directors of the CIA and the Defense Intelligence Agency, the director of the Office of Defense Research and Engineering, the assistant secretary of defense for the Office of Program Analysis and Evaluation (PA&E), the chairman of the Joint Chiefs of Staff, and Marshall. Robert Stone from PA&E directed the interagency working group, with the CIA providing most of the data on Soviet ground forces.[8]

This arrangement did not produce the kind of net assessment Marshall had envisioned in 1972. The steering group was populated with senior officials who lacked the time to devote serious intellectual effort to the assessment, and who also needed to satisfy the views of a wide range of

---

*The Department of the Navy includes the Marine Corps, whose equities were at stake in the assessment of ground forces.

bureaucratic players and organizations. As anyone familiar with the workings of large government bureaucracies knows, the interagency process
generally produces results that reflect compromises on substantive areas of
disagreement among the group's participants. This leads to findings that are
the least objectionable to everyone involved rather than those that are the
most insightful and, not surprisingly, often the most controversial.[9] Such
was the case with this first national net assessment.

The NSSM 186 comparison of the US and Soviet ground forces was not
completed until April 1974 and was, at best, bland. It argued that no important insights or conclusions could be drawn from the major differences, or
asymmetries, between the two sides' ground forces. In particular, it offered
no meaningful observations regarding the question that was increasingly in
the forefront of Marshall and Schlesinger's thinking: whether the United
States or the Soviet Union was more efficient or successful in converting
resources into military capabilities. Instead, the assessment stressed the obvious: that judgments regarding the *overall* balance between US and Soviet
ground forces would have to take into account such things as the US advantages in mobility and tactical air forces, and the forces of both sides' allies.
And since the entire US Army and Marine Corps would not fight the entire
Soviet Army in any plausible scenario, the study also offered no operational
context—such as a conflict between NATO and the Warsaw Pact in Central
Europe—for thinking about possible combat outcomes in realistic contingencies. To make matters worse, the CIA promptly distanced itself from the
assessment's innocuous findings even though the Agency had provided most
of the intelligence data and participated in the interagency working group.

Marshall forwarded results of what became known as the NSSM 186
Phase I assessment to Schlesinger on April 16, 1974. However, his forwarding memorandum did not voice the depth of his disappointment with
its substance. Marshall's foremost objection centered on the assessment's
implication that Soviet ground forces did not have any exploitable weaknesses. Privately, however, he was angry over the assessment. He thought
the analysis was so broad and general as to produce findings that were, in
his eyes, little more than "bullshit." Marshall felt the assessment effectively
concluded that the "Soviets don't have any weaknesses," which he knew was
"nonsense."[10] He also believed that some of the positions taken by participants flew in the face of common sense, particularly DIA's insistence that
the semiannual influx of raw conscripts into the Soviet Army to replace

soldiers who had been serving for several years did not affect its readiness.[11] Making matters worse, when he met with the head of DIA, Lieutenant General Daniel Graham, to discuss the assessment he found that Graham personally agreed with him, contradicting the official position of his organization.[12] This only served to reinforce Marshall's view that net assessments, if they were to be of any value to the defense secretary or other senior officials, would have to avoid the interagency process and its tendency to reduce findings to only those that could be agreed upon by all.

Marshall asked Phillip Karber, who was then working for the BDM Corporation,* to review the assessment. Although his views were not as negative as Marshall's, Karber was by no means enamored of the assessment's findings. He was especially struck by the decision to exclude the US Reserve and National Guard ground forces from US force levels while including the Soviet Army's Category 2 and 3 reserve divisions. This only reinforced Marshall's judgment that the assessment was seriously flawed. Karber was also stunned that the assessment failed to take into account the surprising effectiveness demonstrated by state-of-the-art Soviet equipment used by the Egyptians and Syrians during the recent Yom Kippur War.[13]

It was not until the end of July that Marshall composed a memo to Schlesinger containing a summary of his main misgivings about the NSSM 186 assessment. Marshall called it at best "only a partial success." He also admitted that while he had expected that acquiring the necessary intelligence data from the CIA would be difficult, he had had "little appreciation of how bad the problem was." The assessment revealed that there were serious gaps in the intelligence community's understanding of the qualitative aspects of Soviet forces, and a strong tendency to fill in the gaps with worst-case estimates. He told Schlesinger that he needed good data on such matters as training and logistics, yet he could get little in these areas.

Marshall also noted that the assessment raised a number of issues that were left unresolved. One was the fact that the US Army and Marine Corps had roughly twice as many men per major weapon system as one found in the Soviet ground forces. This suggested that American equipment might be more technically advanced and also better supported and maintained, and thus more capable and reliable than Soviet equipment. But even in this case,

---

*Founded in 1959 by Joseph V. Braddock, Bernard J. Dunn, and Dan McDonald. BDM is now part of the Northrop Grumman Corporation.

when faced with major divergences between how the Soviet and the US military chose to operate their respective forces, the intelligence and military participants in the assessment could not decide whether these differences worked to the United States' advantage. Marshall also noted that while the interagency group found that the Soviets could mobilize and commit their reserves to combat much more quickly than could the US Army and Marine Corps—another major asymmetry between US and Soviet ground forces— it could not agree on the significance of this finding. Marshall's bottom line to Schlesinger: "We cannot leave this subject in this state."[14]

After reading the memo, Schlesinger called Marshall in to discuss the situation. He concurred with Marshall that the ground forces assessment was woefully inadequate. Both men found particularly egregious its overall failure to identify weaknesses in Soviet Union's ground forces that could be exploited to NATO's advantage.[15] The implication that the Soviets had no weaknesses flew in the face of everything Marshall had learned about organizational behavior in general and Soviet organizational behavior in par-ticular during his collaborations with Loftus, Goldhamer, Schlesinger, and others. A "more balanced assessment of Soviet strengths and weaknesses," Marshall later observed, would avoid such mistakes as overestimating the opponent, making wrong choices such as "unnecessary abandonment of defensible positions," and failing to make "more effective use of our own resources."[16] He also felt it was critical to understand the other side's way of "doing business": the psychological-political effects or uses of military forces, both in peace and in war. The assessment generally ignored these qualitative factors, which while important could not be reduced to numerical compari-sons. When they finished reviewing the report Marshall recalled Schlesinger exclaiming, "Enough of this shit. Let's get on and do something serious."[17]

The two men quickly concluded that adequate net assessments—that is, frank and objective analyses of where the United States stood relative to the Soviet Union in various military competitions—could not be left to the interagency process, or to the efforts of individual intelligence agencies, the military services, or even established analytic organizations in the Office of the Secretary of Defense such as PA&E. Instead, Marshall was going to have to develop net assessment as a new analytic discipline, and his small staff in the Office of Net Assessment was going to have to do the bulk of the hard intellectual work needed to produce adequate assessments.

Marshall believed that "most of the things the defense secretary could de-cide or affect were issues that had to do with future forces" and capabilities.[18]

If so, net assessments would have to go beyond the tendency to focus on the problems of evaluating likely outcomes of battles that might occur in the immediate future. There was little a defense secretary could do to influence these battles or campaigns in the sense that the forces, equipment, and the commanders who would fight them were already in place. Nor could they be changed either quickly or easily. What a defense secretary *could* influence to a far greater degree were the US military's characteristics in the mid- to long-term future. A defense secretary was in a position to affect the selection of military officers and leaders who would rise to key command and staff positions in the years ahead. He could also determine the priority that would be given to research into new or more advanced military capabilities, which developmental systems would move forward into production, and in what quantities they would be fielded. As it might well be a decade or longer before these decisions would be realized in the military's force posture, the defense secretary would need to have some sense of what the security environment would look like during that timeframe—in particular, how the future security environment might differ from today's.

To Marshall, therefore, it seemed natural to focus net assessments on providing the Defense Department's most senior leaders with early warning of emerging problems or currently neglected problems that would likely get worse, and of opportunities and advantages the United States already had (or could develop) that it might exploit. He felt that "the kind of perspective you had, the kind of issues you wanted to illuminate, were *strategic management issues* [emphasis added]. We weren't doing this assessment for the theater commander and his immediate problems."[19]

This did not mean that assessments focusing on the longer term would be useless to today's senior military and civilian leaders. But they were not Marshall's principal audience. The assessments would be done specifically for the defense secretary, to help him with strategic management issues facing the Defense Department in the most important existing—and emerging—military competitions. Marshall and his staff would endeavor to highlight one or two of the most pressing problems or attractive opportunities in a given competition, and do so early enough for the defense secretary to make decisions about them that would influence their outcome.

To undertake this kind of work ONA would have a research budget to enable its director to draw on the most talented individuals and organizations anywhere in the United States, including those outside the US government. This reflected Marshall's RAND experience. Especially in the 1950s

RAND's top management had sought out the "best and brightest" talent throughout the country, including outside consultants, to assist in its work. Among other things, he believed this approach could benefit from harvesting some of the thinking done in the area of business strategy, in particular the notion of exploiting one's strengths in order to capture markets as a means of driving rivals out of specific business areas.

Marshall and Schlesinger agreed that ONA's net assessments would be diagnostic, rather than prescriptive. They would strive to diagnose where the United States currently stood relative to the USSR in the key military competitions and where it would likely stand in the next five to eight years. But Marshall's office would not write the prescriptions for which military capabilities might be needed to "treat" a security problem or exploit an opportunity. Those decisions would be left to the defense secretary and other senior DoD officials.

To avoid the risk that assessments would be watered down by having ONA coordinate its products with other parts of the Pentagon bureaucracy, Schlesinger directed that the assessments would go directly to him without being coordinated either within the Pentagon or elsewhere in the government. They would represent the best judgments of the Office of Net Assessment.[20] In addition there would be no set schedule for producing net assessments; the emphasis would be on getting them done well rather than fast. Marshall would be able to devote as much time as necessary to producing full-blown assessments. Nor would he be under any pressure to update major assessments on any regular schedule, although he would always be ready to respond to requests for summaries of existing military balances and those that were under way, as well as to support special projects directed by the secretary of defense.

Recasting net assessments as private documents written for the defense secretary by ONA alone effectively reversed the original process for conducting national net assessments through a coordinated interagency effort. In this way Schlesinger and Marshall set the framework and the conditions under which net assessment would evolve and mature. While originally laid down by Schlesinger, this approach was later accepted and to a great extent institutionalized by his immediate successors, Donald Rumsfeld and Harold Brown.[21]

Marshall was skeptical that he would be able to provide Schlesinger with much in the way of useful assessments in the near term.[22] He and his small staff would have to work their way up a steep learning curve to develop this new form of analysis. The NSSM 186 assessment had shown that the intelligence community could not necessarily be relied upon to provide the kinds of data they would need. Other sources might have to be found. This, too, would take time. Marshall also concluded, after reviewing the state of simulation and modeling, that he could not rely on these analytic tools to estimate or predict likely combat outcomes with any degree of reliability. Success here would require a different approach. Analysis of likely war outcomes would need to rely less on exquisite (and highly expensive) simulations and more on war gaming involving experienced military practitioners.

Schlesinger and Marshall next discussed what assessments should receive top priority. They quickly agreed that ONA would initially concentrate on three areas. First and foremost would be the strategic nuclear balance between the United States and the Soviet Union. Marshall had done extensive work in this area for several decades. More important, the Soviet nuclear arsenal posed the only immediate existential threat to America's survival.

The second assessment would address the military balance between NATO and the Warsaw Pact, an alliance comprising the Soviet Union and its Eastern European satellite states.* This, too, was an obvious choice. Most of the Soviet Union's conventional air and ground forces were opposite NATO in central Europe, and most Soviet reinforcements were located just beyond Poland in the USSR's Western Military Districts. The threat these forces posed to Western Europe was both immediate and clear, as was the need to defend the United States' NATO allies, particularly France, Great Britain, and West Germany.† Were the Soviets to seize Western Europe, the overall military balance between the United States and the USSR would be fundamentally altered in the latter's favor. In addition, a conventional war in central Europe was the most likely trigger for nuclear escalation.

Marshall and Schlesinger decided that the third area would be the maritime balance between the two superpowers. To begin with they viewed the maritime balance as a catchall for strategic mobility and overseas power

---

*The other members of the Warsaw Pact were Bulgaria, Czechoslovakia, the German Democratic Republic ("East Germany"), Hungary, Poland, and Romania.
†West Germany was formally known as the Federal Republic of Germany. Although France had dropped out of NATO's unified military command structure in 1966, it remained within the alliance itself, and continued to station troops in West Germany.

projection, areas of military capability in which the US military was well ahead.[23] But the Soviet Navy was now receiving greater priority, raising the possibility that the Soviets might be looking to move into a new "business area" and begin competing more directly with the United States in the maritime domain. Finally, this assessment would also enable Marshall to examine possible Soviet efforts to engage in power-projection operations far from their borders.

Not long after Schlesinger and Marshall agreed upon these three assessments, the defense secretary added a fourth. Recalling his disagreement with the CIA's estimate of the USSR's military burden when he was DCI, he asked Marshall to pressure the CIA to reconsider its burden estimate. This led to a series of US-Soviet investment balances with particular emphasis on each side's future military capabilities. In terms of American budget categories, this meant focusing on spending for research and development (R&D), procurement, and military construction.[24] In Marshall's lexicon, this assessment would be neither a functional balance like the US-Soviet strategic nuclear competition nor a regional balance such as the NATO–Warsaw Pact competition. Instead it sought to compare both sides' resource allocations to their evolving military forces and capabilities.

Schlesinger's intense interest in the issue of Soviet military expenditures was understandable as the answer had profound implications for the long-term competition between the superpowers. If in fact the USSR could generate substantially more military capability than the United States with an economy half the size, all while maintaining the defense burden at 6 or 7 percent of gross national product, the prognosis for the United States would be bleak indeed. But despite pressure from ONA, the CIA persisted with its 6–7 percent burden estimate into the mid-1970s.[25]

Schlesinger later recalled that while he was DCI he had framed the burden issue for some of the Agency's economists as follows: "Look at those guys [the Soviets]. According to the CIA they're spending 6 percent of the GDP or GNP on the military, and look at all this stuff [they are producing]! . . . [A]re they miracle workers—or is there something wrong with the analysis?"[26] If the US economy was twice the size of the Soviet economy and both were spending 6 percent of their economy on defense, then the US defense budget should be twice the size of the Soviet defense budget. But CIA's efforts to cost Soviet military programs suggested the opposite. Schlesinger told his staff:

[W]e are producing . . . 180 tanks a year . . . And look at these guys, they are producing 3,000 tanks a year—or 2,800. Probably ours are better. They may not be. But if you look at their military production, that's pretty impressive. They are producing "X" number of aircraft a year. We are producing a small fraction thereof. Ours have advanced electronics but, you know, look at the numbers that are coming out over there. . . . *They've got to be spending in dollar terms about 160 percent of what we're spending. . . .* They are devoting a major part of their industrial capability and their economic activity to defense.[27]

Schlesinger and Marshall believed the Soviet buildup was placing far more strain on the USSR's economy than the CIA was willing to admit. Rather than being "miracle workers," the Soviets were devoting a cripplingly large share of their GNP and their industrial base to military purposes, an effort they could not hope to sustain over the long term. The crucial bottom line: If Schlesinger and Marshall were right, then *time was on America's side—it was the Soviet Union that would eventually find itself on the ropes, not the United States.*

Schlesinger's tenure at the CIA had lasted only five months, not long enough to make sufficient headway against its bureaucracy. After getting his feet on the ground as defense secretary, however, he personally told Edward Proctor, the deputy director for intelligence at the CIA, that he remained wholly unconvinced that the Soviet defense burden was as small a percentage of the USSR's GNP as the Agency persisted in maintaining.[28]

While Schlesinger asked Marshall to press the CIA to reexamine its estimates of the USSR's military burden, its economists proved persistently loath to rethink their position.[29] Despite Marshall's persistent efforts to get them to do so, he would have no better luck in getting the CIA to rethink its estimate of the USSR's military burden than Schlesinger had had as DCI.[30] For the remainder of the Cold War, the Agency consistently asserted that the military burden on the Soviet economy was substantially less than Marshall and Schlesinger believed it to be.

After agreeing on the four key areas of the US-Soviet military competition in which ONA would conduct major assessments, Marshall next needed to determine how best to structure them. In 1976, after several iterations, he converged on a basic four-part structure for the balances. The first—the basic assessment—would provide the reader with an overview of the competition under examination: How was the United States faring in the competition? Was its position improving relative to the past, or not? Given current conditions, was its position likely to improve over time, or not? The second section would identify key asymmetries in the competition: Where did the two competitors differ in significant and important ways, particularly in how they were pursuing the competition? These asymmetries could vary widely, to include (but not be limited to) objectives, doctrine, force structure, force posture (e.g., basing of forces), allies, logistics, and modernization efforts. The assessment would then analyze the key asymmetries' significance in terms of their influence on the competition. The third section would identify and discuss major uncertainties that could exert a significant bearing on the conclusions reached in the basic assessment. The fourth and final part would address emerging problem areas in the competition and, equally important, key opportunities, both of which might be exploited to improve the United States' competitive position.[31]

Schlesinger gave Marshall and his office a remarkable degree of autonomy—although this did not free them from dependence on the Pentagon or the intelligence community. Marshall realized that he would need the support of both to conduct his assessments. They had data that he could not obtain from other sources. For example, the CIA was the primary source for order-of-battle data on Soviet forces—everything from nuclear weapons to tank armies to air regiments and naval forces—as well as of dollar-cost estimates of Soviet defense expenditures and the size of the USSR's overall economy. As for the US military services, they were the primary source of historical order-of-battle data on US forces, and could also provide important insights as to how new weapon systems in development would likely be employed. Initially Marshall expected to benefit from his close association with Schlesinger by using the defense secretary's name to gain access to the desired data held by these organizations. Nevertheless, like most large organizations they could be reluctant to share information, particularly when the highest levels of security classification were involved or when the data might be used to support analyses that would challenge their parochial interests.

As it turned out Marshall very much needed Schlesinger's support, or "top cover," to use the parlance of the Pentagon. The Office of Net Assessment was viewed warily by other elements of the government, particularly those that felt its director would challenge their prerogatives or analyses and in so doing undermine their influence. The fact that Marshall already had a track record of challenging the accepted wisdom only increased their anxiety. The general response from OSD's analytic organizations, such as PA&E, as well as the military services was that they either already did, or could, conduct net assessments. In their eyes, there was simply no need for what Marshall proposed to do. This was especially true in the case of PA&E's systems analysts who wanted to fold net assessment's work into their annual Defense Department budgeting and planning cycle.

These organizations did not understand that in both Marshall and Schlesinger's eyes net assessment was intended not to compete with systems analysis but to provide broader, more comprehensive analyses of military issues that looked beyond near-term choices of weapons systems. If they had any doubts, they only had to listen to Marshall talk of his absolute determination that net assessment must not engage in making programmatic recommendations. If his enterprise had been subsumed into the Pentagon's planning, programming, and budgeting process it would have almost certainly lost its broad, long-term focus and been pushed toward the reductionist, near-term prescriptive focus that characterized systems analysis. As for the notion that net assessment would duplicate regular intelligence production processes, as some suggested, this ignored the belief of Marshall, Schlesinger, Kissinger, and many others, including President Nixon, that an independent net assessment group was needed to both evaluate existing national intelligence products and provide balanced, objective assessments of US and allied capabilities relative to those of competitors and adversaries.

While ONA would have received a chilly reception from its bureaucratic cousins—and self-anointed rivals—under almost any circumstances, their lack of comprehension of Marshall's intentions made it downright icy. In the Pentagon (and in other large organizations) there always seems to be someone advancing a new method, a new process, a new way of doing business that will cure what ails the bureaucracy. In nearly all instances these purported fixes prove to be illusory. But until they are rooted out, these new practices often play havoc with the institution's traditional ways of doing business. Armed with these institutional memories and having little if any understanding of what Marshall had in mind, the bureaucracy proved more than willing to give full reign to its fears.

Some of the blame for this rests with Marshall himself, for he did not go out of his way to allay mistrust. With rare exceptions he was extremely reticent to define or to elaborate his views on what a "net assessment" was or would accomplish. While his 1972 paper on "The Nature and Scope of Net Assessments" provided a fairly clear conception of what he had in mind, it was never widely circulated, *even among his own staff*. In fact, not until 2002 was the paper discovered filed away in a binder in Marshall's office.

While Marshall's reticence was unhelpful, his reasons for holding back were understandable. He was literally in the process of trying to create a new analytic discipline. Consequently there was little to gain, and much to lose, were he to lock himself into specific ways of bounding, formally defining, or conducting net assessments that he might later regret.

Marshall had other reasons for his sphinxlike demeanor. Reflecting the enormous value he had received from his own efforts at self-education, he felt that the military officers and civilian assistants on his staff would be better off working out for themselves the details of how to approach their own particular net assessment topic. This attitude would prove intensely frustrating to many of the military officers he would employ. They were accustomed to being given a clear mission to accomplish and provided with guidance—oftentimes detailed in the extreme—as to how to proceed. For those who had grown comfortable operating in such an environment, Marshall's general guidance and light hand when it came to oversight left many feeling as though they had been abandoned in an analytic no-man's-land. He viewed the challenge of producing a good assessment as comparable to writing a doctoral dissertation. As with a PhD dissertation, there was no cookie-cutter formula that could be applied to crafting a net assessment.[32] ONA staff members undertaking assessments were expected to break new ground in the area being examined—to provide some new and original insights that made a significant contribution to the existing body of knowledge. As one of Marshall's military assistants later remarked to a frustrated colleague: "He [Marshall] wants you to tell him things that are worthwhile that he doesn't already know. If he knew what those things are, he wouldn't need us."[33]

In addition to developing an analytic framework for ONA's assessments, Marshall needed good data to draw upon in crafting them. Frustrated by the limits of what the intelligence community and military services could—or would—provide, he began developing his own databases. Toward this end he eventually hired BDM's Phillip Karber to take the lead in building a historical database on NATO and Warsaw Pact forces. In the aftermath of the NSSM 186 Phase I assessment of US and Soviet ground forces, it was decided to conduct a Phase II assessment comparing NATO and Warsaw

Pact tactical air forces. Karber agreed to lead the analysis, even though it was burdened by an interagency structure and process similar to that used in Phase I. Karber was provided with a staff consisting mainly of senior field-grade military officers nearing retirement, individuals who were not well suited for the data-gathering drudgery and analytic rigor required for the assessment. The Phase II study began in the summer of 1974 but was not completed until November 1975.

Because Karber was a civilian contractor, Robin Pirie on the ONA staff was assigned to supervise the tactical air power assessment. Toward the end of the Phase II study a frustrated Pirie suggested to Karber that he modify the contract so that he could bring young BDM analysts on board to begin replacing the military officers who were due to depart once Phase II was completed. Marshall agreed, and decided to use his research budget to break free from bureaucratic constraints by establishing his own independent research effort on the European military balance.

Marshall's new approach became known as Project 186, or simply P-186, the "186" a reference to NSSM 186. P-186 was designed as a long-term research project funded and administered by Marshall's office. It would be run by Karber at BDM. Karber began assembling a small team to support the effort. There would be no more assessments done through an interagency process.

Project 186 would continue to the end of the Cold War. Its principal focus was to assess the military capabilities of NATO and Warsaw Pact forces in central Europe, an area that included Belgium, the Netherlands, Luxembourg, West and East Germany, Poland, and Czechoslovakia.[34] Under ONA, the P-186 effort was shaped and guided by a number of considerations. First and foremost, Karber was to provide Marshall with studies on NATO and Warsaw Pact forces that satisfied the latter's desire for new insights into the military competition in Europe. Frustrated by the lack of data support from the intelligence community and US military, Marshall decided to develop an independent and integrated database on NATO and Warsaw Pact forces, and inserted contractual language that enabled the database work to continue year in and year out. Finally, the effort was informed by guidelines that emerged from a discussion Karber had had with Schlesinger after briefing the defense secretary during the Phase II work.

Schlesinger told Karber that he was looking for three things from an assessment. First, he wanted trend data on the opposing forces over time, so that he could see where the two sides had been and how the competition was developing, as opposed to getting a single snapshot of the current situation. By examining the trends it might be possible to see shifts in the USSR's relative emphasis on various kinds of military forces and thus insights into their intentions and strategy. Second, Schlesinger wanted a sense of the qualitative aspects of the competition affecting the US or NATO position—factors that went beyond simple tabulations or "bean counts" of tanks, aircraft, artillery pieces, numbers of divisions, and such. Both of these points echoed Marshall's desire for the effort to mine for new insights on the character of the two alliances. Third, Schlesinger wanted more meaningful force comparisons. For example, instead of comparing NATO and Warsaw Pact strike aircraft "side by side" with one another, as Phase II assessment had done, Schlesinger wanted each side's tactical aircraft compared against the other's integrated air defenses, which represented their respective real-world opponents in the event of war.[35]

Over time the database work on NATO and Warsaw Pact conventional and theater-nuclear forces proved foundational. As Schlesinger and Marshall knew, comparing the two sides at a single point in time provided no insight into how the competition had gotten to its present state, or where it might be headed in the future. The Project 186 database on NATO and Warsaw Pact forces eventually extended from the mid-1960s through the late 1980s and included reinforcements from the United States and the western military districts of the USSR in addition to the forces stationed in Central Europe. It also acquired enough detail on NATO and Warsaw Pact mobilization and reinforcement capabilities to be able to depict how force ratios would change over time as the alliances began mobilizing prior to war. And, as Schlesinger and Marshall intended, it facilitated more operationally meaningful comparisons between NATO and Warsaw Pact forces, such as armor versus antiarmor and conventional air-strike capabilities versus opposing air defenses.[36] This enabled Marshall and his staff to gain a more complete picture of the military balance than had been possible up to that time. For example, if during a month-long period of mobilization there occurred a few days in which the military balance shifted greatly in the Warsaw Pact's favor, this represented a NATO weakness that needed to be brought to the defense secretary's attention. After all, if the Soviets saw the same weakness, it could encourage them to exploit it by launching their attack at that point in time, and deterrence would have failed.

Developing the database proved to be a monumental undertaking. Oddly enough, obtaining data on the United States' NATO allies was even more challenging than estimating the forces of the Warsaw Pact states. The US intelligence community was formally restricted from "spying" on US allies, and thus did not keep a detailed database on their military forces and programs. Then there was the dispute between Greece and Turkey over Cyprus. Although both countries were NATO members, each viewed the other as an enemy and was reluctant to share information on its forces that might prove useful to the other. The result was that the Greeks and Turks classified their force data at levels that made gaining access difficult.

In the end Marshall's ability to open doors in Europe to provide access for Karber's team proved crucial. It turned out that NATO archives contained historical order-of-battle data that even the Pentagon did not have. As one of Karber's analysts, Diego Ruiz-Palmer, recalled,

> We had incredible access. We tapped in on virtually everything that the U.S. government had in terms of Soviet, Warsaw Pact, U.S., and NATO intelligence and information . . . We had wide access to general officers at the three- and four-star level. Andy [Marshall] was able to open lots of doors in many directions, and we got into the war plans of the U.S., we got into the general defense plans of NATO at all levels, from SACEUR [Supreme Allied Commander Europe] down, and into the special Soviet data. . . . [Polish] Colonel Ryszard Kuklinski . . . was very much a silent member of Project 186 because of the incredible intelligence that for eight years, from 1973 to 1981, he was able to communicate to the CIA, at great risk to himself.[37] He gave the United States a panoramic view of the Warsaw Pact and, thanks to him, the pieces of that huge puzzle, came together, as if by magic.[38]

Marshall was interested in obtaining much more than intelligence on Soviet and Warsaw Pact forces and defense investments. US Cold War strategy focused not only on preserving vital national interests in the event of war, but also on deterring enemies from choosing the path of war in the first place. To *defeat* an enemy of the United States one had to understand the military balance from the US perspective. But to *deter* an enemy meant understanding how the enemy, in this case the Soviets, viewed the balance. Thus it was vital to know how Moscow calculated what it called the "correlation of forces," since it was the Kremlin leadership that had to be deterred.

Doing so led Marshall to pursue what came to be known in ONA as the Soviet assessment. The core questions were: How did the Soviets assess the military competition with the West?* What planning assumptions, analytic methods, models, technical calculations, effectiveness metrics, norms, and dominant scenarios did they use to assess the correlation of forces in each of ONA's main balance areas? Under what circumstances would their assessments lead them to undertake acts of aggression or coercion? If one purpose of undertaking net assessments was to identify opportunities that the United States might exploit to influence Soviet behavior, it was essential to understand what underlay Soviet calculations about the prospective costs and benefits of going to war, especially in Europe.

In looking for ways to address the problem, Marshall came upon John Battilega, who was employed at Science Applications International (SAI), a defense consulting firm then headquartered in La Jolla, California. Battilega had a strong background in quantitative analysis, having earned a doctorate in applied mathematics from Oregon State University. Following his service in the Army during the Vietnam War and a brief stint as an engineer for the Martin Marietta Corporation, a major US aerospace firm, Battilega joined SAI in 1969. There he was given oversight of the development of analytic methods and computer models to assess US and Soviet nuclear forces for Allan Rehm, the branch chief of the CIA's Force Evaluation Analysis Team (FEAT), as part of an effort known as Project Eager.[39]

When funding from the CIA and other sponsors ended, Marshall continued to support Battilega's work on Project Eager—an investment that would, over time, pay big dividends. Battilega's team developed broad insights into how the Soviets did operations research, as well as other forms of analysis, modeling, and simulations bearing on the Soviet assessment of the military competition.[40] As with Project 186 at BDM, Battilega's organization would continue its work for nearly two decades, building up a storehouse of information about how the Soviet military approached and evaluated its competitive position with the West.

Battilega was working a different part of the puzzle from Karber, one that Marshall was attempting to solve, if incompletely and temporarily,

---

*With the help of Nathan Leites, Marshall also undertook to learn how key US allies assessed the military competition. If the United States were to keep them as allies it was important to understand what aspects of the balance most concerned them, and what military capabilities particularly impressed them. Such information could influence what the United States emphasized in dealings with those allies.

given that the military competition was dynamic in character and thus constantly shifting and evolving. Battilega's terms of reference called for him and his group to scour Soviet writings—particularly military writings—to get as good a sense as possible of how they viewed the rivalry in general and how they calculated their version of the military balance in particular. The insights gained over time from this line of research were important for two reasons: (1) They helped senior US policy makers better understand how to deter the Soviets from acts of coercion or overt aggression; and (2) they provided a sense of what and how US actions might shape Soviet behavior in ways favorable to the United States.

Over time Battilega and his team identified three major differences, or asymmetries, between the assessments of the Soviet military and those of their US rivals. The first involved basic aspects of military art. Perhaps not surprisingly, Soviet views on warfare were rooted in the logic of the Marxist dialectic. Battilega concluded that the Soviets truly believed warfare could be understood as a process governed by objective laws. If you could understand what these laws were and use them to plan military operations you would, by definition, be successful in war. Believing as they did, the Soviets were obsessed with identifying these laws, intensely studying historical battles and campaigns to isolate the factors that determined why the winning side had emerged victorious and the losing side had failed. Starting with the General Staff, the Soviets applied these factors through various models and simulations and attempted to come up with "scientific" formulas that would ensure success in combat.

This approach led the Soviets—and by extension, the Warsaw Pact—to take a top-down approach to warfare aimed at ensuring that the objective laws of war were applied correctly. Thus they valued centralized control of forces and frowned on individual initiative from the bottom up. The US military and its NATO allies, by contrast, took the opposite approach. They viewed war more as an art rather than as a science. Western military practitioners were acutely aware of the "fog" and "frictions" of war, which were rooted in human physical and cognitive limits, unavoidable informational uncertainties, and the inherent nonlinearity of combat interactions. Far from looking for specific formulas that would guarantee battlefield success, they believed that war's fog and frictions worked to undermine their ability to conduct operations as they planned or intended. Rather than attempting to wring out the fog and friction of war, the US military accepted them as inevitable and attempted to limit their effects by training junior commanders and noncommissioned officers to exercise initiative and judgment as circumstances changed—a "bottom-up" approach. They drew inspiration from Prussian military theorist Carl von Clausewitz, who observed, "Everything in war is simple. But the simplest thing is difficult," and from another Prussian, General Helmuth von Moltke, who famously declared, "No plan survives contact with the enemy."

Battilega's findings with respect to the differences between Western and Soviet assessments were not unique. Others in the US defense community were coming to similar conclusions. Few if any, however, dug as deeply into the Soviet military's operations research literature and "correlation of forces" calculations as did Battilega's group. Over time his researchers identified many of the norms, rules, and calculations that the Soviet military used in their planning and assessments, all which were in theory based on empirical data from conflicts such as the 1941–1945 Russo-German War and Arab-Israeli conflicts in the Middle East. When they found battles or operations in which the side with the superior correlation of forces did not win, Battilega found that

[T]he Soviet conclusion from that was not that "Our theory is bad." It's that, "We don't understand the dimensions of strength that actually led to success. Our indices were bad." So, they repeatedly would do historical analysis to try and find the actual dimensions of strengths in the situation, and then, from that, draw conclusions about how to characterize that in terms of the correlations of forces. And this went on over and over again. There was a large military institute in Moscow that was focused on historical analysis. Their first objective of historical analysis was always, always to understand the objective laws of war that governed that particular conflict situation. And . . . then determine the dimensions of strengths that would translate that into prescriptive capabilities.[41]

The work of Battilega's Foreign Systems Research Center (FSRC) at SAI helped Marshall's staff identify and evaluate Soviet strengths and vulnerabilities *as the Soviets saw them*, not as United States and its NATO allies saw them. This was crucial to NATO's strategy of deterrence, which ultimately rested not on how the alliance's senior decision makers viewed the correlation of forces, but rather on how the Soviets interpreted it. From a US perspective, this kind of analysis could be very useful to a secretary of defense needing to make decisions about what kind of military capabilities to buy and in what combination. While senior American military leaders can provide the secretary with detailed information on why they believe a particular set of capabilities will enable the United States to achieve its security objectives at an acceptable level of risk, they cannot answer the question of intent: Will this set of capabilities deter the Soviets from taking the path to war in the first place? It was for help in answering this question that Marshall turned to Battilega.

Karber's P-186 effort and Battilega's FSRC program exemplified the sort of long-term research that Marshall's office not only needed but was able to support over periods of many years. Both reflected the kind of analysis Schlesinger sought to help him with the strategic management of the Defense Department. They would not, however, begin to realize dividends until long after Schlesinger was gone.

On November 2, 1975, President Ford dismissed Schlesinger from his position as defense secretary. Apart from his differences with Kissinger, Schlesinger had been directly at odds with his president on several key issues.* The two clearly disagreed on defense funding, with Ford opposed to the higher levels of spending Schlesinger felt necessary. Ford understood the need to stroke the egos of key members of Congress; Schlesinger did not. Of Schlesinger it was said that "he did not suffer fools gladly—if at all," and his straight-talking manner often alienated congressional leaders whose support Ford needed. There were other personality clashes. Ford was offended that Schlesinger "couldn't remember to button his shirt collar and cinch up his tie when he came to see the President of the United States."[42] Not surprisingly, politics were also a factor. Ford was looking ahead to the 1976 presidential election and decided the time was ripe to make some cabinet changes.

Schlesinger was succeeded by Ford's chief of staff, Donald Rumsfeld, whose position at the White House was filled by Richard Cheney. George H. W. Bush was brought in to succeed William Colby at the CIA. Nor did

---

*There were rumors that Ford was angry with Schlesinger over his alleged failure to carry out additional retaliatory strikes the president had directed against Cambodia's Communists after they attacked a US freighter, *Mayaguez*, in May 1975. Prior to Schlesinger's ignoring the order by the commander in chief, American forces did bomb military and fuel installations in Cambodia and rescue the *Mayaguez* crew, at the cost of 41 US troops killed in action.

Kissinger escape unscathed. While he retained his position at the State Department, Brent Scowcroft replaced him as Ford's national security adviser.

Despite having served less than three years as defense secretary, Schlesinger could look back on several impressive accomplishments. He had navigated the dangerous weeks of the October 1973 Yom Kippur War, when US forces were placed on high nuclear alert when the Soviets threatened direct intervention in the conflict. He oversaw the successful evacuation of US personnel from South Vietnam in the spring of 1975 as North Vietnamese forces unleashed a major offensive against South Vietnam and, in a lightning campaign, toppled its government and occupied the country.

It was in nuclear strategy, however, that Schlesinger had perhaps his greatest influence, as he moved the country toward a more flexible nuclear doctrine that took into account the shifting nuclear balance between the United States and Soviet Union. In so doing he rejected the single option of massive assured destruction, which in the event of any Soviet nuclear attack called for the president to respond with an all-out US nuclear counterstrike that would have included Soviet cities and industry along with Moscow's nuclear forces. And, of course, Schlesinger established the Pentagon's Office of Net Assessment and recruited Andrew Marshall to direct it.

In retrospect, Schlesinger may have been the most able strategist ever to serve as defense secretary. But he was not one of the most politically astute occupants of the office, which requires constant attention to the never-ending machinations going on at the White House, among cabinet officials, in Congress, and by the media. Unwilling to temper what he believed to be the right course of action for the nation, he was loath to compromise his principles for the sake of political expediency. One can almost hear him echoing Marshall's words: "We're here to inform, not to please." A man of strong, uncompromising views on national defense, Schlesinger's path was often a lonely one.

Despite Schlesinger's supposed poor relationship with Congress, upon his departure the Senate voted to commend him, appropriately emphasizing not only "his excellence in office," but also "his intellectual honesty and personal integrity. . . . "[43] No doubt reflecting what he and Marshall had concluded regarding the true state of the geostrategic competition between the United States and the Soviet Union, upon his departure Schlesinger retained his optimism about his country's prospects: "I feel like that intelligence officer who was at Pearl Harbor in 1941 and, looking around at the disaster, said, 'We are going to win this war. But God bless my soul if I know how.'"[44]

With Schlesinger's departure, Marshall assumed that he would soon be returning to California. Besides, he had originally promised Mary that the Pentagon job would only last a year or two. Marshall was surprised, then, when Rumsfeld told him that he wanted him to stay.

It soon became clear that Rumsfeld, at age forty-three the youngest defense secretary to date, was not only genuinely interested in assessing the main components of military competition between the United States and the Soviet Union. But he was also willing to accept the agreements Marshall had reached with Schlesinger about ONA's role and functioning.[45] Marshall's assessments would continue to be diagnostic rather than prescriptive. They would focus on the long-term US-Soviet competition rather than on current issues. They would go directly to Rumsfeld. They would not be staffed through the bureaucracy or negotiated with other parts of the Defense Department. For Marshall, what Rumsfeld agreed to would prove to be the first step in a long journey that would result in the institutionalization of the Office of Net Assessment and cement Marshall's role as the Pentagon's *éminence grise*, a behind-the-scenes adviser on strategic issues. Eventually the Russians themselves would recognize Marshall—the "Pentagon's Gray Cardinal"—as one of the most influential thinkers in the US Defense Department.[46]

6

THE MATURATION OF NET ASSESSMENT 1976–1980

What we are involved in is diagnosis, not therapy.
ANDREW MARSHALL

Schlesinger may have departed the Pentagon, but his two immediate successors, Donald Rumsfeld and Harold Brown, both quickly recognized the value of Marshall's new form of analysis. As for Marshall himself, after several years of effort, he was now in a position to begin producing the longer, more complete net assessments he had envisioned. His primary task when he came to the Pentagon had been to establish a net assessment capability for Schlesinger. Initially there had been little need for the long, analytic military balance papers that Marshall's office would begin writing under Rumsfeld. As Schlesinger later observed, Marshall was so bright and the breadth and depth of his knowledge so great that he could "see things without having the data."[1] He could (and did) walk into Schlesinger's office and offer important insights about aspects of the US-Soviet competition without having to provide the detailed background and analysis that most others would have required.[2] Of course, it helped immensely that Schlesinger was, next to Marshall himself, the person who best understood net assessment.

One of the first things that Marshall realized when Rumsfeld came on board at the Pentagon was that ONA's assessments would have to begin providing more of the analytic background and detail that Schlesinger had not required. Rumsfeld proved a good customer for Marshall's products. He not only asked for assessments of what he considered the key balances, but also requested special analyses of the Middle East, US and Soviet mobilization capabilities, détente, and the future of the strategic nuclear competition.[3]

In December 1975, barely a month into Rumsfeld's tenure, Marshall began forwarding to him four- or five-page summaries of the strategic nuclear, naval, power projection, and NATO–Warsaw Pact balances. In the case of the strategic nuclear balance, for example, ONA's basic assessment was that in the mid-1960s the United States had enjoyed a significant margin of superiority. But by the mid-1970s standard static measures of the balance showed that the Soviets had closed the gap. Nevertheless, Marshall judged that there was an adequate balance in the size and capabilities of the US and Soviet strategic forces. By this he meant that the United States' strategic forces were sufficient to deter a Soviet nuclear attack on the US homeland. But he cautioned that this could change in the future because the Soviets had "the more vigorous development program" and appeared "to be strongly motivated to further improve their forces."[4] Looking ahead, Marshall suggested that these and other improvements might one day give the Soviets "a significant advantage in crises" and even "a superior warfighting capability."[5]

Marshall was less sanguine about the US-Soviet maritime balance, which seemed to be shifting in Moscow's favor. "The simultaneous decline of our own naval force levels and the rising capability of the Soviet Navy, he wrote, "have clearly caused and are continuing to cause an adverse shift in the naval balance. However, as of today, the US Navy should be able to fulfill its assigned tasks in most areas of the world, although not without considerable losses in certain situations."[6] Eventually Marshall's basic assessments of these and other key competitions with the USSR would be incorporated as a separate section in an unclassified version of the secretary of defense's annual report to Congress.[7]

Aside from Rumsfeld's requests for these short memos, during his first few months in office he largely left ONA alone. This changed in the spring of 1976 when he tasked Marshall, along with PA&E, to help him in deciding what warships should be included in the Navy's next five-year shipbuilding program.[8] In all likelihood, Rumsfeld's concern with this area was fueled in part by ONA's assessment that the US-Soviet naval balance was shifting in the Kremlin's favor. Of particular concern to Marshall was that the Soviet Navy appeared to be ahead of the United States in the development and fielding of ship-to-ship (or "antiship") guided missiles.

To gain a better understanding of the Navy's shipbuilding program, Rumsfeld decided to convene a Saturday session at which ONA and PA&E

were to give presentations. PA&E's briefing lacked the kind of broad strategic perspective Rumsfeld sought, instead focusing on the cost effectiveness of alterative shipbuilding options. About halfway through PA&E's presentation Rumsfeld brought the briefing to a halt, saying, "Why don't we stop looking at our shoelaces and raise our sights and see where we are going?"[9]

ONA's presentation proved much more to Rumsfeld's liking. Titled "Thinking about the Navy," it placed the issue in its strategic context, and recommended that the United States openly declare its intention to maintain a "blue water" navy able to dominate the world's oceans. Specifically ONA's paper argued for moving the US-Soviet competition into areas where the United States had distinctive advantages. One such area was in the quieting of submarines. The ability of each superpower to identify and track the other's submarines was highly dependent on acoustic detection. The quieter a submarine, the more difficult it would be to locate it and maintain a track. In line with this, Marshall noted that the US Navy had a clear lead over the Soviets in the ability to detect submarine noise, in part through its network of undersea sensors known as the Sound Surveillance System (SOSUS). Concentrating on quieting and acoustic detection, Marshall suggested, could pay big dividends against the Soviet Navy, which placed far greater emphasis on its submarine fleet than did the US Navy. ONA also recommended giving priority to guidance technology, another area in which the United States enjoyed a lead that seemed likely to endure for some time to come. Although precision-guided warfare would not come into its own for another decade, Marshall had already identified its great potential. Underway replenishment—or the ability to resupply and rearm warships at sea without their returning to port—was yet another area ONA recommended be given emphasis. In Pentagon parlance, underway replenishment provided the Navy with a "force multiplier" in that the fleet would not have to waste time and energy returning to base to be resupplied but could remain constantly in action.[10] Here again, the United States enjoyed a significant lead and Marshall urged the Rumsfeld to ensure that this lead was maintained. Marshall's evaluation of the maritime competition was perhaps even more noteworthy than PA&E's presentation for what it did *not* emphasize, namely the number and types of ships and aircraft that should comprise the fleet.

Marshall's coauthor on "Thinking about the Navy" was a young Navy commander, James Roche, who had joined Marshall's staff in 1975. By 1976 Roche had already risen to assistant director of net assessment, owing to his intelligence, bureaucratic skills, and the remarkable similarity between his and Marshall's views on competing with the Soviets. Roche combined a formidable intellect with a dominating, even aggressive personality that was in many ways the opposite of Marshall's. Yet Roche's educational background—which included the study of literature and philosophy, operations research, and business administration—was as eclectic as Marshall's.

In June 1973 Roche had been given command of the USS *Buchanan* (DDG-14), a guided missile destroyer. His tour as the *Buchanan*'s commander was so successful that in 1974 he was awarded the Arleigh Burke Fleet Trophy for the most improved naval combat unit in the Pacific. Then, in 1975, Roche was detailed to the Office of the Chief of Naval Operations' systems analysis staff in the Pentagon. There he was assigned to figure out, in the event of a European conflict, how to maximize the number of ship convoys that could successfully transit the Atlantic against a Soviet submarine force engaged in a commerce raiding campaign. Frustrated by this mundane assignment Roche decided to look for a way to escape from the Navy staff.

Roche heard about Marshall and learned that he was looking for talented officers to fill out his staff. He wrangled an interview. Marshall hired him on the spot. In time the two men became intellectual soul mates and close friends. Over a quarter of a century later, when Rumsfeld was beginning his second tour as secretary of defense in 2001, he asked Marshall to undertake a strategy review. The first person Marshall turned to for help was Jim Roche. When the strategy review started, Roche was the president of Northrop Grumman's Electronic Sensors and Systems sector. By the time the review ended, Roche was secretary of the Air Force.

Given Rumsfeld's positive reaction to "Thinking About the Navy," Marshall decided to draft a strategy paper that addressed in much broader terms the long-term competition with the USSR. Working with Roche, Marshall completed "Strategy for Competing with the Soviets in the Military Sector of the Continuing Political-Military Competition," and sent it to Rumsfeld in July 1976. Rumsfeld found that Marshall had convincingly "demonstrated that the Soviet Union had been gaining ground relative to the United States" in overall military power, that the "trend lines were clearly adverse to America" and that these trends would persist unless US defense spending was increased significantly.[11] Ironically, Pentagon pressure to increase defense spending had been one of the reasons President Ford had fired Schlesinger and replaced him with Rumsfeld.

With the 1976 presidential campaign and general election on the horizon, Rumsfeld's acceptance of Marshall's assessments brought him into conflict with Kissinger, who did not want any public admission of these "unpleasant facts."[12] President Ford sided with Kissinger. He saw no politial advantage to be gained from telling a voting public hostile to defense in the wake of a failed war in Vietnam that the US-Soviet military balance was shifting in the latter's favor.[13] But while Ford was not anxious to discuss the erosion of the US position relative to the Soviets, the issue would not go away.

In 1976 the state of the US-Soviet strategic nuclear balance was generating considerable debate. Conservative critics of the administration had openly accused the CIA's estimates of Soviet strategic nuclear forces of understating the threat. For example, the key judgments in the Agency's 1974 National Intelligence Estimate, NIE 11–3/8–74, stated that Soviet leaders were continuing to develop powerful strategic forces to deter nuclear war, project an image of national power, and support détente.[14] There was no discussion in this or earlier NIEs of whether the Soviets might be building toward a capability to fight and win a nuclear war, as some of the CIA's critics feared. At the urging of the President's Foreign Intelligence Advisory Board (PFIAB), then CIA director George H. W. Bush initiated a Team B competitive analysis (Team A comprising Agency analysts) led by Harvard professor Richard Pipes.[15] The effort began in May, with Team B's members given access to classified intelligence on the Soviet Union's nuclear forces and programs. Marshall was among the experts tapped to brief Team B.

The Team B assessment found that, contrary to the more benign judgments of the NIE 11–3/8 series in the early 1970s, the USSR was striving *"for effective strategic superiority in all the branches of the military, nuclear forces included* [emphasis in the original]."[16] This judgment directly challenged Kissinger's views on the issue. At a Moscow press conference in 1974 the secretary of state had famously asked, "[W]hat in the name of God is strategic superiority? . . . What do you do with it?"[17] In 1977 Pipes's reply was that if the Soviets thought had they sufficient superiority, then they could fight and win a nuclear war.[18]

Interviews with senior Soviet officials after the Cold War ended suggest that Team B exaggerated Moscow's confidence in its nuclear capabilities.[19] But in the mid-1970s the Team B report generated much controversy within the US national security community. Team B's pessimistic conclusions resonated with Rumsfeld. He turned to Marshall and asked for his views on the likely state of the strategic nuclear competition over the next ten to fifteen years (that is, out to 1986–1991).

Marshall's August 26, 1976, response to Rumsfeld remains the closest he has ever come to writing an ONA military balance paper himself. Both then and later, ONA's assessments were written by members of his staff. They, in turn, were given considerable latitude to assess their assigned balances as they saw fit, with Marshall providing only the broadest guidance as to what he wanted.

In his cover memo to the twelve-page "The Future of the Strategic Balance" Marshall noted that neither the usual "static" nor force exchange (or "dynamic") measures adequately captured the essence of the underlying issues.[20] This meant that the inferences one could draw from such measures were of limited utility. Yet, while various static measures—typically side-by-side comparisons of the numbers of US and Soviet strategic warheads, intercontinental delivery vehicles, ICBM payload capacity or "throw-weight," and the like—differed in their portrayals of potential risk, all of them suggested that the balance would grow less favorable to the United States in the immediate future. Similarly, the dynamic measures—the results of modeling all-out exchanges between the US and Soviet nuclear arsenals, which US analysts invariably presumed would begin with a Soviet first strike—indicated increased risk starting in 1976 and continuing well into the future.

Beyond these observations on the limits of the metrics widely used to assess the nuclear balance, Marshall offered three other judgments:

- The Soviets did "indeed seem embarked on a number of nuclear programs to erode our assured destruction capabilities"—the US capability to inflict catastrophic damage the USSR even after absorbing a Soviet first strike.[21]
- The future of this competition would inevitably see both sides continuing to introduce new technologies—primarily greater missile accuracy and increased weapon yields—into their nuclear forces.[22]
- The United States had "not [yet] felt or assessed the likely impact of Soviet nuclear parity on the overall U.S.-Soviet military balance."[23]

Marshall therefore concluded in his forwarding memo that the United States "needed to think through how we should respond to the military *and* political aspects of the trends in the strategic situation" and "develop a more effective strategy for competing with Soviet nuclear forces within the bounds of rough parity in the size of the US and Soviet strategic forces [emphasis in the original]."[24]

These observations reflected Marshall's judgment that the United States' position in the nuclear competition with the USSR was eroding. First, even if static measures of the balance and force exchange calculations did not tell the whole story, one could not escape the fact that public perceptions of the balance often were based on them, and those perceptions mattered. Domestically, members of Congress knew that their constituents tended to form opinions based on simple static metrics, and were wary of being charged by their opponents as being weak on defense. Just as important, the United States' ability to provide shelter under its "nuclear umbrella" to key allies who had foresworn nuclear weapons—such as Germany, Japan, and South Korea— was in no small measure based on their perceptions of the nuclear balance between the two superpowers, whether their perceptions were accurate or not.

Because these static and dynamic measures suggested that strategic nuclear balance was shifting in the Soviet Union's favor, this unpleasant reality needed to be taken into account. In the case of static metrics, the USSR was moving ahead of the United States in ballistic missile throw-weight, equivalent megatonnage (the weapon's yield raised to the 2/3 power), and ICBM and submarine-launched ballistic missile (SLBM) launchers. At the same time, Marshall worried, exchange calculations were likely to "reflect the increasing vulnerability of the [US] silo-based ICBMs."[25] Next, the increased vulnerability of US ICBMs to a Soviet ICBM attack, combined with Soviet efforts to promote the survival of the Soviet economy following a nuclear exchange, would over time cause some erosion in the US capability to maintain assured destruction.[26] If the Soviets could take out a large portion of the Americans' ICBM force, the United States' ability to retaliate to a Soviet first strike would decline over time, perhaps tempting the Soviets to risk such a strike. Third (and by far the most important, in Marshall's judgment), because US leaders may not "clearly enough see the difference in Soviet objectives and their perspective on the military and political competition," they risked ignoring the broader geopolitical leverage that might be derived from the USSR's growing nuclear capabilities, and the longer-term dangers of the USSR's achieving, if only in the its leaders' eyes, sufficient superiority to risk a first strike.[27]

How might the United States deal with these problems? Marshall offered a number of specific suggestions. But his main recommendation was

FIGURE 6.1.   Trends in the US-Soviet Strategic-Nuclear Balance 1966–1976.

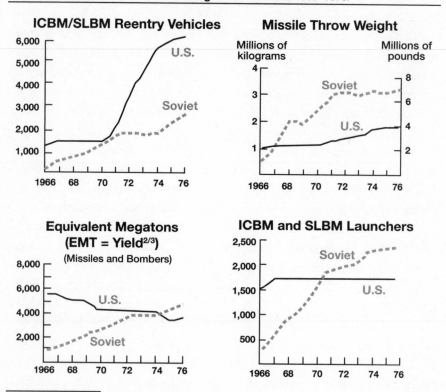

SOURCE: CIA, National Intelligence Estimate 11-3/8-76, "Soviet Forces for Intercontinental Conflict Through the Mid-1980s," December 1976, in Donald P. Steury, *Intentions and Capabilities: Estimates on Soviet Strategic Forces, 1950–1983* (Washington, DC:
Center for the Study of Intelligence, CIA, 1996), p. 357.

the need for thoughtful strategy that would find ways to impose burdensome
costs and difficult choices on the Soviets, including rendering some of their
investments in strategic forces obsolescent. "As in a chess game," Marshall
wrote to Rumsfeld, "one has to think two and three moves ahead."[28] But he
stopped short of telling Rumsfeld what sequence of moves to choose.

D espite a late surge in the polls, President Ford lost his bid for election to
former Georgia governor Jimmy Carter in the 1976 presidential election.
Ford's margin of defeat was so narrow—2 percentage points in the popular vote—that Rumsfeld later ruminated "that almost anything might have
changed the outcome."[29] On Carter's side, his simple campaign promise,

"I'll never lie to you," appealed to a nation that had yet to recover from the traumatic experience of Watergate and Vietnam.[30]

Carter appointed Harold Brown to succeed Rumsfeld as defense secretary. Brown came to office with imposing academic credentials and a wealth of national security experience. He had earned a PhD in physics from Columbia University at the age of twenty-one, joined the Lawrence Radiation Laboratory at Livermore in California in 1952, becoming its director in 1960, and was president of the California Institute of Technology (Caltech) from 1969 to 1977. His defense experience included serving as McNamara's director of defense research and engineering from 1961 to 1965, and as secretary of the Air Force from October 1965 to February 1969. Brown was also the first scientist to become secretary of defense.

Unlike either Schlesinger or Rumsfeld, who often preferred to discuss issues face-to-face, Brown was a reader. He preferred to address strategic issues by reading extended papers, annotating those he found useful with handwritten observations, comments, and guidance. One of those was Marshall and Roche's 1976 paper "Strategy for Competing with the Soviets in the Military Sector of the Continuing Political-Military Competition," which they had originally written for Rumsfeld. Like Rumsfeld, Brown found himself very much in agreement with the paper's recommendation that rather than simply attempting to parry Soviet threats, as the military services were prone to do—especially when arguing for larger budgets—far greater effort should be made to develop ways to exploit Soviet weaknesses. This approach would force the USSR to react to what the United States was doing in the competition, rather than the United States relinquishing the initiative to its opponent.[31]

Many years later Marshall shared this paper with the business strategist Richard Rumelt. At the time Rumelt was a UCLA professor and one of the most influential gurus on management strategy in the private sector.[32] Rumelt understood the fundamental power of leveraging a firm's comparative advantages to impose out-of-proportion costs on its rivals, and saw in Marshall's paper the same approach.[33] "Marshall and Roche's idea," he later wrote, "was a break with the budget-driven balance-of-forces logic of 1976. It was simple. The United States should actually compete with the Soviet Union, using its strengths to good effect and exploiting Soviet weaknesses. There were no complex charts or graphs, no abstruse formulas, no acronym-jammed buzz speak: just an idea and some pointers on how it might be used—the terrible simplicity of the discovery of hidden power in a situation."[34]

If anything, Marshall's influence on both the defense secretary and US strategy was greater under Harold Brown during his tenure from 1977 to 1981 than it had been under Rumsfeld. These years were also among ONA's most prolific in terms of completing net assessments. Marshall forwarded eleven assessments to Brown during these four years as compared with eight reports to Brown's next three successors, Caspar Weinberger, Frank Carlucci, and Dick Cheney from 1982 to 1991, and only four to defense secretaries Les Aspen, William Perry, and William Cohen from 1992 to 2001.

Harold Brown had no hesitation about retaining Marshall and his net assessment program when he took over as defense secretary. However, he had over thirty people in OSD reporting directly to him, which he felt was too many. So he decided to create a new undersecretary of defense position for policy [USD(P)] and put Marshall's office under it.[35] This had little effect on ONA. Brown agreed that Marshall's assessments would still be written for him, go directly to him, and not be coordinated with others in the Pentagon.

With exception of Schlesinger, Harold Brown may well have been the defense secretary who most deeply understood and appreciated the Office of Net Assessment. As he recalled some two decades later, the assessments and analyses he received from Marshall were fundamentally different from those generated by other Pentagon staff elements, primarily because they started from a different premise: that the United States was in a long-term competition with the Soviet Union in which success over time depended on identifying areas of comparative US advantage and using them to exploit areas of comparative Soviet weakness or disadvantage. The kinds of questions embodied by ONA's assessments were: What are we good at compared to the Soviets? What are we trying to do? How can we use what we are good at to gain advantage despite the countervailing actions of the other side?[36] Brown clearly recognized what Marshall had long realized: that the Pentagon's many bureaucracies and power centers were too consumed by the internal competition with one another over budget shares and their own agendas to focus dispassionately on these larger strategic questions that formed the core of ONA's assessments. In Brown's eyes Marshall and his office provided the kind of longer-term strategic focus he needed.

A good example of this can be seen in the strategic rationale Marshall had provided in 1976 for fielding the B-1 bomber. Marshall argued that the Soviet General Staff had been obsessed with the USSR's air defense ever

FIGURE 6.2. United States versus Soviet Bomber Defenses.

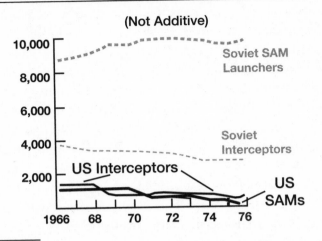

SOURCE: NIE 11-3/8-76 in Steury, *Intentions and Capabilities: Estimates on Soviet Strategic Forces, 1950–1983* (Washington, DC: Center for the Study of Intelligence, CIA, 1996), p. 357.

since its air force had lost some four thousand planes during the opening week of Operation Barbarossa—Germany's invasion of the USSR in June 1941.[37] Consequently, in the late 1940s the USSR's National Air Defense Troops (PVO Strany) were established as a separate military service and began developing the world's most extensive air defense network. The US U-2 reconnaissance over flights of Soviet territory in the late 1950s only served to reinforce the Soviet military's sense of vulnerability and determination to accord high priority to territorial air defenses. From 1945 to the early 1960s the Soviets spent a great deal more on air defenses than on their nuclear forces.[38] Therefore, Marshall concluded, there was good reason to expect that fielding the nuclear-armed B-1 designed to penetrate Soviet airspace would reinforce the USSR's propensity to continue investing heavily in territorial air defenses along borders that stretched across eleven time zones.

The United States, by contrast, had no such tendency. To be sure, in the 1950s the Air Force and the Army had fielded both interceptor squadrons and surface-to-air missile (SAM) batteries, respectively, to defend North America against a Soviet bomber force that was expected to number in the hundreds. But by the late 1960s it was evident the USSR's bomber force would remain relatively small, whereas the Soviets were rapidly expanding their ICBM force. Because neither Air Force interceptors nor Army Nike-Hercules SAMs could defend against Soviet ICBMs, the United States began reducing its investment in its air defenses.[39] Marshall's support for the B-1 was rooted in his belief that fielding the plane would, at a relatively modest cost, enable the United States to continue posing a penetrating nuclear bomber threat to the USSR. Doing so would encourage the Soviets to continue investing far more in territorial air defenses than it would cost to field and maintain a fleet of B-1s. Moreover, the United States could avoid similar costs by abandoning the costly air defense "business," thereby giving the United States "the most leverage" over Soviet defense expenditures.[40]

Marshall's advice fell on deaf ears. In July 1977 the Carter administration stunned the defense establishment by canceling the B-1 in favor of arming B-52s with air-launched cruise missiles (ALCMs). The president argued that his decision constituted a cheaper option and would give the United States "just as good a capability of penetrating Soviet air defenses" as the B-1.[41] Nonetheless, ONA's B-1 memorandum epitomized the kind of "competitive strategies" thinking that impressed Harold Brown. It would later resurface during the administration of President Ronald Reagan.

Marshall's influence was also significantly enhanced by President Carter's restructuring of the National Security Council's staff and its organization. Carter was determined to rectify what he considered the excessive power over foreign affairs that Henry Kissinger had acquired during his years as both national security adviser and secretary of state. The new president's concern was that Kissinger's accumulation of power had shielded Nixon and (particularly) Ford from competing viewpoints within the foreign policy establishment. Carter intended to be the final arbiter of the nation's foreign policy. He set out to maintain access to a broad spectrum of views and information by more fully engaging his NSC cabinet officers in the formulation of national security policy.

The Polish-American political scientist Zbigniew Brzezinski had been Carter's principal foreign policy adviser during his campaign for the presidency. Brzezinski was also an outspoken critic of what he viewed as Nixon and Kissinger's overreliance on détente to slow or constrain the arms race between the United States and the USSR, particularly in nuclear forces. Carter selected Brzezinski as his national security adviser because he wanted an assertive intellectual at his side, one who would provide him with day-to-day advice. The president envisaged the NSC's main functions to be policy coordination and research. Upon taking office he reduced its staff by 50 percent and cut the number of standing NSC committees from eight to two: the Policy Review and Special Coordinating Committees.[42] Brzezinski always chaired the Special Coordinating Committee, but the Policy Review Committee was generally chaired by the department most directly concerned with the issue at hand. By allowing Brzezinski to chair only one of these two committees, Carter believed that his national security adviser and the NSC staff would be precluded from dominating the policy-making process.

Carter also decided to undertake a major reassessment of US security needs. In mid-February 1977, shortly after taking office, he signed Presidential Review Memorandum/NSC-10 (PRM/NSC-10), "Comprehensive Net Assessment and Military Force Posture Review," which directed two studies to be done concurrently. The Policy Review Committee, chaired by Harold Brown, was instructed to "define a wide range of alternative military strategies and construct alternative military force postures" to support each of the alternatives. The Special Coordination Committee under Brzezinski was to conduct "a dynamic net assessment" that reviewed and compared "overall trends in the political, diplomatic, economic, technological, and military capabilities of the United States, its allies, and potential adversaries."[43] Initial results from both efforts were to be completed by early July 1977, although work on PRM/NSC-10 continued into 1978.

Marshall's office was soon drawn into both PRM/NSC-10 reviews. He and Roche were designated the Pentagon's staff leads for Brzezinski's net assessment. This effort was led by Samuel Huntington, a Harvard political scientist Brzezinski had brought in to oversee his portion of the review. Huntington was known for his seminal analysis of US civil-military relations in his 1957 *The Soldier and the State*. Later, in 1993, he presciently predicted in *Foreign Affairs* that the central aspect of global politics would become a civilizational clash between the West and Confucian-Islamic states,[44] a theme he expanded in his 1996 *The Clash of Civilizations and the Remaking of the World Order*. These publications were the bookends of a long and distinguished career by a scholar considered by many to be the preeminent political scientist of his day.

Huntington was assisted in his efforts by Richard Betts and Catherine Kelleher, both also political scientists, and Brzezinski's military assistant, Army colonel William Odom, who had come to him from West Point's Department of Social Sciences. To give a sense of the scale of this assessment, Brzezinski's portion of the enterprise was based on the reports of eleven separate panels as well as special analyses. Drawing on these various reports Huntington, Odom, Betts, and Kelleher generated an overview of some three hundred pages.[45]

Marshall and Roche worked with Huntington and Odom on the Comprehensive Net Assessment portion of PRM/NSC-10. Fortunately, by early 1977 ONA had completed full-blown assessments of the US-Soviet strategic nuclear and antisubmarine warfare (ASW) balances. Brown reviewed and commented on the strategic nuclear assessment at the end of March 1977, liked it, and suggested an abbreviated version be sent to Brzezinski. Brown followed this up by forwarding versions of ONA's ASW, maritime, and NATO–Warsaw Pact balances to Brzezinski shortly thereafter.[46] These balances, along with conversations Marshall and Roche had with the NSC staff, proved helpful to Brzezinski's NSC team. Odom found that listening to Marshall yielded strategic "gems," while Roche provided Huntington with new ways of thinking about power projection.[47]

The PRM/NSC-10 force posture review was done by OSD. This review was led by Lynn Davis, deputy assistant secretary of defense for policy plans, and the NSC's Victor Utgoff. Its aim was to elicit from Carter policy guidance on national military strategy.[48] After being completed in June 1977, Brown's forwarding memorandum stated that the posture review had been useful in focusing attention on the value of developing a strategy to guide the evolution of US military forces over the next decade. But he did not think that any of the study's various alternative military strategies could provide "a sufficient basis for specific decisions on US military force structures or force planning."[49]

As an outside observer Marshall had similar qualms about the force posture exercise, particularly concerning US objectives. He had long argued that US national objectives had never been clearly or precisely articulated, and one of the limitations highlighted by the study was that it was not based on "overall US national objectives because no agreed set of national objectives exists."[50] Were Marshall to have put his concerns in colloquial terms, he might have said, "If you don't know where you want to go, any path will take you there."

After reviewing both the force posture and comprehensive net assessment studies, Carter agreed with Brown's reservations about the force posture recommendations. In Presidential Directive/NSC-18, "US National Strategy," the president concluded that US-Soviet relations would be characterized by both competition and cooperation for the foreseeable future. The national strategy of the United States, he directed, would be to exploit relative US advantages in economic strength, technological superiority, and popular political support. On the military side, US nuclear forces would be needed to deter attacks on the "United States, upon our forces, our allies, and others whose security Washington deemed important to the United States and, if deterrence failed, to inflict [an] appropriate retaliatory response on the Soviet Union."[51]

In light of these judgments, Carter ordered his secretary of defense to undertake a nuclear targeting study. Walter Slocombe, the deputy assistant secretary of defense for international affairs, and Marshall were directed to oversee this effort. Leon Sloss, the assistant director of the US Arms Control and Disarmament Agency, was tasked with leading the effort. Once the targeting study was done, Marshall and Slocombe held a series of meetings with Harold Brown and air force general David Jones, the chairman of the Joint Chiefs of Staff, to help refine its conclusions. Their findings were forwarded to the White House, where they were reviewed and edited by Brzezinski and Odom.

The targeting study led to Presidential Decision/NSC-59, "Nuclear Weapons Employment Policy," which Carter signed on July 25, 1980. PD/NSC-59 retained the Single Integrated Operational Plan (SIOP) as a set of preplanned options for nuclear strikes against the Soviet Union, its allies, and its forces.[52] However, PD/NSC-59 also called for creating the capability to design nuclear employment plans on short notice that would integrate "strategic force employment with theater nuclear force employment and general purpose force employment." Their stated aim was to achieve "theater campaign objectives and other national objectives" when SIOP options were not judged suitable.[53] In the early 1970s Schlesinger had sought to develop options for limited nuclear strikes against the Soviet Union with an eye toward being able to stop nuclear use short of an all-out nuclear exchange, thereby limiting the damage to the United States. But as Odom later emphasized, even nuclear strikes against the USSR involving a small number of weapons seemed likely to trigger a massive nuclear response.

PD/NSC-59's more fundamental change in targeting was aimed at enhancing deterrence. During Sloss's targeting study, the Defense Intelligence Agency discovered that the USSR had constructed extensive facilities intended to protect its leadership in the event of a nuclear exchange. Marshall, among others, pushed the White House to exploit this knowledge.

PD/NSC-59 did so, directing that deterrence could be strengthened by making it clear to Soviet leaders that their efforts to survive a nuclear attack by building facilities to protect themselves could not succeed.[54] Carter's revised targeting policy not only put the economic and social structures of the Soviet state and its external empire at risk, it explicitly targeted the USSR's leaders. Secretary Brown directed and personally cleared certain articles and discussions of PD/NSC-59 to drive this point home to the Kremlin.[55]

Another presidential directive, PD/NSC-18, explicitly called for the US to maintain a posture of "essential equivalence" with the USSR, adding that the United States would not allow its nuclear forces to be inferior to those of the Soviet Union.[56] However, Carter's insistence on essential equivalence raised the perennial question of what analytic measures should be used to determine whether US nuclear forces had met this requirement, either at present or in the foreseeable future.

Marshall had addressed this issue before. In his August 1976 memo to Rumsfeld he had argued against relying on existing static and dynamic measures because they did not adequately capture the evolving relationship between the two sides' nuclear forces. Beyond indicating general trends, static measures such as the numbers of US and Soviet deployed warheads, ICBMs, SLBMs and heavy bombers, he thought, were at best "extraordinarily crude."[57] The same was true of more sophisticated static metrics, such as total ballistic missile throw-weight, equivalent megatonnage and countermilitary potential.* As for calculations of the numbers of US and Soviet warheads likely to survive the initial exchange, or of US and Soviet fatalities, Marshall felt that these metrics ignored too many complexities and uncertainties. Thanks to his collaboration with Joseph Loftus at RAND, Marshall also knew that US intelligence had very limited insight into Soviet assessments of the strategic nuclear competition. If the overriding US objective was to deter a Soviet nuclear attack, he argued, the United States needed to know what metrics and calculations the *Soviets* were employing to assess the risks of nuclear war, for the simple reason that they were the objects of US deterrence strategy. Marshall noted that US and Soviet

---

*Countermilitary potential (CMP) is calculated by taking a weapon's yield raised to the two-thirds power and dividing it by its circular error probable squared: $CMP=yield^{2/3}/CEP^2$. CEP is a measure of accuracy. It is the radius of a circle within which 50 percent of the warheads are expected to fall statistically.

decision makers did not appear to be using the same metrics. Why else would the Soviets continue building up their ICBM forces despite US restraint when both sides had achieved a secure second-strike capability?

These concerns became the focus of one of the panels of a 1978 Defense Science Board (DSB) "summer study" held at the Naval War College in Newport, Rhode Island. Gene Fubini, Brown's mentor, chaired the study. Fubini was a physicist and electronics engineer who had used his insights and understanding of microwave technology to help the Army and Navy jam enemy radars during World War II. Later, starting in 1961, he had been the principal manager of the Pentagon's $7 billion research and development budget. And from 1963 to 1965 he served as an assistant secretary of defense.

Fubini was asked to make recommendations on two issues: improving NATO effectiveness through collaboration on armaments; and the state of the US-Soviet strategic nuclear balance. He organized the participants into four panels, one assigned to examine NATO, and the other three the strategic nuclear balance. The three nuclear panels examined requirements for nuclear systems, the nuclear-relevant technologies, and perceptions and measures of the strategic nuclear balance.

Marshall chaired the last of these panels. His group explored US perceptions and analytic measures of the strategic nuclear competition; allied perceptions of the competition; Soviet perceptions of deterrence; and the operational performance of nuclear forces in the event that deterrence failed. Participants and contributors to Marshall's panel included Walter Slocombe and Leon Sloss, John Battilega, Bruce Bennett and Fritz Ermarth from RAND, Paul Wolfowitz and Thomas Brown from PA&E, Allan Rehm and Sayre Stevens from the CIA, Henry Rowen (Stanford), John Steinbruner (Yale), Major General Jasper Welch (Air Force Studies and Analysis), and Paul Nitze. Besides Marshall and Roche, ONA was represented by Air Force lieutenant colonel Frederick Giessler and Peter Sharfman, who had written ONA's 1977 assessment of the US-Soviet strategic nuclear balance.*

Marshall's summer study panel found that US analyses of the nuclear balance focused on comparing US and Soviet intercontinental nuclear forces in isolation from theater nuclear and conventional forces located in overseas theaters such as Central Europe. By contrast, Soviet writings had made it

---

*Like most of ONA's Cold War assessments, the 1977 strategic balance remains classified.

increasingly evident that the Soviet General Staff's estimates of the military balance, or "correlation of forces," were organized on geographic theaters of military action (*teatry voennykh deistvii*, or TVDs) and strategic directions emanating from Moscow. Thus Soviet assessments of the military balance between the two superpowers included forces that US assessments of the strategic nuclear balance did not. This was but one of many differences between the two sides' assessments. As Ermarth concluded, "Soviet thinking about strategy and nuclear war differs in significant ways from our own."[58] This confirmed what Marshall had long believed: Soviet methods for calculating the military balance did not mirror those of their US rival. Yet, if the principal goal of US strategy was to deter Soviet acts of aggression or coercion, it was the Soviet view of the balance that mattered most. Also, as Marshall had long maintained, US objectives remained vague. Even more troubling, both static and dynamic measures of the nuclear arms race ignored important factors bearing on the balance such as command, control, communications, and intelligence (C3I) vulnerabilities, active and passive defenses, the ability to sustain a fully generated nuclear posture during a protracted crisis, and the survivability of national leaders once the nuclear threshold had been crossed. How, he argued, could one accurately assess the nuclear balance without taking these factors into consideration?

Marshall eventually embraced Thomas Brown's suggestion that a war-gaming approach might enable qualitative and decisional factors to be integrated with quantitative metrics. Brown was the deputy assistant secretary of defense for strategic programs in PA&E. Like Marshall, he had participated in RAND's Strategy and Force Evaluation (SAFE) games in the 1960s, which were essentially force-posture planning exercises played out over a period of ten years. Based on this experience, Brown felt strongly that such exercises, properly crafted, could incorporate key planning factors such as a wide range of nuclear crisis scenarios, various warning times, C3I vulnerabilities, poststrike intelligence, and reconstitution capabilities, all of which traditional analyses of the nuclear balance largely neglected. Thoughtful war gaming, Brown believed, could make a valuable contribution toward better assessments of the US-Soviet competition in nuclear forces.

Marshall and Brown were by no means the only ones in the Pentagon who were dissatisfied with existing measures and methods for assessing the strategic nuclear balance. Major General Jasper Welch, then head of Air Force Studies and Analysis, was another who found existing metrics of the

Andrew Walter Marshall and his younger brother Frederick John ("Jack") Marshall, Detroit. SOURCE: ANDREW MARSHALL.

The mushroom cloud from the first successful test of an experimental thermo-nuclear device. Designated Ivy-Mike, the detonation took place at 07:15 A.M. lo-cal time on November 1, 1952, at the Enewetak Atoll in the Pacific. The explosion had an estimated yield equivalent to over 10 million tons of TNT and the mush-room cloud rose to an altitude of 57,000 feet in less than 90 seconds. Ivy-Mike ushered in the thermonuclear age in which both the United States and the Soviet Union were eventually able deploy thousands of thermonuclear weapons. PHOTO COURTESY OF NATIONAL NUCLEAR SECURITY ADMINISTRATION/NEVADA FIELD OFFICE.

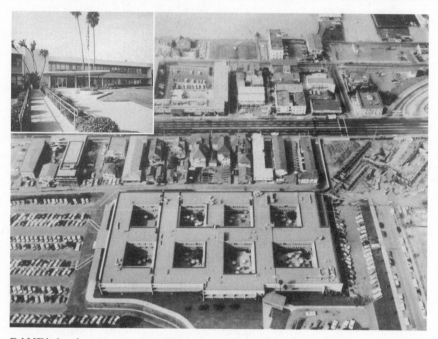

RAND's headquarters at 1700 Main Street, Santa Monica, California. The building was designed by H. Roy Kelly and completed in 1953. The aerial image looks west towards the Santa Monica beach and the Pacific Ocean. The main entrance is shown in the insert (upper left). John Williams, head of the mathematics department, suggested a layout that would encourage chance interactions among RAND's researchers. PHOTOS COURTESY OF THE SANTA MONICA PUBLIC LIBRARY IMAGE ARCHIVES.

Left to right: Mary Beth Weicking, Mary and Andrew Marshall, and Herman Kahn. Marshall and Mary Speer were married in September 1953, just before Marshall returned to the University of Chicago to decide whether to pursue a Ph.D. in statistics. Weickling was the maid of honor and Kahn the best man. SOURCE: ANDREW MARSHALL.

In 1979, as part of the Strategic Air Command's readiness exercise Global Shield 79, two Minuteman III ICBMs were launched twelve seconds apart from Vandenberg Air Force Base in California toward targets in the Marshall Island's Kwajalein Atoll. PHOTO COURTESY OF THE NATIONAL ARCHIVES, STILL PHOTO BRANCH, PHOTO IDENTIFIER 6362313.

Six unarmed Minuteman III Mark 12 reentry vehicles are shown approaching targets near Kwajalein Atoll in the Western Pacific Ocean from the two Minuteman III ICBMs launched as part of Global Shield 79. Despite having invested over $150 billion in ballistic missile defense since President Reagan announced his Strategic Defense Initiative in 1983, US capabilities to defend against more than a handful of rudimentary ballistic missiles remain limited at best. Russian military officials claim that their road-mobile RS-24 Yars heavy ICBM can penetrate even the most sophisticated missile defenses anywhere in the world. PHOTO COURTESY OF THE NATIONAL ARCHIVES, STILL PICTURE BRANCH, PHOTO IDENTIFIER 342-B-08-16-3-K69772.

Evening discussion at the Wohlstetters' house, 1958. Left to right: Daniel Ellsworth, Henry Rowen, Andrew Marshall, Albert Wohlstetter (with back to the camera) and Sidney Winter. PHOTO COURTESY OF LEONARD McCOMBE/TIME LIFE PICTURES/GETTY IMAGES.

This photo appeared in Jay Winik's article "Secret Weapon" in the April 1999 issue of *The Washingtonian*. The article discussed how members of St. Andrew's Prep frustrated defense secretary William Cohen's decision to move ONA from the Pentagon to the National Defense University as part of his Defense Reform Initiative. As Winik summed up the inadvisability of doing so, "Without Andy Marshall, the Pentagon would be depriving itself of its principal source of wisdom and giving license to people who would play all sorts of con games with the Secretary." PHOTO COURTESY OF JAMES KEGLEY.

1999 ONA summer study participants in front of the original Naval War College building in Newport, Rhode Island. Standing (back row): Eliot Cohen, Lionel Tiger, Jim Roche, John Bonsell, Andrew Krepinevich, Jim Callard, Steve Rosen, Chip Pickett, Andrew May, Jeff McKitrick, Mike Vickers, David Spain. Front row: Barry Watts, Sam Tangredi, Andy Marshall, Dakota Wood. PHOTO: BARRY WATTS.

Andy Marshall and Ann Smith Marshall at a November 2006 reception following their marriage. PHOTO: BARRY WATTS.

Donald Rumsfeld honoring Marshall with the DoD Distinguished Public Service Award for
his leadership on defense transformation. December 14, 2006. Dmitri Ponomareff reported that
Marshall was the only recipient at this ceremony who received a standing ovation from those
present. PHOTO: OFFICE OF THE SECRETARY OF DEFENSE.

Dinner during a conference on the past, present and future of net assessment, March 28, 2008. Marshall largely selected the attendees for this conference. The price of admission was to give a paper during the conference. Left to right: Jim Roche, Fred Giessler, Mie Augier, Michael Pillsbury, Andrew May, Charlie Pease, Gerry Dunne, John Battilega, Andy Marshall, Mark Herman, Lionel Tiger, Dmitri Ponomareff, Jaymie Duran, Lance Lord (behind Durnan), Karl Hasslinger, Donna Hasslinger, Phillip Karber, Jan van Tol, Charlie Wolf (in front of van Tol), Barry Watts, Enders Wimbush (behind Watts), Steve Rosen, Aaron Friedberg, David Epstein, James Schlesinger, Diego Ruiz Palmer, Wick Murray, Jeff McKitrick, Chip Pickett. PHOTO: BARRY WATTS.

President George W. Bush honored Marshall with the Presidential Citizens Medal on December 10, 2008. WHITE HOUSE PHOTO BY CHRIS GREENBER.

nuclear balance inadequate. In fact he became so distraught over the stale-ness of the intellectual approach his own organization was taking to strate-gic force adequacy that he disbanded the whole enterprise.[59]

Following the 1978 DSB summer study, Marshall began taking steps to implement his panel's findings. His main thrust centered on building a consensus within the Pentagon in favor of developing more advanced war-gaming methods aimed at improving assessments of the US-Soviet nuclear competition. Marshall, along with Brown, found support among key members of the military, including Generals Richard Lawson (Joint Staff), Jasper Welch, Edward "Shy" Meyer (Army deputy chief of staff/ Operations and Plans), and Admiral William Crowe (deputy chief of naval operations/Plans, Policy and Operations). The idea that emerged was to let two or three small contracts to analytic organizations such as RAND to refine thinking as to how such a gaming system might be structured, organized, and managed. To succeed the enterprise would require the de-fense secretary's support. In an April 1979 memo Marshall informed Harold Brown that the effort would be a multiyear undertaking and would need some funding from the defense secretary's special study fund.[60] Brown promptly agreed, commenting that "this does need to be pushed."[61]

RAND and Science Applications International Corporation (SAIC, formerly SAI) emerged as the leading contenders to develop the new an-alytic tool. Marshall found RAND's conceptual approach far more am-bitious than SAIC's in terms of incorporating state-of-the-art artificial intelligence to produce automated software agents against which human players could, if they desired, play rather than competing against human players.[62] Marshall believed that SAIC's approach would be more respon-sive to the project's central aim of improving US assessments of the strate-gic nuclear competition.[63] But most of the others involved in the selection process favored RAND. Marshall, against his better judgment, acquiesced. It was a decision he would come to regret.

The result was the RAND Strategy Assessment System (RSAS). The RSAS was a "system for analytic war gaming that could be used as a closed model or with one or more human teams playing in a partially or completely automated environment."[64] As Marshall explained to Harold Brown,

As I have mentioned to you in the strategic balance assessments that we have prepared in the past, our capabilities for analyzing and understanding the strategic balance are limited by the narrowness of the kinds of analyses that can now be conducted. For one thing the focus tends to be on large exchanges. Very little that happened before them (for example, crises, LNOs [limited nuclear options], escalation from regional theater war) and little about what may happen after them (recovery and reconstitution of command and control, the use of residual strategic forces) is examined. In addition, while we say that our primary objective is deterrence, the analyses that we carry out are not done in a way that can reflect the Soviet perspective. It's likely that the Soviets do not single out the strategic forces for separate treatment in the way that we have traditionally done so. Moreover, their definition of strategic forces undoubtedly includes a number of their medium range as well as their intercontinental forces.[65]

In the end, however, the RSAS drifted away from Marshall's original goal of improving US analyses of the strategic nuclear balance. Early in the system's development RAND began concentrating on *conventional* combat. By 1985 the RSAS included detailed modules for five combat theaters: Northern Europe or the USSR's Northwestern TVD, Central Europe (Western TVD), Southeastern Europe (Southwestern TVD), Southwest Asia (Southeastern TVD), and Northeast Asia (Far Eastern TVD).[66] The focus of the RSAS' theater modules in playing regional conflicts gradually overshadowed and lost sight of the project's original purpose. Besides the Office of Net Assessment, RSAS users eventually included two Joint Staff directorates responsible for strategy and force planning, the National Defense University, PA&E, the Air University, the Naval War College, CIA, DIA, the Naval Postgraduate School, the Army's Concepts Analysis Agency, and the US European and Pacific Commands. Because most of these organizations also began contributing funding and were mainly interested in conventional warfare, the RSAS development was drawn increasingly toward focusing on nonnuclear regional conflicts rather than nuclear war.

Marshall tried to get the program back on track in late 1985. In a December letter to the head of the RSAS program at RAND, Paul Davis, he reaffirmed that its central objective to develop an analytic tool that could address the problems of global nuclear warfare. "There are plenty of models of particular theaters," he added, "but what we have lacked is both a war game, or other analytic tool, that will allow us to look effectively at global warfare. This to me implies the highest priority in the [RSAS] development is that of the strategic nuclear [warfare] and enough of the theater modeling to allow us to overcome the existing imperfections in our analysis."[67] But Marshall's guidance had little effect in the long run. The momentum toward concentrating on the theater modules was too great for even the director of net assessment to reverse.

Not surprisingly, the limitations of the traditional static and dynamic measures of the US-Soviet strategic nuclear balance had their parallels in Marshall's efforts to assess the balance between NATO and Warsaw Pact forces in Europe. Once Project 186 was converted to an ONA research project under BDM's Phil Karber, the first order of business was to develop a database on the opposing forces in which the same counting rules were applied to both sides. Karber's team at BDM quickly learned that this seemingly straightforward task was anything but. Eventually, though, Project 186 produced "probably the most authoritative NATO–Warsaw Pact database in the West."[68] Its development owed much to Marshall's patience and willingness to sustain Karber's team through the end of the Cold War.

By 1978 Project 186 had accumulated enough comparable data on NATO and Warsaw Pact forces to generate quantitative, or "bean count," comparisons of the two sides' manpower and major weapon systems in central Europe, and these data were displayed in ONA's first detailed assessment of NATO–Warsaw Pact balance. The NATO forces included in this balance were those stationed in West Germany, the Netherlands, and Belgium, Denmark, and Luxembourg as well as the First French Army. The Warsaw Pact Center Region forces were those Soviet and East European forces stationed in East Germany, Poland, and Czechoslovakia.

The theater-level force data displayed in the March 1978 assessment showed that Warsaw Pact forces in central Europe outnumbered NATO's in most categories. The Warsaw Pact's two-to-one advantage in main battle tanks and antitank weapons was a major concern to the NATO alliance. But, as with strategic nuclear forces, there were problems with comparing the raw numbers of weapons in various categories (main battle tanks, artillery, mortars, etc.). First, as Marshall was well aware, static comparisons at a single point in time gave no sense of the trends. Second, these "raw" comparisons ignored the relative quality of individual weapons. They also ignored personnel training and readiness, logistics, tactics, doctrine, command and control, and other variables known to affect combat outcomes.

FIGURE 6.3. NATO/Warsaw Pact Central Region Ground Forces and Ratios, 1978.

	NATO		WARSAW PACT		CENTRAL RATIOS
	TOTAL	CENTRAL	CENTRAL	TOTAL	
Army Manpower	1,328,300	736,300	1,014,000	1,887,000	1 to 1.4
Medium/Heavy Tanks	14,100	8,300	16,400	35,700	1 to 2.0
Light Tanks/Armored Recce	2,200	2,100	800	2,500	2.6 to 1
Anti-Tank Weapons	7,100	2,900	5,800	15,500	1 to 2.0
Air Defense Weapons	7,900	4,400	5,300	14,700	1 to 1.2
Grnd-Grnd Missile Launchers	310	280	390	1,520	1 to 1.4
Tactical Aircraft	5,500	2,200	2,900	6,500	1 to 1.3

SOURCE: OSD/NA, "The Military Balance in Europe: A Net Assessment," March 1978, p. 46. Army Lieutenant Colonel Peter R. Bankson wrote this assessment.

In attempting to address the issue of qualitative differences between the two sides' weapon systems, in 1974 the Army's Concepts Analysis Agency (CAA) published the first version of a qualitative weighting system for ground forces known as Weighted Effectiveness Indices/Weighted Unit Values (WEI/WUV, pronounced "wee-wuv"). It contained subjectively developed WEI scores for NATO and Warsaw Pact weapons in nine categories: small arms, armored personnel carriers, tanks, armored reconnaissance vehicles, antitank weapons, cannons and rockets, mortars, armed helicopters, and air defense artillery.[69] While the original aim of WEI/WUV was to produce "scores suitable for use in current war gaming,"[70] WEIs could also be used to weight the equipment holdings of opposing military forces, as shown in the notional WUV calculations for a US division. Once WEI values had been multiplied by the inventories in each category and the results in each category were multiplied by category weights, the results could be added up to give WUV totals for entire units such as divisions (see Figure 6–4), or for higher-level force aggregations up to and including all NATO and Warsaw Pact forces in the Central Region.

To address the issue of trends, ONA's 1978 European balance also included theater-wide WUV aggregations for 1965, 1970, 1975, and 1977 in the Central Region. These theater WUV totals showed the Warsaw Pact's overall force-ratio advantage increasing since the mid-1960s. Particularly disconcerting was the growth in Warsaw Pact firepower compared to NATO's. Here the NATO WUV for artillery, mortars and multiple rocket launchers had grown 35 percent from 1965 to 1977 whereas the Warsaw Pact firepower WUV had gone up over 80 percent.[71]

FIGURE 6.4. WUV Calculation for a Notional US Combat Division.

Weapon Type		Quantity	WEI	Quantity x WEI	Category Weight	WUV
Tanks	M60A3	150	1.11	166.5		
	M1	150	1.31	196.5		
	Tank WUV Total			363.0	94	34,122
Attack Helicopters	AH-1S	21	1.00	21.0		
	AH-64	18	1.77	31.9		
	Attack Helicopter WUV Total			53.0	109	5,777
Air Defense	Vulcan	24	1	24.0	56	1,344
IFV	Bradley	228	1	228.0	71	16,188
Anti-tank Missiles (launchers)	TOW	150	0.79	118.5		
	Dragon	240	0.69	165.6		
	LAW	300	0.2	60.0		
	Anti-Tank Missile WUV Total			344.1	73	25,119
Artillery & Rocket Launchers	155 mm howitzer	72	1.02	73.0		
	8-inch howitzer	12	0.98	12.0		
	MLRS	9	1.16	10.0		
	Artillery & Rocket Launcher WUV Total			96.0	99	9,504
Mortars	81 mm	45	0.97	43.7		
	107 mm	50	1	50.0		
	Mortars WUV Total			94.0	55	5,170
APCs	M113	500	1	500.0	30	15,000
Small Arms	M16 rifle	2,000	1	2000.0		
	Machine guns	295	1.77	522.2		
	Small Arms WUV Total			2522.2	4	10,088
				Total Division WUV		**122,312**

SOURCE: US Congressional Budget Office, *U.S. Ground Forces and the Conventional Balance in Europe* (Washington, DC: US Government Printing Office, June 1988), p. 15. IFV = infantry fighting vehicle; TOW = tube-launched, optically tracked, wire-guided; MLRS = multiple launch rocket system.

Not surprisingly, there soon emerged a discussion between ONA and Project 186 over the efficacy of such scoring systems as WEI/WUV. Recognizing that WEI indices were basically based on firepower scores, in 1978 Marshall initiated a research effort by The Analytic Sciences Corporation (TASC) to develop a scoring system that would better capture the value of NATO and Warsaw Pact equipment. Since WEI/WUV calculations did not include combat aircraft, the initial focus of the TASC Force

FIGURE 6.5. NATO/Warsaw Pact Central Region WUV Trends.

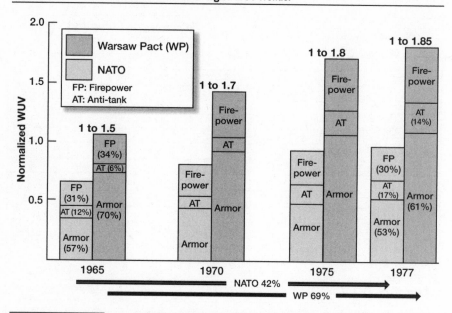

Source: OSD/NA, "The Military Balance in Europe: A Net Assessment," March 1978, p. 52.

Modernization (TASCFORM) effort was to develop scores for fighters, ground-attack aircraft, interceptors, and bombers.

On a more fundamental level, Marshall was concerned with the ability of qualitative weighting methodologies, such as WEI/WUV and TASCFORM, to provide insights into the balance of conventional forces, whether in the European or other theaters. One way to determine this was to see whether the application of WEI/WUV scores to historical battles would reflect actual outcomes. Project 186 set out to address this question by applying WEI/WUV to the Germans' May 1940 rapid and highly successful campaign through France and the Low Countries. But neither bean count comparisons nor WUV aggregations of the German and Allied forces at the theater level appeared to give any significant insight into why the campaign had been so one-sided.

Given this negative outcome, Karber's BDM team refined its efforts, examining various head-to-head comparisons, such as the balance of armor versus antiarmor systems, Allied-versus-German fire support systems, and ground-attack aircraft versus air defenses in the hope of achieving more

FIGURE 6.6. The German Campaign in the West, May–June 1940.

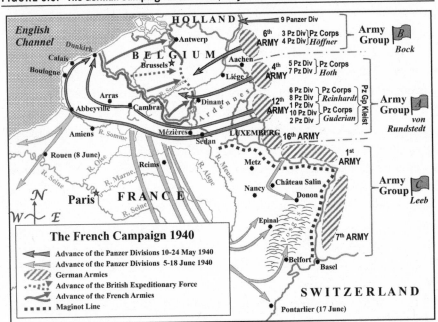

The German Campaign in the West, May-June 1940. Major General F. W. von Mellen-thin, H. Betzler (trans), L. C. F. Turner (ed.), *Panzer Battles: A Study of the Employment of Armor in the Second World War* (Norman, OK: University of Oklahoma Press, 1955).

FIGURE 6.7. Allied/German Theater "Bean Count" and WUV Comparisons, May 10, 1940.

"Bean Counts"				WUV Comparisons		
	Allies	Germans	Ratio	Ratio	Allies	Germans
Manpower	3,368,000	2,758,000	**1.22**	1.03	1,016,697	983,750	Overall Theater WUV
Divisions	140	136	1.03			
Armored Divisions	4	10	**0.40**			
Tanks	4,098	3,227	**1.27**	1.39	56,5689	40,710	Tanks
Antitank Guns	8,832	12,800	**0.69**	0.41	53,745	132,080	Antitank Guns
Artillery	13,326	7,700	**1.73**	1.57	301,944	192,760	Artillery
Armored Carriers	1,830	800	**2.29**	2.29	7.320	3,200	APCs
Mortars	11,912	14,300	**0.83**	0.79	200,120	252,000	Mortars
Rifles	1,160,000	900,000	**1.29**	1.58	397,000	252,000	Small Arms
Machineguns	112,100	147,000	**0.76**			
Aircraft	1,649	3,124	**0.53**	*BDM was unable to extend CAA's WEI/WUV methodology to these systems.*		
AAA	4,232	8,700	**0.49**			

SOURCE: Phillip A. Karber, Grant Whitley, Mark Herman, and Douglas Komer, *Assessing the Correlation of Forces: France 1940* (McLean, VA: BDM Corporation, June 18, 1979), BDM/W-79-560-TR, pp. 2–2 to 2–6.

useful results. Again, however, theater-wide bean-count and WUV comparisons provided no significant insight into why the Germans had been so spectacularly successful.

Next, the BDM analysts explored a number of operational factors—deception, surprise, tactics, air superiority, command and control (C2), and terrain—that were not captured in either the bean count or WUV aggregations, but which "played an important role at some time in the eventual outcome" of the campaign.[72] The assessment of these factors led to a recognition that each of the three attacking German army groups had been given specific missions, and each was confronted by different styles of defense. With these observations in mind, the BDM analysts shifted their focus to a lower level of analysis. They now considered the Allied-German division and WUV ratios in each of the three German army group sectors: Generaloberst Fedor von Bock's Army Group B in the northwest, Generaloberst Gerd von Rundstedt's Army Group A in the center, and Generaloberst Wilhelm Ritter von Leeb's Army Group C in the south.*

The results of the sector-by-sector comparison underscored what has long been known about this campaign. The German *Schwerpunkt* (point of main effort) was in the center, through the Ardennes Forest, terrain that the Allies didn't believe armored forces could cross. Using WEI/WUV, the BDM analysts found that nearly half of the German army's combat power was concentrated in this narrow sector under von Rundstedt's Army Group A. The calculation of WUV totals across the three army groups also found that the Germans were substantially weaker in the northwest and south than a simple aggregation of German versus Allied division ratios suggested, while they were considerably stronger than the Allies in the center. Army Group A's superiority in divisions was 3.1 to 1. When the WUV scores were factored in, Army Group A's advantage increased by roughly one third, to more than 4.2 to 1.

The BDM report conceded that WUV comparisons at the theater level provided little insight into campaign outcomes. But the report went on to suggest that the WEI/WUV methodology, if employed at lower levels of aggregation, was capable of "yielding insights into the dynamics of the campaign" as well as "indicating deficiencies and asymmetries in initial

---

*The term *Generaloberst* is translated as "colonel general," a rank equivalent to a lieutenant (three-star) general in the US military.

FIGURE 6.8. By-Sector Division and WUV Comparisons, May 10, 1940.

	Divisions			Sector WUVs		
Sector	Allies	Germans	Ratio	Ratio	Allies	Germans
Northwest (von Bock)	57	29	2-to-1	1.5-to-1	310,000	205,000
Center (von Rundstedt)	15	45	1-to-3	1-to-4.2	75,000	317,000
South (von Leeb)	44	19	2.3 to 1	1.7-to-1	238,000	136,800

SOURCE: Karber et al., *Assessing the Correlation of Forces: France 1940*, pp. 4–1, 4–6, 4–7.

deployments plus inferring possible outcomes."[73] On the one hand, this conclusion was encouraging. It suggested that the US military's investment in WEI/WUV and P-186's use of this scoring methodology could provide better estimates of conventional force balances at the appropriate level of aggregation below an entire theater. On the other hand, it left one vital question unanswered. In the case of France in 1940, the outcome of the campaign is known, a matter of history. But right to the Cold War's end a conventional war in Europe, while anticipated on both sides, never actually occurred. In the absence of knowing how such a conflict would have turned out in 1978 or later, there wasn't any way to make quantitative comparisons at the right level of analysis. If anything, these results reinforced Marshall's view that the analytic tools needed to make confident predictions of likely war outcomes did not yet exist.

Marshall continued pursuing the possibility that static scoring methodologies might yield insights useful to net assessments. In 1986 he entered into a joint effort with the CIA to fund a project to explore the differences and similarities among the more widely used static indices for conventional forces, which by then included the WEI II and III indices, Generic Weapons Effectiveness Indices, TASCFORM, and the Operational Lethality Indices in Trevor Dupuy's Quantified Judgment Model.[74] The project's objective was to apply the various scoring methodologies to selected NATO and Warsaw Pact force data from 1975 to 1985 to see what insights, if any, might emerge. The study was initiated in part because of growing congressional interest in these various scoring systems.

At the outset of the ONA-CIA project, Marshall's views about what were often termed measures of effectiveness (MOEs) suggest that he appreciated both their uses and their limitations: "[I]t is very clear from past experience in comparing forces that no MOE will solve the net assessment problem. We have found them useful in understanding long-term trends, but they clearly fail as predictors of outcomes of military operations between opposing forces because they reflect only a few dimensions. In particular, historical cases tend to show that other variables often dominate."[75] By then the WEI/WUV methodology was being widely used in theater war games by the military services and the Joint Chiefs of Staff. At least one congressional staffer had requested that ONA provide the TASCFORM methodology to help members of Congress make their own static force comparisons in the context of reviewing annual defense budget requests.

While Marshall remained skeptical of the idea that these sorts of scoring methodologies could provide valid assessments of the military balance in Europe or other theaters, he knew that the Soviets had also developed a variety of quantitative metrics that they used in operational planning to calculate correlations between opposing forces as well as rates of advance for army and front operations.[76] In the early 1980s US intelligence had gained access to some of the Soviet MOEs, enabling ONA to compare them with TACSFORM aircraft and WEI ground force scores. These comparisons revealed significant differences between how the two sides valued certain weapons. For example, Soviet combat potential scores rated US air defense interceptors substantially higher than did TASCFORM while, relative to the US scoring systems, the Soviets undervalued strike aircraft. The Soviets also scored the US M-60A2 main battle tank substantially higher than did US indices.[77] The asymmetries between American and Soviet scoring systems, therefore, provided ONA with insights into Soviet perceptions of the value of various types of equipment and capabilities, which in turn influenced ONA's assessments in the 1980s of the military balance in Central Europe. Thus while static MOEs obviously had limitations, from a net assessment perspective they were not without value.

The US-Soviet strategic nuclear balance was perhaps the preeminent Cold War assessment because, in the event that deterrence failed, the survival of the United States would be at stake. The European balance was in many respects of comparable importance because of the prospect that a successful Warsaw Pact conventional attack could escalate to a general nuclear exchange. Detailed versions of both these assessments were completed in the late 1970s. But as important as these two balances were, Marshall came to view other assessments completed during Harold Brown's tenure as defense secretary as having been even more successful. One of these was Navy commander

Gerald Dunne's assessment of US and Soviet command, control, and communications (C3), which was finished in 1978. This assessment revealed a major asymmetry, if not a gaping lacuna, between US and Soviet preparations for conflict, especially in Europe. For the Soviets, C3 loomed large. They had singled out C3 as a specialized, high-priority "area of warfare" and had developed doctrine, planning processes, tactics, and systems aimed at disrupting or destroying 50 percent of NATO's C3 at every echelon from the theater down to battalions, while investing far more heavily in protecting their own C3 than did NATO forces.[78] By contrast, the US military had a fragmented view of C3. Even more troubling, the Pentagon also lacked the concepts, frames of reference, and tools to evaluate C3 performance in combat.[79]

Marshall and Dunne saw the 1978 C3 assessment as highlighting an area of weakness that the US military needed to address. But the Pentagon's senior military leaders did not react as Marshall would have liked. In the short term the assessment provoked a surge of research into C3 (including five Defense Science Board studies), increased efforts to improve the survivability of US C3, and stimulated thinking about the importance of an "information advantage" in war.[80] In the long run, though, these various studies and research bore little fruit.

Today, over thirty years since ONA's US-Soviet C3 assessment, the US military's thinking about C3 still remains largely focused on tactical-level technical issues, giving short shrift to the overall role of information in future warfare. Marshall remains concerned that the US military still lacks the concepts, frames of reference, and tools to evaluate properly the performance of C3 and intelligence, surveillance and reconnaissance (ISR) systems in combat. These concerns have resurfaced with China's growing efforts since the mid-1990s to modernize its military forces. One could argue that Soviet forces during the Cold War were more reflective of the industrial age than of today's information age. China's ongoing modernization efforts, by contrast, are unquestionably those of a rising power in the information age. The overarching goal of the People's Liberation Army (PLA) is to build an "informationized military" with Chinese characteristics. How successful the PLA will ultimately be in this endeavor remains to be seen. But since the late 1970s Marshall persistantly highlighted the growing importance of information in future warfare.

Possibly the most consequential ONA assessments during the 1970s did not focus directly on military forces. Recall that when Marshall moved to the Pentagon, Schlesinger asked him to continue pushing the CIA to reconsider its estimate of the burden Soviet military programs was imposing on the USSR's economy. In 1974 Marshall hired an Air Force economist, Major Lee Badgett, to develop more inclusive dollar-cost estimates of Soviet military spending. By September 1975 Marshall and Badgett had reached a preliminary conclusion that rather than the Agency's burden estimate of 6 to 7 percent of Soviet GNP, Soviet military activities likely consumed 10 to 20 percent of the USSR's economic output.[81] Over the next decade, as Bob Gough, William Manthorpe, Lance Lord, and David Epstein wrote a series military investment balances for Marshall, the list of indirect costs that Soviet military programs were imposing on the USSR's economy grew. They eventually included expenditures for civil defense, industrial mobilization preparations and dual-use investments as well as the costs of maintaining the Soviet empire.

The direct and indirect costs of the USSR's military efforts constituted the numerator of the burden ratio. It addressed the question: How much are the Soviets spending on their military? The denominator problem, as it came to be known, addressed the question: How large is the Soviet economy? The denominator question was first brought to Marshall's attention in 1979 by the Soviet émigré economist Igor Birman. From 1970 to 1983, the CIA estimated the Soviet GNP to be between 50 and 60 percent of US GNP.[82] In hindsight, the Soviet economy during the 1970s and 1980s was probably never greater than 25 percent of that of the United States. As the Soviet economy was roughly half the size estimated by the CIA, and the total cost of its defense expenditures larger than the Agency's estimates of the USSR's *direct* military expenditures, this suggested that the USSR's military might be consuming as much as 30 to 40 percent of the country's economic output. Furthermore, as became obvious in the 1980s, the Soviet economy, burdened by military spending and the inherent inefficiencies of the USSR's centralized economic planning, was encountering increasingly severe structural problems.

The importance of these insights stemming from ONA's military investment balances cannot be overstated. They effectively demonstrated that Marshall and Schlesinger's instincts about the USSR's military burden had been right from the outset. Consequently, time was not, as Kissinger had feared, on the side of the Soviet Union, but very much on the side of the United States. This shift in understanding opened the door to the possibility of winning the Cold War, something that Carter's successor, Ronald Reagan, would exploit by building up US military capabilities.

While it would be going too far to argue that the US military buildup during the Reagan years caused the collapse of the Soviet Union in 1991, by the late 1980s Marshall was saying privately that the USSR's economy appeared to be on the brink of "Chapter 11" bankruptcy. His pursuit of an accurate estimate of the Soviet defense burden, enabled by both ONA's charter and Marshall's long tenure, enabled him to look beyond the immediate, pressing issues of the day, and may well represent his most important contribution to US strategy during the Cold War's final decade.

7

COLD WAR END GAME
1981–1991

*We're not in the business of saying what ought to be, we're
in the business of giving people something to think about.*
—ANDREW MARSHALL

On November 4, 1980, the American people gave former California governor Ronald Reagan a landslide victory over President Jimmy Carter.
During the election campaign, Reagan argued that Carter had allowed the
nation's defenses to erode to the point where the US military's ability to
deter the nation's enemies and fight effectively should deterrence fail was at
risk. Reagan noted that despite the United States' efforts to bring about stability in the nuclear arms race, the Soviets were modernizing their nuclear
forces at a prodigious rate.

Recent events in the Middle East also undoubtedly influenced some vot-
ers to support Reagan. Critics of the Carter administration's foreign policy
charged that the president had allowed long-standing US ally Mohammad
Reza Pahlavi, the shah of Iran, to be overthrown by radical Islamist elements under Ayatollah Ruhollah Khomeini. The result was the formation
of the Islamic Republic of Iran, whose leaders were unremittingly hostile
to the United States, which they referred to as the "Great Satan." Making
matters worse, the new regime did nothing when Iranian radicals stormed
the US embassy in Tehran and seized its staff as hostages.

When Carter dispatched American military forces in an attempt to rescue
the hostages in April 1980, the operation turned into a fiasco. Eight helicopters were deployed to a desert staging area inside Iran, but only five arrived
in operating condition. A decision was then made to abort the mission. But

one of the departing helicopters crashed into a transport aircraft carrying fuel. In the resulting explosion and fire, eight servicemen were killed. In addition to the destroyed aircraft and helicopter, five other helicopters were abandoned. The operation seemed to confirm fears that the series of cuts in the Pentagon's budget following the Vietnam War had left the United States with a "hollow" military: one that looked strong on paper but whose troops were ill-trained and poorly equipped. Following by less than four years the dramatic and successful rescue of Israeli hostages at Entebbe in Uganda, the aborted US hostage rescue mission appeared an even greater failure. A running joke at the time was that Carter should have outsourced the mission to the Israelis.

In contrast to the pessimistic views of Kissinger regarding the US-Soviet nuclear competition, or the worrisome indicators that the US military was becoming a "hollow" force, Reagan came to the presidency with a more optimistic view of the United States' position in the world. He saw the US-Soviet Cold War as a "struggle of ideas and economic systems." Because the Soviet system was politically illegitimate and economically flawed, Reagan believed it could be challenged and ultimately defeated by an open, representative democracy with a free market economy.[1] In some ways his views of the Soviet Union echoed George Kennan's in that both believed the seeds of the USSR's destruction were inherent in its system and well advanced.

In fact—as Marshall had long known—unlike free market economies, Soviet central economic planning was highly inefficient in allocating resources. The totalitarian government of the USSR suppressed the kind of individual initiative so vital to the functioning of a dynamic economy stimulated by entrepreneurs who were willing to take risks to reap the rewards of success. Over time this produced economic stagnation. Soviet leaders were forced to make increasingly tough decisions regarding the apportionment of resources. Guns or butter? Armaments or consumer goods? They chose military production, thereby imposing increasing burdens on their people and the USSR's economy.[2]

Yet even within Reagan's own administration, few were inclined to believe that the United States could win the Cold War. Marshall's growing suspicions about the economic problems lurking beneath the surface of the Soviet behemoth were neither widely shared by the US intelligence community or the military. Senior military leaders in the Pentagon tended to presume that any resource constraints on Soviet military spending were minimal to nonexistent. In the end, however, Marshall's long-term competition framework would lead the Defense Department to adopt what he called competitive strategies, which placed greater priority on imposing disproportionately large costs on the USSR's military efforts. Coupled with the increases in defense spending under Reagan, the 1980s would find Soviet leaders confronting ever-greater challenges in their attempts to hold up their end of the competition with the United States.

Reagan's belief that history was on the side of the United States rather than the Soviet Union was formalized in US strategy early in his administration. National Security Decision Directive 32 (NSDD 32), which Reagan signed in May 1982, stated that US global goals would include containing and reversing "the expansion of Soviet control and military presence throughout the world," increasing "the costs of Soviet support and use of proxy, terrorist, and subversive forces," while seeking opportunities to foster restraint in Soviet military spending, discourage Soviet adventurism, and weaken Soviet alliances.[3] NSDD 32 was followed in early 1983 by NSDD 75, "U.S. Relations with the USSR," which went even further. Drafted by Richard Pipes, who was then serving on Reagan's NSC staff,[4] NSDD 75 established three objectives for dealing with the Soviet Union: (1) containing and over time reversing Soviet expansionism by competing more effectively; (2) promoting change in the USSR "toward a more pluralist political and economic system in which the power of the privileged elite is gradually reduced"; and (3) engaging the USSR in negotiations leading to agreements that "protect and enhance U.S. interests."[5]

To achieve these objectives, and to remedy the decline in US military readiness over the previous decade, Reagan felt he needed to build up US military strength. He tapped Caspar ("Cap") Weinberger, a longtime political associate from his days as governor of California, to head the effort as his defense secretary. Weinberger's background on defense matters was limited to his service as a junior officer in World War II on General Douglas MacArthur's intelligence staff. He had, however, served in senior positions during the Nixon administration, first as chairman of the Federal Trade Commission, then as director of the Office of Management and Budget, and finally as secretary of health, education and welfare. During his time at OMB Weinberger was given the nickname "Cap the Knife" for his aggressive cost-cutting. Yet as the man chosen by Reagan to lead his defense buildup, Weinberger would become a tireless advocate for increasing the military budget.

Reagan was especially concerned with the strategic nuclear balance. With this in mind, in October 1981 he signed NSDD 12, reversing Carter's cancellation of the B-1 bomber. NSDD 12 also endorsed moving ahead with the Advanced Technology Bomber (the B-2 "stealth" bomber), increasing the accuracy and payload of US submarine-launched ballistic missiles and deploying a newer, larger and more accurate land-based ICBM.[6] These decisions were consistent with NSDD 75's emphasis on sustaining steady, long-term growth in US defense spending and capabilities—both nuclear and conventional—as "the most important way of conveying to the Soviets American resolve and political staying-power."[7]

Yet despite these efforts by the new president to strengthen the United States' military position, as late as March 1983—the same month as his "Star Wars" speech calling for the development of the capability to "intercept and destroy" Soviet ballistic missiles before they could reach American soil—Reagan privately believed that the United States remained "dangerously behind the Soviets" in military capability and was falling still further behind.[8] Meanwhile, the Soviets continued their nuclear buildup. After prolonged debate within the US national security community, especially over basing schemes, the first of fifty Peacekeeper LGM-118A ICBMs were deployed in 1986. But the Peacekeeper deployment was modest and late compared to the USSR's deployment of 308 R-36MUTTH (SS-18) ICBMs, each armed with ten independently targetable thermonuclear warheads.[9] The last of the SS-18s became operational in 1983, three years before the first Peacekeeper's were deployed.

Marshall's impression of Weinberger was that the new defense secretary had little interest in the sorts of net assessments his office had produced under Harold Brown. From Weinberger's perspective, the president's desire to catch up with the Soviets militarily did not require careful net assessments of where the United States stood militarily relative to the USSR. Weinberger seemed to view the country's defenses as having been left in such a sorry state by the previous administration that everything—from military personnel compensation to research and development funding, from training and readiness to the purchase of new equipment—merited large funding increases. Unlike Schlesinger or Brown, Weinberger lacked a background in defense matters in general and in military strategy in particular. While Marshall could be a superb source of strategic insight for a defense secretary who knew how to exploit ONA's potential, he was not adept at engaging those who did not, and consequently did little to promote ONA's work to Weinberger.

Armed with a political mandate following his election victory, Reagan was able to win Congress's support for substantial increases in funding for defense. The growth in the defense budget was so great—around 50 percent from Fiscal Year (FY) 1980 to FY 1985—that Weinberger found himself with an embarrassment of riches. Weinberger's problem was less one of apportioning scarce resources than figuring out how the Pentagon could absorb the flood of money heading its way. Thus for the new defense secretary, Marshall's net assessments had little to offer.

Observations from those who worked with Weinberger during his tenure as defense secretary from 1981 to 1987 indicate that he had very little appreciation of either net assessment or the limits on resources that inevitably constrain strategic choice. During those years Marshall only met with the defense secretary a handful of times.[10] One of those meetings took place in the mid-1980s at Fred Iklé's insistence. As the undersecretary for policy Iklé thought that Weinberger needed to hear some of the insights that had emerged from ONA's work on the US-Soviet military investment balance. Marshall's sense by this time was that the Soviet economy was headed for serious trouble and Iklé wanted the defense secretary to hear about its problems from ONA's perspective. While Weinberger acknowledged the USSR's economic difficulties, he believed that Moscow's military programs did not consume a large percentage of Soviet GNP because the Soviets employed slave labor in their factories and their military conscripts were underpaid relative to American service members.[11] Marshall's conclusion from the meeting was that Weinberger had little understanding of economics.

After his experience with the previous three defense secretaries Marshall found serving Weinberger both disappointing and frustrating. Years later, after Weinberger had stepped down from his post, per tradition a portrait of him was commissioned to hang alongside those of his predecessors. By coincidence, these portraits were displayed along the hallway outside Marshall's office on the Pentagon's A Ring. Each portrait's unveiling was the subject of a formal ceremony, attended by the Pentagon's senior civilian and military leaders, including Marshall. On the day of Weinberger's ceremony, however, a member of the ONA staff noted the event was not on Marshall's calendar. When asked why, Marshall responded, most uncharacteristically, "I might have gone if they were hanging Weinberger instead of his picture."

While ONA was suffering Weinberger's disinterest, it was thrown a lifeline by Fred Iklé. Shortly after he arrived at his post in April 1981 Iklé was preparing the first Defense Planning Guidance (DPG) whose purpose was to provide policy guidance for the military services to follow in developing their annual budgets. When Iklé asked Marshall to take a look at the DPG his main observation was that draft said nothing about exploiting Soviet weaknesses. At Iklé's suggestion Marshall then wrote some guidance to the effect that priority should be given to exploiting opportunities to impose disproportionate costs on the USSR over the long term, something he had originally articulated in a report he had written while at RAND (R-862-PR).[12] Unfortunately the idea was largely negotiated away in later DPGs because the military services argued both that it was too difficult to do and, to the extent it could be done, they were already doing it.[13]

Marshall believed otherwise. He felt the military services had powerful incentives to highlight Soviet strengths and downplay Soviet weaknesses in order argue for increased budgets to cope with Soviet threats. Strategies aimed at exploiting Soviet weaknesses therefore had little appeal to the military during the first Reagan administration. But Marshall was nothing if not patient and persistent in advocating what would emerge in the second Reagan administration as Weinberger's "competitive strategies" initiative.

In the meantime, Iklé filled the void created by Weinberger's indifference to ONA's potential value. He did so by directing Marshall to undertake a series of special projects rather than concentrating on the kinds of net assessments that ONA had produced under Brown.[14] Iklé's use of ONA primarily for special studies and projects led to a 1985 revision of the DoD directive spelling out the responsibilities of the director of net assessment. Among other things, the new directive put Marshall and his office under the direction, authority, and control of the undersecretary of defense for policy.[15]

Moving ONA under the USD(P) was not the only change in how Marshall's office functioned under the Reagan administration. During Harold Brown's tenure as defense secretary the director of central intelligence, Stansfield Turner, had sought to get the CIA into the net assessment business. Brown had flatly rejected this initiative on the grounds that the intelligence community should concentrate on analyzing the adversary— the Soviets—and that getting the Agency involved the DoD's posture and programs would only corrupt the analysis. This response from Brown created hard feelings between the Agency and the Defense Department. The new administration, however, decided to address the issue head on. Early in 1981 Turner's successor, William Casey, and Weinberger decided to take steps to get the Defense Department and the Agency working more closely together.

During World War II Casey had worked for William "Wild Bill" Donovan's Office of Strategic Services (OSS), the forerunner to the CIA, and throughout his subsequent career he sustained a deep interest in foreign affairs. After World War II Casey became a multimillionaire, first working as a corporate lawyer and later as a venture capitalist. During the Nixon administration, he also chaired the Securities and Exchange Commission (1971–1973) and served as an undersecretary of state (1973–1974). As his reward for having directed Reagan's successful 1980 presidential campaign Casey was appointed DCI.

To get the Defense Department and the Agency on the same page, Weinberger and Casey decided that net assessments, "when undertaken, would be published under the joint auspices of the Secretary of Defense and [the] Director of Central Intelligence."[16] This decision was formalized in a June 1981 memorandum signed by Frank Carlucci, Weinberger's deputy defense secretary. A former Foreign Service officer who had served as the US ambassador to Portugal, Carlucci had also worked as the CIA's deputy director under Turner.

Given Reagan's concerns about the US-Soviet strategic nuclear balance, Carlucci's directive designated it as the subject for the first secretary of defense/director of central intelligence (SecDef/DCI) net assessment. The directive gave Marshall primary responsibility within DoD for the assessment. As the lead staff element on the CIA's side Carlucci designated the chairman of the National Intelligence Council (NIC), which produced National Intelligence Estimates. At that time Marshall's former colleague Henry Rowen, who had left RAND after the furor over Daniel Ellsberg's leaking the Pentagon Papers on the Vietnam War, was the NIC's chairman. In July, Marshall reached out to the chairman of the Joint Chiefs of Staff, General David Jones, for his thoughts on the joint assessment. Marshall also met with Rowen to develop a plan on how to proceed. By late August, Rowen and Marshall had agreed on an outline.

The assessment, which was published in November 1983, took over two years to complete. Progress on it was complicated by the fact that the intelligence analysts who were working on the CIA's part of the joint assessment were repeatedly pulled off to work on NIE 11-3/8, "Soviet Capabilities for Strategic Nuclear Conflict," which was intended to both support and precede the net assessment. In addition, two of the key research issues Marshall had identified at the outset required more than technical descriptions and quantitative projections of Soviet nuclear forces out to the early 1990s. Marshall wanted the CIA to develop the closest approximation possible to the Soviet assessment of the strategic nuclear competition and articulate how their views of the correlation of forces differed from Western estimates.[17] His rationale was that US strategists engaged in efforts to strengthen deterrence needed to understand how the Soviets calculated the costs, benefits, and risks associated with this competition. He also wanted the assessment to highlight any emerging problems in the competition that needed high-level attention.

Marshall had long held the view that Soviet assessments were likely to be substantially different from those produced by the United States. As time went on and ONA's research on these assessments matured, it became increasingly clear that he was right. The Soviets made different assumptions about objectives, emphasized different scenarios, used different measures of effectiveness, and highlighted different key variables than did their US counterparts.[18] These differences even extended to the physical effects of atmospheric nuclear detonations. Whereas US test data indicated that the peak blast overpressures on the ground from a nuclear detonation occurred at greater distances from ground zero as the burst height increased, Soviet test data evidently did not.[19] This discrepancy may be one reason why the Soviets generally preferred ground bursts to air bursts in targeting their strategic nuclear forces. In addition, Soviet analysts and planners also assessed the seismic effects of ground bursts against ICBM silos to be greater than did US analysts. This could have a significant influence on Soviet calculations of the prospects of success in executing a disarming first-strike against the US land-based missile leg of the nuclear triad. Marshall's insistence on developing a better understanding how the Soviets assessed this area of military competition was a key reason why it took two years to finish this assessment.

The joint SecDef/DCI net assessment was a hefty two-volume document. Volume 1 provided a relatively short executive summary drafted primarily by US Navy captain Charles Pease in ONA and Lawrence Gershwin, the national intelligence officer for Soviet strategic forces. It contained the key judgments about the nuclear balance and had very limited distribution due to its high level of classification and sensitivity. Weinberger, who was not the reader Harold Brown had been, reviewed the first volume but probably did not spend much time on the second, which ran over 350 pages and contained detailed descriptions of both sides' projected intercontinental nuclear forces and capabilities for nuclear war. But being less sensitive, the second volume received wider distribution than did the first.

Overall Marshall judged the result to have been the "most satisfactory assessment" of this balance that ONA ever produced.[20] ONA's initial strategic nuclear net assessment in 1977 had flagged the need to better understand Soviet assessments but had not been able to provide much detail on how those differed from US assessments. By late 1983 much more was known about how the Soviets perceived and assessed the nuclear competition with the United States, marking a significant step forward in the maturation of net assessment. In fact, the focus of NIE 11-3/8-83 was the "USSR's strategy, plans, operations, and capabilities for strategic conflict" as the intelligence community believed Soviet leaders perceived them.[21] Although this version of NIE 11-3/8 was not published until March 1984, many of the insights into Soviet assessments it contained were available to those who worked on the joint SecDef/DCI net assessment.

While the 1983 SecDef/DCI strategic forces assessment remains classified, most of the NIEs from this period have been released and they offer enough insight to confirm the basic conclusions Marshall had reached about the US-USSR strategic balance as far back as 1976. The February 1983 NIE 11-3/8-82 contained the following assessment of Soviet intentions regarding nuclear conflict: "The Soviets believe that in the present U.S.-Soviet strategic relationship each side possesses strategic nuclear capabilities that could devastate the other after absorbing an attack. Soviet leaders have stated that nuclear war with the United States would be a catastrophe that must be avoided if possible and that they do not regard such a conflict as inevitable."[22] As for the Soviet view of how deterrence might fail Marshall's view agreed with Moscow. A major US-USSR nuclear conflict would most likely arise out of a NATO-Warsaw Pact conventional conflict preceded by a political crisis in Europe. As for US intentions, NIE 11-3/8-83 found that the "Soviets see little likelihood that the United States would initiate a surprise nuclear attack from a normal peacetime posture; we believe it is unlikely that the Soviets would mount such an attack themselves."[23]

Given Marshall's long-standing emphasis on the importance of Soviet assessments and calculations, these insights suggested that the United

States' nuclear posture in the early 1980s was probably adequate to deter a Soviet nuclear attack on the continental United States as well as a Soviet-led conventional assault on Western Europe by the Warsaw Pact. Marshall himself had reached similar conclusions in the late 1970s. His view of the strategic nuclear balance reflected the judgment that the Soviets evaluated their own position more pessimistically than did the United States, and would therefore lack confidence in being able to achieve their goals in either a general nuclear exchange or a NATO–Warsaw Pact conflict that escalated to nuclear use.

That being said, the 1983 and 1984 versions of NIE 11-3/8 both went on to find that the Soviets were making every effort to shift the correlation of strategic nuclear forces more in their favor. This by no means indicated that the Soviet leadership wanted to start a nuclear war with the United States. More likely it reflected the fact that organizations with the USSR's defense structure were working on their own agendas, which may not have conformed to the leadership's priorities. Or perhaps Soviet leaders felt, as Marshall suspected, that if they enjoyed a perceived lead in the strategic nuclear competition, it could be leveraged in other aspects of the competition such as in raising doubts among America's allies regarding the value of US nuclear guarantees. The lack of any Soviet inclination to risk a nuclear war was later corroborated in interviews with Soviet officials such Marshal Sergei Akhromeyev, who from 1984 to 1988 headed the Soviet General Staff. Akhromeyev stated in 1991 that "At no time did the USSR ever intend to make first use of nuclear weapons. In a military sense, the side that attacked preemptively would win, but in practical terms neither side would win. Even to the General Staff it was clear that nuclear weapons were not really military weapons but were political tools."[24]

The SecDef/DCI assessment offered Marshall an opportunity to interact with Weinberger. As Marshall knew at the time, three other areas of US advantage could not be included in the assessment due to their classification. One was the B-2 bomber. In October 1981 the Air Force had decided to develop and build a fleet of B-2s, able to penetrate with high confidence even the most advanced Soviet air defenses.[25] A second advantage was the Navy's edge in submarine detection and quieting. For example, in the late 1970s a Navy nuclear attack submarine had been able to track a Soviet Navaga-class ballistic missile submarine (NATO code-name "Yankee") for weeks without the US sub's presence being detected by the Soviet submarine's crew.[26] These two areas, as well as a third that remains sensitive, were so highly classified that even members of Marshall's staff were not given access to them. Marshall's only recourse was to meet directly with Weinberger and apprise him of them verbally. He told the defense secretary that these three US advantages made the nuclear balance "much more favorable" than the two-volume SecDef/DCI assessment indicated.[27]

After the joint assessment was delivered, Marshall and Rowen discussed whether to begin working together on a second assessment. In light of the heavy burden the effort had imposed on the CIA analysts, Rowen demurred. Neither Casey nor Weinberger pursued the matter. Thus ended the Reagan administration's efforts to have net assessments done jointly between the DoD and the CIA. From then on, for the rest of Reagan's presidency, net assessments defaulted to what they had been before under Schlesinger, Rumsfeld, and Brown: a purely DoD enterprise conducted by ONA.

Again, the long-standing impression of most who worked in ONA during the Weinberger period, including Marshall himself, was that the secretary of defense paid little attention to the office. The irony about this impression is that Weinberger and Carlucci were initially concerned about strategy, if only to counter outside critics who argued that the new administration had no guiding strategy for allocating the additional defense dollars. After meeting with Carlucci on this issue, Marshall recommended the creation of a small core group of five or six people split between military officers and outsiders reporting directly to Carlucci.[28] Weinberger approved Marshall's suggestion and created the Strategic Concepts Development Center (SCDC) at the National Defense University in 1981, appointing Phill Karber as the center's first director. In this capacity Karber reported directly to Weinberger and the chairman of the Joint Chiefs of Staff, and enjoyed "all the access one could possibly want" to the defense secretary.[29]

Having been close to Marshall since the early 1970s, Karber had had considerable exposure to net assessment. During Karber's two years as Weinberger's strategy adviser, Marshall and Karber discussed ONA's strategic and European balances as well as Marshall's thinking about competitive strategies. As head of SCDC, Karber was able to provide a back channel for conveying some of these assessments and ideas to Weinberger.

SCDC's most sensitive project was a war game conducted during two weeks in June 1983. Called Proud Prophet, the game's scenario included a year-long rolling mobilization of NATO and Warsaw Pact forces, followed by a conflict that started in the Mideast and spread to Europe. The game saw intense nuclear counterforce attacks—US strikes against Soviet nuclear forces—the result of NATO's doctrine that called for a deliberate escalation of a conventional conflict between NATO and the Warsaw Pact—as well as large-scale Soviet nuclear strikes in Europe. The exercise ultimately ended in a massive strategic exchange, despite both sides desperately trying to avoid general nuclear war. The actions of two states committing mutual suicide despite the overwhelming desire not to would not have surprised Roberta Wohlstetter or Graham Allison. Nor did they surprise Marshall.

The participation of Weinberger and Joint Chiefs of Staff chairman General John Vessey in the exercise was concealed from virtually all of the more than three hundred participants except for Karber, who ran Proud Prophet 83, and members of his small SCDC staff. In the game, Weinberger consciously tried to execute the existing US military strategy, something that no previous defense secretary had been willing to risk testing even in a war game. In the end the game went, in the argot of the time, "nuclear big time" because Weinberger and Vessey "faithfully implemented the prevailing US strategy," which called for horizontal escalation and employing limited nuclear strikes.[30]

The game culminated with the "Blue" or US/NATO side's decision to execute the full Single Integrated Operational Plan (or SIOP)—the Pentagon's targeting plan for general nuclear war. This decision was personally made by Weinberger playing the role of the US president.[31] The unprecedented direct participation of the secretary and the chairman in the game was deemed so sensitive by Weinberger than he directed that those aware of his and Vessey's participation not to reveal it for twenty-five years. Thus, it was not until 2008 that Karber was able to talk openly about what had occurred behind the scenes during Proud Prophet 83.

It is not difficult to see why Weinberger was so sensitive about the war game. Karber's postmortem of the exercise for the secretary and chairman reviewed how the "Red" (Soviet–Warsaw Pact) team had countered each of the "Blue" (US-NATO) team's escalatory options. Reportedly, Weinberger then turned to Vessey and said, "Our strategy is bankrupt"—a judgment that could have gravely undermined US national security had it appeared, for example, in the *Washington Post* or the *New York Times*.[32] Weinberger's recognition of the defects in key elements of US defense strategy had considerable impact. SCDC's Paul Bracken, now a professor at Yale University, participated as a neutral observer able to talk to both sides in the game. Bracken maintains that Proud Prophet 83 led Secretary Weinberger and

General Vessey to undertake major changes in US strategy, including banishing from Pentagon war planning such strategies as launch on warning, conventional horizontal escalation, the early use of nuclear weapons, and tit-for-tat nuclear exchanges.[33] As for ONA's influence on Proud Prophet 83, Karber maintains that Marshall was primarily responsible for the issues explored in the game.[34]

What troubled Weinberger the most about Proud Prophet 83 was that it showed US Cold War defense strategy, if executed, could not prevent escalation in conventional, much less nuclear, conflicts with the Soviet Union. War between the two superpowers incurred a high risk of leading inexorably to a nuclear Armageddon. Weinberger was hardly the first to reach this conclusion. Still, the strategic problem remained. Weinberger was particularly concerned about the European balance, given that US General Bernard Rogers, the Supreme Allied Commander, Europe, stated in the fall of 1983 that if NATO was attacked conventionally, he could only sustain a defense "for a relatively short time," after which he would have to ask for authorization to use nuclear weapons.[35]

To Weinberger this meant that to avoid crossing the nuclear threshold in the event of a European conflict, the conventional capabilities of the United States and NATO had to be strengthened. This entailed, in the defense secretary's mind, sustained increases in US and allied defense spending. In FY 1981 the Carter administration's last defense budget, DoD's total obligational authority (TOA)* was $175.5 billion (in current dollars). By FY 1985, DoD's TOA had grown to $276.2 billion, a 57 percent increase.[36] Spending on strategic nuclear forces had more than doubled, from $12 billion to $26 billion; and the $47 billion added to the conventional, or "general purpose forces" budget represented a 70 percent increase[37]—in all, an unprecedented peacetime commitment to strengthening the country's military.

Weinberger's concerns over US military strategy persisted into Reagan's second term. The defense secretary continued looking for better ways to prevent the United States from having to resort to nuclear war in contingencies such as a Soviet invasion of Western Europe. Unaware of his concerns, critics of the administration accused Weinberger not only of having

---

*TOA is the amount of funding the Defense Department is authorized to obligate to spend in a given year. DoD also tracks budget authority and outlays.

no strategy for the Reagan defense buildup, but also of seeking a capability to fight a nuclear war.[38] The latter charge, he later wrote, was "nonsense," declaring, "No one who has received as many briefings on nuclear weapons or participated in crisis exercises as I have could hold any doubts about the absolute necessity of avoiding nuclear war."[39] But how, especially in the wake of Proud Prophet 83, was nuclear war to be avoided?

This time Weinberger turned to Graham Allison, then dean of Harvard's Kennedy School of Government, for help in answering this question as well as in countering public criticism that the DoD's defense strategy could be encapsulated in one word: "More."[40] In mid-1985 Allison began dividing his time between Harvard and the Pentagon as Weinberger's special assistant on strategy. Given an office near Weinberger's, Allison began spending two or three days a week in Washington in the summer and one day a week after classes resumed in the fall.

Marshall had known Allison for two decades. They had been so close that when Allison married in 1967, the Marshalls had hosted a reception for the newlyweds. And of course Marshall had been a mentor to Allison when the latter served as a junior member of the May Group. When Allison arrived at the Pentagon it was natural for him to explore whether Marshall could help with the strategy issues that concerned Weinberger. Marshall immediately offered the idea he had suggested to Iklé four years earlier: cost-imposing or "competitive" strategies.[41]

Weinberger quickly embraced the idea. In his February 1986 annual report to Congress he announced that competitive strategies would be a major DoD theme for the rest of the Reagan administration.[42] And it was. When Carlucci succeeded Weinberger as defense secretary in November 1987, he continued the effort to institutionalize competitive strategies in the Department of Defense.[43]

The competitive strategies concept was not complicated. The idea had grown out of a larger set of Marshall's ideas about the long-term competition between the United States and the Soviet Union. The pertinent question became: What sorts of strategies should the United States adopt to be a more effective competitor in the continuing peacetime competition?[44] Marshall's answer, going back to 1969, when he had replaced James Schlesinger as RAND's director of strategic studies, was to develop strategies that could capitalize on the United States' enduring strengths (those easiest to sustain over time) while exploiting the enduring weaknesses and vulnerabilities of the USSR (those most difficult for the Soviets to overcome).[45]

Like Marshall, Weinberger saw competitive strategies as a way to compel the Soviets to perform less efficiently or effectively by (1) moving the competition into areas where the USSR would have to expend far more resources than the US to remain competitive; and (2) creating conditions whereby the USSR would be incentivized to invest disproportionately in less threatening capabilities.[46] Marshall had, of course, been urging the adoption of such strategies for at least a decade, as in the case of his arguments for going ahead with the B-1 bomber program.

Weinberger created three organizations to implement the competitive strategies initiative. At the top was a Competitive Strategies Council, chaired by Weinberger himself, which also included the chairman of the Joint Chiefs of Staff, the service secretaries and chiefs, the undersecretaries of defense, the directors of the National Security Agency and the Defense Intelligence Agency, and the assistant secretary of defense for PA&E. He assigned Allison chairmanship of the Competitive Strategies Steering Group,[47] which included Marshall, the assistant defense secretaries for policy and international security affairs along with representatives of the undersecretary for acquisition, the service secretaries and chiefs, and the DIA director. For day-to-day management of the initiative, a competitive strategies office, headed by a colonel, was established within OSD in June 1987.[48] Subsequently, two intradepartmental task forces were established. Task Force I explored competitive opportunities in a mid- to high-intensity European conventional conflict. In large measure Task Force I recommended expediting what the Soviets termed reconnaissance-strike complexes based on "smart" conventional munitions, wide-area sensors, and battle networks.[49] Task Force II was asked to explore nonnuclear strategic capabilities based on precision conventional munitions and long-range systems.[50] However, its recommendations proved much too general and abstract to be given serious consideration for action. Both lines of development would capitalize on US strengths but neither would be brought to fruition before the Cold War ended.

As sound as the thinking behind Weinberger's competitive strategies initiative was, its implementation proved difficult. Within the Pentagon, the military services and the Joint Chiefs of Staff began quietly implementing a "paralysis by analysis" approach to competitive strategies to frustrate Weinberger from taking programmatic actions that might disrupt the their own budget priorities. In November 1988, not long after Weinberger's departure, they succeeded in getting deputy defense secretary William Taft to sign a memo to the steering group chairman that effectively derailed the competitive strategies initiative.[51]

The issue that prompted this memo was whether the War Game Committee charged with evaluating specific acquisition programs to implement competitive strategies would be permitted to use special-access programs (SAPs, highly classified programs also known as "black" programs) for its computer-based modeling and simulation analysis. The military services opposed this, and Taft's memorandum placed a hold on allowing SAPs in competitive strategies work for the remainder of the Reagan administration. This rendered the War Game Committee's programmatic recommendations too general and abstract to be actionable. Despite this outcome, competitive strategies was by no means the only initiative during the Reagan years that caused great concern in Moscow by threatening to exploit US technological advantages to move the US-Soviet military balance in the United States' favor.

Reagan's Strategic Defense Initiative (SDI) also put pressure on the Soviets, and Marshall's analysis of this program made a stronger case for the value of pursuing ballistic missile defenses than did the arguments of those who were actually charged with doing so. His ability to conduct this contrarian assessment was only possible because ONA had substantial study funds for independent research. In SDI's early days many observers, including both critics and proponents, presumed that to be successful any missile shield would have to be able to stop almost all incoming Soviet warheads, as even a handful of thermonuclear weapons falling on US cities would inflict catastrophic damage. Short of meeting that criterion, the conventional wisdom held that SDI represented an expensive road to nowhere.

Marshall, never inclined to accept the conventional wisdom at face value, decided to think the problem through and draw his own conclusions. Starting in 1984 he entered into a teaming arrangement with Guy Barasch from the Los Alamos Scientific Laboratory to explore the potential effects of missile defenses on the US-Soviet strategic nuclear balance. Barasch was working with the newly established Strategic Defense Initiative Office (SDIO). The thrust of their effort was to use seminar war-gaming to assess various missile-defense architectures.[52] The games were played using Booz Allen Hamilton's Strategic Analysis Simulation (SAS), which Mark Herman, a former colleague of Phill Karber's at BDM, and others had automated on a personal computer.[53] Charlie Pease served as Marshall's point man for the games.

Going into the SDI games the players, like most observers, estimated that US missile defenses would need effectiveness levels of 90 percent or better in order to have a significant effect on the US-Soviet nuclear relationship.[54] The working assumption was that as little as ten percent leakage would still find hundreds of Soviet warheads getting through to US targets. To explore this assumption a total of fourteen of SDI games were conducted with Soviet specialists from the intelligence community playing the "Red" or Soviet side.

When the "Blue," or US, side had layered defenses capable of reducing leakage to 10 percent (that is to say, when 90 percent of the incoming warheads were successfully engaged), the Red players were "deterred at every level of war much more" than they were in games in which the Blue side lacked missile defenses.[55] The real surprise, however, came when Barasch and Pease decided to run a game to investigate the effectiveness threshold for a "Small Strategic Defense." What they discovered was that SDI effectiveness levels as low as 15 percent—that is, leakage as high as 85 percent—exerted a "profound impact" on the US-Soviet nuclear balance.[56] The reason, as John Battilega's efforts have shown, was the uncertainty that even minimally effective defenses imposed on the attacking side. Soviet military theory and practice demanded very high probabilities of mission success in nuclear as well as in conventional conflicts. The Red players used these planning norms in the games.[57] The upshot was that Red players had to allocate so many warheads to ensure a sufficiently high success rate against the US Minuteman ICBM force that they risked exhausting their own ICBM forces. Even modest missile defenses combined with the Soviet military's overly ambitious planning norms created a "missile sink" for the Soviet ICBMs. This suggested that even very "leaky" US missile defenses could have a strong deterrent effect on the Soviets.[58]

As with a number of other Marshall initiatives, this insight about the potential influence of missile defenses on attacker uncertainty never became a major part of the public debate over SDI. Moreover, as in the cases of competitive strategies and the US-Soviet investment balance, Marshall could provide senior policy makers with insights derived from ONA's assessments, yet he could not compel these officials to act on them. Put another way, he could lead the policy-making horses to water, but could not make them drink—or, perhaps, think.

It remains something of a mystery as to why the findings of ONA's SDI games were not used to counter the criticism that missile defense systems needed to be near perfect, if not impenetrable, to affect the balance between US and USSR nuclear forces, or to influence Soviet thinking about the risks associated with attempting a disarming first-strike against US land-based missile forces. Interestingly, while Marshall's assessment did not enter the mainstream of discussions among senior US policy makers, there is at least circumstantial evidence that he had a good fix on how the USSR viewed the prospect of American missile defenses. Like their US counterparts, the Soviets knew the limitations of prospective missile defense systems, which were the subject of intensive debate. But despite these limitations, from 1983 until the USSR's collapse constraining SDI became "the single most important object of Soviet diplomacy and covert action."[59] And even after the Soviet Union's collapse in 1991, Russian concern over even limited US missile defenses against a small attack from, say, North Korea or Iran has not abated. As recently as February 2011, when the New Strategic Arms Reduction Treaty (New START) officially entered into force, Soviet deputy prime minister Sergey Ivanov warned that any attempt to build a shield against ballistic missiles would inevitably provoke the creation of a "better sword" in the form of increasingly accurate Russian ICBMs.[60]

Particularly for those outside ONA, the varied and complex relations between its external research program and its formal balances were often opaque. But as Marshall and Schlesinger recognized at the outset, the research program was a necessary, vital component of Marshall's development and maturation of net assessment. Without it, ONA's assessments would have been confined to official government data. But as Marshall found time and again, the data available from official sources could be nonexistent, incomplete, or simply wrong.

The debate between the CIA and ONA over the burden that Soviet military programs imposed on the USSR's economy is perhaps the most consequential example of official intelligence estimates simply getting it wrong and, hence, the need for independent research outside the government. During the 1970s most of ONA's efforts to estimate the ratio of Soviet military spending to the USSR's GNP focused on getting the numerator—how much the Soviets were spending on their military forces—right. Again, Marshall's view was that the CIA's estimates of Soviet defense spending concentrated on the visible elements of the USSR's military forces: ICBMs, naval combatants, shipyards and naval bases, fighter and bomber bases and the aircraft on them, surface-to-air missile batteries, tanks, armored fighting vehicles, military design bureaus, manufacturing plants, and so forth. With the advent of satellite photographic reconnaissance in 1960, the US intelligence community was able to build up relatively accurate estimates of the Soviet military's equipment holdings. Rightly suspicious of official Soviet figures for defense expenditures, the CIA adopted a building-block approach to estimating the USSR's military spending, based on the concept that *prices × quantities = spending*.[61]

Identifying prices presented the greatest challenge because the USSR spent rubles, not dollars, on its military programs. Establishing a valid ruble–dollar exchange ratio proved difficult, as ruble prices in the Soviet Union were not set by market forces as were dollar prices in the United States.[62] In contrast, getting the quantities of military goods to be priced was simpler because over time the CIA was increasingly able to estimate the numbers of units in the USSR's order of battle, tables of organization and equipment for Soviet units, manpower levels, and production rates for weapons and equipment.[63] In 1967 the CIA's Office of Strategic Research (OSR) was responsible for estimating Soviet defense expenditures. A different Agency staff element, the Office of Economic Research (OER), was tasked with estimating Soviet GNP.[64] Because of this division of labor there was ambiguity about which of the two offices was responsible for estimates of the USSR's military burden. This ambiguity seems to have persisted even after OSR and OER were absorbed into the CIA's Office of Soviet Affairs (SOVA) in 1981.

In 1983 ONA analyst David Epstein completed a two-volume assessment of the US-Soviet investment balance. Epstein's assessment built on the efforts of Major Lance Lord and retired Navy captain William Manthorpe who had inherited the military investment portfolio from Major Robert Gough in the late 1970s. The assessment broadly accepted CIA estimates of the direct costs of Soviet weapon systems that had been generated with the Agency's building-block approach. But Soviet production rates were hard to square with estimates of the USSR's military burden. In 1986 the CIA and the DIA estimated that over the years 1974–1985, the USSR had procured three times as many ICBMs and SLBMs as had the United States, nine times as many surface-to-air missiles, three times as many tanks, and ten times as many artillery pieces.[65] Even though US systems were generally more costly than their Soviet counterparts, the USSR's dramatically higher production rates suggested that the burden imposed on the Soviet economy should be higher than the CIA's estimate of less than 14 percent, which had been revised upward from its earlier estimates of roughly 6–7 percent.[66]

There were also at least two sources of "indirect" military costs. One consisted of costs incurred outside the country's defense budget where the Soviet military acquired resources or influenced their allocation to satisfy wartime requirements. Here Marshall cited as examples the fact that Aeroflot passenger aircraft and the USSR's merchant marine fleet incorporated additional features—at additional cost—to enable them to transport men and equipment in time of war. Marshall also pointed to the costs incurred by the Soviets in providing economic and military aid to its satellites and clients—in effect, the costs of sustaining the Soviet Union's external empire.[67]

There was yet another tranche of expenditures beyond the direct costs of Soviet military programs. In the spring of 2001 Marshall met in Paris with Colonel Vitaly V. Shykov, who had been in one of the major planning sections of the Soviet General Staff. Shykov revealed that the Soviet military leaders had accumulated and incurred the cost of maintaining "gigantic war reserve stocks" intended to help match their estimates of US production if the country mobilized fully as it had done in World War II.[68]

Epstein contended that the CIA's estimates of the numerator for the Soviet defense burden clearly left out the indirect costs of the USSR's military efforts. He estimated that these indirect costs added another 5 to 8 percent of GNP to the USSR's defense burden.[69] After the Cold War former CIA analysts Noel Firth and James Noren recalculated the CIA's historical burden estimates. They estimated the average burden for 1981–1990 to have been 14.8 percent, using constant 1982 ruble prices (and 15.8 percent for 1981–1989, using current prices). Their revised burden for the 1970s was 16.8 percent, using constant 1982 ruble prices. Firth and Noren conceded, therefore, that the 6 to 7 percent in the early 1970s had been a substantial underestimate.[70]

There was, however, another issue—estimates of the denominator (the actual size of the Soviet economy)—where the disagreement between the CIA and ONA was even more pronounced. Soviet GNP eventually turned out to be not 55 to 60 percent of US GNP, as the CIA believed during most of the Cold War, but closer to 25 or 30 percent. Igor Birman was one of the first to raise this possibility with Marshall. Before immigrating to the United States in 1974, Birman had been a member of the Soviet Communist Party and had worked as an economist in several Soviet industrial institutes; he had also published a number of books in Russian on economic issues.[71] Sometime in the early 1970s Birman got into trouble with the Party over provocative statements he made about the Soviet economy and centralized planning during a lecture on Gosplan.* As a result he decided to leave the Soviet Union.

In the early 1980s Birman began arguing that Soviet GNP was as low as 20 to 25 percent of US GNP, thereby directly challenging the CIA's much higher estimates and the prevailing conventional wisdom in the West concerning the Soviet economy.[72] Consequently he found himself engaged in numerous professional disputes with Western Sovietologists and economists, not least those at the CIA. Marshall, long accustomed to challenging the conventional wisdom and, given his abiding interest in how the world *really* works, was one of the few who took Birman seriously enough to support his research.

Time proved Marshall—and Birman—right. After the Cold War ended, records released from Russian state archives showed Birman's analysis to have been largely correct. Yet even he actually *underestimated* the proportion of national wealth being swallowed by the Soviet military.[73] As late as 1990 Birman put the USSR's defense burden as a least 25 percent of Soviet GNP.[74] Marshall had reached roughly the same estimate in 1987, prompted in large part by articles such as Vasiliy Selyunin and Grigoriy Khanin's "Cunning Figures," which appeared in the February 1987 issue of *Novyy Mir* (New World). Their contention was that Western estimates of recent Soviet economic growth were overstated; in fact, the USSR's economy had actually stagnated.[75]

Birman was by no means the only researcher who developed contrarian views on the size of the USSR's economy during the 1980s. Other researchers who did so included Henry Rowen, Charles Wolf, Anders Åslund, and Stephen Meyer.[76] All received encouragement and in some cases funding support from Marshall's office. Inevitably these outside research efforts reinforced Marshall's long-standing conviction that the CIA's estimate that Soviet GNP was 55 percent of US GNP was "total hokum."[77]

In his efforts to alert senior US policy makers to his conclusions, Marshall also found some allies at the CIA whose judgments were closer to his

---

*"Gosplan" is an abbreviation of Gosudarstvenniy Komitet po Planirovaniyu (State Committee for Planning).

than those of the SOVA economists. Among them were Herbert Meyer and, ultimately, William Casey himself. Casey had hired Meyer as a special assistant and deputy director of the NIC. Prior to joining the CIA Meyer had been an associate editor at *Fortune* magazine, where he specialized in the Soviet economy. He had also traveled extensively in the USSR. In late 1983, Meyer wrote a memorandum to Casey arguing that the Soviet economy was "heading toward calamity" and, with an average annual growth rate of less than 2 percent, could not sustain an estimated 4 percent growth rate in military spending.[78] Another notable skeptic about SOVA's burden estimates was Robert Gates, who served Casey as deputy director for Intelligence and, later, as the DCI and eventually as secretary of defense.[79]

In the end, intelligence community estimates of the USSR's military burden by the 1980s were understated by at least a factor of two. In 1975, Marshall had estimated the burden as "10 to 20 percent of Soviet GNP" versus the 6 to 7 percent then estimated by the CIA.[80] By 1987 he thought the burden had been "somewhere between 20 and 30 percent" during the preceding ten years.[81] In 2001, after Shykov's revelations, he concluded that the burden had probably been even higher: "somewhere in the range of 35 to 50 percent of Soviet GNP."[82] Without an office as independent of the intelligence community as ONA and a director with Marshall's emphasis on rigorous analysis and facts, US senior policy makers would have had to rely solely on the CIA's flawed estimates of the USSR's military burden.[83]

The economic burden imposed by Soviet military programs was not the only area where ONA's study funds for independent research paid dividends. Starting in 1970, the Soviet Union temporarily loosened emigration restrictions for Jewish emigrants, allowing nearly 250,000 people to leave the USSR. By the mid-1970s the flow of former Soviet citizens into the United States had reached significant numbers.

A young RAND analyst, Enders Wimbush, approached Marshall and suggested that these émigrés might prove a source of useful information regarding the role of ethnic factors in the Soviet Army and, by extension, its effectiveness as a fighting force.[84] Marshall asked Wimbush to put together a proposal for an émigré interview project. Marshall sent it to both the CIA and the DIA. Neither intelligence agency expressed any interest in it. Their view was that any information gleaned from Soviet émigrés could not be trusted.

Marshall decided to fund the project himself. Eventually some 200 to 250 émigrés were interviewed about their military experiences. The effort, Wimbush concluded, "taught us not just about the ethnic factor in the Soviet armed forces, it taught us about their staffing requirements; it taught us about violence in the ranks; it taught us about the alcohol problem; it taught us about the political oversight problem. And when we finished with this, we had a profoundly different view of what the inside of the Soviet military looked like. . . . "[85]

The conscript personnel that formed the backbone of the Soviet armed forces clearly were not comparable to the volunteer soldiers, sailors, marines, and airmen that composed the US military. Moreover, in the aftermath of Vietnam the US military began investing in realistic combat training with such innovations as the Navy's Topgun training program for its fighter crews, the Air Force's Red Flag exercises at Nellis Air Force Base in Nevada, and the Army's National Training Center at Fort Irwin in California. The Soviets had nothing to match these initiatives.

By the mid-1980s President Reagan was halfway through his second administration. Having voted for dramatic increases in the defense budget throughout the early part of the decade, Congress was showing a growing reluctance to continue the rate of growth advocated by Weinberger. As a result, Marshall's influence increased, especially during the Commission on Integrated Long-Term Strategy (CILTS). The Defense Department formed CILTS in the fall of 1986, stimulated in part by Weinberger's efforts to silence critics who accused him of having no strategy.

Chaired by Iklé and Albert Wohlstetter, both long-standing Marshall colleagues, CILTS was intended to chart those broad trends shaping the future security environment that were likely to affect US defense strategy over the next fifteen or twenty years, particularly with an eye to preventing catastrophic technological or geopolitical surprises.[86] Among the commission's eleven members were Zbigniew Brzezinski, Andrew Goodpaster, Samuel Huntington, Henry Kissinger, and John Vessey, former chairman of the Joint Chiefs of Staff. To support the Commission's deliberations Iklé and Wohlstetter established four working groups. Retired Army general Paul Gorman examined low-intensity conflict; Fred Hoffman and Henry Rowen looked at offensive and defensive power projection on the periphery of the USSR; Charles Hertzfeld headed the technology working group; and

Marshall and Charles Wolf explored the overall security environment into the first decade of the twenty-first century.

Marshall had worked with Iklé, Wohlstetter, Hoffman, and Rowen at RAND and later in government. In 1987 Wolf was still at RAND. Herzfeld had inspired Marshall's first net assessment in 1970 for Kissinger's Special Defense Panel, and Marshall had collaborated with Gorman on a net assessment of US and Soviet tank crew training in the early 1970s. So the CILTS chairmen and the heads of its working groups knew one another well and had extensive experience in strategy.

The commission's report, *Discriminate Deterrence*, appeared in January 1988. The more detailed working group reports followed in October. From Marshall's perspective, his work on the future security environment with Wolf raised two fundamental issues. First, their working group concluded that the Soviets were correct in their assessment that the advent of new technologies would revolutionize the conduct of war, not merely make current forces marginally more effective.[87] Their finding made its way into *Discriminate Deterrence,* which concluded that the "further exploitation of microelectronics, in particular for sensors and information processing," combined with low-observable (stealth) technology, extremely accurate conventional weapons, and improved means of locating targets, would revolutionize war.[88] The implications of this conclusion became a central focus of ONA's work during much of the 1990s, after the Soviet Union had collapsed.

Second, in 1988 the USSR was still seen as the United States' major competitor going forward, and the long-standing habit of seeing the future through the lens of that rivalry had the effect of pulling the commission members toward a short-term focus. Most refused, as Marshall later noted, "to admit publicly that the Soviet had had it."[89] To his frustration, Iklé was unwilling to state in *Discriminate Deterrence* just how weak Marshall believed the Soviet Union had become.[90]

Notwithstanding the apparent distance between Marshall and Weinberger, and despite Iklé's desire to have ONA focus on projects other than net assessments, work on a number of the Cold War balances continued during the 1980s. Two years after the joint DoD-CIA net assessment of US and Soviet strategic nuclear forces, ONA analyst Dmitry Ponomareff updated the executive summary of this balance.[91] It was ONA's third and final look at the US-Soviet competition in intercontinental nuclear forces. In 1984 Marshall forwarded to Weinberger three more assessments: the US-Soviet maritime and power-projection balances, and an East Asian assessment undertaken by Stephen Rosen. All were fairly lengthy reports, and thus not the sorts of documents that Weinberger was inclined to read from front to back, if at all, which the absence of any feedback seemed to confirm to Marshall. A similar fate awaited the NATO–Warsaw Pact military balance assessment that was forwarded to Weinberger in 1986. This was the last major assessment ONA completed during the Cold War.

While Marshall could not compel an incumbent defense secretary to pay attention to ONA's assessments, his thinking on various areas of military competition nevertheless found other, less direct ways of entering the public debate on national security. In particular, Marshall's "hidden hand" approach could be found in his mentoring of promising young scholars and analysts. At RAND Marshall had been a mentor to researchers such as Roberta Wohlstetter and Graham Allison. Once in the Pentagon he continued to mentor both members of his staff and others through ONA's contract research. Over time his gentle guidance produced a cadre of individuals who understood enough about net assessment to appreciate its value and endeavor to apply this analytic discipline in their own work on defense issues.

Inside ONA these individuals came to be loosely referred to as members of St. Andrew's Prep. Years later, when asked about his most important contribution as ONA's director, Marshall declared his major achievement to have been the influence he had on the people who had served on his staff. Because the majority of ONA's net assessments remain classified, the work outside ONA by some members of St. Andrew's Prep whom Marshall mentored provides perhaps the best window currently available into how net assessment worked in practice. Their work also reveals how, through them, Marshall was able to influence the debate over US strategy even when Weinberger was apparently paying scant attention to ONA's balances.

Three of the more distinguished members of St. Andrew's Prep were brought to his attention in the late 1970s by Sam Huntington. The three—Eliot Cohen, Aaron Friedberg, and Steve Rosen—were among Huntington's best students at Harvard. Their writings are particularly useful in understanding Marshall's thinking and on how he viewed military competitions since each of them spent time in the Office of Net Assessment working under Marshall.

Rosen had graduated from Harvard in 1974, and not long after earned his PhD at that university. Early in his career Rosen was hired by Marshall as a civilian assistant. After a few years he left ONA to become the director of political-military affairs on President Reagan's NSC staff and later served on the faculty at the Naval War College in Newport, Rhode Island. Whatever position Rosen held, he was never far from Marshall or his fellow members of St. Andrew's Prep. He participated with Marshall in the CILTS work on the future security environment in the late 1980s and, along with fellow ONA alumni Eliot Cohen and Barry Watts, on the secretary of the Air Force's Gulf War Air Power Survey following the 1991 Persian Gulf War. Rosen later earned tenure at Harvard as the Beton Michael Kaneb Professor of National Security and Military Affairs. During his summers he often led one of the panels of experts exploring an issue of particular interest to Marshall at one of ONA's two-week "summer studies" at the Naval War College. In the early 1990s his book *Winning the Next War* would play an influential role in ONA's effort to assess what Marshall suspected was a discontinuous shift in the character of warfare and, correspondingly, the need for military innovation in preparing for it.

Aaron Friedberg had trailed Rosen at Harvard by four years, graduating in 1978. Like Rosen, he then earned a PhD from Harvard. Friedberg first met Marshall in April 1979 when working as a twenty-three-year-old intern at the journal *Foreign Policy*. When Huntington left his position on President Carter's NSC staff as director of long-range planning to return to Harvard, he was succeeded by Fritz Ermarth, who shortly thereafter hired Friedberg to do a classified history of US nuclear doctrine. Friedberg needed a place to work, and Ermarth was able to get Marshall to provide him with some space at ONA. In 1987 Friedberg joined the faculty at Princeton University, and in 1999 he was appointed professor of politics and international affairs. Like Rosen, Friedberg has combined scholarship and public service, including service as deputy assistant for national security affairs and director of policy planning on the staff of Vice President Richard Cheney during 2002–2005. As in the case of Rosen, once Friedberg had worked for Marshall, he found himself permanently drawn into the ONA director's orbit.

Starting in the late 1980s Friedberg began focusing much of his formidable intellect on an issue of great interest to Marshall: how dominant powers preserve their position in the face of challenges from rising powers, a topic Friedberg addressed in his 1988 *The Weary Titan: Britain and the Experience of Relative Decline, 1885–1905*. As the subtitle suggests, the book explored how British statesmen became aware of unfavorable shifts in Britain's relative power at the turn of the twentieth century and how they sought to mitigate them. Over a decade later Friedberg returned to the subject of a dominant nation's being challenged by a rising power. As with Marshall, it had become clear to Friedberg that China would pose a growing challenge to US primacy, and he endeavored to assess how the People's Republic of China (PRC) would seek to assert itself and how the United States might best respond.

The third Huntington protégé that came to Marshall's attention was Eliot Cohen. Cohen was a contemporary of both Friedberg and Rosen while an undergraduate at Harvard, where he also earned his doctorate. Like Rosen, Cohen would later teach strategy at the Naval War College. After serving a brief stint in the secretary of defense's policy planning staff at the beginning of the Bush administration in 1989, Cohen left the government to become the Robert E. Osgood Professor of Strategic Studies at the Johns Hopkins University's Nitze School of Advanced International Studies. Along with Friedberg and Rosen, Cohen has combined his pedagogical career with frequent, albeit temporary, forays into public service. Following the 1991 Persian Gulf War Cohen was tapped by Air Force secretary Donald Rice to lead the Gulf War Air Power Survey, an assessment of air power's performance in the war. The multivolume survey was widely praised as one of the most insightful and impartial studies of air operations since the US Strategic Bombing Survey at the end of World War II. During George W. Bush's administration Cohen returned to serve on Defense Policy Board, which advises the secretary of defense. In 2007 Cohen was appointed to serve as counselor to Secretary of State Condoleezza Rice, a position he held until the transition to the Obama administration in 2009.

In 1983, shortly after earning his doctorate, Cohen, who had also been commissioned a lieutenant in the Army Reserve, was assigned to the Office of Net Assessment to fulfill his reserve duty requirements. As was the case with all new arrivals to the ONA staff, Cohen was instructed to sit and read—to self-educate himself in the workings of the office and the analytic discipline of net assessment. He soon impressed Marshall, and for years afterward was invited to serve his reserve duty time working in ONA.

This was the case when, in early 1988, Cohen was drawn into a debate encouraged by the journal *International Security*. Although the Berlin Wall's fall was less than two years off, at the time the Cold War seemed to have no end in sight and few disputed that the Soviet threat to Western Europe was both real and formidable. Just how formidable was the subject of considerable dispute. Analysis of the military balance in Central Europe focused on the forces facing each other along a line stretching from Denmark in the north, moving south along the intra-German border down to the West German-Czech border.

In the event of war Soviet military doctrine called for Warsaw Pact forces to advance rapidly into Western Europe to seize West Germany and the Low Countries by employing blitzkrieg-style operations, with fast-moving armored forces supported by air and missile forces. NATO's objective was to block the Soviets from achieving a quick victory while not giving up much territory and avoiding escalation to nuclear use. If the alliance's conventional forces could accomplish these goals, it was hoped that NATO could mobilize its superior industrial base and manpower and compel the USSR to seek peace. Of course, NATO's ultimate objective was not to fight at all but to convince the Soviets that the risks of taking military action were unacceptably high—that is, to deter them from attacking in the first place.

With this in mind the editors of *International Security* commissioned papers to assess the Central European military balance. Three distinguished scholars—Joshua Epstein, John Mearsheimer, and Barry Posen—were engaged.[92] Each was asked to present his assessment of the balance. In conducting their assessments, the three reached generally the same conclusion: The balance between NATO and Warsaw Pact conventional forces favored NATO because the Soviets and their Warsaw Pact allies lacked the combat power to win the breakthrough battles on which their campaign strategy depended. Mearsheimer declared, "The chief question in assessing the European balance is whether the Soviets have the wherewithal to launch a successful blitzkrieg against NATO. This question can never be answered with certainty, but there is ample reason for thinking the Soviets cannot overrun Germany with conventional forces."[93] Moreover, his assessment led him to conclude that "contrary to the conventional wisdom, NATO's forces probably can stymie a Pact offensive in Europe without surrendering much German territory."[94]

Posen was even more optimistic, declaring that his analysis indicated "that the widespread impression of *decisive* Pact quantitative superiority is a myth" [emphasis in the original]. He concluded that NATO forces "are *fully competitive* with the Warsaw Pact in Central Europe" and that "it is clear that predictions of early NATO defeat based on Pact quantitative superiority should be treated with great skepticism. NATO actually is in a very good position to defeat a Pact attack [emphasis in the original]."[95] Similarly, Epstein wrote that "overwhelming Warsaw Pact superiority has not been demonstrated using serious analytical methods," and that even based on his "conservative" assumptions regarding its forces, *"NATO has the material wherewithal to stalemate the Warsaw Pact"* [emphasis in the original].[96]

Despite their common findings, the articles triggered a heated debate among the three authors. Although coming to similar conclusions regarding the state of the Central Front balance, each found their colleagues' methodology lacking.[97] After all, the value of an assessment's findings is heavily dependent on the line of argument used in reaching them—the methodology—and the evidence provided in support of the argument.

Three members of St. Andrew's Prep—Eliot Cohen, Jim Roche, and Barry Watts—also had serious issues with the methodologies employed by the three authors and proceeded to make their concerns a matter of public record in two articles, one by Cohen and the other by Roche and Watts.[98] Their concerns echoed how Marshall approached the problem of estimating this key military balance, and reaffirmed the apprehensions the ONA director expressed in his 1966 seminal paper on the difficulties of developing accurate measures of relative military power.

Having served in ONA, Cohen, Roche, and Watts knew that net assessment is very much about identifying and exploiting favorable asymmetries in key areas of the competition, and finding ways to mitigate the effects of those asymmetries that work in the enemy's favor. Net assessment also relies heavily on reliable data—here, "garbage in" really does result in "garbage out." It also requires a good understanding of the value—and limitations—of what the intelligence community can provide in the way of "good data."

Extending all the way back to Marshall's master's thesis that found Klein's economic model severely wanting, he has always urged those engaged in crafting net assessments to be extremely wary of the ability of models of any kind to predict the behavior of highly complex phenomena, whether it be the factors shaping a nation's economy or those influencing a war's outcome. And as those familiar with Marshall's approach to net assessment know, "Not everything that can be counted counts; and not every thing that counts can be counted." That is, Marshall advised his staff that the impulse of many political scientists to quantify the main elements of military balances risked ignoring important qualitative and intangible factors. Shaped by their time spent under Marshall's tutelage, Cohen, Roche, and Watts applied these and other Marshall insights in their critiques of the Epstein, Mearsheimer, and Posen assessments.

For his part, Cohen began his critique by stating that the "Optimists"—the term by which he referred to Epstein, Mearsheimer, and Posen—discounted qualitative "fundamental asymmetries between West and East with respect to coalition unity and purpose" that could significantly affect war outcomes in Central Europe and, therefore, the balance of forces. As an example, Cohen noted that "Unlike the Soviet Union, the United States cannot dictate to its allies the fact, let alone the timing, of their mobilization, nor their choices of arms and doctrine."[99] Yet NATO's ability—or *inability*—to mobilize all its members' forces promptly once warning of Warsaw Pact mobilization had been received could significantly influence the outcome of a NATO-Warsaw Pact conflict.

Cohen acknowledged the Optimists' point that the armed forces of the Soviet satellite states, particularly those of East Germany, Poland, and Czechoslovakia, might not prove reliable. Yet Cohen noted that their reliability would be most likely to come into question if NATO forces were winning the war, not merely trying to stave off a Warsaw Pact offensive, a factor left unaddressed by the Optimists.[100] Cohen also pointed out that the Optimists generally relied on a single scenario to inform their assessment: a mobilization race between the two coalitions that assumed the Soviets would only strike at the moment when the balance of forces was most heavily in their favor. Yet Marshall would never approve an assessment that self-limited itself to a single "canonical" scenario. At the time at least two other scenarios would have engaged Marshall's attention. One emerged from President Carter's pronouncement in January 1980 following the Soviet invasion of Afghanistan that the United States would commit itself to the defense of the Persian Gulf region against external aggression. The question that soon arose was how the United States would react if the Soviets launched an incursion into Iran. Would Washington mobilize and move forces earmarked for NATO to the Persian Gulf region instead? If so, what did it portend for the Central Front balance?* The concern arose that a Soviet attack on Iran could be used as a diversion to draw US forces away from a coming Warsaw Pact offensive in Europe.

---

*In the 1980s many US military officials believed that the Soviets could mount an offensive against Iran and the Persian Gulf without redeploying forces earmarked for operations in Central Europe.

Another alternative scenario was the so-called Hamburg Grab in which the war began as envisioned by the Optimists; however, the Warsaw Pact's goal was not to defeat NATO outright but to grab enough NATO territory to fracture the alliance politically. A short, limited offensive to seize Hamburg, a major city in West Germany roughly forty miles from the border with East Germany, would also minimize the risk that NATO would escalate the conflict by employing nuclear weapons.[101] Indeed, it might be possible to seize the city before NATO could mobilize its forces. Once Hamburg had been overrun, the Soviets could offer a cease-fire, calculating that NATO would prefer a negotiated end to the fighting in light of the obvious difference between the value of Hamburg and the cost (to include the prospect of nuclear war) of retaking it. If the offer were accepted, it was feared that NATO members—West Germany in particular—would conclude their pledge to consider an attack upon one of them as an attack upon all was hollow. This could create political fissures in the alliance that the Soviets could exploit.

Cohen's critique turned next turned to the issue of mobilization. Because both NATO and the Warsaw Pact could significantly enhance their combat forces by mobilizing those not in a high state of readiness, mobilization was an important factor in assessing the Central Front balance, and each of the three Optimists addressed this issue. While Posen asserted that he assessed the situation "more realistically" than did others, Cohen found that many of his assumptions about how quickly the two alliances could mobilize reserves and bring them to bear—including the entry of French ground forces— yielded an advantage to NATO.[102]

Besides challenging Posen's sanguinary assumptions regarding the two sides' mobilization rates, Cohen again noted that the Soviet Union could compel its allies to mobilize, whereas the United States could not. Cohen then turned to the issue of surprise: the possibility that NATO intelligence would either fail to provide timely warning of a Warsaw Pact attack or the warnings would be ignored. Cohen recalled that the commander of the US Army in Europe first heard about the Warsaw Pact's August 1968 invasion of Czechoslovakia, involving over 200,000 Soviet, Bulgarian, Hungarian, and Polish troops, not from his intelligence staff, but from an Associated Press dispatch. He also noted that despite a number of intelligence warning indicators, the Israelis were surprised by the Egyptian and Syrian attacks in October 1973 that initiated the Yom Kippur War.[103] Cohen reiterated Roberta Wohlstetter's warning that it is risky to assume that accurate intelligence will reach senior decision makers promptly and that they will be able to filter it from the "noise" of less relevant information. To this might be added Graham Allison's observation in *Essence of Decision* that individuals and organizations can, at times, filter out useful intelligence when it does not match their preferred view of how their "rational" rivals would behave.

In assessing a military balance such as that between NATO and the Warsaw Pact in the 1980s, Marshall's view has long been that the first task is to compare the quantities of men and equipment (tanks, artillery, troops, etc.) each side has at its disposal. Second, an assessment needs to capture qualitative differences between the opposing men and equipment (such as the firepower, mobility, and survivability of a US main battle tank versus that of its Soviet counterpart, Soviet conscripts versus the professional soldiers of an all-volunteer army, differences in command and control, etc.). Third and most crucial, in Marshall's judgment, a good net assessment needed to incorporate intangible, often uncertain, variables such as geography, weather, logistics, warning times, surprise, and readiness along with asymmetries between the two sides in training, tactics, military doctrine, campaign strategy, and theater objectives.

To address the first two of these requirements, Posen used the US Army's WEI/WUV methodology. Mearsheimer did the same, asserting that, "The best measures of relative conventional strength are those that capture the full range of the combat capabilities of the forces, including their mobility, survivability, and firepower (including the rate and lethality of their fire). The measure that best captures these capabilities in ground forces is the 'armored division equivalent' (ADE) score that the Pentagon uses as its basic measure of ground force capability."[104]

An Armored Division Equivalent (ADE) is based on the WUV score of a standard US armored division. If the WUV aggregate for a US armored division was 120,000 and that of a Soviet tank division was 96,000, then dividing both units by the WUV score of the US division would yield ADEs of 1.0 and 0.8 for the US and Soviet units, respectively. ADEs could then be calculated for both sides' ground forces throughout the European theater, thereby producing a quantitative force ratio between NATO and Warsaw Pact ground forces. Using this methodology both Mearsheimer and Posen concluded that the Warsaw Pact had an ADE advantage over NATO of 1.2 to 1.[105]

Setting aside the fact that the Army's Concepts Analysis Agency that first developed the WEI/WUV scoring system discounted its utility as a valid means for assessing the relative effectiveness of opposing forces in actual combat, Posen adjusted the theaterwide force ratio by assigning a multiplier of 1.5—an increase of 50 percent—to NATO ADEs because NATO allocated "1.2 to 2 times the personnel as the Pact to generate a given unit of firepower."[106] Here Posen was endeavoring to reflect NATO's higher investment in support forces, or logistics, than the Warsaw Pact in the theaterwide force ratio.

Cohen questioned Posen's use of the amount of invested resources as the proper metric for gauging relative military effectiveness. He noted that NATO logistics forces were larger, in part, because of the greater emphasis given by the alliance's governments to providing their troops with creature comforts, which do not exhibit a high correlation to overall military effectiveness. He also noted that while Warsaw Pact forces operated with a common set of equipment and spare parts established by the Soviet Union, the major NATO militaries typically fielded their own major items of equipment, greatly complicating the challenge of providing logistics support while causing considerable duplication of effort and outright waste, further diminishing the value of investment levels as a surrogate for military effectiveness.[107]

Finally, as Marshall appreciated, there were major asymmetries in the two sides' military objectives and the doctrines by which they hoped to achieve their objectives in time of war. These differences exerted a substantial influence on their respective logistics systems. The Soviets planned on achieving their objectives in a short campaign; thus their need for spare and replacement parts and major repair facilities was far less than those needed for the NATO forces, whose major weapon systems were generally more sophisticated than those of the Warsaw Pact forces and thus more difficult—and expensive—to maintain in an operational state. NATO forces also had to be prepared to defend against an attack for as long as it might take to prevail, and could not risk assuming the war would be short. Consequently Cohen concluded "The merits of NATO's logistical and organizational practices require discussion, not an assumption that the West's practices are invariably correct, and certainly not an increase of NATO firepower scores by fifty percent."[108]

Remarkably, the Optimists accorded relatively little attention to the role of air power in their assessments, even though air forces had played a major role in conventional warfare at least since the beginning of World War II. Cohen noted that Mearsheimer "simply excludes air power from his analysis."[109] Posen also omitted air forces, asserting that NATO's were superior to the Warsaw Pact's. His justification was that because he had assessed NATO ground forces as "fully competitive" with the Warsaw Pact's, adding aircraft to the assessment would only reinforce his judgment that the European conventional balance did not favor the Soviets.[110]

Cohen responded that a true net assessment of the balance would reject the Optimists' notion that air forces are just another input into the combat power layered atop ground forces. In particular he cited Soviet air doctrine regarding the "initial air operation" at the beginning of a war.[111] In fact, the Soviets had concluded by the mid-1980s that NATO air forces constituted the greatest threat to the success of a Warsaw Pact ground offensive in a conventional war in Central Europe.[112] Hence the Soviets developed the theater, or strategic, air operation, which called for massive attacks not on NATO's front-line ground forces but on its air forces. They planned to employ tactical ballistic missiles to attack NATO air bases within minutes of the onset of war, so as to pin down the allies' aircraft until Warsaw Pact attack aircraft arrived. These attacks would also be supported by chemical weapons attacks and Soviet special forces raids to finish the job of destroying most of NATO's air forces on the ground. Although NATO fielded a network of surface-to-air missile batteries, there were concerns that in the chaos of war, these forces were as likely to engage NATO aircraft as they were the enemy's. Given that NATO commanders viewed Soviet success in the initial air operation as a "recipe for disaster" in terms of their ability to blunt a Warsaw Pact offensive, Cohen's criticism of the Optimists' discounting of this aspect of the European balance was certainly justified.[113]

Coming back to theater-wide ADE ratios, a debate ensued over what kind of a force ratio advantage was required for either side to achieve its war objectives. While Epstein and Posen relied to a significant extent on models designed to simulate the dynamic interactions between NATO and Warsaw Pact forces, Mearsheimer eschewed models and focused on the ratio of the forces measured in terms of ADEs. He concluded that while "it is difficult to say precisely what ratio represents a decisive advantage for an attacker . . . the defender would probably be in serious trouble if the overall balance of ADEs in a theater of the size and geography of Central Europe favored the attacker by 2:1." Mearsheimer went on to assert that as a rule of thumb: "A theater-wide balance of 3:1 or more would almost surely mean rapid defeat for the defender. The attacker could then easily concentrate forces along various breakthrough sectors and simply steamroll over the defender's forces, regardless of how well the defender fought."[114] Yet as

Marshall knew, historical data from some 571 land battles reviewed by the military analyst Trevor Dupuy indicated that force ratios "do not make any significant difference" in which side ultimately won.[115]

Mearsheimer's colleagues Joshua Epstein and Barry Posen also rejected his use of the 3:1 rule. Unlike Mearsheimer, however, they employed models as part of their methodology. As Epstein explained: "For purposes of theater-level net assessment, the most revealing way to evaluate the conventional balance is through *dynamic analysis*. In a thorough dynamic analysis, an explicit mathematical model—a formal idealization—of warfare is used to simulate the mutual attrition of engaged forces, the flow of reinforcing units into the battle, and the movement of battlefronts over time" [emphasis in the original].[116]

Epstein, like Marshall, expressed skepticism about the Pentagon's models for conducting dynamic assessments. He observed that the British polymath and engineer "Frederick William Lanchester's mutual attrition equations are the core of virtually all dynamic models used by the Pentagon, its contractors, and prominent independent analysts."[117] Lanchester's so-called N-Square law, which he derived from gunfire duels between opposing lines of World War I era capital ships, postulated that outcomes would be in response to the casualties incurred over time.[118] Yet the evidence shows that battles have been resolved largely on the basis of other considerations: "No matter how casualties are measured, battles have been given up as lost when casualties ranged from insignificant to overwhelming."[119] As with force ratios, the results of historical battles do not support casualty rates as a driver of outcomes. Epstein deemed this form of modeling "absurd" for several reasons and had developed his Adaptive Dynamic Model to help overcome these and other shortcomings of the Lanchester theory.

Epstein's Adaptive Dynamic Model, however, had its owns problems, as two other members of St. Andrew's Prep, Jim Roche and Barry Watts, pointed out in a 1990 article published in the *Journal of Strategic Studies*. In it they concluded that underlying Epstein's model were two assumptions. First, that changes in combat outputs are directly proportional to changes in inputs. In other words, the relation between inputs and outputs in war is linear. Second, Epstein assumed that the overall dynamics of a battle or campaign is the sum of the dynamics of its various components, which is to say that warfare does not include emergent phenomena. Roche and Watts found that "even the most cursory inspection of the equations underlying

Epstein's Adaptive Dynamic Model reveals his 'calculus of conventional war' embraces both these assumptions. . . . "[120] They argued that in reality war is fundamentally and relentlessly a *nonlinear* enterprise.* To back this up, they looked to Marshall's emphasis on history and data, reviewing the disconnects between inputs and outputs in the strategic bombing of Germany during 1943–1945 and the US B-25 raid on the Japanese home islands led by Colonel Jimmy Doolittle in April 1942. The latter was particularly striking in that the immediate damage the Doolittle raid had inflicted on Japanese targets was negligible, but the fact that the sacred soil of home islands had been attacked led the Japanese to make subsequent strategic decisions that culminated in their defeat at the June 1942 Battle of Midway, where the Imperial Navy lost four fleet carriers in exchange for a single American flat top.[121]

Epstein's model attempted to capture the dynamics of a hypothetical situation in which NATO forces were attempting to trade space for time so as to improve their position. Yet the model failed to account for what Andrew Krepinevich experienced when, as an Army staff officer, he was temporarily assigned to NATO's Northern Army Group in 1977 for a field exercise.† As the exercise progressed he found NATO's ground forces trading space for time—all of them, that is, except for the three West German corps, which were interspersed between the other national corps along the alliance's "layer cake"‡ defense. Owing to political considerations, the Germans felt they could not embrace a military doctrine that called for ceding territory—German cities, towns, and fellow citizens—to the Soviets in the hope that it would eventually be retaken. Consequently, not long into the war game NATO's front line showed a series of undulations comprising large salients where the allied corps had conducted a fighting withdrawal,

---

*The fact of war's nonlinearity is neither new nor novel. It can be linked to modern chaos theory, which addresses how small changes in initial conditions can produce highly divergent outcomes.

†NATO's Central Front forces were organized into the Northern Army Group (NORTHAG)—Belgian, British, Dutch, and West German units—deployed along the border between the two Germanies from Denmark to near Bonn; and the Central Army Group (CENTAG)—US and West German forces—which assumed responsibility for covering the border down through the German-Czech border.

‡The term *layer cake* comes from the arrangement of NATO corps forces, which were aligned from north to south, giving the appearance of a layer cake.

trading space for time, save for the three German corps, which had held fast to protect their land and countrymen.

The result of the battlefield decisions Krepinevich anticipated was nothing like what might be expected from Epstein and Posen's models, which implicitly assumed that NATO's members would act "rationally" to optimize their military effectiveness, when in fact bureaucratic and organizational forces were very much involved in the outcome—a conclusion Marshall had reached thirty years earlier in reviewing his RAND colleagues' projections as to where the Soviets would locate the bases for their bomber forces. Roche and Watts captured the point well in pointing out that "Human involvement alone argues that combat interactions and processes cannot be universally linear, that effects can be all out of proportion to their causes. As a result, the measures and analyses by which we attempt to deal with such complex interactions . . . cannot be . . . adequately captured by explicit, linear mathematical formulas any more than can chaotic dynamic systems."[122] In summing up their thoughts, Watts and Roche brought their mentor Marshall explicitly into the discussion, noting his "concern . . . that as the stockpile of quantitative measures and models has grown, it has become easier to deal with whatever analytic problems happen to occur simply by pulling old measures and models off the shelf and applying them with little or no thought as to their applicability or appropriateness."[123]

While Marshall applauded the *efforts* of such scholars as Epstein, Mearsheimer, and Posen to assess the European balance, he was not impressed with their results. He had decided long ago, in writing his master's thesis on Klein's economic model, that analytic measures and models, no matter how sophisticated they might appear to be, or how much effort and talent had been committed in their construction, did not overcome the simple fact that, as he had written in 1966, "The conceptual problems in constructing an adequate or useful measure of military power have not yet been faced. Defining an adequate measure looks hard, and making estimates in real situations looks even harder."[124] Epstein, Mearsheimer, and Posen had each come up against exactly the sorts of difficulties Marshall and members of St. Andrew's Prep had become attuned to, and their attempts at net assessments fell short of ONA's Cold War balances.

In little more than a year after this debate, the Soviet Union's position in Eastern Europe began gradually to collapse, bringing with it an end to the four-decade Cold War. In a December 1988 speech to the United Nations,

Mikhail Gorbachev announced his decision to reduce the USSR's armed forces by 500,000 personnel within two years, withdraw and disband six tank divisions then stationed in Eastern Europe, and cut Soviet forces there by 50,000 personnel and 5,000 tanks.[125] The following November the Berlin Wall came down, and in December 1991 the Soviet Union itself collapsed. These developments were part of a rapid succession of world-changing events that obviated the original impetus for competitive strategies against the USSR and left the United States standing alone as the world's preeminent power.

Although the economic and political disintegration of the Soviet Union into fifteen separate countries brought the United States a respite from years of rivalry with a major adversary, it did not bring an end to such competitions. New security challenges would emerge in the years following the Cold War. Remarkably, they would be along the lines of what had been predicted by Marshall years earlier.

Marshall was by no means egotistical enough to suggest, as some did after the fact, that he had foreseen the USSR's demise in 1991. To be sure, he had felt for some years that the Soviet economy was headed for bankruptcy, but he did not predict precisely when or how the Soviet Union would unravel. When the end finally came in the same year as the 1991 Persian Gulf War, what surprised him was its rapidity and completeness.

Granted, many elements contributed to the USSR's collapse. One was surely the spreading loss of confidence among Soviet elites in the future that Soviet experts, such as James Billington and Peter Reddaway, began to sense in the early 1980s—a spiritual malaise that the 1986 nuclear disaster at Chernobyl only reinforced.[126] Still, Gorbachev was probably right to complain that US policies, especially Reagan's SDI initiative, sought to "exhaust the Soviet Union economically."[127]

The Reagan defense buildup did indeed put pressure on the Soviets, but to begin to understand how much one needs to appreciate the magnitude of military burden that the Soviet's own choices had imposed on the USSR's economy. Marshall's insights into the true burden enabled him to provide Weinberger, Iklé, and many others with a more accurate and nuanced assessment of how the long-term competition with the Soviets was going and whether deterrence was likely to hold.

Looking ahead, the 1980s proved to be a period in which Marshall's office made great strides in understanding Soviet assessments and anticipating the likelihood of a disruptive shift in the military competition based on the marriage of precision munitions with wide-area surveillance and automated command and control. In many respects these insights flowed directly from Marshall's willingness to relentlessly challenge the Pentagon's bureaucracy and its conventional, but often self-serving, wisdom. Combined with his own lifelong quest to better understand how the world really worked, these intellectual inclinations are what made him and ONA so valuable during the latter decades of the Cold War—and what would make these same proclivities so vitally important during the tumultuous security transition that followed its end.

8

THE MILITARY REVOLUTION
1991–2000

*The next twenty years are likely to be a period of transition
to what will be a new situation in the global political-
military game. . . . [T]he management of our relations with
China and Japan will be a major aspect of U.S. strategy. . . .
[as will be coping with the] military technical revolution.*

ANDREW MARSHALL

The abrupt and surprising end of the Cold War generated new challenges
for Marshall and the Office of Net Assessment. The Soviet Union's
breakup seemed likely to consign Russia to the sidelines for a considerable period of time. This left the United States with a wide margin of military superiority. At the same time, the internal logic that had long united
ONA's Cold War balances had evaporated along with the USSR. Almost
overnight the issue of *what* key military balances to assess became a genuine
question to which there were no immediate or obvious answers.

But even before a diminished Russian Federation had succeeded the
Soviet Union, Marshall was already anticipating how the security environment was likely to change over the next couple of decades. In a September 1987 memo he sent to Iklé discussing the work he and Charlie Wolf
were doing to support the Defense Department's Commission on Integrated Long-Term Strategy Marshall wrote: "[T]he world really is going
to be quite different twenty years from now. . . . [T]he structural changes
connected with the rise of China and the military technical revolution do
not seem to be getting across to the Commission or to the other working
groups as fully as they might. Their focus appears still to be on the Soviet

Union, the US-Soviet competition, the European theater, etc."[1] By contrast, Marshall suggested to Iklé, in the decades ahead US strategy will have to deal with a rising China as well as changes in warfare stemming from the military technical revolution."[2] These two issues—the rise of China and the military-technical revolution (MTR)—would dominate much of ONA's work over the next quarter-century.

Since the 1960s Soviet military theorists had been writing openly about their belief that scientific-technical progress produces successive revolutions in military affairs (RMAs). Marshal V. D. Sokolovskiy's *Soviet Military Strategy*, which first appeared in 1962, argued that just as airplanes, tanks, and massed artillery linked by radio had given rise to a new operational concept—blitzkrieg—that revolutionized land warfare during World War II, so, too, had "modern nuclear weapons" ushered in another RMA during the 1950s and 1960s.[3] By the 1970s Soviet theorists were anticipating that "automated reconnaissance-and-strike complexes, long-range high-accuracy terminally guided combat systems . . . and qualitative new electronic control systems" would bring about still another military-technical revolution. The common characteristic of these revolutions was the dramatic increase in the combat potential they offered to those militaries that exploited them. Moreover, Soviet military theorists argued, the advantages for those militaries that embraced the new ways of fighting first could be decisive.[4]

Marshall thought it crucial that the Defense Department determine whether the Soviets were right. Three issues animated his concern. First, if the US military also came to the conclusion that disruptive changes in the character of warfare were likely over the next several decades, then it would need to engage in a period of intense innovation to develop competence in the new warfare regime. Second, whether or not the Pentagon leadership agreed with the Soviets that a new MTR was under way, as long as the Soviets thought so US policy makers would have to take that into account when pursuing efforts to deter Soviet coercion or aggression. Third, if the United States and the Soviet Union had fundamentally opposed views on the character of future warfare, it would be important to identify ways in which the United States could hedge its bet against the possibility of being wrong, lest the Soviets gain a major advantage in the military competition.

Marshall felt the Soviets were onto something. During his work on the future security environment for CILTS he, Charlie Wolf, and their working group concluded that the Soviets were "correct in their assessment that the advent of new technologies" would revolutionize warfare.[5] With this in mind Marshall began tapping his modest research budget to fund historical assessments of how military innovation had occurred during past periods of revolutionary changes in warfare. He contracted Williamson Murray and Allan Millett, two eminent military historians at the Ohio State University, to produce a three-volume study of military effectiveness during the two world wars and, most relevant, between the wars when intense military innovation took place.[6] Leading the revolution on land was the German military, which developed the blitzkrieg form of warfare by leveraging developments in mechanization, aviation, and radio communications. At sea the rise of naval aviation led to the battleship's being displaced in World War II by the aircraft carrier as the capital ship of the major naval powers. Land-based air power also came into its own during the interwar years 1918–1939, enabling the emergence of an entirely new mission: strategic aerial bombardment. To defend against the strategic bombing of a country's war economy the British (and later the Germans as well) leveraged modern sensors and communications to field integrated air defenses—the first modern battle networks. Marshall hoped this research would provide some clues as to why some militaries were able to exploit a major shift in warfare while others—to their great peril—lagged behind.

Around the same time he encouraged Steve Rosen to explore the topic of military innovation. Rosen's award-winning book *Winning the Next War*[7] would be an important source of insights on the factors that enabled, or retarded, innovation in military institutions. Marshall also suggested to Jim Roche and Barry Watts that they might consider examining what he saw as problems associated with the metrics, or measures of effectiveness, used to choose among the alternatives under consideration or, in the case of historical battles or wars, judge the results. Marshall knew that while identifying the right MOEs was difficult under the best of circumstances, doing so was especially daunting during periods of disruptive changes in the character of war and the competitive environment. Later, after Marshall had tasked Andrew Krepinevich to assess the MTR, the work of Rosen, Roche, and Watts would become important sources of insights for his assessment.

As with his light-handed supervision of ONA's Cold War balances, Marshall suggested topics bearing on the MTR and encouraged members of St. Andrew's Prep to look into them. But he certainly never told them what to think or what conclusions to reach. As Andrew May, another member of St. Andrew's Prep who would become Marshall's right-hand man at ONA in the early 2000s, aptly put it, Marshall "never, that I can remember, instructed me on what to write, or still less on what to think. He has never come out and said something I had written was wrong. He instead has offered only the most indirect of guidance."[8] Aaron Friedberg seconded May's observation, recalling, "Like all the best teachers Andy never tells you what to think, but instead has a way of drawing your attention to what he considers to be important questions and offering encouragement when he senses that you may be headed in a fruitful direction."[9] Marshall's mentoring approach has been successful in no small part because, as his friend James March observed, "Very few smart people can tolerate anonymity, but Andy can."[10]

With the Cold War apparently winding down, Marshall decided his office would undertake an assessment as to whether the Defense Department should accept the Soviet view that a military-technical revolution was underway. He told Krepinevich that it would be done "in a very, very different way" from ONA's previous Cold War assessments.[11] Krepinevich, an Army officer, had joined Marshall's staff in October 1989, having served on the defense secretary's personal staff since 1986. A West Point graduate, Krepinevich had been sent to Harvard by the Army to earn his master's degree prior to returning to teach at the US Military Academy at West Point. There he and Jeffrey McKritick, both of whom would later work for Marshall, served in the Social Sciences Department.

Krepinevich had been brought onto Weinberger's staff in 1986 partly at the behest of Graham Allison, who was then the dean of Harvard's Kennedy School of Government and working part-time as a consultant to Weinberger on strategy. Allison had encountered Krepinevich when the young officer was a student at Harvard and felt that he could help the defense secretary in preparing his annual Department of Defense report to the Congress. Krepinevich was later given responsibility for preparing Weinberger's other leading annual public document, *Soviet Military Power*, which summarized the ongoing buildup of the Soviet Union's military capabilities. When Weinberger asked Krepinevich what he thought of the early *Soviet Military Power* publications, he responded by pointing out that because they focused exclusively on the Soviet side of the competition, they failed to provide the reader with a sense of where the United States stood relative to the USSR or where the NATO countries stood relative to the Warsaw Pact. A discerning reader could not gauge whether the United States and its allies were improving their position or not. What *Soviet Military Power* needed, Krepinevich said, was a net assessment. Weinberger agreed and Krepinevich then turned to ONA for help, the same office in which McKitrick was serving as Marshall's lead analyst on the NATO–Warsaw Pact military balance. In briefing the European assessment to members of Congress, McKitrick had impressed then senator Daniel Quayle. After Quayle was elected vice president, he asked McKitrick to join his personal staff. McKitrick's abrupt departure led to Krepinevich's joining ONA as McKitrick's replacement.

Even before Krepinevich had finished the latest edition of *Soviet Military Power* for Weinberger and moved to ONA, Marshall recognized that his office would need to begin looking beyond the Soviet-oriented assessments that ONA had been producing since the 1970s. Thus when Marshall met with his new military assistant in September 1989, he emphasized that Krepinevich would not be doing a traditional assessment of the military balance in Central Europe. The next NATO–Warsaw Pact balance would require a new structure, he said, with greater emphasis on longer-term trends. The Soviets, Marshall told Krepinevich, were talking about a coming military-technical revolution. Your job, he said, will be "to look at the ten- to fifteen-year time horizon and ask yourself: Who will think through this period of change correctly?"[12]

In the months that followed, in addition to his research on military revolutions, Krepinevich worked to come up with an outline or structure for the European Central Front assessment that would satisfy Marshall. As fate would have it, he was to gain access to considerable data and some insights into what the coming revolution might look like from the 1991 Persian Gulf War. On August 2, 1990, the Iraqi dictator Saddam Hussein ordered his armed forces to launch a full-scale invasion of Kuwait. Only three years earlier Iraq had agreed to a ceasefire with Iran after eight years of brutal warfare. The fighting had left Iraq heavily in debt, primarily to Kuwait and Saudi Arabia. Saddam pressured both countries to forgive Iraq's war debts, but was rebuffed. Faced with little to show for the costly war he had started, other than debt and growing internal instability, the Iraqi leader began accusing Kuwait of exceeding its production quota for the Organization of Petroleum Exporting Countries (OPEC), which he declared constituted a form of economic warfare. Tensions escalated during the spring and summer of

1990. After Saddam Hussein failed to receive what he considered sufficient concessions from Kuwait, Iraq invaded. Within two days nearly all Kuwaiti resistance had ceased and the small country was occupied by Iraqi forces.

Condemnation of Iraq's aggression was swift and widespread. Even Saddam's traditional sponsor, the Soviet Union, supported UN Resolution 660, which demanded that Iraq withdraw its forces from Kuwait. Simultaneously, President Bush began assembling a coalition to forcibly evict the Iraqis if diplomacy failed. While Iraqi forces secured their hold on Kuwait and began preparing defenses along the Kuwaiti-Iraqi border with Saudi Arabia, the coalition began a massive military buildup in the region. Although diplomatically isolated and facing overwhelming military power, Saddam Hussein maintained his position that Kuwait was now a part of Iraq.

On January 17, 1991, the US-led coalition, having exhausted all diplomatic options, launched Operation Desert Storm against Iraq. American forces led the way, with the Navy launching highly accurate Tomahawk cruise missiles while the Air Force struck with its new F-117A stealth fighters armed with precision-guided munitions (PGMs) to cripple the Iraqi air defense network and fracture its command and control systems. It was the first large-scale use of stealth aircraft against a significant military power,[13] and the first intense application of PGMs to achieve the operational and strategic objectives of a campaign.[14] Within days the coalition established clear air superiority over Iraq. By the war's second week, Iraqi aircraft began abandoning the fight and flying to Iran for sanctuary. Over the next six weeks the air campaign continued in the skies over Iraq, followed on February 24 by a US-led coalition ground force offensive. The combined air-ground operation produced one of the most one-sided engagements in modern times, as coalition forces quickly drove the Iraqi Army from Kuwait in what became known as the "100-Hour War." On February 28 President Bush declared a ceasefire and proclaimed the liberation of Kuwait.

For many, Marshall included, the 1991 Gulf War provided strong evidence of the boost in military effectiveness made possible by the use of stealth aircraft, precision-guided munitions, advanced sensors, and the global positioning system (GPS) constellation of satellites the United States had deployed in the 1980s. Following the war Soviet military theorists, working in the shadow of the collapsing USSR, concluded that "the integration of control, communications, reconnaissance, electronic combat, and delivery of conventional fires into a single whole" had been realized for the first time,[15] essentially crediting the US military with being the first to field a reconnaissance-strike complex. This was not quite true. Although the necessary components had been present in the theater they had not been integrated into a comprehensive battle network.[16] Nonetheless, the evidence was growing ever harder to ignore that advances in military technology were starting to change in fundamental ways how future wars would be fought.

The US military's performance in Desert Storm confirmed for many senior US military leaders the wisdom of the changes they had made since Vietnam. Given their success, they saw little need to change their existing doctrines, operational concepts, organizations or military systems. To quote a well-known military aphorism: Why fix it if it ain't broke?

Marshall, who was looking much further ahead, had a different reaction. He was concerned that the changes the American military would need to make were unlikely to occur until the Pentagon's leadership articulated "a convincing case for the declining utility of current approaches to war as well as the benefits of transformation."[17] Despite the progress Krepinevich was making on the MTR assessment, Marshall worried about the feasibility of trying to project how the competition in reconnaissance-strike operations would unfold over the next fifteen to twenty years. ONA's Cold War balances had generally only looked five to eight years ahead. Marshall therefore began pressing Krepinevich on how he was structuring the assessment.

Marshall also began soliciting opinions and advice from outside ONA, something he had not done in the past with the office's Cold War balances. In August 1991 he convened a meeting of external experts to brainstorm how the MTR assessment might best be approached. Eliot Cohen and Barry Watts were in attendance, as was Chip Pickett. Frank Kendall,[18] OSD's director of tactical warfare programs participated, along with Air Force colonel John Warden, head of the Air Force's Checkmate staff element, which had played a prominent role in planning the Desert Storm air campaign.[19]

Marshall began the meeting by stressing the potential importance of this assessment for the United States' long-term competitive position. The military that "gets the MTR right," he said, would have a major advantage over its enemies in the next war, similar to the edge that the Germans' development of blitzkrieg had given them over France and Great Britain in May 1940. Another point that emerged from the discussion was that the United States was at a very early stage in the emerging precision-strike regime. Using the analogy of blitzkrieg's development during the interwar years, Marshall believed that US precision strike capabilities during Desert

Storm were, at best, analogous to where the development of blitzkrieg was in the early 1920s. Krepinevich even speculated that Desert Storm might be closer to Great Britain's first large-scale use of tanks in the November 1917 Battle of Cambrai. There was also discussion of the likelihood that the precision-strike regime would threaten a lot of service "rice bowls," Pentagon jargon for the military's preferred programs and forces. The group also agreed that different nations might follow different paths in pursuing the MTR, which meant that Krepinevich's assessment had to take into account the divergent paths open to various US competitors. Finally, as with all ONA's assessments, Marshall reminded everyone that his office was not in the business of telling the services what to do. The assessment would be purely diagnostic in character.[20]

Shortly thereafter, Marshall approved the general structure for the assessment. The outline argued that the process leading to an MTR can be initiated when militaries field new capabilities made possible by advanced technologies. But the sort of discontinuous leap in military effectiveness associated with a true MTR generally requires not only new capabilities but the development of new operational concepts (or ways of employing the new capabilities) as well as new organizational arrangements. Marshall thought this "formula" would work, and instructed Krepinevich to refine the outline with an eye toward having a detailed draft by the end of the year. He set late 1992 as the target date for a completed assessment.[21]

By late 1991 word was beginning to circulate around the Pentagon about Marshall's MTR assessment, including his intention to involve a wide range of military officers and civilian defense experts to help with the analysis. Given Marshall's reputation for challenging the conventional wisdom and his direct line to the defense secretary, he soon found himself approached by senior officials offering advice. One such official was Vic Reis, the Pentagon's director of defense research and engineering (DDR&E). Reis had a broad background in both advanced technologies and government. Having earned his doctorate at Princeton, he had served at MIT's prestigious Lincoln Laboratory, and in government as deputy director of the Defense Department's Defense Advanced Research Projects Agency (DARPA).

Reis met with Marshall and Krepinevich in mid-November. He described the rapid advances in information technology, referencing Moore's law about the rate at which the power of microprocessors was growing.[22]

Advances in information-related technologies, Reis said, were almost certain to continue beyond the next decade. He went on to say that once use of the Internet reached critical mass around the world, it would bring about profound changes in the way people lived, with uncertain implications for America's security. These developments in information technology, Reis concluded, *were* the military-technical revolution.

After some reflection, Marshall and Krepinevich disagreed with Reis's perspective. Information technology per se was certainly important, they conceded, but the MTR was also about how those advances might be exploited by various nations to gain advantage in military competitions. They reiterated their view that to master the emerging precision-strike regime the US military services would need more than technological advances or their applications to hardware. They would also need to explore new operational concepts and associated changes in military organizations aimed at enabling them to execute new ways of fighting.

A related insight, which emerged from a DARPA brainstorming session on the MTR that Marshall had Krepinevich attend, was that the potential for dramatic growth in the ability to scout over great distances would enable precision munitions to be employed at longer and longer ranges, even against mobile targets. As a result, the new warfare regime would very much become a contest between "hiders" and "finders." Wars involving rival reconnaissance-strike complexes would be waged not by individual systems but by networks linking systems together—by a "system of systems."[23] In such an environment anything that could be seen and targeted was at high risk of destruction—especially force elements that remained stationary.

After the DARPA session Marshall decided to convene a group of senior experts to solicit their views on the MTR. Invitations went out to some retired Army leaders such as General (Ret.) Edward "Shy" Meyer, General (Ret.) Paul Gorman, General (Ret.) Donn Starry, along with Admiral William Owens, and Colonel John Warden. Some members of St. Andrew's Prep—Graham Allison, Eliot Cohen, Chip Pickett, Jim Roche, and Stephen Rosen—were also brought in, along with several distinguished senior defense civilians including Al Bernstein, Johnny Foster, and Frank Kendall.

Gorman, Meyer, and Starry had been regarded as among the Army's brightest and most capable general officers during the turbulent period of the Vietnam War and the "hollow Army" that resulted. After the war Gorman established the Army's National Training Center, which revolutionized training. Meyer became one of the Army's youngest and brightest

chiefs of staff, and Starry was the animating force behind the AirLand Battle doctrine that had proved so successful in the 1991 Persian Gulf War.
Like his Army counterparts, Bill Owens was considered among his service's brightest officers. Owens had commanded the Navy's Sixth Fleet in
the Mediterranean during the 1991 Gulf War, and went on to serve as vice
chairman of the Joint Chiefs of Staff. As dean of the Naval War College's
Strategy Department, Al Bernstein had helped build it into the most respected higher educational institution in the US military. Also prominent
among the attendees was Johnny Foster, a legend in defense science circles
due in large part to his contributions as the director of the Lawrence Livermore National Laboratory, director of the Pentagon's DDR&E office, and
chairman of the Defense Science Board, among other senior posts.

In the end this group supported Marshall's conviction that an MTR
assessment was needed and should be an ONA priority. It was becoming evident that in a mature precision-strike regime, achieving "information dominance" over the enemy would be critical. Achieving information
dominance, in turn, would require by fielding a "systems architecture" that
could facilitate identifying targets over the breadth and depth of the theater and move that information quickly and reliably to those who needed
it—especially to the "shooters." Against mobile or moving targets the time
between sensing a target and engaging it would have to be greatly com-
pressed. Finally, information dominance could not be achieved until these
capabilities were denied to the enemy.

In addition to meetings with senior military and civilian defense officials
Marshall also used war gaming to advance the assessment. The idea was to
explore how a NATO-Warsaw Pact conflict might be affected if US forces
had more mature reconnaissance-strike capabilities than they had enjoyed
in the 1991 Persian Gulf War. Even before Desert Storm began, Marshall
asked Krepinevich to begin reorienting the P-186 effort in this direction.
The BDM staff had been developing a detailed simulation for the Central Front. So Krepinevich directed them to incorporate the planned Soviet
ground force withdrawals announced by Gorbachev as well as an enhanced
version of the primitive US reconnaissance-strike complex that had made
its debut in the First Gulf War.[24]

Krepinevich's baseline scenario assumed that the Soviets had withdrawn
their forces from Eastern Europe back into the USSR, and that NATO
forces, per the reunification treaty, were prohibited from basing in the territory of the former East Germany.[25] This created a large no-man's-land

between the NATO and Soviet forces. This was done to put a premium on the information dimension of warfare, enabling an examination of the "hider-finder" competition between two forces when they started the conflict hundreds of miles apart.

As with any war game, the results were not definitive but suggestive. Marshall and Krepinevich were not looking to predict the outcome of a future war in Europe in which one side or both had reconnaissance-strike complexes. Rather, they hoped to glean insights into a novel situation, and they were not disappointed.

Thanks to NATO's clear advantage in extended-range precision-strike forces linked by battle networks, neither the Warsaw Pact's long-standing "WUV advantage" in armored division equivalents nor its greater numbers of tactical aircraft translated into success on the battlefield, as it had in the Cold War–era games. In part this was due to the shift in how the two sides' forces were positioned. Unlike the scenarios in which the forces started out toe-to-toe along the Central Front, now Soviet forces—tanks, armored troop carriers, and self-propelled artillery—that had been withdrawn to the western USSR had to cross hundreds of miles before they could effectively engage NATO forces at close range. While attempting to transit this distance the Soviet forces were subjected to repeated attacks by US extended-range precision-strike forces. These attacks so decimated the Soviet forces that only remnants of those that left the USSR were able to transit the no-man's-land and engage NATO forces in close combat. The ability of US forces to see deep and to strike deep, with precision, had a profound influence on the game's results.

With WEI/WUVs and other Cold War metrics offering a poor explanation for the BDM simulation's results, it was clear that precision strike required new measures of effectiveness. During the Cold War in Central Europe the primary measures of combat potential had been metrics, such as armored division and tactical fighter wing equivalents (ADEs and TFWEs). In the BDM simulation ADEs and TFWEs simply failed to reflect the devastating potential of one side possessing reconnaissance-strike complexes when the other did not. And if both sides had these advanced capabilities, and gaining information dominance would assume even greater importance and would require still more new metrics. The results seen in the BDM simulation suggested not only that some key military service programs should be accorded lower priority, but that the dominant service cultures would be challenged as well. Frank Kendall pointed out that when this happened the resistance to the idea of an MTR from the services would be intense. Thus even before ONA's MTR assessment was finished, it seemed likely that the military services would be inclined to resist making the changes needed to master the new way of fighting.

Concern over service resistance to revolutionary change led Marshall to begin thinking about the problem of bringing about innovation in large organizations—in this case the US military. As Steve Rosen asked in 1988, "When and why do military organizations undergo major innovations in the way that they operate?"[26] Convinced that a major shift in how future wars would be fought was in the offing, and recognizing that in the wake of Desert Storm the services would see little need for major innovation, Marshall began encouraging members of St. Andrew's Prep and other scholars to explore past examples of successful innovation with an eye toward answering Rosen's question.

Rosen's initial research suggested that a military did not have to lose a war to embrace innovation.[27] Subsequently, in his 1991 *Winning the Next War*, he explored twenty-one cases of successful and unsuccessful military innovation, ten of which he examined in detail, and six of which occurred in peacetime.[28] The case that most intrigued Marshall was the US Navy's development of carrier aviation during the interwar years 1918 to 1941.

This case study revolved around a simple question: Why during this period had the US Navy succeeded in developing carrier aviation while Great Britain's Royal Navy, despite having developed an early, commanding lead in carrier aviation during World War I, fell behind not only the United States but Japan by the eve of World War II? Rosen's answer was that "peacetime military innovation occurs when respected senior military officers formulate a strategy for innovation, which has both intellectual and organizational components."[29] Specifically, "Peacetime innovation has been possible when senior military officers with traditional credentials [i.e., members of the military service's dominant culture] . . . reacting to a structural change in the security environment, have acted to create a new promotion pathway for junior officers practicing a new way of war."[30] He went on to argue that "Rather than money, talented military personnel, time, and information have been the key resources for innovation,"[31] The talented people, time, and information were to be found in the military services. Civilian political leaders, he added, "do not appear to have had a major role in deciding which new military capabilities to develop."[32]

Rosen's conclusions were clear. The United States could not count on its huge advantage in resources to guarantee it would master reconnaissance-strike and be the first to transform its military to the new way of war. Since the services were the engines of innovation, it would be important to get them to buy in to the idea that a major shift in the character of war was not only possible but, indeed, likely. And ways would have to be found to gauge progress in this endeavor. This meant that new measures of effectiveness would need to be identified and adopted by the services if they were to make sound decisions regarding future capabilities. As Schlesinger had argued in the late 1960s, and Roche and Watts reiterated in 1991, choosing appropriate analytic measures is seldom easy, particularly for higher-level, strategic problems. This point was hardly news to Marshall in the early 1990s. He had known it since the 1950s. But the work of Rosen on innovation, and of Roche and Watts on MOEs, underscored the difficulties of getting the US services, fresh from their triumph in the 1991 Gulf War, to embrace the MTR.

In July 1992 Krepinevich completed the first version of the MTR assessment. Throughout the rest of the decade the paper would have an enduring influence on the post–Cold War defense debate, both within the United States and abroad. The assessment benefited greatly from Marshall's mentoring of Krepinevich and the contributions of St. Andrew's Prep and many others outside ONA. But it especially benefited from Marshall's intellectual flexibility to approach a strategic question—Is an MTR in the offing?—in a way that was radically different from how ONA had assessed the key military competitions of the Cold War.

The first issue the MTR assessment tackled was explaining what constituted a military-technical revolution. As Krepinevich wrote,

> A Military-Technical Revolution occurs when the application of new technologies into military systems combines with innovative operational concepts and organizational adaptations to alter fundamentally the character and conduct of military operations. Therefore, such revolutions are characterized by:
> Technological Change
> Military Systems Evolution
> Operational Innovation
> Organizational Adaptation

These elements combine to produce a dramatic improvement in military effectiveness and combat potential. The rate of transition into a new military-technical regime will also be influenced by the geopolitical environment, and the nature of the military-technical competition.[33]

The assessment went on to suggest that once the current MTR matured, armed forces that embraced the new way of war might see their "military capabilities increase as much as an order of magnitude or more" compared to pre-MTR forces that existed over the previous 10–20 years.[34]

In the early 1990s it was unclear to Marshall or Krepinevich how the military-technical revolution of the late twentieth century would play out although history offered some possibilities. Competitors might be slow to grasp and exploit the full potential of revolutionary technologies and systems, as occurred in the American Civil War. Then both sides persisted in trying to wage war in the open, Napoleonic-style, but ended up fighting in trenches around Petersburg, Virginia, in a manner not terribly dissimilar from the trench warfare along the Western Front in World War I. Or one side might recognize and exploit the potential of emerging technologies to gain a decisive military advantage, as happened with Germany's use of blitzkrieg during the first few years of World War II. Or the leading military competitors might all exploit the power of an MTR, as happened with the development of nuclear weapons and ballistic missiles by the United States and the Soviet Union after 1945.

The MTR assessment suggested that in embracing transformation military organizations would experience the "progressive blurring of the distinction between—and the increasing fusion of—space air, land, and maritime operations, to the point where most operations become multidimensional in nature."[35] This would be facilitated in part by the "growing importance of space as a major medium for conducting and supporting military operations." Leading militaries would benefit from the "emergence of aerospace operations; i.e., the linking of space systems with extended-range air systems (e.g., UAVs [unmanned aerial vehicles], cruise missiles) and a variety of sensors in an entirely new type of military operation." These developments would lead to an "increase in non-LOS [line-of-sight] fires relative to LOS fires" because "direct contact will generally be avoided by those who have achieved information dominance and who possess the means to exploit it."[36]

In these areas the 1992 assessment anticipated with remarkable accuracy many of the steps that US military would take over the next two decades to develop precision-strike capabilities and information networks. But those steps by no means guaranteed that the United States would continue to lead the revolution. As Krepinevich assessed the situation in July 1993:

> The revolution seems to have arrived *operationally*, at least in part, in the [1991] Gulf War. There various systems and networks began tentatively to realize the enormous potential of integrated operations to the point where deep-strike architectures (DSAs), or reconnaissance-strike complexes (to use the old Soviet parlance) made their first appearance. However, we have yet to integrate the information networks we have developed for reconnaissance, surveillance, . . . target acquisition (RSTA), and battle-damage assessment, with the network(s) of weapon systems ("shooters").[37]

The last point was especially illuminating with regard to much of what transpired subsequently within the US military. Integrating sensors and precision-strike elements into battle networks that could respond in near-real time to strike relocatable, moving, emergent, or fleeting targets proved far more difficult than anyone imagined in the early 1990s. The US military is still working on this problem, however much success Special Forces and more traditional shooters, such as strike aircraft, have had against insurgents and terrorists in Afghanistan, Iraq, and elsewhere.

From a US perspective the saving grace up until fairly recently has been the fact that no other country has had the technology, resources, or inclination to try to match the United States in precision-strike and battle networks. Only over the last decade or so have China's development of anti-access/area-denial (A2/AD) capabilities[38] based on long-range sensors, highly accurate ballistic and cruise missiles, and the pursuit of "informationized" operations has begun to pose a serious challenge to US power-projection forces in the western Pacific. Even so, China's A2/AD capabilities, while exploiting MTR technologies and weaponry, are regionally focused, whereas US precision-strike capabilities can span the globe. Consequently Marshall's view has consistently been that a *mature* MTR regime has not yet arrived, and will only do so once "the other guys would have a lot of the same precision-strike capabilities" as the United States.[39]

Nevertheless, the 1992 MTR assessment was prescient in anticipating a growing challenge to long-standing US approaches to overseas power projection. Whether in Europe and the Pacific during World War II, in Korea during 1950–1953, in South Vietnam and Thailand during the Vietnam

War, or in Saudi Arabia and Kuwait during the 1991 Persian Gulf War, the United States' approach to projecting power has been the same: American forces would deploy into the theater of operations through major ports and air bases that were effectively sanctuaries from enemy attack. Then, once forces had been built up to a sufficient level, offensive operations would be undertaken against the enemy, using ground forces and strike aircraft operating from forward bases. This basic approach was again utilized in the Second Gulf War in 2003. Foreshadowing the emergence of A2/AD threats, the assessment warned that the price of projecting power in this manner

> will change markedly as this military revolution matures. Forward bases— those huge, sprawling complexes that bring to mind such places as Malta, Singapore, Subic Bay, Clark Air Base, and Dhahran—will become great liabilities, not precious assets. The reason is simple: as Third World states acquire significant numbers of . . . [long-range strike] systems (i.e., ballistic and cruise missiles, high-performance aircraft) and enormously more effective munitions (i.e., smart bombs; nuclear[,] chemical, and biological weapons), these bases will become very lucrative targets.[40]

Thus,

> Rather than deterring potential aggressors, these bases' "sudden" vulnerability will deter their owners [i.e., countries hosting US forces at these bases] from acting to deter or thwart aggression. Their occupants will find themselves in the uncomfortable (and certainly unintended) role of hostages to the growing military capabilities of Third World nations. Rather than acting as a source of assurance to friends and allies in the region, these bases will be a source of anxiety. . . . Rather than a source of stability in a crisis, the bases will likely encourage one side or both toward pre-emptive strikes: either against the base before its assets can be dispersed, or against the potential aggressor in an attempt to disarm it of its . . . [long-range] strike capability.[41]

As for naval forces operating close to an enemy's homeland, the assessment found that

> Forward-deployed naval forces may be able to offset the future liabilities of forward bases, but only partially and probably not for very long,

as currently configured. The traditional carrier task force or surface action group possesses neither the mobility nor the stealth to function as the spear tip of forcible entry operations.[42]

Although these and other problems were anticipated in ONA's 1992 and 1993 MTR assessments, two decades later the US military is still searching for ways to deal with them. The Air Force's posture remains heavily biased toward short-range fighters and fighter-bombers tied to a few increasingly vulnerable overseas forward bases, while the Navy continues to accord primacy to aircraft carriers equipped with short-range strike aircraft for force presence and power projection. These institutional preferences have persisted even though China, the country Marshall had identified in 1987 as the United States' next major rival, has continued fielding increasingly advanced A2/AD capabilities. These observations underscore the difficulties of bringing about innovative changes in large organizations.

ONA's 1992 MTR assessment raised the possibility that the paths various American competitors might choose in adapting to the emerging changes in warfare could be different from that taken by the US military. One possibility was that the US military might retain a substantial advantage in long-range conventional precision strike for a decade or more, which turned out to be the case. This reading of how the MTR could unfold led directly to Admiral William Owens's notion of dominant battlefield awareness (later dominant battlespace awareness or DBA), which envisioned the emerging US "system of systems" providing near-perfect information on enemy forces throughout an area roughly the size of North Korea, thereby dissipating the fog of war.[43] ONA conducted a number of war games and simulations aimed at exploring DBA. However, these efforts raised more questions than they answered.[44] Worse, as Marshall and Krepinevich realized early on, crushing American dominance in long-range precision strike was likely to incentivize adversaries that could not compete with United States in this new way of warfare to be drawn to nuclear weapons as a way of offsetting American conventional dominance.[45]

A second possibility of how the MTR might unfold was that the United States would eventually face one or more competitors with comparable precision-strike capabilities. In that case, as Marshall suggested in 1993, "long-range precision strike" would become "the dominant operational approach" of militaries sufficiently advanced to exploit the MTR and would play prominent roles in power projection, war at sea, and in space.[46] In other words, future wars between major powers could be decided primarily by opposing reconnaissance-strike complexes engaging one another over long distances and achieving information dominance would become increasingly central to the outcomes of battles and engagements.

Yet another possibility was that in the interim lesser US adversaries might devise other, less sophisticated ways of offsetting the US military's enormous advantage in precision strike. Krepinevich labeled this kind of enemy the "Streetfighter State." What he had in mind was a Third World enemy that combined "some of the sophisticated technologies of the Cold War era with . . . unconventional strategies and operational concepts" and a willingness "to accept a disproportionate amount of punishment (to include collateral and environmental damage) if necessary to accomplish its strategic objectives."[47] To achieve its objectives the Streetfighter State would

> pursue its plans for aggression by emphasizing the social dimensions of strategy. That is to say, the aggressor would attempt to exploit those aspects of the U.S. social culture that would inhibit the effective application of American military power. Specifically, acts of aggression would be low-intensity in nature and ambiguous in execution, with emphasis on terrorism, subversion, and insurgency. The objective would be to commit acts of aggression in such a way that they fall beneath the threshold that would trigger a U.S. military response.[48]

Given its early lead in exploiting the MTR, the 1992 MTR assessment judged this sort of opponent to be the "most formidable threat" the US military was likely to face over the next ten to twenty years, a prediction that has been amply borne out in Afghanistan, Iraq, and Ukraine.

The first person to receive the July 1992 MTR assessment was Paul Wolfowitz, then the undersecretary of defense for policy. His response was encouraging. With Wolfowitz on board, Marshall sent the assessment to a veritable who's who of the Pentagon's top leaders. Copies went out to Defense Secretary Richard Cheney, and to the country's senior military leaders, including the chairman of the Joint Chiefs of Staff, and the Army and Air Force service chiefs, among others.

Marshall expected the assessment to generate "a lot of resistance and flak." So he was pleasantly "surprised at the degree to which people tended to agree that we were probably in a period" of revolutionary change.[49] Encouraged by the response, Marshall directed Krepinevich to undertake another cut at the assessment and pursue further research on military revolutions. The target for the next version would be late 1993 or early 1994. To get the word out and solicit more feedback he asked Krepinevich to begin presenting the findings of the MTR assessment in national security venues outside Washington, DC. That fall Krepinevich spoke at Sam Huntington's Olin Center at Harvard, the Naval Postgraduate School (NPS) in Monterrey, California, and the Los Alamos National Laboratory, among other venues. Like Marshall, Krepinevich was met with general acceptance of the idea that an MTR was possible, along with some helpful suggestions. Huntington, who heard the MTR presentation at an NPS conference, pressed Krepinevich to look more broadly at the Streetfighter problem, as did Rear Admiral Dennis Blair, then serving in the Joint Chiefs of Staff's J-8 directorate, which was responsible for providing the Joint Chiefs with assessments on new capabilities and nontraditional warfare areas.

Vic Reis encouraged Marshall to convene a high-level meeting to explore aspects of innovation. On November 10, 1992, Marshall and Krepinevich drove to Annapolis, where the meeting would be held the following day. At dinner that evening Marshall voiced his impression that feedback on the MTR assessment had been so encouraging that the issue was no longer whether a military revolution was possible; rather, the question was: What should be done about exploiting it? Terminology was a concern, however. Krepinevich recalled that his MTR presentation at the Naval War College had been introduced as the "military *technology* revolution." But as the assessment had stressed, the most difficult and important component of the MTR was not technology, but how to develop appropriate operational concepts for the new military systems and to organize forces to best employ them. By the summer of 1993 Marshall began referring to the "revolution in military affairs" as opposed to the "military-technical revolution" for precisely this reason.

The focus of the November 11 meeting was innovation in large organizations. Marshall had invited leaders from the corporate world who had struggled with how to stay ahead of the competition in rapidly changing business environments: Dr. James McGroddy from IBM, Dr. Richard Roca of AT&T, Dr. Ivan Sutherland of Sun Microsystems, and Dr. Robert Spinrad from the Xerox Corporation. Joining them were senior Pentagon military leaders—the audience Marshall most wanted to convince of the need for a vigorous program of innovation. The Air Force was represented by General Merrill McPeak, its chief of staff. The Marine Corps sent a future commandant, Lieutenant General Charles Krulak, then serving as head of the Marine Corps Combat Development Command. The Army was represented by its vice chief of staff, General Dennis Reimer who, like Krulak, would soon become head of his service. Reimer also brought along Major General John Tilelli, who would succeed him as vice chief of staff. Also attending was Vice Admiral William Owens and Rear Admiral Dennis Blair. Several key members of the OSD staff, including Paul Wolfowitz and Vic Reis, were also present.[50]

Marshall opened the meeting by noting that there had been an "amazingly good response" to the assessment, especially since in the long term "it gores everyone's ox." He went on to say that the assessment identified "a long list of areas in which we should focus." They ranged from evaluating prospective competitors to examining the potential of computer-driven simulations to support imaginative war gaming, and enhancing individual and unit training. Above all, Marshall said, was the need to identify ways to institutionalize innovation. War colleges could play a key role, he noted, again emphasizing that the assessment found the greatest challenges during past periods of revolutionary change had been primarily intellectual, not technical.[51]

After some brief comments by Vic Reis on how emerging technologies could support innovation, the industry participants discussed innovation in the business world. McGroddy led off, comparing innovation to a breakpoint—like water freezing when its temperature drops to 32 degrees Fahrenheit—whereupon everything seems to change very quickly. Progressive advances in information technology had created such a breakpoint for IBM. The proprietary technologies that had been a major source of IBM's competitive advantage were now being eclipsed by other technologies that were available to all. So, he asked: Where do you derive competitive advantage? How do you differentiate? His answer: It's in the application! When the technologies are available to all, it's in the way you *apply* the technology.

McGroddy asked the military leaders present: What technologies will you choose to emphasize? In what way? He declared that corporations that successfully innovate have organizations that are willing to take major risks. If you do not take risks, you cannot change. From his vantage point, McGroddy concluded, many organizations fail to change until crises force them to do so. This was especially true of highly successful military ones because, thankfully, they are not constantly at war and thus do not benefit from constant market feedback like corporations.

McGroddy was followed by Roca, who emphasized the need to think about what measures of effectiveness would define the new competitive environment. This starts, he declared, with identifying what you are trying to do. What are your objectives? From that, you ask yourself: How will I measure success? He cited AT&T as an example. It had undergone a culture shock after losing its telephone monopoly and having to deal with serious competitors. Prior to losing its monopoly AT&T had measured its success in terms of providing "universal service" that maximized the number of subscribers, not by the profits generated from its customers. After AT&T was broken up some executives simply could not make the mental transition from the old business model to a new and very different one. Those executives were retired because they could not accept, let alone pursue, new measures of success.

Sutherland, following Roca, emphasized the need for creative destruction, which he argued was essential to innovation. He advanced two key measures of success for the military in pursuing innovation: a willingness to let certain parts of a service "die" or fall into "bankruptcy"; and the foresight to promote and protect individuals who showed a knack for innovation from the organization's "antibodies," as he called those who benefited from the status quo and thus sought to prevent any change in it.

Spinrad was the last to present, and used his firm as a case study to reinforce McGroddy's views. As IBM had done with computers, he said, Xerox had developed a near monopoly in the copier business. It also had the deepest pockets when it came to research and development. Nonetheless Xerox was attacked by innovative competitors and saw its market share fall to 20 percent, though it had since recovered to 40 percent. Alluding to the point made by Roca, Spinrad said Xerox dramatically changed its measures of success when it began losing its monopoly. Formerly his company had focused on minimizing cost and meeting detailed product specifications. Now, he declared, the firm's independent variable was "time to market." Product specifications and cost were dependent variables.

Following a mid-morning break, the military leaders gave their presentations. Their observations were generally in line with the main themes of the MTR assessment and did not challenge the arguments about the prerequisites for innovation made by the industry participants. The industry participants were generally unimpressed by what they heard from the senior

military officers. Sutherland, for one, expressed amazement at their relatively benign reaction to the ongoing advances in information technology,
noting that by the year 2000 something the size of a small matchbox would
be able to record images, and that remotely guided robotic "rats" could be
made to carry payloads—sensors or weapons. How did the military intend
to exploit these new capabilities and defend itself against them? By 2000,
Sutherland added, computing power would increase by three orders of
magnitude. The military, he said, needed to move beyond generalizations
about advances in information technology to examine specifically how these
advances could best be applied to their advantage—that is, to engage in
creative destruction, create winners and losers, and let some parts of their
organizations, like the horse cavalry of old, die out.

At the conclusion of the presentations Marshall felt that the industry
executives had given the military leadership a very different way of looking
at the challenges of innovation, along with some stern warnings as to how
even the most dominant organizations could be brought low in a period of
dynamic technological change. But were the generals and admirals merely
paying lip service to innovation, or were they truly committed to the changes
necessary to lead their services into a new era of warfare? Some senior military leaders, notably Army chief of staff General Gordon Sullivan, subsequently made a real effort to go into business with Marshall on the MTR.
But even with a service chief on board, substantially changing the overall
direction of an entire military service proved extraordinarily difficult.

The 1992 presidential election produced additional resistance within the
Pentagon to Marshall's efforts to foster innovation in the military services. Eight days before the Annapolis meeting Bill Clinton was elected
president, turning George H. W. Bush out of office after one term. With
the change in administrations came changes in the Pentagon's senior civilian leadership, along with some shifts in the military's senior ranks.

By late November the president-elect was filling out his cabinet. He
nominated Les Aspin, chairman of the House Armed Services Committee,
to be defense secretary. During his time in Congress Aspin had earned a
reputation as an expert on defense issues. Following the 1991 Persian Gulf
War he had engaged several members of RAND's staff in an ambitious
effort to craft a post–Cold War US defense posture. Among them was Ted
Warner, who would become assistant secretary of defense for strategy and
threat reduction, a position that placed him in a position to identify future

US defense requirements. Over the years Aspin had also approached Marshall several times for assistance in tackling issues pertaining to military strategy and policy. The ONA director had always tried to be helpful, and the two had developed a friendly, if not close, relationship.

Despite their previous interactions Marshall was concerned about Aspin's stated defense priorities. The incoming defense secretary wanted to emphasize planning for near-term threats. Aspin saw this as the only way to put a floor under rapidly declining defense budgets. With the Cold War over, the new president and members of Congress were talking about reaping a "peace dividend" through dramatic reductions in defense spending. The idea that the US military, now far and away the world's most powerful, would need to adapt itself to sustain its advantage was simply not on Aspin's radar, or on that of his closest advisers. To address the problem, in January 1993 Marshall sent a copy of the MTR assessment to Aspin. He also sent copies to the incoming deputy undersecretary of defense for policy, Walter Slocombe, and to Graham Allison, who had been tapped to serve as assistant secretary of defense for policy and plans.

Quickly confirmed by the Senate, Aspin arrived at the Pentagon on January 21, 1993, the day after President Clinton's inauguration. He was immediately beset by policy and personal challenges. One concerned Clinton's campaign promise to accept homosexuals for military service. The controversial issue dragged on until December, when Aspin approved what became known as the "Don't Ask, Don't Tell" policy.[52] Gays could serve in the US armed forces so long as they did not disclose their sexual orientation. The new policy fulfilled Clinton's campaign promise but by no means entirely resolved the issue.

Aspin also found himself immersed in a crisis in the Balkans stemming from the breakup of Yugoslavia at the end of the Cold War. The country split into several new states, one of which was the multi-ethnic Socialist Republic of Bosnia and Herzegovina, formed in February 1992. The move was opposed by Bosnian Serbs, who established their own state with the support of the Serbian government. War soon broke out. The Croats and Muslims were badly outgunned, in part due to a United Nations resolution imposing an arms embargo on the region. Not wanting to oppose the British, French, and Russians, who also supported the embargo, President Clinton vetoed two congressional resolutions calling on the United States to lift it. He did, however, approve humanitarian aid (and, as later revealed, covert military assistance).

Beyond these policy challenges Aspin also experienced major medical problems early in his tenure as defense secretary that limited his activities. A serious heart ailment put him in the hospital for several days in February, after barely a month in office. In March he returned to the hospital to have a pacemaker implanted.

Given these short-term issues and developments, Marshall's concerns about the MTR and innovation were consigned to the back burner. He discovered this in mid-March when Clark Murdock, one of Aspin's aides from his days on the House Armed Services Committee, called to discuss the MTR assessment. As the new head of OSD's Policy Planning Staff, Murdock was responsible for mid- to long-range planning.

Murdock was known for his blunt manner, and his talk with Marshall proved no exception. He told Marshall that despite the assessment's initial positive reception, "Most people are not with you on where we are on the MTR. Look at our prospective competitors, they won't spend to get there." The majority of senior Pentagon leaders weren't worried about any major challenge to US military dominance arising anytime soon, he said; neither was Congress or the American people. And as for people concerned with the future of defense, well, those "people aren't looking at the interwar period, they're looking at the Gulf War" as a basis for shaping the post–Cold War military. At the end of the day, Murdock told Marshall, what the MTR assessment was talking about wasn't going to help "diddly shit in Bosnia or Somalia, and that's what people care about now." Marshall responded by reiterating his view that the United States "can exploit the potential of the MTR to derive decisive advantages against smaller opponents and to hedge against or dissuade the rise of a peer competitor."

Murdock concluded the meeting by telling Marshall that his chances of getting a hearing for his ideas would improve if ONA worked through Graham Allison rather than by trying to go directly to the defense secretary. Aspin was reading what Allison was giving him, Murdock said, but he was also very concerned about the coming deep cuts in the defense budget. If Marshall could get Allison to sign a memo to Aspin saying that the MTR challenge did not require changes in equipment or additional investments but was primarily an intellectual challenge, he might get Aspin to sign up.[53]

Afterward Marshall asked Krepinevich to draft a short memo from him to Allison along the lines suggested by Murdock, emphasizing the strategic importance of the MTR effort. Murdock took a look at the draft memo and told Marshall that to resonate with Aspin it needed to be redrafted to link the MTR to the findings of the recent Gulf War. The memo, Murdock said, needed to emphasize near-term implications of dealing with challenges along the line of the Streetfighter State, and using air power as a tool of compellance.[54]

Marshall next sent Krepinevich to meet with Ted Warner, who was leading the new administration's review of US defense strategy and programs, formally known as the Bottom-Up Review. Murdock's views on the MTR were confirmed. Warner informed Krepinevich that he was less interested in the MTR than in how Marshall's office might help him deal with near-term regional conflicts and peacekeeping contingencies, with emphasis on how to fight them more cheaply.[55]

A series of meetings between Krepinevich, Warner, and Murdock followed. At times their discussions grew rather spirited. On one occasion Murdock told Krepinevich that if there was going to be a military revolution, it would be decided in the Pentagon. Krepinevich replied that if there was going to be an *American* military revolution that was up to the Pentagon, but how other nations would deal with the MTR was up to them. Murdock reminded Krepinevich that Congress was telling Aspin that to avoid major additional cuts to the defense budget the Pentagon needed to accord top priority to dealing with near-term threats. "Only a threat-based approach sells," Murdock said. As for Murdock himself, he didn't see that MTR was "doing a good job on low-intensity conflict." As an example, alluding to the challenges US troops were encountering in their efforts to bring order to the Horn of Africa, Murdock noted, "The MTR didn't do a goddamn thing for marines in Somalia." While Krepinevich sympathized with the problems OSD's leaders were facing, he saw Murdock's objections as presenting a false choice. It was not a question of meeting either near-term requirements or preparing for a coming discontinuity in the character of warfare. Ways would need to be found to do both.

During a meeting in which Krepinevich briefed Warner and his staff on the state of his research, Warner was incredulous at his statement that systems such as the Air Force's joint surveillance and target attack radar system (JSTARS) would be vulnerable once the revolution had matured. Krepinevich's point was that any aircraft based at a fixed point on land would become vulnerable to precision-guided weaponry, which offered accuracy independent of the range to the target. Warner had a hard time accepting that an expensive system barely in production and designed to last for decades would confront such a problem.[56] He conceded that the

MTR assessment had a logic to it, but that the challenge it presented was in the distant future. Krepinevich agreed, but also noted that the scale and scope of innovation involved meant that it would take a long time to bring about.

This tension between the need to balance short- and long-term considerations was to persist over the next two decades, even as the US military's dominance began to fade. While intellectually many senior civilian and military leaders appreciated the need to stay out in front of efforts to master the coming changes in warfare, for much of the 1990s declining budgets; the pressure to deal with the recurring crises in the Balkans, Haiti, and Somalia; and the rise of two nuclear powers, India and Pakistan, drew attention from the long-term issues of the MTR toward the problems of the moment. This tendency to focus on the immediate problems at hand would persist after the 9/11 attacks, when hundreds of thousands of troops and over a trillion dollars would be spent on fighting the wars in Afghanistan, Iraq, and in global operations against terrorist groups.

In late May 1993 Marshall and Murdock met again. The latter had good news to report. Aspin had read the assessment and saw value in it. The defense secretary wanted to know how to translate its findings into action.

Marshall reiterated his position that, at least in the near-term, determining the way forward was primarily an intellectual problem for the military services. Deciding how they could best meet the challenges of the military revolution would not immediately require much in the way of funding, although some modest initiatives might be pursued. Murdock thought Marshall would be on safe bureaucratic ground in requesting funding for MTR war games and simulations. He might also get a high-level oversight body that would enable him to engage senior leaders and, if he were able to win them over, gain support for his efforts to get the services to accord higher priority to innovation.

Hoping to generate stronger support for his efforts with Aspin, Marshall met with the Pentagon's second-ranking official, deputy defense secretary William Perry. An engineer and mathematician, Perry had served in the Pentagon during the Carter administration as the undersecretary of defense for research and engineering. During Perry's tenure in that position significant advances had been made in so-called stealth technologies that promised to reduce radically the radar signatures of aircraft. Over time Perry would often, with substantial justification, be described as "the Father of

Stealth." In the late 1970s he had also initiated the DARPA Assault Breaker program that demonstrated the technical feasibility of reconnaissance-strike operations using the Pave Mover radar and missiles with terminally guided submunitions. Assault Breaker's success had led NATO to adopt Follow-on-Forces Attack as a mission concept.

In August 1992, just after the initial MTR assessment was completed, Marshall held a meeting of all the then-living directors of defense research and engineering. Perry had participated and been supportive when Marshall made the case for prioritizing and institutionalizing innovation, and had agreed with Marshall that the issues raised by the assessment were the right ones. Yet Perry was also of the view that the military revolution had largely already happened, that it had emerged from the work he had done under Harold Brown on stealth and Assault Breaker during the Carter administration. Unlike Marshall, who believed the MTR was in its very early stages, Perry believed the opposite.[57] While voicing support for Marshall's efforts at the August 1992 meeting, as Aspin's deputy Perry subsequently proved unwilling to advocate the need for major innovation, preferring instead to follow Aspin's lead. Later, after becoming defense secretary in February 1994, Perry continued to regard stealth, precision-strike systems, JSTARS, GPS, and high-fidelity simulations for training as evidence of a nearly complete MTR.[58] Marshall would have to change perceptions like these if the need for innovation was to be taken seriously by either the Pentagon's civilian leadership or the military services.

At the end of July 1993 Krepinevich completed an updated MTR assessment. Marshall read through the assessment and, over a weekend, dictated a memorandum in which he set forth his sense of how the MTR was progressing. The memo reveals his frustration with the Pentagon's new leadership: "My impression is that a lot of people sign up to the notion that a military revolution is underway, *but very few draw the significant consequences that flow from that belief*" [emphasis added].[59] Noting that Perry and John Deutch, the undersecretary for acquisition and technology, seemed "quite interested" in the idea that a military revolution might be possible, if not under way, Marshall's memo sought to describe more fully "the kinds of things that might be undertaken if they and other top-level officials become convinced that, in fact, we are in the early stages of a period of major change in warfare."[60] Marshall restated his strongly held belief that, at least early on, the principal challenge was intellectual.

The most important goal is to be the first, to be the best in the intellectual task of finding the most appropriate innovations in concepts of operation and making organizational changes to fully exploit the technologies now available and those that will be available in the course of the next decade or so. The most important thing that we can focus on in the next several years is the investigation of, and experimentation with, novel concepts of operation and new organizations to exploit the technologies available now and likely to be available in the next 20 years.[61]

Marshall acknowledged that the United States had an enormous lead in military capabilities. But he also knew that in periods of disruptive change even a large lead could vanish quickly. The corporate executives at the Annapolis meeting had described how their dominant positions had evaporated almost overnight as the competitive environment changed. And there was plenty of historical research on past military revolutions to show how dominant military advantages could be lost in short periods of time, whether it was the Royal Navy's huge advantage in naval aviation in 1918 or the US monopoly in nuclear weapons after World War II. What, he asked in the memo,

[I]s our strategy for doing well? We have to think about [the] potential emergence of major threats in the future and how we could postpone their emergence. How are we going to deal with them as they emerge? How can we position ourselves to maintain our preeminent position? A large part of this preeminence will reside in superior ideas with respect to concepts of operation and organizational innovation. Indeed, being ahead in concepts of operation and in organizational arrangements may be far more enduring that any advantages in technology or weapon systems embodying them, although designing the right systems may depend on having good ideas about concepts of operations.[62]

Marshall went on to raise several aspects of the emerging military competition he believed would be particularly important. In addition to the growing impact of long-range precision strike, a second aspect "that seems an area of major change is the emergence of what might be called information warfare."[63] The latter was especially challenging, he noted, because US modeling and simulations had done a very poor job of capturing partial or massive disruptions of command, control, and communications networks.

Finally, alluding to the issues raised in the July 1993 MTR assessment, Marshall argued that the central military problems facing the US military in the first phase of the MTR, meaning the near-to mid-term, "are power projection and peace making," dealing with emerging A2/AD capabilities and low-intensity conflicts.[64] Beyond that he foresaw a second phase of the MTR as involving "the possible emergence of a major competitor or perhaps a coalition that may challenge us."[65] Over time it would become clear just how right he was.

During the next few years, Marshall and his office became deeply involved in efforts to encourage the US military to explore the potential of what he now referred to as a revolution in military affairs. ONA would not be alone in this effort. In September 1993 Defense Secretary Les Aspin approved a DoD-wide initiative on the RMA. After succeeding Aspin the following February, Perry established a group to coordinate the effort.[66]

To explore the possible implications of the RMA five separate task forces were formed: (1) Combined Arms and Maneuver; (2) Deep Strike; (3) Naval Forward Operations, Crisis Prevention, and Response; (4) Low-Intensity Conflict; and (5) Fostering/Institutionalizing Long-Term Innovation. Marshall was given leadership of the innovation task force with the explicit goal of trying to overcome the barriers to military innovation.[67] The effort quickly absorbed most of his energies along with that of his small staff, leaving little time to pursue the sorts of balances ONA had concentrated on during the Cold War.[68] Among other things, the initiative led to a number of efforts by the military services to explore various aspects of the RMA.

For his part, Marshall continued to encourage scholarly research on military innovation. In 1996, with his sponsorship, Williamson Murray and Allan Millett published *Military Innovation in the Interwar Period*, a survey of the principal changes in war's conduct during the years between the two world wars. After considerable back and forth with Marshall over the lessons of the individual cases, Murray and Barry Watts concluded in their final chapter that, as with net assessment, no methodology or set of rules could ensure innovation would succeed. Peacetime military innovation appeared to be a highly contingent endeavor in which factors such as visionary leaders with the talent to operate effectively in bureaucracies, and plain good luck could play—and often had played—decisive roles.[69] From a management standpoint, "genuine innovation, like democratic government," was rarely "a tidy process," much less one that could be tightly managed and

controlled by senior defense officials. Indeed, attempts to eliminate the inherent messiness—including the tendency for innovation to proceed in fits
and starts—emerged as "one of the surest ways to kill innovation."[70]

Perhaps the most vocal senior military officer who supported the RMA
in the mid-1990s was the vice chairman of the Joint Chiefs of Staff, Admiral William Owens. The Goldwater-Nichols DoD Reorganization Act
of 1986 had made the vice chairman head of a special council on military
requirements—the Joint Requirements Oversight Council (JROC)—and
Owens's inclination was to try to use it to address the emerging RMA from
a joint perspective.[71] Yet, contrary to Marshall's instincts, Owens tended to
emphasize the technologies underlying the RMA at the expense of the requisite operational concepts and organizational adaptations. Owens stressed
how technological improvements in three areas—(1) sensors or ISR (intelligence, surveillance, and reconnaissance); (2) C4I (command, control, communications, computers, and intelligence); and (3) precision force—would
be the heart of the emerging "American RMA."[72]

Owens's support of this view of the military revolution led to the publication in July 1996 by the Joint Chiefs' chairman, General John Shalikash-
vili, of *Joint Vision 2010*, a conceptual template or vision statement that
committed the US armed forces to harnessing the potential capabilities of
the system-of-systems to "gain dominant battlespace awareness, an inter-
active 'picture' which will yield much more accurate assessments of friendly
and enemy operations within the area of interest."[73] Despite Owens's belief
that DBA would dissipate the fog of war, *Joint Vision 2010* stopped short of
this claim, saying more sensibly that while DBA would improve situational
awareness, decrease response times, and make the battlespace more transparent, it could not eliminate the fog and friction of war.[74]

While Marshall himself voiced no opinion on *Joint Vision 2010*, both
Krepinevich and Watts saw it as excessively focused on technology and
lacking of any sense of how other militaries would compete to offset US advantages. Watts was especially troubled by Owens's insistence that the fog
and friction of war could be largely or completely eliminated by technology.[75] He went on to publish a lengthy paper that updated the arguments
of the military theoretician Karl von Clausewitz that "friction" was inherent
in the nature of war.[76] Indeed, from NATO's 1999 intervention in Serbia to
the United States' wars in Afghanistan and Iraq, there is little, if any, evidence to support the view that technology per se can banish Clausewitzian
friction.

No matter. Marshall had lost control of the RMA "narrative." What began with a *Foreign Affairs* article by William Perry stating his views on the RMA four years earlier had blossomed into a cottage industry. Although ONA's 1992 MTR assessment had certainly started the debate and provided the lexicon in which it was conducted, alternative interpretations from all over the US security community now abounded. Such thinkers as Owens had their own version of the RMA. The services, in developing their own responses to the challenges of the RMA, often sought to use the terms and rhetoric of the debate more to protect their existing programs and budgets during the post–Cold War drawdown than to move forward along the lines Marshall was advocating. Defense consulting firms, sensing business opportunities, began passing themselves off as RMA "experts."

Given that Marshall sought a far broader audience for the MTR assessment than did the senior Pentagon leaders he had focused on at the outset, this posed a fundamental problem for him as the RMA's self-proclaimed "herald."[77] His job, he insisted, was not to tell the services how to respond to the MTR—what particular operational concepts they should embrace, what systems they should buy, or what mix of forces they should field. As he later observed, "I've been very leery about saying, 'And here is the answer for us.' In fact, I think . . . that it is the officer corps that has the moral responsibility to find the best way, and only they can do it. But in addition they're better positioned, if they really go about it. [And] . . . apart from that they have the *moral* responsibility to the people they are going to lead."[78]

If, as Marshall believed, the services were ultimately responsible for undertaking the innovations necessary to cope with the RMA, what could he and his small office do to get the military focused on the challenge as he saw it? Toward this end he devoted much of ONA's efforts in the 1990s to supporting war gaming, further case studies, and professional and academic writings on the RMA. These methods yielded some progress, although far less than he would have liked.

For instance, Marshall used some of his modest budget to establish an RMA essay contest in the military journal *Joint Forces Quarterly*.[79] He supported additional work on the development of carrier aviation during the interwar years, having been impressed by the excellent research of Tom Hone, Norman Friedman, and Mark Mandeles on how the US Navy had succeeded in developing this new form of naval warfare. A talented member of the ONA staff, Navy Commander Jan van Tol, condensed their research into a short paper so that Marshall could hand it out to others as an example of what he had in mind.[80] Van Tol and James FitzSimonds, another naval officer on ONA's staff during this period, found themselves increasingly involved in teasing out some of the implications from various RMA workshops and war games ONA sponsored. By mid-1995 they had concluded that the data fusion problem at the heart of effective battle networks was "the long pole in the tent of achieving and exploiting" Admiral Owens' notion of dominant battlefield awareness.[81]

ONA's RMA war-gaming efforts also owed much to Michael Vickers, a former Army Special Forces officer who later became a CIA case officer and eventually the Pentagon's undersecretary of defense for intelligence in 2011.[82] Vickers is that rare combination of the man of action who is also a first-rate strategic thinker. During the late 1980s he had been instrumental in the successful US campaign to support the Afghan mujahideen (guerrillas) in their insurgency against Soviet occupation forces, a role later made famous in the book *Charlie Wilson's War*.[83] Having left the CIA to pursue his master's degree under Eliot Cohen at Johns Hopkins's Nitze School of Advanced International Studies, Vickers had signed up for a net assessment course being taught by Krepinevich. Vickers's term paper for the course examined the issue of military revolutions. This 1993 paper so impressed Krepinevich that he shared it with Marshall, who too was taken by Vickers's work. This led to an internship for Vickers in ONA. Through his discussions with Marshall, Vickers developed the idea for a series of war games looking out to the time when the RMA had "matured"; that is, when both the United States and its major rivals had fielded the long-range precision strike capabilities described in ONA's MTR assessments. Vickers called the game series "20XX," given that the warfare regime he had in mind would not likely emerge until some indefinite time in the early twenty-first century. He ran the games at the Center for Strategic and Budgetary Assessments (CSBA), the think tank Krepinevich had established in 1995 shortly after retiring from the Army.[84]

Another avenue Marshall pursued in trying to foster innovative thinking about the RMA was to establish fellows programs that would expose promising young officers to the challenges of the MTR. Two such programs were the Secretary of Defense Strategic Studies Group (SecDef SSG) and the Secretary of Defense Fellows Program. Marshall had originally raised the issue with Robin Pirie in December 1992 and shortly thereafter with Admiral Owens. Pirie had run the Chief of Naval Operations' Strategic Studies Group (CNO SSG) and as a young officer Owens had been selected as a member of the group. Each year the CNO SSG identified a handful of midcareer Navy officers who had shown great promise of reaching flag rank. Over the course of the year they spent in the CNO SSG, they were assigned to assess an issue of strategic importance to the Navy's leadership. They were given access to senior Navy leaders to get their views on the issue. At the end of the year they reported their findings to the chief of naval operations. The program's principal objective, said Owens, was not to have the officers produce an excellent assessment; rather it was to stretch their minds, to get them to think on a strategic level, rather than within their familiar world of operations and tactics. Marshall liked the idea and persuaded Secretary Perry to establish his own SSG.

Marshall then went one step further, recommending to Perry that he establish a Secretary of Defense Fellows program. Like the SecDef SSG, the program would involve a small number of hand-picked officers from all the services. Unlike the SecDef SSG, however, each of these officers would spend a year at a civilian corporation challenged by the need to conduct strategic planning in a field characterized by rapidly emerging technologies and shifting forms of competition. In brief, such companies faced challenges similar to those that would be confronted by a military organization doing planning in an environment of dynamic change and, hence, great uncertainty.

Both the SecDef SSG and the Fellows program were approved by Perry in September 1995.[85] The SecDef SSG was eventually discontinued under Perry's successor, William Cohen. However, the Defense Fellows program has endured, with an unusually high percentage of its officers later selected for flag rank.

By 1996, with the RMA debate fully under way, Marshall began thinking about the long-term character of the Office of Net Assessment in the post–Cold War security environment. He felt that by the end of 1997 his office would have done what it could to jump-start DoD's innovation efforts. By then, he thought, ONA could begin refocusing its time and energy on more traditional net assessments.[86]

It says much about the durability of Marshall's 1972 conception of net assessment, which he had originally developed for assessing the long-term competition with the Soviet Union, that it remained relevant in the post–Cold War era. Marshall felt that despite the "slightly greater level of uncertainty about potential opponents and [the] vagueness of national goals," the long-term-competition framework remained "appropriate" and with it the analytic framework he had originally developed while in charge of the Net Assessment Group on Kissinger's National Security Council.[87] Marshall also retained his belief formed in the late 1980s that Asia would "be an increasing focus of attention for us." As for the RMA,

> The potential RMA is important, but we need to shift to address the net assessment issues and questions it raises. This could include a focus on areas that we think, based on our broader analysis, are going to be key areas of competition between military establishments. These now look like long-range precision strike and information warfare, but we should consider additional areas.
>
> Power projection as impacted by the proliferation of weaponry of all kinds (but in particular, nuclear, chemical, biological weaponry) is a very important issue. Indeed it seems that it interacts with the likely near term focus of some RMA efforts within the United States military. New technology and new operational approaches may allow us to deal more effectively with small or intermediate powers who possess a small number of nuclear, chemical, biological systems. It is only later that larger opponents may arise in Asia, with China a specific possibility.[88]

While Marshall would continue to devote attention to RMA-related issues, by the late 1990s he was redirecting ONA's focus to China—the other long-term challenge he had foreseen in his 1987 memo to Fred Iklé—and to the spread of advanced military capabilities, including weapons of mass destruction, and nuclear weapons in particular. Although the military revolution would not occupy a central place in US defense strategy that Marshall had hoped during the early 1990s, by 2000 he had succeeded in framing the terms of the debate regarding the character of future warfare. But he was also frustrated by the absence of a well-defined US national security strategy, one that could enable him to craft net assessments that would be of greatest benefit to senior Pentagon leaders in dealing with the long-term strategic management of the Defense Department and the military services. His frustration would continue during the next administration headed by President George W. Bush.

THE PIVOT TO THE ASIA-PACIFIC REGION
2001–2014

*I see the function of net assessment being to provide to top
leadership a frank, well thought out, unbiased diagnosis of
major problem areas and issues that they should pay more
attention to. Because of the situation we are in, those people
are going to have a lot of problems.*
                                        —ANDREW MARSHALL

The first decade of the twenty-first century saw major changes in Marshall's personal life. In December 2004, after a long struggle with cancer, Mary Marshall died. Their marriage had lasted just over fifty years. The two of them had been exceptionally close due in no small part to Mary's keen intelligence and her ability to accurately assess people at first meeting. Like her husband, Mary Marshall was able to distinguish lesser minds from those worth listening to, and she had little patience for the former

When Mary died they were still living in the same rental apartment on Virginia Avenue near the Watergate complex that they had moved into "temporarily" in 1972—or so they thought at the time. The Marshalls had always planned to return to their house in Los Angeles. But as the years in Washington turned to decades Mary had become involved the Washington scene. Among other things she became active with the capital's Textile Museum and had run its membership program for many years. Despite her husband's recurring declarations that they would return to California within the next year or so, the couple never did.

Marshall did not remain a widower for long. Mutual friends prevailed upon him to him to take Ann Smith, who was also widowed, to dinner. They met at the Foggy Bottom Metro near the State Department and walked to Marshall's favorite French restaurant. During dinner Ann found herself doing most of the talking until she finally asked her date to tell her about himself. She soon discovered that they had much in common. They were both born and raised in the Midwest, came from English stock, claimed the same religion, and could even have passed each other on Michigan Avenue in Chicago after Ann had dropped out of college to study dance in the late 1940s. After dinner, as they walked back to the Metro, Marshall asked Ann whether she would be his companion for an occasional dinner or social event and she agreed.

A few weeks later he invited Ann to accompany him on a trip to France. Although the trip had to be rescheduled, soon thereafter he asked her whether she would go with him to Normandy, to the beaches where American forces had invaded the Continent on D-Day. Ann demurred, saying she'd cry all over the beach and embarrass him. But Marshall, who had been there five times before, persisted, saying that the Americans buried there were his and Ann's generation and they owed it to them to pay their respects.

Ann did go to Normandy, and their relationship deepened quickly after that. She and Marshall married in November 2006. Soon after the wedding Marshall finally relinquished the apartment on Virginia Avenue he had shared with Mary. He moved into Ann's apartment on Prince Street in Alexandria, a few miles south of the Pentagon, and rented an adjacent apartment to serve as a library for his large collection of books. The apartment complex was just a few blocks from the King Street Metro Station, allowing Marshall to continue commuting daily to the Pentagon by Metro as he had been doing since the Blue Line had opened in 1977.

The new century found Marshall continuing to think about how best to make the transition back to the kinds of net assessments his office had done during the Cold War. This by no means meant ignoring the RMA, but his intention was to return to analysis that more closely resembled ONA's Cold War balances than the 1992 MTR assessment. But what kind of assessments should be undertaken, and against which competitors? The United States suddenly no longer faced a major, long-term adversary armed with thousands of nuclear weapons. In 1972 Marshall had characterized net assessment as a careful comparison of where the United States and its allies stood militarily relative to the USSR and its allies. But now, with the Soviet Union a memory and no other large competitor in sight, what useful comparisons could be made? And what assessments would be most valuable to the Pentagon's top decision makers?

In the early 1970s the overarching imperative to avoid general nuclear war had led Schlesinger and Marshall to agree instinctively on the strategic nuclear, European, maritime, and military investment balances as the key Cold War assessments. In the post–Cold War security environment careful net assessments were no longer needed to realize that the US military enjoyed wide margins of advantage, especially in conventional conflicts against lesser adversaries such as Saddam Hussein's Iraq. This was one unmistakable lesson of 1991 Persian Gulf War, and it would be reiterated in Serbia in 1999, Afghanistan in 2001–2002, and Iraq in 2003.

Nevertheless, as Marshall began thinking about ONA's future, it seemed to him that the goal of net assessment—to highlight "for the top-level decision makers emerging or already existing problems" or, equally important, "opportunities that they might wish to focus on"—remained the same as it had been during the Cold War.[1] He also thought that his long-term competition framework from the late 1960s was still appropriate. What had changed was the United States' external security environment.

In 1996, in preparation for considering ONA's future direction, Marshall had offered some tentative suggestions on possible future assessment topics. Asia seemed likely to matter more to US security in the years ahead than Europe. The maturation of the RMA would continue to be of interest. The proliferation of weaponry of all kinds would certainly challenge the US military's ability to project power overseas, and in the wake of Deng Xiaoping's economic reforms China had become a rising power.[2] But his initial attempt to define the future focus and direction of ONA was derailed by the office's continued absorption with issues related to the RMA.

Marshall returned to the issue of future net assessments in October 1999. This time he convened a two-day offsite with his staff. Again, however, little progress was made toward deciding on the right topics for future assessments or how best to pursue them. In fact, much of the discussion did not get beyond some of the observations Marshall had offered in his 1996 memorandum: that US attention would shift from Europe to Asia, especially to China; that maturation of the RMA would greatly alter how future wars would be fought, and that the proliferation of advanced weaponry—nuclear weapons in particular—would likely continue. Due to the lack of progress toward articulating a future focus and direction for ONA, Marshall ended the offsite early on the second day.[3]

The following spring Marshall made another attempt to set down his thoughts about the character of future net assessments. He noted that for the moment the United States' military capabilities dominated those of all other nations, especially in conventional warfare. Although US leaders had not sought military preeminence, it was understandably something that they were reluctant to give up.[4] This observation suggested that future ONA assessments might center on prospective changes in the competitive environment, particularly those that could degrade or offset the United States' military preeminence. Through their public declarations, military writings, or both, countries such as China, Russia and Iran had clearly demonstrated a strong desire to erode the US position.[5]

One prospect that emerged from this line of thought was that the United States should focus on a prioritized portfolio of key military competitions and try to remain well ahead in them as long as possible. Going down this path would require OSD and the services to reach some degree of consensus on a manageably short list of the strategically important military competitions. At the same time Pentagon leaders would need to identify capabilities of declining value and reduce funding in these areas. Finally, in those military competitions that appeared to be gaining in importance, the United States would want to establish (or maintain) an early lead through appropriate investments.

Despite his periodic attempts to reassess ONA's long-term research agenda, Marshall still had not settled on a way forward by late 2002. The following March, as another US-led coalition was preparing to invade Iraq, he held a one-day workshop on the role and focus of ONA over the next decade.[6] At the workshop's end he articulated several conclusions. First, ONA needed to increase its efforts on aspects of the future that others in the national security establishment were not considering, but which could profoundly influence US security. Meanwhile, the office would continue its analysis of issues relating to a mature precision-strike regime and a world in which the spread of nuclear weapons had not been contained. Second, he reaffirmed the need to pursue efforts to identify those areas of military competition that would dominate the future security environment and how the United States might best position itself to prevail in these competitions.[7]

Yet it was not until mid-2004 that Marshall formally committed ONA to a new long-term research agenda. He identified three main balances: a regional assessment focused on the military balance in Asia, emphasizing the need to hedge against the rise of China; a functional assessment of power projection in an anti-access/area-denial environment; and an assessment of the durability of the US advantage in realistic combat training that had emerged after the Vietnam war.[8] To these balance areas he added a series of studies aimed at foreseeing how the security environment might be changed by advances in undersea warfare, the biological and human sciences, directed energy weapons, demographic decline in Russia, and possible calamities, such as an AIDS epidemic in Asia. He also mentioned the possibility of supporting studies in new areas such as policing and stability operations, understanding the kinship societies that dominate the Muslim world, and assessing the United States' long-term economic prospects.[9]

The time Marshall had taken to decide on the direction that ONA should take in the post–Cold War security environment reflected several considerations. One, of course, was his own long-standing view that it was important to determine the right issues—the right "questions"—for ONA's future work before beginning the effort to look for "answers" to these questions. A second issue concerned the extent to which the framework for net assessment that he had originally developed in 1972 could be adapted to the post-Cold War security environment. Instead of being able to focus on a single, large competitor, the United States was confronted with a much more complicated world, especially after al Qaeda terrorists succeeded in flying airliners into the Pentagon and both towers of the World Trade Center on September 11, 2001. The final factor was the frustrating outcome of the defense strategy review Marshall conducted in the months before 9/11.

In early 2001, soon after Donald Rumsfeld had returned to the Pentagon for a second tour as defense secretary under President George W. Bush, he asked Marshall to conduct a review of US defense strategy. Given the mutual respect that had emerged between the two men during Rumsfeld's first tour at the Pentagon, it was natural for Rumsfeld to ask Marshall for such an assessment.

The circumstances in which the ONA director received this assignment reveals much about Rumsfeld and his view of Marshall's value. Instead of asking Marshall to meet with him in the privacy of his office, Rumsfeld invited him to lunch in a Pentagon dining room where senior officials often ate. As Rumsfeld later wrote, he wanted to send a message to others in the Pentagon that he "valued Marshall's thinking," particularly on strategy.[10] Rumsfeld also recalled that during the lunch Marshall had warned him that the Pentagon bureaucracy was as resistant as ever to change.

On Saturday morning, February 3, only two weeks after Bush's inauguration, Marshall met with Jim Roche and Barry Watts to begin outlining a defense strategy based on the idea of maintaining US military dominance for as long as possible. Marshall's senior military assistant, Navy captain Karl Hasslinger, soon joined the effort along with Jeffrey McKitrick and Andrew May, who were both then at the consulting firm Science Applications International Corporation doing work for ONA.

By late February the rapidly evolving outline for the review had identified four goals for an advantage-driven defense strategy based on the premise that the United States enjoyed a remarkably dominant and favorable geostrategic position:

1. Preserve and extend [key or vital] U.S. military advantages as long as possible;
2. Use the dominant U.S. position to secure a prolonged peace;
3. Keep future American wars small, limited in means, and far away by maintaining strategic buffers and overseas allies;
4. Discourage or delay the emergence of a major or "peer" competitor.[11]

As sensible and straightforward as these goals seemed at the time, it was not long before the strategy review started to lose focus. In a February meeting with Rumsfeld's deputy, Paul Wolfowitz, to discuss the strategy review, Marshall was informed that Rumsfeld and others did not like such terms as *dominance*. Successive rounds of wordsmithing ensued, rapidly undermining the document's clarity as more and more OSD political appointees began to make inputs. Along with responding to this guidance, Hasslinger and May were soon making slides to convert the strategy paper into a briefing for President Bush.

On March 21, 2001, Rumsfeld and Marshall met with the president to present the strategy review. Rumsfeld did the briefing. Afterward Hasslinger reported that the briefing had gone better than even the most optimistic among the Department of Defense staff could have hoped. The session had lasted about ninety minutes. The president had been interested, engaged, and had asked probing questions. And at the end Bush had said he was "very pleased" with the effort so far and told Rumsfeld and Marshall to continue developing the strategy.[12]

In response to some of Bush's questions, Rumsfeld gave Marshall an opportunity to say what he thought needed to be done. The ONA director stressed the importance of experimentation and engaging bright young officers who could think creatively about the future. The president replied that he had talked to a lot of officers but had not found very many of them who thought innovatively about the future.[13]

The responses of the service chiefs to the strategy review were not nearly as supportive as Bush's had been. They had received copies of the evolving draft the same week as the presidential briefing by Rumsfeld and Marshall. By then comments on earlier drafts had generated requests for examples of the key areas of advantage to be maintained going forward. The version of the review that went to the service chiefs listed five candidate areas: air superiority, undersea warfare, space, robotics, and realistic combat training. This list was intended to be illustrative—at most tentative examples of the sorts of areas of military competition in which the US military would want to remain well ahead. Marshall certainly did not intend for this list to be the final word. Nevertheless, the morning after this version of the strategy review was circulated to the service chiefs, Karl Hasslinger found himself in the office of the Army chief of staff, General Eric Shinseki, trying to explain why mechanized ground forces had not been included in the list of key areas of competitive advantage. In short order the other service chiefs began voicing similar objections, naming dozens of areas they considered vital and wanted to protect at all costs. Inexplicably Marshall, who should have known better, had been bushwhacked by the Pentagon bureaucracy.

At this juncture the easiest thing to have done bureaucratically would have been to let the services expand the portfolio of key military competitions. But there were compelling reasons to resist doing so. First there was the reality that resources are always limited in relation to perceived wants and needs—in this case to those of the Pentagon. The advantage-based strategy was designed in part to compel hard choices—to set priorities— regarding which military competitions would be most important over the next ten to fifteen years and therefore the ones to invest in preferentially. The other side of this coin was, of course, that over time the Defense Department would need to make the necessary divestitures and reductions in funding to military competitions of lessening value.[14]

Second, to be of genuine value, it was impracticable for such a list to comprise dozens or scores of "top" priorities. Back in 1976 Marshall and Roche had argued that nations had distinctive competencies, and part of formulating a long-term US strategy was using one or more of the United States' distinctive competencies to develop competitive advantage.[15] But they were also aware that nations, like corporations, do not have dozens or scores of distinctive competencies. As the business strategists C. K. Prahalad and Gary Hamel had pointed out in the case of corporations, "Few companies are likely to build world leadership in more than five or six fundamental competencies. A company that compiles a list of 20 to 30 capabilities has probably not produced a list of core competencies."[16] Adding even a portion of all the war-fighting areas and capabilities that each of the four military services deemed important would be tantamount to trying to do everything rather than making strategic choices. The result would not be a coherent strategy—it would not be a strategy at all.

Recognizing these realities, Marshall encouraged the services to embrace a portfolio of no more than nine or ten truly key military competitions. If such a consensus could be reached it would also resolve the problem of deciding what areas ONA should assess going forward. The portfolio of key military competitions would be the areas in which senior decision makers would want to know how the United States was doing relative to the competition: Were the competitors catching up, making no progress, or falling further behind? How could the United States improve its position in the key competitions? How might it hedge against the possibility it had chosen the wrong competitions to emphasize?

During the strategy review Marshall failed to get the services to agree on a short list of key competitions. Nevertheless, he persisted in his efforts. After 9/11 Marshall made further attempts to develop a consensus. In both 2002 and 2003 he had Chip Pickett head ONA summer studies on defense portfolios as a way of moving from a threat-driven to a capability-based planning paradigm. In 2005 Andrew May led another summer study that focused on the sources of US advantage rather than on the key military competitions themselves.

None of these efforts succeeded in pushing the services toward agreement on a short list of key military competitions. Preoccupied with the ongoing wars in Afghanistan and Iraq, and determined to protect their preferred programs and budgets, the services resisted developing the defense strategy that the president had initially encouraged. The short list of candidate areas for preferential investment ONA had suggested became so controversial that it was deleted from the body of the final version of Marshall's strategy review, appearing only in an annex.[17]

Other events, starting with 9/11, undoubtedly limited the time and energy Rumsfeld was able to devote to advancing an advantage-based defense strategy. The 9/11 attacks were quickly followed by Operation Enduring Freedom, the campaign against the Taliban in Afghanistan. In 2003 came the turn of Iraq. The previous year the UN Security Council had passed Resolution 1441, calling upon Iraq to cooperate with UN weapon inspectors to verify that it had completely eliminated any stocks of weapons of mass destruction (WMDs) and was not engaged in trying to create any more. After months in which Iraqi dictator Saddam Hussein failed to conform to the resolution despite repeated demands that he do so, a US-led coalition invaded Iraq, overthrowing Saddam's regime in a mere three weeks of major combat operations.

The Second Gulf War—Operation Iraqi Freedom—drew the United States and its allies into what became a protracted counterinsurgency campaign in Iraq just as Operation Enduring Freedom did in Afghanistan. A key caution in Marshall's late February 2001 strategy outline had been to "keep future American wars small, limited in means, and far away" from US shores.[18] Operations Enduring Freedom and Iraqi Freedom were indeed fought far from American shores, but the Bush administration neither kept these conflicts small, nor the means required to wage them limited. Especially in the case of Iraq, prior to the initial three weeks of major US combat operations too little thought or planning were given in advance to dealing with the long-term consequences of overthrowing Saddam Hussein and occupying the country.

Only two days before Operation Iraqi Freedom began, Watts asked Marshall whether there was any evidence that senior Pentagon decision makers might embrace either the strategy of advantage or the specific areas of US competitive advantage that had been discussed since 2001. His response was, "No."[19] As Iraq began descending into lawlessness and insurgency, the war increasingly occupied the time and energies of senior Pentagon leaders. By the time Robert Gates replaced Rumsfeld as defense secretary in November 2006, the situation in Iraq had deteriorated into a civil war between the majority Shiites and the minority Sunnis, with al Qaeda and covert Iranian elements engaged as well. Marshall's efforts on strategy formulation had been overtaken by the combination of deep-rooted resistance of the military services to change and external contingencies stemming from the protracted wars in Afghanistan and Iraq. In the final analysis, the 2001 strategy review serves primarily as a cautionary tale about just how difficult it can be to bring about fundamental changes in the thinking and priorities of large organizations.

Crafting good strategy in competitive situations is rarely, if ever, easy. One reason is that the adversary seeks very different outcomes, and the interaction between the two sides is never predictable.[20] The post–Cold War efforts by a succession of administrations to develop national security and defense strategies have been no exception.

After the 2001 strategy review, two topics dominated ONA's work: the rise of China and the maturation of the revolution in military affairs, particularly as they related to the challenges that would arise in a mature precision-strike regime. From a net assessment perspective, China's rise and the spread of nonnuclear precision munitions were intimately entwined. Over time China's development of long-range precision strike capabilities would provide it with the means to begin shifting the military balance in the western Pacific progressively in its favor, increasing the risks that the PRC would one day be tempted to undertake coercive or aggressive acts against US allies and partners in the region.

China's pursuit of A2/AD counterintervention capabilities was part of a wholesale military modernization effort that the People's Liberation Army (PLA) began in the mid-1990s. But even before China's A2/AD capabilities and military modernization grew into major concerns in the Pentagon, the issue of how best to cope with China's economic resurgence became a political lightning rod. The impetus behind this controversy went back to the *New York Times*'s publication in March 1992 of excerpts from a classified draft of the Pentagon's Defense Planning Guidance (DPG).[21] By then the 1991 Persian Gulf War and the abrupt collapse of the USSR had made it clear to senior US policy makers that the era of containing Soviet power was over and the United States was at a historical turning point. This was reflected in a speech President Bush delivered at the Aspen Institute on August 2, 1990, in which he announced that by 1995 US active forces could be safely reduced by 25 percent. Unfortunately Bush's effort to articulate a post–Cold War security strategy was immediately lost in the noise of Iraq's invasion of Kuwait, which began that same day.

The national security strategy that the White House published the month after the end of the 1991 Gulf War only mentioned what became known as the military's Base Force as an afterthought. A more comprehensive formulation of a national security policy and defense strategy for the post–Cold War world was clearly needed. To address this Defense Secretary Dick Cheney and Paul Wolfowitz, Cheney's undersecretary for policy, directed Wolfowitz's deputy, I. Lewis "Scooter" Libby, to begin developing a DPG that would go beyond what Bush had enunciated at Aspen and in the administration's earlier, March 1991, National Security Strategy.

Libby and others involved in drafting the new strategy looked at the Truman administration's crafting of the containment policy and the Eisenhower administration's development of massive retaliation. Both Truman's NSC 68 (containment) and the Solarium exercise that led to Eisenhower's NSC 162/2 (the "New Look" and massive retaliation) had been major efforts to formulate grand strategy at a critical juncture in US history. The DPG Libby and others drafted in 1992 offers a third example of government officials "attempting to step back and think strategically about the nation's future at a very dramatic turning point in US foreign policy."[22]

The tempest that followed the *New York Times*'s publication on March 8, 1992, of excerpts from the February 18 version of the DPG draft lost sight of this broader purpose. The headline and opening sentence of Patrick Tyler's *New York Times* article highlighted the primary objective of the DPG's proposed defense strategy as being "to ensure that no rival superpower is allowed to emerge in Western Europe, Asia or the territories of the former Soviet Union."[23] Critics, even thoughtful ones, read this statement as "an unrealizable attempt at imposing global hegemony in the face of a rising China."[24] This reading of the DPG suggested that the administration's intent was for the United States to arrogate to itself the role of the world policeman and eschew collective security with allies and friends.

Later versions of the DPG were not leaked, and subsequent drafts moved further and further away from this interpretation. For example, the version forwarded to Cheney later in March instead emphasized US and allied efforts to "shape" the future security environment to "preclude hostile, nondemocratic domination of a region critical to" US interests, "and also thereby to strengthen the barriers against the reemergence of a global threat to the interests of the US and its allies."[25] Nine years later, in the Pentagon's September 2001 Quadrennial Defense Review (QDR), the idea of shaping the future security environment so it would be less threatening emerged as the US policy goal of dissuading "adversaries from undertaking programs or operations that could threaten US interests or those of our allies and friends."[26] (The QDR's other three policy goals were to assure friends and allies, deter threats to and coercion against US interests, and decisively defeat any adversary should deterrence fail.)

The notion that targeted strategy and policy choices could dissuade other prospective adversaries from competing militarily with the United States was not, of course, anything new under the sun. At the heart of Marshall's 2001 strategy review was the idea of maintaining US military preeminence in order to achieve a long peace. But the underlying notion of shaping the security environment so as to dissuade prospective competitors from mounting major military challenges to the United States went back much further. The 2001 QDR's strategy goal of dissuading military competitions can be traced back to Weinberger's adoption of competitive strategies in the mid-1980s, which in turn had its origins in Marshall's 1972 RAND paper on a long-term competition framework for competing with the USSR. The leaking of the February 1992 draft DPG had clearly created controversy over the proposed strategy of trying to dissuade potential adversaries from trying to compete with the US military. While the strategy was sound, the image of the United States as the world's policeman generated strident political opposition.

While the controversy surrounding the 1992 DPG swirled, Marshall, as usual, was looking further ahead than most everyone else. The lure of China as a vast untapped market led many in the United States, both during the 1990s and the early 2000s, to dismiss the possibility of the PRC emerging as major military competitor to the United States even within East Asia. Marshall's inclination, by contrast, has been to concentrate on what the Chinese were actually thinking and doing, ignoring the "popular wisdom" of the time. His focus was on data—on empirical research into China's long-term goals, strategic culture, history, and the evolving military capabilities of the People's Liberation Army (PLA).

To him, the starting point for any coherent long-term strategy for dealing with China's rise was, as Aaron Friedberg put it in 2000, to "see the situation plain—namely, that in several important respects a US-PRC strategic competition is already underway."[27] It would be going too far to claim that ONA's research has determined the United States' strategy toward the PRC. Yet, on the surface at least it has undoubtedly helped to frame the context of US strategy toward China in much the same way that ONA's MTR paper framed the debate over the military revolution. In the late 1990s ONA was one of the first offices in the US government to warn of Chinese efforts to begin fielding A2/AD capabilities aimed at limiting the ability of US forces to project power into the Asia-Pacific region, long considered an area of vital interest to America's security. In 2002 Marshall stated in a memo to Secretary Rumsfeld that US defense strategy required "some redirection of attention within DoD towards Asia."[28] In the same memo he recommended that the military services be directed "to plan for the types of military challenges a malevolent China may pose over the long-term, and incorporate these into service and joint war games, training and exercise programs, including routine wide-area USN-USAF [Navy-Air Force]-special forces exercises."[29]

Since then the US-China Economic and Security Review Commission has published a series of annual reports on the national security implications of China's rise, including the PLA's "area control" strategy in the western Pacific.[30] Eventually, in 2012, President Barack Obama directed a rebalancing of the United States' posture toward the Asia-Pacific region. If nothing else, this rebalancing suggests that, as with the MTR, Marshall once again managed to peer further into the future than most others in the US government.

The net assessments that Marshall's office has produced since the early 1970s remain classified except for the 1978 European and 1992 MTR assessments. However, since the Cold War ended much of ONA's outside research on Chinese economic development and strategic culture, the maturation of precision strike, and the proliferation of nuclear weapons has been unclassified. ONA's research in these and other areas provides a window into Marshall's thinking about various military competitions since 2000.

One of ONA's most fruitful areas of research during the Cold War was the long-term effort of John Battilega's Foreign Systems Research Center to translate and understand the Soviet literature on operations research. Over time this line of research produced systematic insights into Soviet military strategy, doctrine, planning, and technical calculations by revealing just how different Soviet assessments of the USSR's competition with the United States were from US and NATO assessments.[31] Once the Cold War ended, Marshall directed Battilega to reorient his research center to focus on China and continued to fund research into China's strategic culture by other scholars such as Michael Pillsbury.

There was every reason for Marshall to expect that Chinese modes of thought would be even more alien to American ways of thinking than the Soviet leadership's had been, and that some insights into the thinking of China's political and military leaders could be gleaned from surveying open source writings. Pillsbury's work on China, which Marshall had encouraged and supported since the early 1970s, illustrates both points. In 1995 the PLA's Academy of Military Science (the equivalent of DoD's National

Defense University) hosted a delegation from the Atlantic Council in Beijing.* Pillsbury, who was then a fellow at the Council, returned with one hundred-odd Chinese books and professional military journals.[32] While he was told that PLA officers could not publish on current military issues for security reasons, they were free to write about the future of war. The eventual result was the 1998 *Chinese Views of Future Warfare*, which contained Pillsbury's summaries and translations of a selection of the PLA writings on war's future that he had acquired in 1995.

Chinese Views contains articles on the RMA, two of which approvingly cite the ONA director concerning future warfare.[33] As Major General Wang Pufeng wrote, "Andrew Marshall of the Pentagon believes the information era will touch off a revolution in military affairs, just as the cannon in the 15th century and the machine in the past 150 years of the industrial era touched off revolutions."[34] Wang concluded that for the PLA, figuring out how to "adapt to and achieve victory in . . . information warfare," which China would face from now on, "is an important question" that its military would "need to study carefully."[35]

The evidence is now convincing that the PLA has since studied this question intensely and drawn its own conclusions. Chinese military theorists have concluded that "informationalized" war is a new type of war, dominated by "informationized" forces.[36] As a result China's rulers have firmly committed the country to building an "informationized military"— one that can dominate local wars under "high-tech conditions" by having more and better information than the opponent, even against an opponent such as the United States that is stronger in most other respects.[37] Significantly the Chinese have not only been developing a comprehensive theory of informationized warfare, but the PLA's General Staff Department has recently made organizational changes to reflect this theory.[38]

Marshall and Krepinevich, of course, had concluded in the early 1990s that the information dimension of warfare might become increasingly central to combat outcomes. If it did, then establishing information superiority over one's opponent would become a major focus of the operational art. But in making this point in 1993 Marshall's intended audience was the US military,

---

*The Atlantic Council is a nonpartisan think tank founded in 1961 to encourage cooperation between North American and European experts in the fields of political science, economics, and security studies.

not China's. Pillsbury's research, however, made it clear that the PLA had adopted Marshall's definition of the current RMA. In a sequel to his 1998 volume on Chinese views of future war, Pillsbury noted that Wang Zhenxi, a senior adviser to the China Institute of International Strategic Studies, used the same definition of the RMA as had ONA's MTR assessment.[39]

The fact that the Chinese have embraced Marshall's definition of the RMA does not mean that Chinese views on informationized operations are a mirror image of US views on cyber and information operations. To the contrary, Chinese writings about informationized war in the early twenty-first century are couched in the idioms and framework of statecraft from the Warring States period (475–221 BC) in China's ancient history.[40] The lessons the Chinese military have drawn from this period include accumulating comprehensive national power while avoiding destruction at the hands of a predatory hegemon and, should war become unavoidable, winning before the first battle by exploiting superiority in selected areas such as information superiority.

The differences between Chinese and US modes of military thought and strategic culture go even deeper than seeing the lessons of the Warring States period as being applicable to China's situation today vis-à-vis the United States. Marshall has been particularly impressed by François Jullien's analysis of Chinese thought and strategy. On the former Jullien writes, "Chinese thought . . . never constructed a world of ideal forms, archetypes, or pure essences that are separate from reality but inform it. It regards the whole of reality as a regulated and continuous process that stems purely from the interaction of the factors in play (which are at once opposed and complementary: the famous *yin* and *yang*)."[41] As for Chinese strategic thought in the Warring States era as well as in the twenty-first century, he explains, "Two notions lie at the heart of ancient Chinese strategy, forming a pair: on the one hand, the notion of a *situation* or *configuration* (*xing*), as it develops and takes shape before our eyes (as a relation of forces); on the other hand, and counterbalancing this, the notion of *potential* (*shì*), which is implied by that situation and can be made to play in one's favor."[42] *Shì* can be viewed as achieving a positional advantage that can be exploited now or in the future. While this notion resonates with Marshall's notion of gaining competitive advantage, the Chinese perspective grounded in *shì* is not regularly found in US strategic thought—especially in the area of decisions regarding the value of new military capabilities.

In light of the chasm between US and Chinese worldviews, Marshall's support of Pillsbury's work on Chinese strategic thought and culture was a natural line of long-term research for ONA. In fact it followed the same general path as ONA's efforts to understand Soviet assessments had done during the Cold War. Characteristic of Marshall's approach is that he has sought insight into Chinese strategic thought and culture from a number of researchers besides Pillsbury, to include Battilega's Foreign Systems Research Center, Jacqueline Newmyer Deal's Long Term Strategy Group, the Hudson Institute's Laurent Murawiec, and Princeton's Aaron Friedberg.

Marshall's relations with Friedberg illustrate both the former's influence as a mentor as well as the subtle impact on US strategy he has exerted through the members of St. Andrew's Prep. In the late 1970s Marshall provided office space for Friedberg in ONA to do an unclassified history of US strategic doctrine while serving as a consultant to both the NSC and ONA.[43] At the time, Friedberg was a doctoral candidate in government at Harvard University. In 1986 he completed his dissertation on Great Britain's relative decline as the world's dominant power during 1895–1905, which was published two years later as *The Weary Titan*.[44] In the preface he credited Marshall for planting the seeds for his work, adding that he was very pleased to add one more item to the long list of studies for which Marshall has been directly or indirectly responsible.[45]

Two decades after its publication *The Weary Titan* was followed by Friedberg's *A Contest for Supremacy: China, America, and the Struggle for Mastery in Asia*. Friedberg dedicated this book to the two men whom he believes have had the most profound impact on his intellectual development: Andrew Marshall and the late Samuel Huntington.[46] *A Contest for Supremacy* was motivated by Friedberg's experience late in the Clinton administration, when he was asked to review the US intelligence community's assessments of China's economic development, political stability, strategic intentions, and military power. The experience left him puzzled and frustrated by what seemed to him to be a willful, blinkered optimism that Sino-US rivalry was highly unlikely, in part because it was too dangerous to contemplate.[47] By 2011, however, the thesis Friedberg had advanced in 2000—that "there is a good chance that United States will find itself engaged in an open and intense geopolitical rivalry with the People's Republic of China"—had become more widely accepted.[48]

Friedberg summarized China's post–Cold War grand strategy for dealing with the United States and with the outside world with three axioms:

- Avoid confrontation with the global hegemon.
- Build China's comprehensive national power.
- Advance incrementally.[49]

Put somewhat differently, and reflecting the views of such Chinese military theorists as Sun Tzu, China's leaders hope to achieve hegemony in the Asia-Pacific region without fighting. But should war become unavoidable in the meanwhile, the PLA plans to achieve "victory before the first battle" through such stratagems as developing "secret weapons that strike the enemy's most vulnerable point (called an acupuncture point) at precisely the decisive moment" and mastering informationized operations.[50] Particularly against a foe as technically superior as the United States, PLA theorists increasingly see winning the information confrontation as the key to winning before the first battle.

All three elements of China's strategy are served by the PLA's development of A2/AD capabilities aimed at making it ever more difficult and costly for US air and naval forces to project power close to China's shores. The most conspicuous element of these capabilities has been the PLA's Second Artillery Force's growing inventory of highly accurate, land-based ballistic missiles, which are now estimated to number over 1,100. This missile force has the potential to place fixed targets on Taiwan and, eventually, Kadena Air Base in Japan and Anderson Air Force Base in Guam under threat of ballistic-missile bombardment. When operational the Deng-Feng-21D anti-ship ballistic missile (ASBM), now under development, could eventually threaten moving targets such as US carrier strike groups operating in the western Pacific. The Second Artillery's missiles, however, are just one component of the PLA's A2/AD capabilities. Other systems aimed at denying access to China's littoral waters, coastal areas, and airspace include over-the-horizon (OTH) radars, HQ-9 (HongQi-9) surface-to-air-missiles, ocean surveillance satellites for real-time target tracking, advanced fighter interceptors, submarines, hit-to-kill antisatellite weapons, radio-frequency jammers, cyber weapons, and ground-based lasers. Viewed in their entirety, these various systems and capabilities are intended to disable or destroy the United States' battle networks and precision-strike forces, the core elements of the RMA outlined in ONA's 1992 assessment.

As China accumulates these capabilities, and as they proliferate over time to other nations, major US rivals will be able to employ their own A2/AD forces to establish "no-go" zones into which it would be too difficult

and costly for the United States to project military power using the overseas bases and forward-deployed expeditionary forces its military has relied
upon since World War II. Granted, the costs in blood and treasure that
US decision makers might be willing to bear would depend on the United
States' stakes in any future conflict in the Asia-Pacific region. But as Marshall has repeatedly warned, the diffusion of A2/AD capabilities poses a
growing challenge to long-standing US approaches to power projection.

What are the implications for traditional power projection in a future
in which a number of nations, starting with China, possess robust reconnaissance-strike capabilities? And what might this ultimately mean for
America's role in the world? These are the kinds of first-order questions
Marshall has always raised and is still posing to the military and OSD civilians through war games, workshops, and studies. Arguably Marshall's
persistence in raising these questions has influenced US defense strategy.
The Air Force and Navy have looked at China's evolving anti-intervention
strategy in the western Pacific and concluded that there will come a day
when neither service, fighting more or less independently of the other, will
be able to project power effectively in the face of China's mounting A2/
AD capabilities. This possibility has led them to develop Air-Sea Battle as
an operational concept to defeat A2/AD threats. As the heads of the Navy
and Air Force, Admiral Jonathan Greenert and General Mark Welsh, have
written, Air-Sea Battle seeks to take down the enemy threat to US power-
projection forces by "first, disrupting an adversary's command, control,
communications, computers, intelligence, surveillance, and reconnaissance
(C4ISR) systems; second, destroying adversary weapons launchers (including aircraft, ships, and missile sites); and finally, defeating the weapons an
adversary launches."[51] To a great extent, the Air-Sea Battle concept de-
scribes the clash of reconnaissance-strike complexes envisioned in ONA's
1992 MTR assessment. Air-Sea Battle, in turn, is nested within the overarching Joint Operational Access Concept that the US military services are
developing to deal with A2/AD threats.

Marshall's views on these developments are perhaps most apparent in
the assessment of the future security environment through 2030–2040 he
offered at a 2008 dinner talk he gave to business leaders from the Chicago
Council on Global Affairs. He began by stating the obvious: the future
security environment will be shaped by such factors as demographic trends,

differential rates of economic growth, and technological developments. Second, he cited three long-term challenges confronting the United States: the long "war" with Islamic extremists; the rise of China, whose military modernization is proceeding more rapidly than anticipated; and the likely proliferation of nuclear weapons to Iran, which many think could trigger a proliferation cascade in the volatile Middle East.[52] Third, Marshall pointed out that there is an alternative—less obvious—way of looking at the future security environment. The United States is in the midst of a period of enormous change. Geopolitically these changes include the relative decline of Europe, Russia, and Japan; the rise of China; and possibly the rise of India as well. At the same time warfare itself is undergoing profound transformation due to the maturation of long-range precision strike, the military use of highly vulnerable satellites, the growing importance of undersea warfare, the blossoming of cyber threats, and the spread of advanced weaponry, including nuclear weapons as a counter to US conventional preeminence.[53] How, he asked, should the United States prepare for these developments should they play out? What is the United States' long-term strategy? Unfortunately, he noted, the crafting of an effective long-term strategy appears to be an area of growing American weakness when compared to the Truman administration's development of containment or the Eisenhower administration's adoption of massive nuclear retaliation. Consequently, Marshall concluded, much hard intellectual work remains to be done.

Pentagon decision makers would do well to take Marshall's views to heart. His observations on such matters over three score years reveal a brilliant strategic mind with an uncanny ability to peer into the long-term future and see the situation "plain"—for what is—more clearly than most around him despite the enormous uncertainties involved. His influence on US strategy over time has been closely associated with his development and practice of net assessment. That influence, though real, has mostly been indirect, but then net assessment was always intended to be diagnostic rather than prescriptive. Marshall's goal has not been to tell secretaries of defense how to respond to emerging strategic problems or opportunities, but to identify them far enough ahead that Pentagon leaders would still have time to act on the problems and opportunities net assessment revealed.

Much has changed since Marshall arrived at the Pentagon in October 1973. Yet the value of a net assessment organization able and willing to ask the hard questions about the national security environment, the future of warfare, and the state of various military competitions has not diminished despite the profound geopolitical and military-technical changes that have occurred since President Truman established the Special Evaluation Subcommittee in January 1953. Indeed, given the complexities of the security environment the United States faces today, well-crafted net assessments may be more valuable than ever before.

CONCLUSION

I think my major achievement is the training or impact I've
had on the people who have come through the office.
                                        —ANDREW MARSHALL

A ndrew Marshall's thinking about—and assessments of—long-term military competitions involving the United States have exerted a subtle but
indelible influence on American defense strategy for over half a century.
Although his development of net assessment initially focused on the Cold
War between the United States and the Soviet Union during the early
1970s, the conceptual framework he developed on the NSC has also proven
useful in assessing subjects as diverse as the ongoing military revolution, the
rise of China, and the proliferation of advanced weaponry. In all these areas, the Office of Net Assessment sought to provide the secretary of defense
and other senior defense officials with early warning of emerging strategic
problems or opportunities to gain comparative advantage over rivals.

Those who have been close to Marshall over the years—the authors
included—have been as impressed with his unique personal qualities as with
his penetrating intellect. Gifted with an extraordinary memory for people,
places, events, and substantive issues involving strategy and the future security environment, his recollections have rarely been contradicted by archival
material or other documentary sources. The accuracy of Marshall's memory is nothing short of astonishing. Time and again his exceptional recall
has enabled him to make connections between national security issues that
would elude many of today's best defense analysts.

Another of Marshall's unique qualities is that he has never been inclined
to tell senior defense officials what decisions they should make in response

to strategic problems or opportunities. His willingness to serve as an in-fluential behind-the-scenes adviser, or *éminence grise,* reflects a modest, self-effacing personality. Egos as big as Texas are hardly uncommon in na-tional security affairs, but they all too often get in the way of dispassionate consideration of the empirical facts or a willingness to challenge institu-tional shibboleths and assumptions. Despite his remarkable prescience in anticipating, far earlier than most everyone else, major strategic issues likely to affect US national security, an overinflated ego has never been part of Marshall's makeup.

In keeping with his low-key, unassuming personality, both at RAND and in the Pentagon, Marshall has resisted empire building. The Office of Net Assessment has never been a large organization. Even including sec-retaries and other support personnel, its staff never exceeded twenty and often was significantly less. Yet over the years scores of individuals have benefited from working in ONA. Over the four decades of the office's ex-istence roughly ninety people have served on Marshall's staff in various ca-pacities. Many went on to hold senior positions in the Defense Department or elsewhere. Jim Roche, who was the twenty-first Air Force secretary, is an obvious example, but so are Eliot Cohen, Aaron Friedberg, General Lance Lord, Steve Rosen, Dennis Ross, and Mike Vickers, among many others.

Rather than providing detailed guidance to members of his staff, Marshall has always been reluctant to tell them how to craft their assessments. His 1972 NSC memo "The Nature and Scope of Net Assessment" articulated a clear conception of what he envisioned net assessment to be: namely an analytic framework that would complement and, hopefully, transcend the limits of earlier, more quantitative forms of analysis. Yet, although he brought a copy the memo with him when he moved from the National Security Council to the Pentagon in 1973, he did not show it to members of his Pentagon staff. Instead of using it to explain net assessment to new members of his office, he rarely went beyond emphasizing the need for research and data, and asking for outlines. During the 1970s and 1980s Marshall was content to describe net assessment vaguely as being similar to the notion of "scanning the environ-ment," which provided little real illumination, especially to military members of his staff who had come to ONA from operational assignments and were accustomed to following specific orders.[1]

When "The Nature and Scope of Net Assessment" was finally discovered in a binder in Marshall's office in 2002, Barry Watts's first question was why it had not been shown to him when he first joined ONA in 1978. Marshall replied—with his usual wry smile—that he would have gladly shown it to anyone in his office who had asked to see it. But not knowing that the memo existed, no one had asked. Beyond modesty about his own ideas Marshall had a deeper, more pedagogical reason for not pushing his 1972 memo on members of his staff as they came aboard. He far preferred for them to work out for themselves what net assessment was, much as he himself had done over the years through relentless self-education and intellectual introspection.

This is not to suggest that Marshall would assign balance areas to new members of his office and then simply leave them twisting in the wind with respect to how to proceed. He invariably pressed his net assessors to start with outlines of their balances before attempting any drafting, and he was rarely satisfied with the first, second, or even third iteration. It was not uncommon for members of his staff to iterate through a dozen or more outlines before Marshall was persuaded that the assessment was headed in the right direction. And even after an outline had garnered his approval, it was not unknown for him to read the resulting draft and direct that it be abandoned in favor of starting over again with a fresh outline.

Yet there were also times when Marshall did not hesitate to offer fairly pithy and pointed guidance to those on his staff. In the early 1980s he brought Steve Rosen to ONA and asked him to work on an East Asian assessment. After taking an initial cut at an outline, Rosen approached Marshall expecting the same kind of praise he had invariably received throughout his career. Never using two words when one would do, Marshall responded, "Why don't you go out and do some research for a change?" adding, "You keep giving me solutions. Stop giving me solutions. Why don't you tell me what the problem is?"[2]

Marshall's emphasis on solid research and ascertaining the nature of a problem goes to the heart of his conception of net assessment. It also points to another proclivity: the importance he has always attached to asking the right questions. In this he had a rather different perspective than a number of the other leading thinkers of his day. Recall, for example, how acidly the head of RAND's mathematics division, John Williams, criticized Brodie, Hitch, and Marshall for preferring questions to concrete answers in their in their 1954 paper "The Next Ten Years," which sought to plot a course for RAND's research on strategic nuclear forces. Marshall probably never agreed with Williams's strong preference for answers versus questions. In Marshall's view higher-level issues of strategic choice were inevitably riddled with uncertainties that had to be faced, rather than avoided by jumping ahead to possible solutions. Efforts to go beyond diagnosis and produce prescriptions, he came to feel after becoming Schlesinger's director of net assessment, was likely to corrupt balanced, objective analysis. He thought it far better to concentrate on asking the right questions and leave the prescriptions to others. Returning to our medical analogy, Marshall has been the preeminent strategic "diagnostician" of his generation, identifying "security maladies" earlier than most for senior policy makers, thus enabling them to write the proper "prescriptions" in establishing the proper defense priorities.

Good questions, then, were—and remain—the core of Marshall's approach to net assessment. It is a priority that he shared with some of the most brilliant men of his time. When the Nobel laureate in economics Ronald Coase died in 2013, *The Economist* magazine began its obituary by recalling Coase's capacity to ask the right questions: "The job of clever people is to ask difficult questions. The job of very clever people is to ask deceptively simple ones. Eighty years ago a young British economist wondered: why do companies exist? The answer that he gave remains as fascinating as it was back then." Firms exist because they can reduce or eliminate the "transaction cost" of going to the market by doing things in-house.[3]

Marshall's long intellectual journey from the Great Depression and the Second World War to the University of Chicago, RAND, Kissinger's National Security Council under Nixon, and finally the Office of Net Assessment has been entwined with a series of deceptively simple but difficult and illuminating questions, among them:

- What measures, exchange calculations, war games, scenarios, and analytic methodologies can be used to assess where the United States stands relative to a given opponent in various areas of military competition?
- Did the Soviets make different assumptions about objectives, emphasize different scenarios, use different measures of effectiveness, and focus on different variables than did their US counterparts?
- Why did Soviet choices about strategic nuclear forces diverge so much from the predictions of the rational-actor model of human and organizational behavior?

- Did Herbert Simon's notion of bounded rationality and the behavior of large organizations, such as private business firms, provide a better framework for understanding actual Soviet strategic choices than the rational-actor model?
- Do anthropology, ethology, and evolutionary biology support the belief that conflict and war are part of the human condition, in which case war is unlikely to be banished from international relations?
- Should US force posture decisions during the long-term competition with USSR have focused less on arms race stability and, instead, more on how the United States might be a better, more effective competitor by exploiting areas of US advantage and Soviet weakness?
- How did USSR's gross national product compare with that of the United States and what was the burden of Soviet military programs on the USSR's economy?
- Were the Soviets right in their belief that advances in precision munitions, wide-area sensors, and computerized command and control would give rise to a late-twentieth-century revolution in military affairs?
- What would a mature precision-strike regime be like and would it constrain traditional US approaches to overseas power projection?
- If even medium-size countries will eventually be able to field anti-access/area-denial capabilities sufficient to make intervention in their regions too difficult and costly for the United States to bear, would US leaders be forced to reassess the country's role in the world, or would it be possible, through a combination of new capabilities, operational concepts, and innovation to restore the American military's freedom of maneuver?
- How has the role of nuclear weapons changed since the Cold War ended? How does the second nuclear age differ from the first? Is the "firebreak" between nuclear use and conventional precision strike narrowing?
- What are the implications—for the US military and the West as a whole—of China's rise?
- Are Chinese assessments of the military balance even more different from US assessments than were those of the Soviet General Staff during the Cold War, or as Russian assessments are today?
- Are Chinese military theorists right in thinking that being "richer" in information than the adversary will increasingly be the most critical source of advantage in future crises and conflicts?

- During the Cold War the global political-military competition was dominated by two "players," the United States and the Soviet Union. Is the world moving toward an era of a three-or four-player multipolar competition and, if so, what might that imply for strategic stability?

These are all profound questions. And, characteristically, Marshall has not asked them once or twice but again and again in the belief that they were of enduring relevance for the Pentagon's most senior leaders. He has been indefatigable in seeking better and better answers to such "simple" questions.

Marshall's development of net assessment rests on a number of intellectual themes or lines of research that he has pursued since he left the University of Chicago in 1949. In discussing these themes over the years, the one he has most often mentioned first is the importance of resource constraints in national security decisions—a fact that has increasingly eluded both civilian and military leaders in recent years due to the growing tendency to conflate the stating of desired objectives with the wherewithal to accomplish them. As Hitch and McKean famously put it in 1960, resources are always limited compared to our wants and therefore constrain our choices.

Marshall's appreciation for the ways that economics can constrain defense strategy dates back to his early days at RAND. The think tank's original mission focused on assessing the military worth of alternative force postures for the Air Force's intercontinental nuclear forces. RAND's economists recognized early on that such judgments had to take into account not merely the costs and effectiveness of various alternatives but the share of the Air Force's overall resources that each option consumed. A choice that left the Air Force unable to meet its other missions and responsibilities was not viable no matter how much bang it delivered for the buck. Such macroeconomic constraints meant, for example, that there were real limits to how many bombers and aerial refueling tanker aircraft the Strategic Air Command could buy and operate in the 1950s. Later, resource limits imposed similar tradeoffs between heavy bombers, land-based intercontinental ballistic missiles, and sea-based submarine-launched ballistic missiles.

These sorts of tradeoffs, in turn, required choices to be made about decision criteria or metrics, which RAND economists termed the "criterion problem." The engineers who dominated the think tank during its early years were inclined to specify decision criteria for judging alternative Air

Force nuclear postures in ways that ignored the fact that total resources were always limited in relation to the service's wants. The work on the criterion problem by Hitch and his economists sought to infuse RAND's analyses with a healthy appreciation of the reality of resource constraints. Yet even today, sixty years later, one finds defense analysts who argue that US defense strategy should not be "resource constrained."

Because the USSR's strategic nuclear programs were similarly constrained by available resources, this issue was also relevant to US forecasts of Soviet strategic nuclear forces, which was Marshall and Loftus' main concern in the 1950s. To be realistic, projections of the USSR's nuclear forces needed to take into account the resource tradeoffs that the Soviets themselves faced. Doing so proved easier said than done. At least part of the reason that in 1953 the CIA established a five-person branch to begin estimating the costs of the USSR's military establishment was to address this issue.[4] Nevertheless, disagreement over the magnitude of the USSR's military burden would persist to the Cold War's end.

In their early thinking about the burden issue in late 1950s Marshall and Loftus expected that excessive military spending would lead to penalties in either current consumption or investment in the USSR's economic infrastructure. But they did not yet anticipate how burdensome Soviet military programs would prove to be. In hindsight the USSR's military burden probably approached 40 percent of GNP in the 1980s and was one of the major factors that led to the collapse of the Soviet economy and the USSR itself. Interestingly, though, Marshall's experience was that even late in the Cold War some very senior US military leaders believed that Soviet military efforts did not face resource constraints. General Lew Allen, a nuclear physicist who was the Air Force's chief of staff from 1978 to 1982, doubted the viability of US strategies that sought to impose costs on the Soviets. The USSR, he believed, would always be able to find the extra resources to counter any strategic challenges that the United States might pose.[5] Through sustained intellectual effort informed by experience, Marshall knew better.

There were more subtle effects of resource constraints than those that could be measured in rubles or dollars. In the late 1970s, Marshall began supporting Murray Feshbach's research on Soviet demographics. By 1982 Feshbach was reporting that male life expectancy in the USSR had dropped from a high of 67 years in 1964 to 61.9 years in 1980.[6] Influenza, alcoholism, and limited and shoddy medical care were blamed by Western Sovietologists for this unprecedented decline in male longevity in a supposedly advanced nation. In Marshall's eyes the decline in male longevity was a concrete manifestation of the reality of macroeconomic resource constraints.

A second intellectual theme in Marshall's career—one that emerged during his collaboration with Loftus—was the importance of understanding the adversary, including the possibility that the opponent could change significantly over an extended period of time. This understanding required appreciating the bureaucratic, budgetary, and historical factors constraining incremental decisions by various stakeholders in peacetime that affected the adversary's force posture (rather than decisions made in crises or wars). Good net assessments required appreciation of the needs and objectives of the various power centers able to influence force posture decisions as well as a sense of the adversary's strategic culture. During the Cold War, the recurring inclination of most US analyses was to assume that Soviet force-posture decisions were made by a rational, utility-maximizing central authority with complete information and consistent goals. But none of these elements were commonly found in business firms or other large organizations such as military services. The sheer size and complexity of large organizations, Marshall and Loftus realized, precluded any single central authority from having either enough time or all the information needed to make all the important decisions optimally. Yet that is precisely what the rational-actor model of Soviet decision-making presumed. Beyond this view of decision making being simply mistaken, embracing the rational-actor model encouraged worst-case analyses that painted the Soviets as being "ten feet tall," to use the popular Cold War euphemism.

Widespread reliance by Western defense analysts on the rational-actor model was also connected in Marshall's mind with the reasons that both systems analysis and game theory had eventually failed to provide a satisfactory basis for higher-level strategic choices. In the case of systems analysis, James Schlesinger was right to point out that the highest strategic objectives or utility preferences "must in large part be imposed from the outside," thereby limiting the applicability of systems analysis to higher-level strategic choices.[7] The truth of the matter, he insisted, is that "for such goals as deterrence, assured destruction, controlled nuclear warfare, damaging-limiting, to say nothing of welfare benefits, we fall back, not on a firm technical base, but on what may be scientific mush."[8] As for game theory's ability to answer the complex problems of strategic choice, Marshall's judgment was that warfare was "just too complex" for such methods to have much utility.[9]

Given the limits of systems analysis and game theory, Marshall became convinced that in any long-term military competition it was vital to understand the opponent's assessments, including the weaknesses and proclivities of the adversary, such as the Soviet obsession with territorial air defenses. That is why as the Pentagon's director of net assessment he invested in Project Eager and John Battilega's Foreign Systems Research Center, funded Enders Wimbush's émigré interview project, and supported Feshbach's research into Soviet demographics and Igor Birman's work on the Soviet economy. But Marshall also paid attention to what could be learned about the perceptions and assessments of Soviet elites. Here he was influenced by Soviet émigrés such as sociologist Vladimir Shlapentok as well as by American Russian specialists including George Washington University's Peter Reddaway, the Woodrow Wilson International Center's James Billington, and Duke University's Vladimir Treml. All of these individuals and their research efforts contributed to Marshall's growing understanding of how much Soviet perceptions and assessments differed from those of most US defense officials and academics. Caspar Weinberger's competitive strategies initiative, which among other things sought to use such US advantages as precision munitions and stealth to devalue the USSR's reliance on second-echelon or follow-on forces and territorial air defenses grew directly out of the ONA's sustained efforts over more than a decade to understand Soviet perceptions and assessments.

More generally, Marshall recognized that bounded rationality—the limits of problem-solving routines and man's capacity to generate alternatives and process information—applied to US strategic choices as well as to those of prospective opponents, thereby constraining the decision-making of individuals and organizations on both sides of the Cold War. Bounded rationality also helps explain why ONA's 1992 military-technical revolution assessment was unclassified and developed with the active participation of midgrade military officers and civilians from the military services, the Office of the Secretary of Defense, and the intelligence community. Recognizing how difficult fundamental change in large organizations could be, Marshall sought to "infect" midcareer officers and analysts with the lexicon and concepts of the late-twentieth-century revolution in military affairs. Still, he never felt it was his place to prescribe the changes that the US military should make to prepare for a mature precision-strike regime or what many termed information warfare. Those choices, he believed, should be left those officers when they had reached more senior positions.

A third theme that has run throughout Marshall's career has been his approach to framing or structuring thinking about military competitions. To begin with, there are the actors, which at the most abstract level are states. But particularly from an organizational behavior perspective, it is usually necessary to consider some of the more specific actors and organizations able to influence a state's strategic choices. In the case of the United States, for instance, influential actors might include the president, Congress, the Defense Department, the Joint Chiefs of Staff, individual military services, or even certain war-fighting communities (e.g., submariners, fighter pilots, special forces operators, etc.). The actors have different strengths, weaknesses, access to resources, vested interests, and patterns of behavior. They also have goals—and strategies for attaining those goals—stemming from their histories and life experiences or cultures. Some of these factors can change more rapidly than others. Intentions and some aspects of technology can change virtually overnight, whereas demographics, differential rates of economic growth, and the earth's climate not only change more slowly but may not be entirely under the control of the actors.

The players or states, in turn, are embedded in the prevailing international security environment: the Cold War, whether it be the second nuclear age, or the conditions flowing from such things as Russian revanchism or China's rise. In this context nations develop over time a complex set of goals and seek to attain them by competing individually or by forming coalitions. The geo-strategic context of a competition can, of course, change, sometimes rapidly and radically, as happened in 1991 when the Soviet Union collapsed to the surprise of almost everyone. But the broader point is that opposing states "need to be treated entirely symmetrically" within this framework.[10] Note, too, that there is no reason to restrict the actors to states. Terrorist organizations, such as al Qaeda, its affiliates, and its offshoots are increasingly relevant actors because, since the 1950s, technology has dramatically increased the damage that small groups of dedicated individuals can inflict on nations and societies.

A fourth theme that emerges from Marshall's intellectual journey is the importance of looking at particular issues from the perspective of the long-term-competition framework that he developed during 1969–1970 after succeeding Schlesinger as RAND's director of strategic studies. This framework had antecedents, especially in George Kennan's analysis of the sources of Soviet conduct, from which the guiding principle of containment emerged. But when Marshall resurrected the idea of viewing the US-Soviet rivalry as an extended competition, he was struck by the change in perspective that resulted from this shift in focus. Up to that point in time, the standard analyses of the US-USSR strategic nuclear balance had largely focused on quantifying the immediate requirements for deterrence and the likely deaths and destruction the United States would suffer if deterrence failed. For both Pentagon decision makers and strategic analysts this focus tended to narrow attention to specific force posture and programmatic choices. Insufficient attention was paid to the more complex, evolving goals that both sides developed and pursued over the course of their extended military competition.

What Marshall realized was that embracing a long-term-competition framework allowed US strategists to broaden their focus from trying to quantify deterrence by calculating arsenal exchanges to, instead, viewing the rivals' relationship as a series of moves in peacetime aimed at improving the United States' position relative to the USSR's. This perspective would focus attention on leveraging areas of the United States' enduring comparative advantage, exploiting enduring Soviet weaknesses, imposing disproportionate costs on the USSR, and otherwise complicating the Moscow's efforts to compete effectively. The genesis of Weinberger's competitive strategies initiative is not difficult to discern in this framework which, as Marshall later recalled, transformed the way in which he subsequently viewed many defense issues, not just the US-Soviet strategic nuclear balance. The long-term-competition framework has been central to Marshall's approach to net assessment ever since.

A fifth intellectual theme that has persisted throughout Marshall's career concerns what might be termed the nonrational aspects of human behavior. This theme can be traced back to Herbert Simon's conclusion that evolution had adapted organisms to make "good enough" decisions rather than "optimal" ones.[11] This view of human decision making was reinforced by Marshall and Loftus's realization that Soviet organizations often made suboptimal decisions about the USSR's strategic-nuclear forces—such as the location of their bomber bases—that could not be explained by the rational-actor, utility-maximizing model of human behavior.

Marshall's conclusions about human decision-making led him to begin exploring the then-emerging literature on the behavior of business firms and, in the 1960s, to initiate research into organizational behavior as a way of transcending the limitations of traditional systems analysis. This line of thought was reinforced by reading and discussing with Schlesinger works on the evolutionary roots of human behavior, including Robert Ardrey's *The Territorial Imperative*, and, later, meeting Ardrey through the anthropologist Lionel Tiger, who became a regular participant in Marshall's Newport summer studies. Marshall's conviction that human behavior has inherently irrational components was reinforced by Tiger and Robin Fox's *The Imperial Animal*, which argued that evolution had wired "identifiable propensities for behavior" into the human genome.[12] Man, Tiger insists, is an "action animal" rather than a "thinking animal"; human behavior is dominated by the ability to make quick, astute choices to survive. Further evidence of human irrationality was provided by the seminal work on judgment under uncertainty by Daniel Kahneman and Amos Tversky.[13] Among other things, they found that even experienced researchers trained in statistics were prone to fallacies in making intuitive judgments about probabilities in more intricate and less transparent problems.[14] Given all this evidence, Marshall agreed with Fox's conclusion that that the human race is as likely to have a future of peace and nonviolence as one of chastity and nonsexuality.[15] Fox's conclusion in 1991 was that war is neither an institution like slavery that can be outlawed, nor a disease that can be cured, "but part of the normal human nature."[16] Hence Marshall's belief that war is an integral part of human nature. The use of military force might be controlled but never banished.

A sixth intellectual theme that has influenced Marshall's approach to analysis in general and net assessment in particular concerns the difficulties of thinking about the future. Net assessments were supposed to look ahead and highlight emerging strategic problems and opportunities that could be leveraged to gain competitive advantage. Nevertheless, his long-standing conviction has been, and remains, that it is not possible to predict either the strategic outcomes of actual conflicts or the course of military competitions. There is simply too much uncertainty. Despite the desire of senior leaders for accurate forecasts of what the future holds, the stubborn fact that the future is unpredictable has to be faced. As the economist Douglass North has written, the reality is that in human affairs we "cannot know today what we will learn tomorrow which will shape our tomorrow's actions," and the world itself is "nonergodic," meaning that statistical time averages of future outcomes can be and, more often than most people appreciate, are persistently different from the averages calculated from past observations.[17] Some of the most concrete evidence for unpredictability in protracted competitions comes from astrophysics. We now know, for instance, that the clockwork view of the planetary motion suggested by Isaac Newton's mechanics is wrong. The movement of the planets around the sun is in fact chaotic. If one looks far enough into the future—say 100 or 200 million years—computer models lose "all ability to predict planet trajectories."[18] And in strategy and international affairs as in planetary science, unpredictability can take us by surprise literally overnight.

Over the years, Marshall has advanced three main suggestions for how net assessment can look ahead to identify emerging challenges and opportunities for the United States, given that the uncertainty of the future cannot be eliminated. First, some aspects of the future are surer than others over time spans of years or decades. Examples include demographics, long-term macroeconomic trends such as differential rates of economic growth, and some aspects of technology. In the latter case, in 1997, four years before al Qaeda's successful attacks on the World Trade Center and the Pentagon, Martin Shubik pointed out that since the 1950s, the technology of killing, combined with advances in finances, communications, and logistics, had increased the lethality of a small organized group (say ten to twenty trained, dedicated individuals) by orders of magnitude.[19] Creating large-scale death and destruction are no longer the exclusive purview of nations with huge economies, large militaries and weapons of mass destruction.

Second, the use of scenarios can be valuable not as predictions so much as tools to help decision makers envision alternative futures and think through how to respond to particular situations or challenges. Here Marshall often pointed to Pierre Wack's adaptation of the theories of futurist Herman Kahn to create the scenario approach that prepared Royal Dutch/Shell's managers to cope better than their industry rivals with the abrupt quadrupling of oil prices precipitated by the October 1973 Arab-Israeli war.[20] Scenario planning, Marshall maintains, is a viable way, in Wack's formulation, of "reperceiving" reality in turbulent times or, as Peter Schwartz later put it, of taking the long view in a world of great uncertainty.[21]

Third, since the 1950s Marshall has viewed war-gaming as a useful way of exploring higher-level strategic problems. In 1950 the RAND mathematicians Merrill Flood and Melvin Dresher first posed the prisoner's dilemma, a fundamental problem in game theory that demonstrated two people might not cooperate even if it was in the best interests of both to do so. Marshall recalls that early in Flood's RAND career he observed that human beings are very good at playing games, and well-structured games can generate insights into reasonably effective strategies for coping with situations that elude the closed mathematical solutions of formal game theory.[22] Flood's observations led to a number of insightful competitive games played at RAND in the 1950s. Herbert Goldhamer was an early innovator in political or crisis games, and RAND's Strategy and Force Evaluation (SAFE) game was used to explore US and Soviet alternative budgetary options for planning and programming force postures.

Marshall has continued to fund war games as a way of gaining insights into the strategies competitors might adopt in specific situations, usually articulated through scenarios that included both well-established trends along with possible discontinuities. One of the more successful examples of scenario-based war games that provided strategic insight was ONA's Strategic Defense Initiative (SDI) series in the mid-1980s. It revealed that ballistic missile defenses with far less than near-perfect effectiveness might make the US-Soviet nuclear balance more stable. Due to the high probabilities of success—upward of 90 percent—Soviet planners insisted upon, ONA's SDI games suggested even leaky US missile defenses would require Soviet planners to target so many warheads against the US ICBM force that they could not be confident of executing an effective counterforce strike against even one leg of the US nuclear triad.

A final intellectual theme throughout Marshall's career, which is also reflective of his personality, is his realization that one should be modest about one's expectations of what can be accomplished in large organizations such as the Defense Department. Inevitably there are a lot of less-than-ideal, if not deleterious, activities and choices on defense issues that are made by the military services, the Joint Chiefs of Staff, OSD, and Congress. Only so much of this dysfunctional behavior can be prevented, an outlook captured in what has been perhaps Marshall's best-known saying: "There's only so much stupidity one man can prevent."

Because most of the assessments produced by ONA have been highly classified and written primarily for the use of the secretary of defense, any understanding of what Marshall's office has accomplished over the last four decades has been limited, even within the Defense Department. This, combined with Marshall's aversion to publicity and his refusal to define what he sees as an ever-evolving form of analysis, has led even some of those close to him to define net assessment simply as "what Andy Marshall does." Similarly, a recurring question many in the Pentagon and the strategic studies community have asked about ONA has been: What did Marshall ever accomplish?

Perhaps the most obvious accomplishment to point to is Marshall's work on estimating the burden that Soviet military programs imposed on the USSR's economy during the 1970s and 1980s. This was one of the first issues Schlesinger asked Marshall to pursue. Schlesinger told Marshall to push the CIA to reconsider its estimate that only 6 to 7 percent of the USSR's economic output was going to military programs. If the CIA's economists were correct and Soviet central planners were "miracle workers," then time was on the Soviet Union's side in their long-term competition with the United States. If Schlesinger and Marshall were right, then the situation over the long-term was more favorable to the United States, with important implications for the development of strategy.

Right to the end of the Cold War the economists at the CIA resisted Marshall's arguments on the need for a fundamental rethinking of their burden estimates. To be sure, there was the May 1976 "bombshell" when, virtually overnight the agency abruptly doubled its estimate of the USSR's military burden to 11 to 13 percent.[23] But as late as 1987, both the CIA and the DIA insisted that the burden had risen to only 15 to 17 percent of the USSR's GNP in the early 1980s.[24]

Marshall never gave up on this issue, never stopped questioning the official estimates. In 1975, Marshall estimated the USSR's military burden to be roughly double the CIA's estimate.[25] By 1988 he and David Epstein thought it was in the vicinity of 32 to 34 percent of Soviet GNP when indirect military costs and spending on the USSR's external empire were included.[26] These estimates proved closer to the truth than the intelligence community's by at least a factor of two. In the end, Marshall's small office, aided by its ability to fund outside research on Soviet military spending and the size of the USSR's economy, produced more accurate estimates of the USSR's military burden for senior Pentagon leaders than did the US intelligence agencies.

ONA's long-term research on the USSR's military burden had other consequences. In the mid-1970s the Office of Net Assessment's military investment assessments persuaded Rumsfeld that the Soviet military was outspending the Defense Department, that the trends were adverse, and that the US defense budget needed to be increased.[27] Later, under Ronald

Reagan, Marshall's work on the USSR's defense burden inspired Weinberger's decision in the mid-1980s to embrace competitive strategies as a
way of imposing disproportionate costs on the Soviets.

A second area in which Marshall has unquestionably had a profound
and enduring influence on US strategic thought was his instigation of debate over the revolution in military affairs. ONA did not merely start the
debate over whether, as the Soviets believed, advances in precision munitions, wide-area sensors, and computerized command and control were
giving rise to changes in war's future conduct comparable to the emergence
during 1918–1939 of blitzkrieg, carrier aviation, and strategic bombing.
Marshall and his staff also managed to set the terms of the debate. They
provided the debate's lexicon as well as operational concepts such as reconnaissance strike, anti-access/area-denial and AirSea Battle—terms that
have become central to debates about national security both in the United
States and abroad.

In assessing the RMA, as in many other phases of his career, Marshall
proved himself willing to push ONA in an entirely new direction from its
original focus on the key Cold War balances. Those balances had all tried
to assess where the United States stood relative to the USSR in various
areas of military competition. The MTR assessment, by contrast, was not
a balance per se but an attempt to alert Defense Department officials to
the possibility that a military revolution was under way. ONA's 1992 and
1993 assessments of the military-technical revolution differed from the Cold
War assessments in other ways because they were neither classified nor
written privately behind the closed doors of ONA, which was a sensitive
compartmented information facility. Even the most cursory comparison
of the MTR assessment with the Cold War assessments that preceded it
reveal a rare flexibility of mind and openness to new possibilities on Marshall's part that very few individuals or organizations manage to achieve.

The issue of defense transformation that emerged from the MTR debate is still with us. When Rumsfeld returned to the Pentagon in 2001 for
his second term as defense secretary, he argued in his first annual report to
Congress that, despite al Qaeda's attacks on 9/11, he viewed transformation
of the US armed forces as necessary because the challenges confronting
the United States in the twenty-first century were "vastly different" from
those of the twentieth century.[28] To be sure, the United States needed to
win the war against al Qaeda and like-minded terrorists, but Rumsfeld also
insisted that the military's transformation had to proceed at the same time.

Thus he ostensibly committed himself to transformation, just as his predecessor, William Cohen, had, at least rhetorically, during the second Clinton administration.

One can, of course, question how serious the commitments of Cohen and Rumsfeld to transformation were. As Marshall foresaw in 1987, the issue was the pace at which the United States might pursue transformational technologies and capabilities at the expense of fully funding and fielding existing programs.[29] In Cohen's case the bulk of the Pentagon's programmatic emphasis remained on existing systems and capabilities. As for Rumsfeld, in the wake of 9/11 his paradigm for transformation was the combination of air-delivered precision-guided munitions being called in against the Taliban in Afghanistan by Special Forces operators on horseback.[30] This paradigm hardly called for the transformation of even a small portion of the US military's capital stock. At the end of the day, Marshall's influence has always been limited by the willingness of senior defense officials not only to take his advice to heart but to act upon it.

His influence has been more evident with respect to the United States' emerging competition with China. Drawing from Marshall's 2001 strategy review, Rumsfeld was on solid ground in arguing that the security challenges of the twenty-first century were dramatically different from those of the previous century. In the mid-1990s China's leaders began a military modernization program that included developing A2/AD capabilities in the western Pacific, which its strategists refer to as enabling "counter-intervention operations."[31] Sustained investments aimed at denying US forces access to China's periphery have ranged from deploying over a thousand advanced short-range conventional ballistic missiles opposite Taiwan to developing medium-range antiship ballistic missiles (notably the DengFeng-21D), land-attack and antiship cruise missiles, long-range SAMs such as the HQ-9, counterspace (antisatellite) weapons, and military cyberspace capabilities.

As far back as the late 1980s Marshall had begun thinking about how the rise of China and the proliferation of precision weaponry might affect the United States' position in the Asia-Pacific region. Toward this end he began funding research aimed at better understanding the Chinese as a military competitor. A good example of such ONA-directed research is Michael Pillsbury's *China Debates the Future Security Environment*, which explored divergent schools of thought on the RMA within the PLA.[32] Despite the research into the PLA that Marshall sponsored, however, it took a decade before the US defense establishment began to respond openly to the

PLA's growing A2/AD capabilities for counterintervention operations—capabilities that ONA had been exploring in war games and through other research for more than a decade.

As the US military began recognizing China as a military competitor, however, Marshall's fingerprints were evident, especially in the responses of the Navy and the Air Force. One explicit manifestation of his concerns about China occurred when Air Force chief of staff General Norton Schwartz and chief of naval operations Admiral Gary Roughead signed a memorandum of understanding to develop Air-Sea Battle, which sought to find ways of countering China's A2/AD capabilities in the western Pacific by having the two services work together rather than separately. There is now an Air-Sea Battle Office in the Pentagon.[33] And in 2012 President Barack Obama went a step further by calling for a rebalancing the US military toward the Asia-Pacific region.[34] In short, US security policy and defense strategy is finally beginning to catch up with Marshall long-standing view that the rise of China presents a security challenge that the United States will not be able to ignore in the long run. In this respect, Marshall's contributions to US strategic thought and national security may outlast his actual career—a career that is unlikely to be surpassed in its duration and influence anytime soon.

After a long and productive career at RAND, Marshall has served every defense secretary since Schlesinger and every president since Nixon. Insofar as ONA's core mission since 1973 has been to identify emerging problems and opportunities in time for the Pentagon's top leaders to address them, he has been extraordinarily successful and influential, even if most of his success and influence has occurred behind the scenes. Characteristically Marshall has never sought credit or public acknowledgment for all that he and his office have achieved. But time and again he has managed to ask the right strategic questions and see further and more clearly into the uncertain future than those around him.

GLOSSARY OF ACRONYMS

A2/AD	anti-access/area-denial
AAF	Army Air Forces
ABM Treaty	Anti-Ballistic Missile Treaty
ACDA	Arms Control and Disarmament Agency
ADE	armored division equivalent
ALCM	air-launched cruise missile
ASW	antisubmarine warfare
ATGM	antitank guided missile
C2	command and control
C3I	command, control, communications, and intelligence
C4I	command, control, communications, computers, and intelligence
C4ISR	command, control, communications, computers, intelligence, surveillance, and reconnaissance
CAA	Concepts Analysis Agency
CBO	Combined Bomber Offensive
CENTAG	Central Army Group
CIA	Central Intelligence Agency, a.k.a. the Agency
CILTS	Commission on Integrated Long-Term Strategy
CNO SSG	Chief of Naval Operations Strategic Studies Group
COMINT	communications intelligence
CONUS	continental United States
CSBA	Center for Strategic and Budgetary Assessments
DARPA	Defense Advanced Research Projects Agency
DBA	dominant battlespace awareness
DBP	Defense Budget Project
DCI	director of central intelligence
DCS	deputy chief of staff
DCS/R&D	deputy chief of staff/research and development
DDR&E	Office of Defense Research and Engineering
DIA	Defense Intelligence Agency
DPG	Defense Planning Guidance
DSB	Defense Science Board
FEAT	Force Evaluation Analysis Team
FY	Fiscal Year

GPS	global positioning system
HEW	Department of Health, Education and Welfare
ICBM	intercontinental ballistic missile
IEDs	improvised explosive devices
ISA	International Security Affairs
ISR	intelligence, surveillance and reconnaissance
JSTARS	joint surveillance and target attack radar system
LGB	laser-guided bomb
LNO	limited nuclear option
LRA	Long Range Aviation
MIT	Massachusetts Institute of Technology
MOE	measure of effectiveness
MTR	military-technical revolution
NATO	North Atlantic Treaty Organization
NESC	Net Evaluation Subcommittee
New START	New Strategic Arms Reduction Treaty
NIC	National Intelligence Council
NIE	National Intelligence Estimate
NORTHAG	Northern Army Group
NPS	Naval Postgraduate School
NSA	National Security Agency
NSC	National Security Council
NSCIC	National Security Council Intelligence Committee
NSDD 32	National Security Decision Directive 32
OER	Office of Economic Research
OMB	Office of Management and Budget
ONA	Office of Net Assessment
ONE	Office of National Estimates
OPEC	Organization of the Petroleum Exporting Countries
OR	operations research
OSA	Office of Systems Analysis
OSD	Office of the Secretary of Defense
OSD/NA	Office of Net Assessment in the Office of the Secretary of Defense
OSR	Office of Strategic Research
OSRD	Office of Scientific Research and Development
OSS	Office of Strategic Services
OTH	over-the-horizon [radar]
PA&E	Office of Program Analysis and Evaluation
PFIAB	President's Foreign Intelligence Advisory Board
PGM	precision-guided munition
PLA	People's Liberation Army
PPBS	Planning, Programming, and Budgeting System
PRM/NSC-10	Presidential Review Memorandum/NSC-10
QDR	Quadrennial Defense Review

R&D	research and development
RAND	Research ANd Development Corporation
RMA	revolution in military affairs
ROTC	Reserve Office Training Corps
RSAS	RAND Strategy Assessment System
RUK	reconnaissance-strike complex
SAC	Strategic Air Command
SACEUR	supreme allied commander in Europe
SAFE	Strategy and Force Evaluation
SAI	Science Applications International
SAIC	Science Applications International Corporation
SALT	Strategic Arms Limitation Talks
SAM	surface-to-air missile
SAP	special-access programs
SAS	Strategic Analysis Simulation
SCDC	Strategic Concepts Development Center
SCIF	sensitive compartmented information facility
SDI	Strategic Defense Initiative
SDIO	Strategic Defense Initiative Office
SecDef SSG	Secretary of Defense Strategic Studies Group
SecDef/DCI	secretary of defense/director of central intelligence
SESC	Special Evaluation Subcommittee
SHAPE	Supreme Headquarters Allied Powers Europe
SIOP	Single Integrated Operational Plan
SLBM	submarine-launched ballistic missile
SOC	Strategic Objectives Committee
SOSUS	Sound Surveillance System
SOVA	Office of Soviet Affairs
SSG	strategic studies group
TASC	(the) Analytic Sciences Corporation
TASCFORM	TASC Force Modernization
TFWE	tactical fighter wing equivalent
TVD	geographic theater of military action
UCLA	University of California–Los Angeles
USAFE	US Air Forces in Europe
USD(P)	undersecretary of defense position for policy
USSBS	US Strategic Bombing Survey
WARBO	"Warning and Bombing" [study]
WEI/WUV	Weighted Effectiveness Indices/Weighted Unit Values
WMD	weapon of mass destruction

NOTES

Chapter 1: A Self-Educated Man, 1921–1949

1. Ford Madox Ford, *The March of Literature: From Confucius' Day to Our Own* (New York: The Dial Press, 1938).

2. Richard Courant and Herbert Robbins, *What Is Mathematics? An Elementary Approach to Ideas and Methods*, 4 vols. (New York: Oxford University Press, 1941).

3. *A Study of History*: 2nd edition [1st edition, 1934] (London: Oxford University Press, 1945), vols. 1–3; vols. 4–6 published in 1939, reprinted in 1940; and *A Study of History*, abridgment of vols. 7–10 by D. C. Somervell (New York: Oxford University Press, 1957).

4. "Murray Body Corp.; Murray Corp. of America," available at http://www.coach built.com/bui/m/murray/murray.htm.

5. Andrew W. Marshall, "A Test of Klein's Model III for Changes of Structure," master of arts thesis submitted to the faculty of the Department of Economics, University of Chicago, March 1949, 29.

6. F. A. Hayek and W. W. Bartley III, ed., *The Fatal Conceit: The Errors of Socialism* (Chicago and London: University of Chicago Press and Routledge, 1988), 14.

7. A. W. Marshall, "Early Life to 1949," interview by Kurt Guthe, January 13, 1994, 1–16. (The reference "1–16" refers to page 16 of the transcript of the first of twelve taped interviews Guthe did with Marshall.)

Chapter 2: Early RAND Years, 1949–1960

1. Angus Maddison, "Historical Statistics for the World Economy: 1–2003 AD," 2007, available at http://www.ggdc.net/maddison/historical_statistics/horizontal-file_ 03–2007.xls.

2. Stewart M. Powell, "The Berlin Airlift," *AIR FORCE Magazine*, June 1998, 50–63.

3. Harry R. Borowski, "A Narrow Victory: the Berlin Blockade and the American Military Response," *Air University Review*, July–August 1981, available at http://www .airpower.maxwell.af.mil/airchronicles/aureview/1981/jul-aug/borowski.htm, accessed November 16, 2013.

4. S. Nelson Drew, ed., *NSC-68: Forging the Strategy of Containment* (Washington, DC: National Defense University, September 1994), 23.

5. X [George Kennan], "The Sources of Soviet Conduct," *Foreign Affairs* 25, no. 4, July 1947, 575.

6. Steven J. Zaloga, *The Kremlin's Nuclear Sword: The Rise and Fall of Russia's Strategic Nuclear Forces, 1945–2000* (Washington and London: Smithsonian Institution Press, 2002), 10.

7. Thomas C. Reed and Danny B. Stillman, *The Nuclear Express: A Political History of the Bomb and Its Proliferation* (Minneapolis, MN: Zenith Press, 2009), 34–35.

8. Walter Isaacson and Evan Thomas, *The Wise Men: Six Friends and the World They Made* (New York: Simon & Schuster, 1986), 489–90, 495–97.

9. Robert R. Bowie and Richard H. Immerman, *Waging Peace: How Eisenhower Shaped an Enduring Cold War Strategy* (Oxford: Oxford University Press, 1998), 16–17.

10. George Orwell, "You and the Atomic Bomb," *Tribune*, October 19, 1945, available at http://orwell.ru/library/articles/ABomb/english/e_abomb.

11. Vannevar Bush, foreword in Irvin Stewart, *Organizing Scientific Research for War: The Administrative History of the Office of Scientific Research and Development* (Boston: Little, Brown and Company, 1948), ix.

12. James Phinney Baxter, III, *Scientists Against Time* (Cambridge, MA: The MIT Press, 1946), 31–36.

13. C. J. Hitch, amended by J. R. Goldstein, "RAND: Its History, Organization and Character," Project RAND, B-200, July 20, 1960, 1–2.

14. Hitch "RAND: Its History, Organization and Character," 4.

15. Ibid., 3–4.

16. Ibid., 5.

17. Ibid., 7.

18. "Conference of Social Scientists: September 14 to 19, 1947—New York," RAND R-106, vii–viii.

19. Hitch, "RAND: Its History, Organization and Character," 8.

20. RAND, "History and Mission," available at http://www.rand.org/about/history/, accessed November 16, 2013.

21. Andrew W. Marshall, "Strategy as a Profession in the Future Security Environment," in *Nuclear Heuristics: Selected Writings of Albert and Roberta Wohlstetter*, Robert Zarate and Henry Sokolski, eds. (Carlisle, PA: Strategic Studies Institute, January 2009), 628.

22. Bernard Brodie, "The Development of Nuclear Strategy," *International Security* Spring 1978, 67.

23. Henry S. Rowen, "Commentary: How He Worked" in *Nuclear Heuristics: Selected Writings of Albert and Roberta Wohlstetter*, Robert Zarate and Henry Sokolski, eds. (Carlisle, PA: Strategic Studies Institute, January 2009), 101.

24. A. W. Marshall, "Talk for Book Project," interview by Kurt Guthe, September 16, 1993, 11–4.

25. A. W. Marshall, "1950–1969," interview by Kurt Guthe, October 29, 1993, 3–39; A. W. Marshall, "Second Talk on Themes" interview by Kurt Guthe, October 6, 1995, 12–26.

26. Alan L. Gropman, "Mobilizing U.S. Industry in World War II," McNair Paper 50, National Defense University, August 1996, 109; and Maddison, "Historical Statistics for the World Economy: 1–2003 AD."

27. Office of the Undersecretary of Defense (Comptroller), "National Defense Budget Estimates for FY 2015," April 2014, table 7–5, 254.

28. Herbert Goldhamer and Andrew Marshall, *Psychosis and Civilization: Studies in the Frequency of Mental Disease* (Glencoe, IL: The Free Press, 1949, 1953), 91–93.

29. Hitch, "RAND: Its History, Organization and Character," 3.

30. A. W. Marshall, interview with Barry D. Watts, April 12, 2011, 6–7.

31. Reed and Stillman, *The Nuclear Express*, 36.

32. Ibid., 37.

33. "Implications of Large-Yield Nuclear Weapons," RAND R-237, July 10, 1952, 1–2.

34. Gian P. Gentile, "Planning for Preventive War, 1945–1950," *Joint Force Quarterly*, Spring 2000, 69.

35. Hans M. Kristensen and Robert S. Norris, "Global Nuclear Weapons Inventories, 1945–2013," *Bulletin of the Atomic Scientists*, September/October 2013, 78. Kristensen and Norris believe that United States had only 170 atomic weapons in 1949. However, the US stockpile expanded rapidly, growing to over 1,100 weapons in 1953 and peaking at over 31,000 in 1967.

36. A. W. Marshall, "Early 1950s," interview by Kurt Guthe, September 16, 1993, 4–5.

37. Marc Trachtenberg, *History and Strategy* (Princeton, NJ: Princeton University Press, 1991), 7–8.

38. J. D. Williams, "Hunting the Tiger (and Other Aspects of the Active Life)," RAND S-16, March 25, 1954, 31–32.

39. Neil Sheehan, *A Fiery Peace in a Cold War: Bernard Schriever and the Ultimate Weapon* (New York: Random House, 2009), 181.

40. Bernard Brodie, "A Moratorium on Similes," memorandum to J. D. Williams, M-5484, November 1, 1954, 1.

41. Roger G. Miller, *To Save a City: The Berlin Airlift 1948–1949* (Washington DC: Air Force History Support Office, 1998), 18.

42. Ibid., 16–17.

43. Gregory W. Pedlow, ed., *NATO Strategy Documents 1949–1969* (Brussels: Supreme Headquarters Allied Powers Europe, October 1997), xii.

44. Sheehan, *A Fiery Peace in a Cold War*, 193.

45. H. Kahn and A. W. Marshall, "Methods of Reducing Sample Size in Monte Carlo Computations," *Journal of the Operations Research Society of American* (November 1953): 263–78.

46. Marc Peter Jr. and Andrew Marshall, "A Re-examination of Hiroshima-Nagasaki Damage Data," RAND RM-820, May 1, 1952, 1–4.

47. Marshall, "1950–1969," interview by Guthe, 3–11.

48. Bernard Brodie, ed., with Frederick S. Dunn, Arnold Wolfers, Percey E. Corbett, and William T. R. Fox, *The Absolute Weapon: Atomic Power and World Order* (New York: Harcourt, Brace, 1946), 74.

49. Bernard Brodie, "Strategy Hits a Dead End," *Harper's Magazine*, October 1955, 36.

50. Marshall, "1950–1969," interview by Guthe, 3–22.

51. Robert R. Bowie and Richard H. Immerman, *Waging Peace: How Eisenhower Shaped an Enduring Cold War Strategy* (Oxford: Oxford University Press, 1998), 137; and B. Brodie, C. J. Hitch, and A. W. Marshall, "The Next Ten Years," RAND, December 30, 1954, 27–28.

52. Brodie, Hitch, and Marshall, "The Next Ten Years," 3–9.

53. Ibid., 10.

54. Ibid., 16.

55. A. J. Wohlstetter, F. S. Hoffman, R. J. Lutz, and H. S. Rowen, *Selection and Use of Strategic Air Bases,* RAND R-266, April 1954, x.

56. Ibid., vii. R-266 estimated, accurately, that the Soviets would have around four hundred atomic bombs in 1956 (Ibid., 271).

57. Ibid., vi–viii, xxxvii.

58. Ibid., vii.

59. Andrew D. May, "The RAND Corporation and the Dynamics of American Strategic Thought, 1946–1962," unpublished revision of PhD dissertation as of July 2003, chap. 4, 21.

60. E. S. Quade, "Principles and Procedures of Systems Analysis," in Quade's edited volume *Analysis for Military Decisions* (Santa Monica, CA: RAND R-387-PR, November 1964), 37.

61. Henry S. Rowen, "Commentary: How He Worked," in *Nuclear Heuristics*, ed. Zarate and Sokolski, 116.

62. Marshall, "Strategy as a Profession in the Future Security Environment," in *Nuclear Heuristics*, ed. Zarate and Sokolski, 629–30.

63. May, "The RAND Corporation and the Dynamics of American Strategic Thought, 1946–1962," chap. 2, 13.

64. Wohlstetter et al., *Selection and Use of Strategic Air Bases*, v.

65. Brodie, Hitch, and Marshall, "The Next Ten Years," 38.

66. Ibid., 37.

67. Ibid., 39.

68. J. D. Williams, "Unkind Comments on the Next Ten Years," memo to B. Brodie, C. J. Hitch, A. W. Marshall, RAND M-4419, September 2, 1954, 1.

69. Ibid., 1.

70. Roberta Wohlstetter, *Pearl Harbor: Warning and Decision* (Stanford, CA: Stanford University Press, 1962), xi.

71. National Security Agency, "Professional Reading: Books Briefly Noted," 123, n.d., accessed at http://www.nsa.gov/public_info/_files/tech_journals/book_review_pearl _harbor.pdf (emphasis in the original).

72. Dr. Alfred Goldberg and Maurice Matloff, OSD Historical Office, "Oral History Interviews, Director, Net Assessment," June 1, 1992, 5.

73. Roberta Wohlstetter, *Pearl Harbor*, 401.

74. Ibid., viii–ix.

75. Dennis Hevesi, "Roberta Wohlstetter, 94, Military Policy Analyst, Dies," *New York Times*, January 11, 2007, accessed at http://www.nytimes.com/2007/01/11/obituaries /11wohlstetter.html?_r=0.

76. James C. DeHaven, "The Soviet Strategic Base Problem," RAND RM-1302, August 16, 1954, vii.

77. A. W. Marshall, "Improvement in Intelligence Estimates Through Study of Organizational Behavior," RAND D-16858, March 15, 1968, 1.

78. Security Resources Panel of the Science Advisory Committee, "Deterrence and Survival in the Nuclear Age," Washington, DC, November 7, 1957, 1.

79. Ibid., 4.

80. Zaloga, *The Kremlin's Nuclear Sword*, 50.

81. Security Resources Panel, "Deterrence and Survival in the Nuclear Age," 11.

82. Herbert Goldhamer and Andrew W. Marshall, "The Deterrence and Strategy of Total War, 1959–1961: A Method of Analysis," RAND RM-2301, April 30, 1959, iv.

83. Ibid., vii.

84. Ibid., vi, 189.

85. Richard Nixon, "Policy for Planning the Employment of Nuclear Weapons," National Security Decision Memorandum 242, January 17, 1974, 2.

Chapter 3: The Quest for Better Analytic Methods, 1961–1969

1. Frances Acomb, *Statistical Control in the Army Air Forces* (Maxwell Air Force Base, AL: Air University, January 1952), 1.

2. Acomb, *Statistical Control in the Army Air Forces*, 95.

3. John A. Byrne, *The Whiz Kids: Ten Founding Fathers of American Business—and the Legacy They Left Us* (New York: Doubleday Business, 2008), 39–44.

4. Charles R. Shrader, *History of Operations Research in the US Army*, Vol. II, *1961–1973* (Washington, DC: US Government Printing Office, 2008), Center for Military History Publication 70–105–1, 17.

5. Phil Rosenzweig, "Robert S. McNamara and the Evolution of Modern Management," *Harvard Business Review*, December 2010, 3.

6. Tim Weiner, "Robert S, McNamara, Architect of a Futile War, Dies at 93," *New York Times*, July 6, 2009, available at http://www.nytimes.com/2009/07/07/us/07mcnamara.html?pagewanted=all, accessed December 7, 2013.

7. Byrne, *The Whiz Kids*, 13–16, 80–86.

8. Ibid., 17–19.

9. Ibid., 107, 108, 365.

10. Ibid., 171–73, 206, 228.

11. Ibid., 213, 229.

12. Ibid., 143–48.

13. "Robert S. McNamara Oral History Interview," Arthur M. Schlesinger (interviewer), April 4, 1964, 6–8, available at http://archive2.jfklibrary.org/JFKOH/McNamara,%20Robert%20S/JFKOH-RSM-01/JFKOH-RSM-01-TR.pdf, accessed December 7, 2013.

14. Alain C. Enthoven and K. Wayne Smith, *How Much Is Enough? Shaping the Defense Program, 1961–1969* (New York: Harper and Row, 1971), 325; and John A. Byrne, *The Whiz Kids: Ten Founding Fathers of American Business—and the Legacy They Left Us* (New York: Doubleday Business, 2008), 396–400.

15. Enthoven and Smith, *How Much Is Enough?*, 32–33.

16. Stephen Budiansky, *Blackett's War: The Men Who Defeated the Nazi U-Boats and Brought Science to the Art of War* (New York: Alfred A. Knopf, 2013), 221–226.

17. For in-depth accounts of RAND's approach to systems analysis, see E. S. Quade, ed., *Analysis for Military Decisions* (Santa Monica, CA: RAND R-387-PR, November 1964); and E. S. Quade and W. I. Boucher, eds., *Systems Analysis and Policy Planning: Applications in Defense* (Santa Monica, CA: RAND R-439-PR, June 1968). Both can be downloaded from RAND's website.

18. RAND, "50th: Project Air Force 1946–1996," 1996, 23.

19. Charles J. Hitch, "Decision-Making in the Defense Department," Gaither Memorial Lectures, University of California, April 5–9, 1965, 15–18.

20. Ibid., 19. An outline for what became PPBS can be found in Charles J. Hitch and Roland N. McKean, *The Economics of Defense in the Nuclear Age* (Santa Monica, CA: Project RAND R-346, March 1960), 54–59.

21. Hitch, "Decision-Making in the Defense Department," 28.

22. The Office of Systems Analysis became the Office of Program Analysis and Evaluation (PA&E) in 1973 and PA&E was renamed the Office of Cost Analysis and Program Evaluation (CAPE) in 2009.

23. Charles J. Hitch and Roland N. McKean, with contributions by Stephen Enke, Malcolm W. Hoag, Alain Enthoven, C. B. McGuire, and Albert Wohlstetter, *The Economics of Defense in the Nuclear Age* (Cambridge, MA: Harvard University Press, 1960), 23.

24. Hitch, "Decision-Making in the Defense Department," 28.

25. James R. Schlesinger, *The Political Economy of National Security: A Study of the Economic Aspects of the Contemporary Power Struggle* (New York: Praeger, 1960).

26. "Interview with James R. Schlesinger," February 8, 2006, in Barry D. Watts, "Interviews and Materials on the Intellectual History of Diagnostic Net Assessment," July 2006, 97.

27. R. Nelson and J. Schlesinger, "A Long-Range Basic Research Program for the Department," RAND M-6527, September 10, 1963, 1. This memo was addressed to Gustave H. Shubert, who had succeeded Burton Klein as head of RAND's Economics Department. Copies went to Marshall, Klein, and McKean. Mai Elliot, *RAND in Southeast Asia: A History of the Vietnam War Era* (Santa Monica, CA: RAND, 2010), xx.

28. Nelson and Schlesinger, "A Long-Range Basic Research Program for the Department," 2.

29. James R. Schlesinger, "On Relating Non-Technical Elements to Systems Studies," RAND P-3545, February 1967, 1.

30. Ibid., 1

31. Ibid., 2.

32. James R. Schlesinger, "Uses and Abuses of Analysis," in *Selected Papers on National Security 1964–1968* (Santa Monica, CA: RAND P-5284, September 1974), 106.

33. Enthoven and Smith, *How Much Is Enough?*, xii.

34. James March and Herbert Simon, with the collaboration of Harold Guetzkow, *Organizations* (Cambridge, MA: Blackwell, 2nd ed. 1993, 1st ed. 1958), 3.

35. March and Simon, *Organizations*, 4.

36. Richard M. Cyert and James March, *A Behavioral Theory of the Firm* (Cambridge, MA: Blackwell, 2nd ed. 1992), xi–xii, 120–22, 214–15.

37. Herbert A. Simon, "A Behavioral Model of Rational Choice," RAND P-365, January 20, 1953. Also Herbert A. Simon, "Rational Choice and the Structure of the Environment," *Psychological Review* 63, no. 2 (1956): 129.

38. A. W. Marshall, "1950–1969," interview by Kurt Guthe, October 29, 1993, 3–27.

39. Ibid., 3–28.

40. Burton H. Klein, *Germany's Economic Preparations for War* (Cambridge, MA: Harvard University Press, 1959).

41. "Burton H. Klein, 92," available at http://www.caltech.edu/content/burton-h-klein-92, accessed December 11, 2013.

42. A. W. Marshall, discussion with Barry Watts, July 17, 2013.

43. Ibid.

44. Joseph Bower, e-mail to Barry Watts, July 8, 2013.

45. A. W. Marshall, "The Formative Period of the Office of Net Assessment," OSD/NA memorandum for Andrew May and Barry Watts, September 3, 2002," 3.

46. Robert Ardrey, *The Territorial Imperative: A Personal Inquiry into the Anima Origins of Property and Nations* (New York: Atheneum, 1968), ix, 333, 337.

47. Konrad Lozenz, *On Aggression*, trans. Marjorie Kerr Wilson (New York: Harcourt, Brace and World, 1966), x, 237, 243, 271, 276, 333, 337.

48. Richard E. Neustadt, *Presidential Power and the Modern Presidents: The Politics of Leadership from Roosevelt to Reagan* (New York: The Free Press, 1990), 11.

49. Graham T. Allison, *Essence of Decision* (Boston: Little, Brown and Company, 1971), 67.

50. Ibid., 88–90.

51. Ibid.

52. Dennis Hevesi, "Roberta Wohlstetter, 94, Military Policy Analyst, Dies," *New York Times*, January 11, 2007.

53. A. W. Marshall, "The Improvement in Intelligence Estimates Through Studies of Organizational Behavior (U)," seminar background paper for Board of Trustees meeting, March 15, 1968, 1–7.

54. A. W. Marshall, "Problems of Estimating Military Power," RAND P-3417, August 1966.

55. Ibid., 2.

56. Ibid., 9.

57. Ibid., 17.

58. Ibid., 16.

59. Ibid., 21.

60. Marshall, "1969–1975," interview by Guthe, 5–21.

61. A. W. Marshall, letter to Ivan Selin, RAND L-23604, December 15, 1967, 1.

62. A. W. Marshall and S. G. Winter, "Program of Studies in the Analysis of Organizational Behavior," RAND L-4277, draft March 3, 1967. A. W. Marshall and S. G. Winter, "A RAND Department of 'Management Sciences'—the Case in Brief," RAND L-4277, draft March 3, 1967.

63. A. W. Marshall and S. G. Winter, "A RAND Department of 'Management Sciences'—the Case in Brief," RAND M-8668, December 29, 1967, 1.

64. A. W. Marshall, "Attachment II: Problems and Hypotheses Concerning Soviet Behavior (U)," RAND, July 16, 1968.

65. A. W. Marshall, "Comparisons, R&D Strategy, and Policy Issues," RAND WN-7630-DDRE, October 1971, 25.

Chapter 4: The Birth of Net Assessment, 1969–1973

1. James S. Lay, "Directive for a Net Capabilities Evaluation Subcommittee," NSC 5423, June 23, 1954 (originally top secret; declassified February 1987).

2. William Z. Slany, chief ed., Lisle A. Rose and Neal H. Petersen, eds., *Foreign Relations of the United States, 1952–1954*, vol. 2, part 1, *National Security Affairs* (Washington, DC: US Government Printing Office, 1984), 332–33. We now know that this report overstated the capability of LRA's bombers. Steven J. Zaloga, *The Kremlin's Nuclear Sword*, 15–16, 24, 26, 28.

3. Robert R. Bowie, NSC 140/1, "Summary Evaluation of the Net Capability of the USSR to Inflict Direct Damage on the United States up to July 1, 1955" memorandum for the secretary of state, June 2, 1953 (originally top secret; declassified March 1976), 1.

4. Ibid., 2.

5. David S. Peterson, *Foreign Relations of the United States, 1964–1968*, vol. 10, National Security Policy (Washington, DC: US Government Printing Office, 2002), 202.

6. Ibid.

7. McGeorge Bundy, "Discontinuance of the Net Evaluation Subcommittee of the National Security Council," National Security Action Memorandum No. 327, March 18, 1965.

8. General Leon W. Johnson, memorandum to R. B. Foster, December 9, 1968.

9. John F. Kennedy, Inaugural Address, January 20, 1961, available at http://www .jfklibrary.org/Asset-Viewer/BqXIEM9F4024ntFl7SVAjA.aspx?gclid=COznv9bwt7s CFa9lOgod2kcAkw, accessed December 18, 2013.

10. Thomas Powers, *The Man Who Kept the Secrets: Richard Helms and the CIA* (New York: Alfred A. Knopf, 1979), 200–206.

11. See comments by Russell Jack Smith (then deputy director for intelligence) in his *The Unknown CIA: My Three Decades with the Agency* (Washington, DC: Pergamon-Brassey's, 1989), 205.

12. For a discussion of ONE and its decline, see Harold P. Ford, *Estimative Intelligence: The Purposes and Problems of National Intelligence Estimating*, rev. ed. (Lanham, MD: University Press of America, 1993), 81–105. See also William Colby and Peter Forbath, *Honorable Men: My Life in the CIA* (New York: Simon and Schuster, 1978), 351; and Ray S. Cline, Secrets Spies and Scholars: Blueprint of the Essential CIA (Washington, DC: Acropolis Books, 1976), 135–40.

13. Andrew Marshall, "Outline for DIS Presentation, November 15, 1972"; and Andrew Marshall, notes for "Talk to CIA Training Course" (section on new methods), February 15, 1973.

14. Andrew Marshall, "Intelligence and Crisis Management," in *Crisis Decision Making in the Atlantic Alliance: Perspectives on Deterrence*, Gen. Jack N. Merritt, Gen. Robert Reed, and Roger Weissinger-Baylon, eds. (Menlo Park, CA: Strategic Decisions Press, n.d.), 8–1, 8–2.

15. A. W. Marshall, "Intelligence Inputs for Major Issues: A Substantive Evaluation and Proposal for Improvement," memorandum for Henry A. Kissinger, NSC, May 1, 1970, 2; and Marshall, "1969–1975," interview by Guthe, 5–12.

16. Marshall, "Intelligence Inputs for Major Issues: A Substantive Evaluation and Proposal for Improvement," memorandum for Henry A. Kissinger, NSC, May 1, 1970, 4–5, 7–9.

17. Ibid., 3.

18. A. W. Marshall, "Net Assessment of US and Soviet Force Posture: Summary, Conclusions and Recommendations," 2.

19. Marshall, "1969–1975," interview by Guthe, 5–14.

20. Ibid.; K. Wayne Smith, "Meeting of Special Defense Panel," memorandum for Dr. Kissinger, September 29, 1970, top secret sensitive (declassified August 17, 2000), 1.

21. A. W. Marshall, "Net Assessment of US and Soviet Force Posture," NSC, 1970, top secret (declassified March 26, 2004), 7.

22. A. W. Marshall, "Net Assessment of US and Soviet Force Posture: Summary, Conclusions and Recommendations," NSC, 1970, top secret (declassified March 26, 2004), 1.

23. Marshall, "Net Assessment of US and Soviet Force Posture," 10.

24. Marshall, "Net Assessment of US and Soviet Force Posture: Summary, Conclusions and Recommendations," 2.

25. Blue Ribbon Defense Panel, *Defense for Peace: Report to the President and the Secretary of Defense on the Department of Defense*, July 1, 1970, 7, 59, 215–16.

26. Marshall, "1969–1975," interview by Guthe, 5–15.

27. Ibid., 5–16.

28. Barry D. Watts, "Net Assessment at CIA; Nixon's Intelligence Reorganization," interview with A. W. Marshall, July 26, 2005.

29. J. R. Schlesinger, "A Review of the Intelligence Community," March 10, 1971, redacted copy, 1, available at http://www.gwu.edu/~nsarchiv/NSAEBB/NSAEBB144/, accessed January 6, 2013. For a discussion of Schlesinger's study from CIA's perspective, see Garthoff, *Directors of Central Intelligence as Leaders of the US Intelligence Community, 1946–2005*, 65–69.

30. Schlesinger, "A Review of the Intelligence Community," 5, 8, 9, 10. A 1974 CIA review of major studies of the intelligence community going back to 1960 argued that the "cumulative impact" of these studies was "necessarily more negative than the intelligence community's record of achievement would warrant"; CIA, "An Historical Review of Studies of the Intelligence Community for the Commission on the Organization of the Government for the Conduct of Foreign Policy," December 1974, preface, available at http://www.gwu.edu/~nsarchiv/NSAEBB/NSAEBB144/.

31. "Comments on 'A Review of the Intelligence Community.'" undated, 2–3, also available at http://www.gwu.edu/~nsarchiv/NSAEBB/NSAEBB144/.

32. Schlesinger, "A Review of the Intelligence Community," 29–30.

33. "Comments on 'A Review of the Intelligence Community,'" 31–33; and Richard M. Nixon, "Organization and Management of the US Foreign Intelligence Community," memorandum, November 5, 1971, 4–5.

34. Marshall, "1969–75," interview by Guthe, 5–16.

35. Barry D. Watts, "Marshall's Role in Nixon's Intelligence Reorganization; the Interagency Process," interview with A. W. Marshall, July 31, 2005.

36. Nixon, "Organization and Management of the US Intelligence Community," 5–6.

37. Marshall, "1969–1975," interview by Guthe, 5–17; and Nixon, "Organization and Management of the US Foreign Intelligence Community," 6; "Net Assessment Group," March 8, 1972; and memo, J. Fred Buzhardt, general counsel of the Department of Defense, to the secretary of defense, subject: Establishment of Net Assessment Group, n.d.

38. "Director of Net Assessment," DoD Directive 5015.39, December 6, 1971. The directive established the net assessment director as "the principal staff advisor and assistant to the Secretary of Defense on net assessment," and included among his responsibilities developing assessments of current and projected US and foreign military capabilities as well as preparing the net assessment portion of the defense secretary's annual report to Congress.

39. Letter, Andrew Marshall to Michel Crozier, November 2, 1973.

40. A. W. Marshall, memorandum for the record, "Definition of the National Net Assessment Process," NSC, March 26, 1972, 1.

41. Andrew W. Marshall, "The Nature and Scope of Net Assessments," NSC memorandum, August 16, 1972, 1.

42. Ibid., 2.

43. Ibid. [Authors' emphasis.]

44. Ibid.

45. Ibid., 1–2.

46. Ibid., 1.

47. Ibid., 2. [Authors' emphasis.]

48. Dwight D. Eisenhower, *Crusade in Europe* (Baltimore, MD: Johns Hopkins University Press, 1948), 36.

49. Richard Rumelt, *Good Strategy, Bad Strategy* (New York: Crown Business, 2011), 62.

50. Marshall, "The Nature and Scope of Net Assessments," 2.

51. Ibid., 2.

52. Ibid., 2–3.

53. Marshall, "1969–1975," interview by Guthe, 5–2.

54. Henry A. Kissinger, "Program for National Net Assessment," NSSM 178, March 29, 1973.

55. National Security Decision Memorandum (NSDM) 224 ("National Net Assessment Process"), and NSSM 186 ("National Net Assessment of Comparative Costs and Capabilities of US and Soviet Military Establishments"). The titles and dates of all Nixon administration NSDMs and NSSMs can be found on the Federation of American Scientists' website, http://www.fas.org/irp/offdocs/direct.htm.

56. Henry A. Kissinger, "National Net Assessment of the Comparative Costs and Capabilities of US and Soviet Military Establishments," NSC, NSSM 186, September 1, 1973.

57. Kissinger became secretary of state on September 22, 1973, a position he held until January 20, 1977. However, he continued as national security adviser to the president until November 1975, the only period since 1947 in which the same individual has held both positions.

58. A. W. Marshall, "Departure Planning," memorandum for Brent Scowcroft, October 3, 1973, 1.

59. Andrew Marshall, "Dinner Remarks," March 28, 2008, cited in Mie Augier and Barry D. Watts, "Conference Report on the Past, Present, and Future of Net Assessment," unpublished paper, 2009, 151.

Chapter 5: Moving to the Pentagon, 1973–1975

1. A. W. Marshall, "Departure Planning," memorandum for Brent Scowcroft, October 3, 1973, unclassified.

2. J. R. Schlesinger, "Net Assessment," memorandum for the secretaries of the military departments, the chairman of the Joint Chiefs of Staff, the director of defense research and engineering, the assistant secretary of defense (intelligence), the assistant secretary of defense (international security affairs), the director of defense program analysis and evaluation, and the assistant to the secretary and deputy secretary, October 13, 1973, unclassified.

3. Henry A. Kissinger, "National Net Assessment Process," National Security Council, NSDM 239, November 27, 1973.

4. Henry A. Kissinger, *White House Years* (Boston: Little, Brown & Co., 1979), 195–204.

5. Harold Brown, testimony, January 31, 1979, *Department of Defense Appropriations for Fiscal Year 1980*, hearings before a Subcommittee of the Committee on Appropriations, United States Senate, 96th Congress, 1st session, 278.

6. President Richard M. Nixon, broadcast to the nation, January 23, 1973, accessed at http://www.presidency.ucsb.edu/ws/?pid=3808#axzz2gm8H8SaS.

7. "Watching Birds and Budgets," *Time*, February 11, 1974, 16.

8. A. W. Marshall, "1969–1975," interview with Kurt Guthe, December 14, 1993, 5–31; Barry D. Watts, notes from telephone discussion with Phillip A. Karber, August 13, 2005. The position of assistant secretary of defense (systems analysis) changed to the director, program analysis and evaluation, on April 11, 1973.

9. Barry D. Watts, "Selecting Key Balances, Coordination," interview with A. W. Marshall, July 22, 2005.

10. A. W. Marshall, "1973–1980," interview by Kurt Guthe, April 9, 1994, unclassified, 6–11.

11. The Soviet Union required its conscripts to serve for two years. One might expect soldiers at the end of that time to be considerably more proficient at soldiering than those who has just been inducted.

12. Watts, "Early Days of Net Assessment Discussion," October 1, 2002, 5.

13. Barry Watts, notes from a discussion with Phillip Karber, A. W. Marshall, and Andrew May, September 19, 2005.

14. A. W. Marshall, memo to Schlesinger on Project 186 Phase I, July 30, 1974.

15. Barry D. Watts, "Early Days of Net Assessment Discussion," October 1, 2002, 5.

16. "Project 186, Phase 1 Report (Ground Forces)," secretary of defense talking points for a meeting with the Joint Chiefs of Staff, September 30, 1974, unclassified, 2.

17. Marshall, "1973–1980," interview by Guthe, 6–9.

18. Barry D. Watts, "Early Days of Net Assessment Discussion," 3.

19. Marshall, "1973–1980," interview by Guthe, 6–33.

20. Marshall, "The Formative Period of the Office of Net Assessment," 4.

21. Marshall, "The Formative Period of the Office of Net Assessment," 5.

22. On the grounds that methodologies for doing net assessments "are virtually nonexistent," and because data problems abounded, Marshall's August 1972 NSC paper, "The Nature and Scope of Net Assessments," observed, "Initial assessments are bound to be crude, tentative, and controversial."

23. A. W. Marshall, "Comments on the US/Soviet Navy Net Assessment," memorandum for Rear Admiral Harry Train, February 7, 1974, 1 (declassified August 6, 2004).

24. ONA's military investment balance did not, of course, ignore each side's total military consumption, including resources allocated to operations and maintenance. However, Robert Gough, who drafted three versions of this balance in the late 1970s, points out that the term *investment* was deliberately chosen to emphasize Soviet military spending aimed at producing future military capability. Robert G. Gough, e-mail to Barry D. Watts, September 27, 2004.

25. Andrew May and Barry D. Watts, Interview with Dr. James Schlesinger, February 8, 2006.

26. Ibid.

27. Ibid.

28. Marshall, "1969–1975," interview by Guthe, 5–40.

29. Barry D. Watts, interview with A. W. Marshall, July 23, 2004.

30. Marshall recalled some meetings with CIA representatives. He was finally given a paper on the subject that he found "totally unconvincing." In it the CIA conceded that its estimates could at the most be off by about 1 percent—in *either direction*!

31. A. W. Marshall, "Memo for NA Staff," November 17, 1976.

32. More than thirty years after the establishment of ONA, when former staff member Andrew Krepinevich was teaching a graduate course on net assessment, he showed Marshall a draft of a "notional" structure of what he intended to give the students, asking him whether it was accurate. Marshall's only reply was that the structure was generally correct.

33. The source is Krepinevich, who made the statement to a colleague while serving on Marshall's staff.

34. As Project 186 evolved, it eventually added assessments of the forces on NATO's northern and southern flanks and explored reinforcements from the United States and the western military districts of the USSR.

35. Barry D. Watts, notes from, discussion of P-186 with Phillip A. Karber, Andrew Marshall, Barry D. Watts, and Andrew May, September 19, 2005, 2.

36. Andrew May, "RE: P-186 and the Balances," e-mail to Barry D. Watts, October 19, 2005.

37. During the 1970s and early 1980s Kuklinski, an army officer on the Polish general staff who also acted as a liaison with Moscow, provided the CIA with thousands of secret documents as well as insights into the plans and thinking of the Warsaw Pact. James Risen, "Ryszard Kuklinki, 73, Spy in Poland in Cold War, Dies," *New York Times*, February 12, 2004.

38. Diego Ruiz-Palmer in "Conference Report on the Past, Present and Future of Net Assessment," by Mie Augier and Barry D. Watts, "Conference Report on the Past, Present and Future of Net Assessment," unpublished paper, 2009, 79–81. Other prominent members of Karber's Project 186 team included John Milam, A. Grant Whitley, Douglas Komer, Graham Turbiville, and Jon Lellenberg. When Karber left BDM in 1988, Milam succeeded him and continued to run Project 186 until 1996.

39. Allan Rehm, "The Background of Project Eager," March 2002, 4–5. Marshall, along with the CIA's Strategic Evaluation Center and Pat Parker, the Pentagon's assistant secretary of defense for intelligence, had sponsored Rehm's earlier research on Soviet operations research while he was at the Center for Naval Analyses.

40. See, for example, Judith K. Grange and John A. Battilega, "The Soviet Framework for Planning and Analysis, (U)," Foreign Systems Research Center SAI-83–103-FSRC-B, SAI, October 31, 1983.

41. John Battilega, in "Conference Report on the Past, Present and Future of Net Assessment," by Mie Augier and Barry D. Watts, unpublished conference report, 2009, 95.

42. Peter W. Rodman, *Presidential Command* (New York: Alfred A. Knopf, 2009), 93–94.

43. Hugh Sidey, "We Are Going to Win—But How?," *Time*, December 1, 1975, 16.

44. Ibid.

45. A. W. Marshall, "The Formative Period of the Office of Net Assessment," OSD/NA memorandum, September 3, 2002, 5.

46. Sergey Modestov, "The Pentagon's Gray Cardinal (Éminence Grise) Andrew Marshall—Ideologist of the New American Revolution in Military Affairs," *Nezavisimaya Gazeta*, December 14, 1995.

Chapter 6: The Maturation of Net Assessment, 1976–1980

1. "Interview with James R. Schlesinger," February 8, 2006, in Barry D. Watts, "Interviews and Materials on the Intellectual History of Diagnostic Net Assessment," July 2006, 110.

2. A. W. Marshall, "Future Directions for Net Assessment," OSD/NA memorandum for Eugene Fubini, February 28, 1977, 1.

3. Ibid., 2.

4. A. W. Marshall and J. G. Roche, "Strategy for Competing with the Soviets in the Military Sector of the Continuing Political-Military Competition," OSD/NA paper, July 26, 1976, A-2.

5. Ibid., A-4.

6. Ibid., B-1. These basic assessments were followed by discussions of the trends and asymmetries in each competition.

7. Donald H. Rumsfeld, *Annual Defense Department Report FY 1978*, January 17, 1977, 105–20.

8. Ibid., 178.

9. A. W. Marshall, "1973–1980," interview by Kurt Guthe, April 8, 1994, 6–13.

10. A. W. Marshall, "Thinking About the Navy," OSD/NA memorandum for the secretary of defense, March 1, 1976, 5.

11. Donald Rumsfeld, *Known and Unknown: A Memoir* (New York: Sentinel, 2011), 224–25.

12. Ibid., 228.

13. Ibid., 229.

14. CIA, NIE 11–3/8–74, Soviet Forces for Intercontinental Conflict in Intentions and Capabilities: Estimates on Soviet Strategic Forces, 1930–1983, Donald P. Steury, ed. (Langley, VA: Center for the Study of Intelligence, 1996), 330–31.

15. The associate members of Team B were Professor William Van Cleave, Lt. Gen. Daniel O. Graham (USA, Ret.), Thomas Wolfe from RAND, and General John Vogt (USAF, Ret.). CIA, "Soviet Strategic Objectives: an Alternative View: Report of Team 'B,'" December 1976, iv.

16. CIA, "Soviet Strategic Objectives: an Alternative View: Report of Team 'B,'" 6. There were three teams, one each to examine Soviet air defenses; Soviet ICBM accuracy; and Soviet strategy, policy, and objectives. This last subject, studied by Team B, generated the greatest debate.

17. Murrey Marder, "Summit Clouded by Watergate," *Washington Post*, July 4, 1974.

18. Richard Pipes, "Why the Soviet Union Think It Could Fight and Win a Nuclear War," *Commentary*, July 1977, 21–34.

19. John G. Hines and Daniel Calingaert, "Soviet Strategic Intentions, 1973–1985: A Preliminary Review of US Interpretations," RAND WD-6305-NA, December 1992, v–vii. Hines was a member of Marshall's staff during the mid-1980s.

20. A. W. Marshall, "The Future of the Strategic Balance—INFO," OSD/NA memorandum for the secretary of defense, August 26, 1976, 1.

21. Marshall, "The Future of the Strategic Balance—INFO," 1.

22. A. W. Marshall, "The Future of the Strategic Balance," OSD/NA memorandum for the secretary of defense, August 26, 1976, 2.

23. Marshall, "The Future of the Strategic Balance—INFO," 2.

24. Ibid., 2.

25. Marshall, "The Future of the Strategic Balance," 4.

26. Ibid.

27. Ibid., 5–6.

28. Ibid., 6, 8.

29. Rumsfeld, *Known and Unknown: A Memoir*, (New York: Sentinel, 2011), 237.

30. Ibid., 233, 235.

31. Marshall and Roche, "Strategy for Competing with the Soviets in the Military Sector of the Continuing Political-Military Competition," 34.

32. Tim Hindle, *Guide to Management Ideas and Gurus* (London: The Economist with Profile Books, 2008), 299. In December 2008 Rumelt was highlighted in *The Economist* as one of the fifty most influential strategic management "gurus."

33. Richard P. Rumelt, *Good Strategy Bad Strategy*, 30.

34. Ibid., 29.

35. "Interview with Harold Brown," January 27, 2006, in Barry D. Watts, "Interviews and Materials on the Intellectual History of Diagnostic Net Assessment," 77–78.

36. Ibid., 80.

37. Von Hardesty, *Red Phoenix: The Rise of Soviet Air Power 1941–1945* (Washington, DC: Smithsonian Institution Press, 1982), 15. By contrast, Luftwaffe losses during the first week of Barbarossa came to around 150 aircraft.

38. Trachtenberg, *A Constructed Peace*, 182.

39. By 1974 Schlesinger had begun phasing out all the Nike-Hercules surface-to-air-missiles and reducing the fighter interceptor force to twelve squadrons. James R. Schlesinger, *Annual Defense Department Report FY 1975*, March 4, 1974, 68.

40. OSD/NA memorandum, "B-1 DSARC [Defense Systems Acquisition Review Council] III Decision," 1976, 2.

41. "Carter's Big Decision: Down Goes the B-1, Here Comes the Cruise," *Time*, July 11, 1977, available at http://content.time.com/time/subscriber/article/0,33009,919040,00.html, accessed January 7, 2014.

42. Office of the Historian, Bureau of Public Affairs, Department of State, "History of the National Security Council 1947–1997," August 1997, available at http://www.fas.org /irp/offdocs/NSChistory.htm#Nixon.

43. Jimmy Carter, Presidential Review Memorandum/NSC-10, "Comprehensive Net Assessment and Military Force Posture Review," February 18, 1977, 1–2.

44. Samuel P. Huntington, "The Clash of Civilizations," *Foreign Affairs*, Summer 1993, 45–48.

45. Brian Auten, *Carter's Conversion: The Hardening of American Defense Policy* (Columbia, MO: University of Missouri Press, 2008), 157; Lieutenant General (Ret.) William Odom, interview by Barry Watts, November 3, 2004.

46. A. W. Marshall, "Net Assessment Products," OSD/NA memorandum for David E. McGiffert, March 11, 1977.

47. A. W. Marshall, "1989–1993," interview by Kurt Guthe, January 25, 1995, 9–30; and William Odom, interview by Barry Watts, November 3, 2004.

48. PRM/NSC-10, "Military Strategy and Force Posture Review: Final Report," June 1977, 1.

49. Harold Brown, "PRM-10 Force Posture Study," June 5 1977, 1.

50. PRM/NSC-10, "Military Strategy and Force Posture Review: Final Report," 8.

51. "US National Strategy (Presidential Directive/NSC-18)," August 24, 1977, 2.

52. Jimmy Carter, "Nuclear Weapons Employment Policy," PD/NSC-59, July 25, 1980, 2.

53. Ibid.

54. Summaries of interviews with Harold Brown and Andrew W. Marshall in *Soviet Intentions 1965–1985*, vol. 2, *Soviet Post–Cold War Testimonial Evidence*, by John G. Hines, Ellis M. Mishulovich, and John F. Shull (McLean, VA: BDM Federal, September 22, 1993), 13–14, 118.

55. Marshall in *Soviet Intentions 1965–1985*, by Hines, Mishulovich, and Shull, vol. 2, 18.

56. "US National Strategy (Presidential Directive/NSC-18)," August 24, 1977, 2.

57. A. W. Marshall, interview with Barry Watts and Andrew May, April 9, 2010.

58. Fritz W. Ermarth, "Contrasts in American and Soviet Strategic Thought," *International Security*, Autumn 1978, 138.

59. Jasper Welch, e-mail to Barry Watts, May 24, 2007.

60. Andrew W. Marshall, "Improving Analysis Methods for Strategic Forces," memorandum for the SecDef, April 17, 1979, 1.

61. Brown's handwritten comments on the OSD/NA's file copy of "Improving Analysis Methods for Strategic Forces."

62. Paul K. Davis and James A. Winnefeld, "The Rand Strategy Assessment Center: An Overview and Interim Conclusions about Utility and Development Options," RAND, R-2945-DNA, March 1983, v.

63. Barry D. Watts, "AWM Comments on the 1st Draft of Chapter I, Methodology Essay; RSAS," telephone discussion with A. W. Marshall, April 14, 2005, 3.

64. Bruce W. Bennett, "Project Description: Improving Methods of Strategic Analysis: Evolutionary Development of the RSAS," draft, September 13, 1988, 1.

65. Marshall, "Improving Analysis Methods for Strategic Forces," 1.

66. Bruce Bennett, "Reflecting Soviet Thinking in the Structure of Combat Models and Data," RAND, P-7108, April 1985, 4.

67. A. W. Marshall, letter to Paul K. Davis, December 20, 1985, 1.

68. Diego Ruiz-Palmer in Mie Augier and Barry D. Watts, "Conference Report on the Past, Present, and Future of Net Assessment," 2009, 83.

69. CAA, *Weapon Effectiveness Indices/Weighted Unit Values (WEI/WUV)*, vol. 2, *Basic Report*, April 1974, II-2, III-1. WEI/WUV II appeared in 1976, and WEI/WUV III in 1980.

70. Ibid., I-1.

71. ONA, "The Military Balance in Europe: A Net Assessment," March 1978 (declassified December 31, 1988), 48–49.

72. Phillip A. Karber, Grant Whitley, Mark Herman and Douglas Komer, "Assessing the Correlation of Forces: France 1940," BDM Corporation, BDM/W-79–560-TR, June 18, 1979.

73. Karber et al., *Assessing the Correlation of Forces: France 1940*, 4–9.

74. Paul K. Davis, "Influence of Trevor Dupuy's Research on the Treatment of Ground Combat in RAND's RSAS and JICM Models," *International TNDM Newsletter* 2, no. 4 (December 1988): 6–12.

75. Ibid., 2.

76. Andrew F. Krepinevich, "RAND Symposium—A Discussion with Dr. Vitaly Tsygichko," June 27, 1990, 1–2.

77. See Steven Zaloga, "Soviets Denigrate Their Own Capabilities," *Armed Forces Journal International*, July 1991, 18, 20.

78. Gerald Dunne in Augier and Watts, "The Past, Present, and Future of Net Assessment," 116.

79. Ibid., 118.

80. Gerry Dunne, "Cold War Net Assessment of US and USSR Military Command, Control and Communications (C3)," 2008, draft, unpublished.

81. Andrew W. Marshall, "Comparisons of US and SU Defense Expenditures," letter to Richard F. Kaufman, Joint Economic Committee of the US Congress, September 18, 1975, 2; also table A, 4.

82. Office of Soviet Analysis, CIA, "A Comparison of Soviet and US Gross National Products, 1960–83," SOV 84–10114, August 1984, 3, 5.

Chapter 7: Cold War End Game, 1981–1991

1. James Mann, *The Rebellion of Ronald Reagan: A History of the End of the Cold War* (New York: Viking, 2009), 23–24.

2. Ronald Reagan, speech to the House of Commons, June 8, 1982, available at http://www.fordham.edu/halsall/mod/1982reagan1.html, accessed October 10, 2013.

3. Ronald Reagan, "U.S. National Security Strategy," NSSD 32, May 20, 1982, 1, 2.

4. Peter W. Rodman, *Presidential Command*, 152.

5. Ronald Reagan, "U.S. Relations with the USSR," NSSD 75, January 17, 1983, 1.

6. Ronald Reagan, "Strategic Forces Modernization Program," NSDD 12, October 1, 1983, 1.

7. Reagan, "U.S. Relations with the USSR," NSSD 75, 7.

8. Douglas Brinkley, ed., *The Reagan Diaries* (New York: Harper, 2007), 135.

9. Pavil Podvig, ed., Oleg Bukharin, Timur Kadyshev, Eugene Miasnikov, Igor Sutyagin, Maxim Tarasenko, and Boris Zhelezov, *Russian Strategic Nuclear Forces* (Cambridge, MA, and London: MIT Press, 2001), 137, 218.

10. A. W. Marshall, "1981–1984," interview by Kurt Guthe, July 26, 1994, 7–46.

11. A. W. Marshall, "1985–1988," interview by Kurt Guthe, December 16, 1994, 8–22.

12. A. W. Marshall, "Long-Term Competition with the Soviets: A Framework for Strategic Analysis (U)," RAND R-862-PR, April 1972.

13. Marshall, "1981–1984," interview by Guthe, 7-15.

14. Ibid., 7-24.

15. William H. Taft IV, Deputy Secretary of Defense, "Director of Net Assessment," DoD Directive 5105.39, September 27, 1985, 1.

16. Ibid., 1–2.

17. A. W. Marshall, "Secretary of Defense/DCI Net Assessment," ONA memorandum for record, August 24, 1981, 1, 2.

18. A. W. Marshall, "A Program to Improve Analytic Methods Related to Strategic Forces, *Policy Sciences* 15, no. 1 (1982): 48.

19. Barry D. Watts, Notes from discussion with A. W. Marshall and Dmitry Ponomareff, October 17, 2003. US experts have generally been skeptical about the idea that there could be differences between the two sides over the physical effects of nuclear detonations.

20. Marshall, "1981–1984," interview by Guthe, 7-21.

21. NIE 11-3/8-83, "Soviet Capabilities for Strategic Nuclear Conflict, 1983–93," vol. 1, "Key Judgments and Summary," CIA, March 6, 1984, 1.

22. NIE 11-3/8-82, "Soviet Capabilities for Strategic Nuclear Conflict, 1982–92," vol. 1, "Key Judgments and Summary," CIA, February 1983, 5.

23. NIE 11-3/8-83, "Soviet Capabilities for Strategic Nuclear Conflict, 1983–93," vol. 1, 13.

24. John G. Hines, Ellis M. Mishulovich and John F. Shull, *Soviet Intentions 1965–1985*, Vol. II, *Soviet Post–Cold War Testimonial Evidence* (McLean, VA: BDM Federal, September 22, 1993), 5–6. At the time of this interview in February 1991 Akhromeyev was the personal national security adviser to Soviet president Mikhail Gorbachev.

25. Rick Atkinson, "Project Senior C.J.: The Story Behind the B-2 Bomber," *Washington Post*, October 8, 1989, A39.

26. Thomas B. Allen, "Run Silent, Run Deep," *Smithsonian Magazine*, March 2001, abstract at http://www.smithsonianmag.com/history-archaeology/sub-abstract.html.

27. Marshall, "1973–1980," interview by Guthe, 6-38.

28. A. W. Marshall, "How to Organize for Strategic Planning," memorandum for the deputy secretary of defense, April 6, 1981, 3.

29. Phillip Karber in Mie Augier and Barry D. Watts, "Conference Report on the Past, Present, and Future of Net Assessment," Center for Strategic & Budgetary Assessments, Contract HQ0034-07-D-1011-0006, 2009, 55.

30. Paul Bracken, *The Second Nuclear Age: Strategy, Danger, and the New Power Politics* (New York: Henry, Holt and Company, 2012), 88.

31. Phillip A. Karber, "Re: Net Assessment and Proud Prophet," e-mail to Barry Watts, September 7, 2008.

32. Karber in Augier and Watts, "Conference Report on the Past, Present, and Future of Net Assessment," 55.

33. Bracken, *The Second Nuclear Age*, 89.

34. Karber, "Re: Net Assessment and Proud Prophet."

35. General Bernard W. Rogers, interview by Anthony H. Cordesman and Benjamin E. Schemmer, *Armed Forces Journal International*, September 1983, 74.

36. OUSD/Comptroller, "National Defense Budget Estimates for FY 2014," May 2013, p. 92.

37. Ibid., 110.

38. Bill Keller, "Pentagon; Thinker-in-Residence Brought from Harvard," *New York Times*, August 15, 1985.

39. Caspar W. Weinberger, "US Defense Strategy," *Foreign Affairs*, Spring 1986, 681.

40. Bill Keller, "Pentagon; Passing the Cerebral Ammunition," *New York Times*, February 11, 1986.

41. David J. Andre, "New Competitive Strategies Tools and Methodologies," vol. 1, "Review of the Department of Defense Competitive Strategies Initiative 1986–1990," Science Application International Corporation, SAIC-90/1506, November 1990, 2.

42. Caspar W. Weinberger, *Annual Report to the Congress, Fiscal Year 1986* (Washington, DC: US Government Printing Office, February 5, 1986), 87.

43. Andre, "New Competitive Strategies Tools and Methodologies," 9.

44. A. W. Marshall, "Competitive Strategies—History and Background," March 3, 1988, 1.

45. Ibid., 2.

46. Caspar W. Weinberger, *Annual Report to the Congress, Fiscal Year 1988* (Washington, DC: US Government Printing Office, January 1, 1987), 65–66.

47. Andre, "New Competitive Strategies Tools and Methodologies," 13–14.

48. Ibid., 15.

49. Ibid., 29.

50. Ibid., 46.

51. Ibid., 36–37, 47, 52.

52. Charlie Pease and Kleber S. "Skid" Masterson, "The US-Soviet Strategic Balance: Supporting Analysis, a Retrospective," unpublished conference paper, September 30, 2008, 14. At the time Masterson, a navy admiral, had recently retired from the Joint Staff's Strategic Analysis and Gaming Agency.

53. Ibid., 10–12.

54. Ibid., 15. Assuming 90 percent effectiveness of each interceptor missile, firing two at an incoming missile or its warhead would yield an effectiveness of 99 percent. Yet even at this level, a hundred or more Soviet nuclear warheads would strike the United States in an all-out exchange. Moreover, the USSR could increase its nuclear forces at far less cost than the United States could offset them with more defenses, putting the United States on the wrong side of a cost-imposing strategy.

55. Ibid., 15.

56. Pease and Masterson, "The US Soviet Strategic Balance: Supporting Analysis, a Retrospective," Ibid. 15.

57. A typical example is Lieutenant Colonel Yu. Kardashevskiy, "Plan Fire Destruction of Targets by Fire Creatively," *Voennyi Vestnik* (Military Herald), July 1978, 64–67.

58. Pease and Masterson, "The US Soviet Strategic Balance: Supporting Analysis, a Retrospective," 16.

59. Robert M. Gates, *From the Shadows: The Ultimate Insider's Story of Five Presidents and How They Won the Cold War* (New York: Touchstone, 1996), 539.

60. Tom Z. Collina, "New START in Force; Missile Defense Looms," Arms Control Association, March 2011 available at http://www.armscontrol.org/act/2011_03/New START_MissileDefense, accessed on November 10, 2013.

61. Noel E. Firth and James H. Noren, *Soviet Defense Spending: A History of CIA Estimates, 1950–1990* (College Station, TX: Texas A&M University Press, 1998), 25.

62. Ibid., 21, 23.

63. Ibid., 25–26.

64. Ibid., 42.

65. CIA and DIA, "The Soviet Economy Under a New Leader," March 19, 1986, 6.

66. CIA, Office of Soviet Analysis (SOVA), "A Comparison of Soviet and US Gross National Products, 1960–83," SOV 84-10114, August 1984, 5.

67. A. W. Marshall, "Commentary," in Joint Economic Committee, Congress of the United States, *Gorbachev's Economic Plans*, vol. 1, *Study Papers* (Washington, DC: US Government Printing Office, 1987), 483.

68. A. W. Marshall, letter to Thomas C. Reed, September 27, 2001, 3.

69. David F. Epstein, "The Economic Cost of Soviet Security and Empire," in *The Impoverished Superpower: Perestroika and the Soviet Military Burden*, Henry S. ("Harry") Rowen and Charles Wolf Jr., eds. (San Francisco, CA: Institute for Contemporary Studies, 1990), 130–39, 153.

70. Firth and Noren, *Soviet Defense Spending*, table 5.10, 129–30.

71. Robert W. Campbell, *A Biobibliographical Dictionary of Russian and Soviet Economics* (London, Routledge, 2012), 37–39.

72. Igor Birman, "Who Is Stronger and Why?" *Crossroads*, Winter/Spring 1981, 117–26. A shorter version of this article, entitled "The Way to Slow Down the Arms Race," appeared in the *Washington Post* on October 27, 1980.

73. "Igor Birman," *The Telegraph*, June 8, 2011, available at http://www.telegraph.co.uk/news/obituaries/politics-obituaries/8564376/Igor-Birman.html, accessed November 11, 2013.

74. "Conversion of Soviet Military Industry: An Interview with Igor Birman," *Perspective* 1, no. 2, December 1990, available at http://www.bu.edu/iscip/vol1/Interview.html, accessed November 13, 2013.

75. A. W. Marshall, "Estimates of Soviet GNP and Military Burden," Memorandum for the Secretary of Defense Through the Assistant Secretary of Defense (ISA)," August 2, 1988. Carlucci succeeded Weinberger as defense secretary in 1987 and Richard Armitage was then the assistant secretary of defense (international security affairs).

76. Essays by these researchers can be found in Rowen and Wolf, *The Impoverished Superpower*. See especially 1–12, 127–154.

77. Marshall, "1985–1988," interview by Guthe, 8-35.

78. Herbert E. Meyer, "Why Is the World So Dangerous?" memorandum for the director of central intelligence, unclassified, NIC# 8640-83, November 30, 1983, 5.

79. Gates, *From the Shadows*, 564.

80. A. W. Marshall, letter to Richard Kaufman, Joint Economic Committee, September 18, 1975, 1.

81. "Commentary," in Joint Economic Committee, *Gorbachev's Economic Plans*, vol. 1, *Study Papers*, 484.

82. Marshall, letter to Thomas C. Reed, 2.

83. CIA and DIA, "Gorbachev's Modernization Program: A Status Report," DDB-1900-140-87, August 1987, 8.

84. S. Enders Wimbush in Augier and Watts, "Conference Report on the Past, Present, and Future of Net Assessment," unpublished, 2009, 84.

85. Wimbush in Augier and Watts, "Conference Report on the Past, Present, and Future of Net Assessment," 85. See also Alexander Alexiev and S. Enders Wimbush, "The Ethnic Factor in the Soviet Armed Forces: Historical Experience, Current Practices, and Implications for the Future—An Executive Summary," RAND R-2930/1, August 1983.

86. John H. Cushman Jr., "Applying Military Brain to Military Brawn, Again," *New York Times*, December 17, 1986, available at http://www.nytimes.com/1986/12/17/us /washington-talk-pentagon-applying-military-brain-to-military-brawn-again.html, accessed November 15, 2013.

87. Andrew W. Marshall and Charles Wolf Jr., *The Future Security Environment* (Washington, DC: DoD, October 1988), 26.

88. Report of the Commission on Integrated Long-Term Strategy, *Discriminate Deterrence*, January 11, 1988, 8.

89. Barry Watts, notes from a discussion with A. W. Marshall on CILTS, 1996.

90. Marshall, "1985–1988," interview by Guthe, 8-33.

91. Barry Watts, interview with Dmitry Ponomareff, May 27, 2003.

92. Joshua M. Epstein, "Dynamic Analysis and the Conventional Balance in Europe," *International Security*, Spring 1988, 154–65; John Mearsheimer, "Numbers, Strategy, and the European Balance," *International Security*, Spring 1988, 174–185; and Barry R. Posen, "Is NATO Decisively Outnumbered?" *International Security*, Spring 1988, 186–202.

93. Mearsheimer, "Numbers, Strategy, and the European Balance," 174.

94. Ibid., 184.

95. Posen, "Is NATO Decisively Outnumbered?," 187, 189.

96. Epstein, "Dynamic Analysis and the Conventional Balance in Europe," 163, 165.

97. The debate among the authors, and later with Eliot Cohen, would persist in several successive issues of *International Security*.

98. Eliot A. Cohen, "Toward Better Net Assessment: Rethinking the European Conventional Balance," *International Security*, Summer 1988, 50–89; and James G. Roche and Barry D. Watts, "Choosing Analytic Measures," *Strategic Studies*, June 1991, 165–209.

99. Cohen, "Toward Better Net Assessment: Rethinking the European Conventional Balance," 56.

100. Ibid., 55.

101. Waltz, "Thoughts on Virtual Arsenals," in *Nuclear Weapons in a Transformed World*, Michael J. Mazarr, ed. (New York: St. Martin's Press, 1997), 314–15.

102. Barry R. Posen, "Is NATO Decisively Outnumbered?," 189. The French withdrew from the alliance's military command in 1966, and all allied troops in France were

told to leave. Among other things, this significantly shifted—for the worse—NATO's ability to send Germany supplies and reinforcements, which would now have to arrive by sea much further forward in Belgium and the Netherlands. It also led to concerns regarding the reliability of French forces in time of war.

103. Eliot A. Cohen, "Toward Better Net Assessment: Rethinking the European Conventional Balance," 60.

104. John Mearsheimer, "Numbers, Strategy, and the European Balance," 175, 180.

105. Ibid., 181; and Barry R. Posen, "Is NATO Decisively Outnumbered?," 187.

106. Posen, "Is NATO Decisively Outnumbered?" 196.

107. Eliot A. Cohen, "Toward Better Net Assessment: Rethinking the European Conventional Balance," 76–77.

108. Ibid.

109. Ibid., 66.

110. Ibid., 200.

111. CIA, *Warsaw Pact Forces Opposite NATO*, NIE 11-14-79, vol. 2, *The Estimate*, January 31, 1979, IV-11.

112. CIA, *Warsaw Pact Air Forces: Support of Strategic Air Operations in Central Europe*, SOV 85-10001 CX, January 1985, iii.

113. Christopher J. Bowie, "How the West Would Have Won," *Air Force Magazine*, July 2007, accessed at http://www.airforcemag.com/MagazineArchive/Pages/2007/July%202007/0707west.aspx. During his service at Rand, Bowie wrote classified assessments of aspect of the NATO–Warsaw Pact air balance, and later served as the Air Force's senior civilian strategic planner.

114. John Mearsheimer, "Numbers, Strategy, and the European Balance," 176.

115. Robert McQuie, "Force Ratios," *Phalanx*, June 1993, 27.

116. Joshua M. Epstein, "Dynamic Analysis and the Conventional Balance in Europe," Spring 1988, 154.

117. Ibid., 159. However, Epstein was correct in arguing that Pentagon dynamic models, such as TACWAR, were based on the Lanchester attrition model. Skeptics of such modeling were hardly limited to ONA. In 1997 Krepinevich, then serving as a member of the National Defense Panel, asked the Marine Corps' General Charles Krulak for his reaction. Krulak responded: "Whenever I see TACWAR, I raise the 'Bullshit Flag.' We don't plan on fighting on a linear battlefield and we sure as hell don't plan on fighting a war of attrition."

118. F. W. Lanchester, *Aircraft in Warfare: The Dawn of the Fourth Arm* (London: Constable and Company, 1916), 39–53.

119. Robert McQuie, "Battle Outcomes: Casualty Rates as a Measure of Defeat," *Army*, November 1987, 33.

120. Roche and Watts, "Choosing Analytic Measures," 194. Their critique stems from the presentation of the Adaptive Dynamic Model in Joshua M. Epstein, *The Calculus of Conventional War: Dynamic Analysis Without Lanchester Theory* (Washington, DC: Brookings, 1985), 21–31.

121. Roche and Watts, "Choosing Analytic Measures," 185.

122. Roche and Watts, "Choosing Analytic Measures," 194.

123. Ibid., 194–95.

124. Andrew W. Marshall, *Problems of Estimating Military Power*, 9.

125. Mikhail Gorbachev, Speech to the United Nations General Assembly, December 7, 1988, available at http://legacy.wilsoncenter.org/coldwarfiles/files/Documents /1988-1107.Gorbachev.pdf, accessed November 6, 2013.

126. Barry Watts, "Soviet Assessments," notes from discussions with A. W. Marshall, September 23, 25, 2002, 2.

127. Mikhail Gorbachev, *Perestroika: New Thinking for our Country and the World* (New York: Harper and Row, 1987), 220, 234.

Chapter 8: The Military Revolution, 1991–2000

1. A. W. Marshall, Memorandum for Fred Iklé, "Future Security Environment Working Group: Some Themes for Special Papers and Some Concerns," September 21, 1987. In this memo, Marshall also voiced concerns regarding the long-term prospects for stability in Mexico, and the potentially huge affect of the AIDS epidemic were it not contained.

2. Ibid.

3. Marshal V. D. Sokolovskiy, chief ed., *Soviet Military Strategy*, Harriet Fast Scott, trans. (New York: Crane, Russak & Company, 3rd ed. 1975), 227. The second and third editions of *Soviet Military Strategy* appeared in 1963 and 1968.

4. Marshal N. V. Ogarkov, "The Defense of Socialism: Experience of History and the Present Day," *Red Star*, May 9, 1984, trans. FBIS, *Daily Report: Soviet Union*. 3, no. 091, annex no. 054 May 9, 1984, R19.

5. Marshall and Wolf, *The Future Security Environment*, 26. The working group included Eliot Cohen, David Epstein, Fritz Ermarth, Lawrence Gershwin, James Roche, Thomas Rona, Stephen Rosen, Dennis Ross, Notra Trulock, and Dov Zakheim.

6. Williamson Murray and Allan R. Millett, eds., *Military Effectiveness: vol. 2, The Interwar Period* (London: Unwin Hyman, 1988). Volumes 1 and 3 concerned World War I and World War II respectively.

7. Stephen Peter Rosen, *Winning the Next War* (Ithaca, NY: Cornell University Press, 1991). Rosen's book would be awarded the prestigious Furniss Award as the book making the "most outstanding contribution to security studies" for that year.

8. Andrew May, "Happy Birthday, Andy!" unpublished paper, 2011, 51.

9. Aaron Friedberg, "Happy Birthday, Andy!" unpublished paper, 2011, 20–21.

10. James March, "Happy Birthday, Andy!" unpublished paper, 2011, 43.

11. A. W. Marshall, "1989–1993," interview by Kurt Guthe, January 25, 1995, 9–14.

12. Andrew Krepinevich, meeting with Andrew Marshall, September 11, 1989.

13. The United States had first employed two F-117s in Operation Just Cause during December 1989 and January 1990, which deposed Panamanian dictator Manuel Noriega.

14. The Vietnam War saw the first widespread use of PGMs, with over 10,500 laser-guided bombs (LGBs) employed between February 1972 and February 1973. Barry D. Watts, *Six Decades of Guided Munitions and Battle Networks: Progress and Prospects* (Washington, DC: Center for Strategic and Budgetary Assessments, 2007), 9.

15. Defense Intelligence Agency, "Soviet Analysis of Operation Desert Shield and Operation Desert Storm," trans. LN 006–92, October 28, 1991, p. 32.

16. Thomas A. Keaney and Eliot A. Cohen, *Revolution in War? Air Power in the Persian Gulf* (Annapolis, MD: Naval Institute Press, 1995), 212.

17. Thomas Mahnken and James FitzSimonds, "Strategic Management Issues," memorandum for record, August 26, 2001. Krepinevich thought a fundamental question would center on the difference between using emerging military technologies to enhance existing forms of warfare, which he referred to as "innovation," as opposed to displacing these forms of operation to bring about a major discontinuity, or "transformation," in the character of warfare.

18. Kendall, a West Point graduate, would later go on to serve as the undersecretary of defense for acquisition, technology and logistics, replacing Ashton Carter in October 2011.

19. Project Checkmate was formed in the 1970s by General David Jones to provide candid assessments by experienced operators of how a NATO–Warsaw Pact conflict might playout. Warden was viewed by many as a latter-day Billy Mitchell—a brilliant, forward-thinking air power theorist who also had a habit of rubbing people the wrong way.

20. Andrew F. Krepinevich, MTR working group meeting, August 1, 1991.

21. Andrew F. Krepinevich, meetings with Andrew Marshall, August 26 and 28, 1991.

22. Moore's "law" is the observation, first made by Gordon E. Moore in 1965, that since the invention of the integrated circuit in the late 1950s, the number of transistors that can be squeezed onto an integrated circuit or microchip had doubled roughly every two years. As of 2011 Moore's "law" continued to hold.

23. Andrew F. Krepinevich, Meeting at DARPA, November 22, 1991.

24. Andrew F. Krepinevich, meeting with Andrew Marshall, January 14, 1991.

25. Formally known as the Treaty on the Final Settlement with Respect to Germany, it was signed by Britain, France, the USSR, the United States, and the two Germanies on September 12, 1990. It stipulated that no foreign armed forces, nuclear weapons, or carriers for nuclear weapons would be stationed or deployed in the six states composing the former East Germany, or in Berlin. In accordance with the treaty, all Russian forces were withdrawn by August 1994.

26. Stephen Peter Rosen, "New Ways of War: Understanding Military Innovation," *International Security* 13, no. 2, Fall 1988, 134.

27. Ibid., 135.

28. Stephen Peter Rosen, *Winning the Next War*, 6.

29. Ibid., 21.

30. Ibid., 251.

31. Ibid., 252.

32. Ibid., 252.

33. Andrew F. Krepinevich Jr., *The Military-Technical Revolution: A Preliminary Assessment* (Washington, DC: Center for Strategic and Budgetary Assessments, 2002), 3. This published version of the July 1992 assessment will henceforth be cited as Krepinevich, *The Military-Technical Revolution: A Preliminary Assessment*, July 1992. Updated versions will be cited as unpublished ONA papers with their dates.

34. Krepinevich, *The Military-Technical Revolution: A Preliminary Assessment*, July 1992, 3.

35. Ibid., 20.

36. Ibid.

37. Andrew J. Krepinevich Jr., "The Military-Technical Revolution: A Preliminary Assessment," unpublished OSNA paper, July 1993, 7.

38. Anti-access capabilities are those that deny access to major fixed-point targets, especially large forward bases, whereas area-denial capabilities threaten mobile targets over an area of operations, including maritime forces, such as aircraft carrier battle groups. See Andrew Krepinevich, Barry Watts, and Robert Work, *Meeting the Anti-Access and Area-Denial Challenge* (Washington, DC: Center for Strategic and Budgetary Assessments, 2003); and Christopher J. Bowie, *The Anti-Access Threat and Theater Air Bases* (Washington, DC: Center for Strategic and Budgetary Assessments, 2002).

39. A. W. Marshall, comments at a workshop on a mature precision-strike regime, July 17, 2012.

40. Andrew F. Krepinevich Jr., "The Military-Technical Revolution: A Preliminary Assessment," unpublished paper, July 1993, 30.

41. Ibid.

42. Ibid.

43. Admiral William A. Owens, "Systems-of-Systems: US' Emerging Dominant Battlefield Awareness Promises to Dissipate the 'Fog of War,'" *Armed Forces Journal International*, January 1996, 47. At the time, Owens was vice chairman of the Joint Chiefs of Staff.

44. Commander Jan van Tol, "Brief on Early RMA Gaming Insights," prepared for the Joint Requirements Oversight Council, OSD/NA, July 14, 1995.

45. Krepinevich, "The Military-Technical Revolution: A Preliminary Assessment," July 1993, 27–28.

46. A. W. Marshall, "Some Thoughts on Military Revolutions—Second Version," OSD/NA memorandum for the record, August 23, 1993, 3–4.

47. Krepinevich, *The Military-Technical Revolution: A Preliminary Assessment*, July 1992, 56.

48. Ibid., 57.

49. Marshall, "1989–1993," interview by Guthe, 9–15.

50. Other attendees included several retired flag officers, including General Larry Welch, who had preceded McPeak as the Air Force's chief of staff, and Wolfowitz's military assistant, Captain Lynn Wells.

51. The account of the November 11 meeting is based on Krepinevich's notes, compiled on that day, and a summary provided to Marshall by SAIC, a consulting firm. Ron C. St. Martin and Leine E. Whittington, "The Military Technical Revolution: Opportunities for Innovation," Draft Report, Science Applications International Corporation, January 25, 1993.

52. The policy essentially declared that military personnel would be judged on their suitability for service, not on their sexual orientation provided that orientation was not manifested by homosexual conduct.

53. Andrew F. Krepinevich, meeting with Andrew Marshall and Clark Murdock, March 18, 1993.

54. Andrew F. Krepinevich, meeting with Andrew Marshall and Clark Murdock, March 22, 1993.

55. Andrew F. Krepinevich, meeting with Ted Warner, March 26, 1993.

56. Andrew F. Krepinevich, meeting with Ted Warner, May 21, 1993.

57. William J. Perry, "Desert Storm and Deterrence," *Foreign Affairs*, Fall 1991, 66–82.

58. William J. Perry, "Defense in an Age of Hope," *Foreign Affairs*, November–December 1996, 64–79. Absent from Perry's 1991 and 1996 *Foreign Affairs* articles was any sense of a competition—in regard to adversaries' reaction to a US advantage, or what the United States should do if rivals acquired similar advantages.

59. A. W. Marshall, "Some Thoughts on Military Revolutions," OSD/NA memorandum for the record, July 27, 1993, 4.

60. Ibid., 1.

61. Ibid., 2.

62. Ibid., 3.

63. Ibid.

64. Ibid., 4.

65. Ibid.

66. Theodor W. Galdi, "Revolution in Military Affairs? Competing Concepts, Organizational Responses, Outstanding Issues," Congressional Research Service, 95–1170 F, December 11, 1995, 10, available at http://www.fas.org/man/crs/95–1170.htm, accessed March 2014.

67. Ibid.

68. After Krepinevich's 1993 assessment, the next balance completed by Marshall's staff appears to have been one of undersea warfare in 1998; however, it is unclear whether it was forwarded to William Cohen, who replaced Perry as defense secretary in January 1997, at the beginning of the second Clinton administration.

69. Williamson R. Murray and Allan R. Millett, eds., "Military Innovation in Peacetime," in *Military Innovation in the Interwar Period* (New York and Cambridge: Cambridge University Press, 1996), 414.

70. Ibid., 415.

71. Admiral William A. Owens, "JROC: Harnessing the Revolution in Military Affairs," *Joint Force Quarterly*, Summer 1994, 55–57.

72. Admiral William A. Owens, "The Emerging US System-of-Systems," *Strategic Forum*, Institute for National Strategic Studies, National Defense University, No. 63, February 1996; available at http://www.ndu.edu/inss/strforum/SF_63/forum63.html, accessed May 2, 2014. For an especially interesting critique of Owens's system-of-systems notion, see Lieutenant General (Ret.) Paul K. Van Riper and Lieutenant Colonel F. G. Hoffman, "Pursuing the Real Revolution in Military Affairs: Exploiting Knowledge-Based Warfare," *National Security Studies Quarterly*, Summer 1998, 1–7.

73. Chairman of the Joint Chiefs of Staff (CJCS), *Joint Vision 2010*, July 1996, 13.

74. Ibid. *Joint Vision 2020*, which appeared in May 2000, was even more adamant that Clausewitzian friction is inherent in military operations and it sources cannot be eliminated.

75. See Admiral William A. Owens with Ed Offley, *Lifting the Fog of War* (New York: Farrar Straus Giroux, 2000), 12–15.

76. Barry D. Watts, *Clausewitzian Friction and Future War* (Revised Edition), McNair Paper Number 68 (Washington, DC: National Defense University Institute for National

Security Studies, 2004). The first edition of *Clausewitzian Friction and Future War* was McNair Paper 52 published in 1996.

77. A. W. Marshall, taped interview with Barry D. Watts, January 9, 2006.

78. Ibid.

79. For details on the RMA essay contest, see *Joint Force Quarterly*, Spring 1994, 31; and *Joint Force Quarterly*, Summer 1994, 58.

80. See Jan M. van Tol, "Military Innovation and Carrier Aviation—The Relevant History," *Joint Force Quarterly*, Summer 1997, 77–87; and Jan M. van Tol, "Military Innovation and Carrier Aviation—An Analysis," *Joint Force Quarterly*, Winter 1997–98, 97–109.

81. James FitzSimonds, memo Jan van Tol commenting on van Tol's "Brief on Early RMA Gaming Insights," July 17, 1995, For an overview of RMA war gaming through the late 1990s, see William J. Hurley, Dennis J. Gleeson, Jr., Col. Stephen J. McNamara and Joel B. Resnick, "Summaries of Recent Futures Wargames," Joint Advanced Warfighting Program, Institute for Defense Analyses, October 21, 1998.

82. From 2007 to 2011 Vickers was the first and only assistant secretary of defense for special operations/low-intensity & interdependent capabilities (ASD SO/LIC&IC).

83. George Crile, *Charlie Wilson's War: The Extraordinary Story of the Largest Covert Operation in American History* (New York: Atlantic Monthly Press, 2003).

84. Upon retiring, Krepinevich became director of an organization called the Defense Budget Project (DBP). Drawing upon what he had learned from Marshall during his service in ONA, he recast it into the Center for Strategic and Budgetory Assessments to address issues of strategic importance.

85. The Fellows program was established in DoD Directive 1322.23, September 2, 1995.

86. A. W. Marshall, "The Character of Future Net Assessments," memorandum for distribution, June 10, 1996, 1.

87. Ibid., 3.

88. Ibid., 4.

Chapter 9: The Pivot to the Asia-Pacific Region, 2001–2014

1. A. W. Marshall, "The Character of Future Net Assessments," 2.

2. Marshall, "The Character of Future Net Assessment," 4.

3. Andrew May, e-mail to Barry Watts, August 23, 2002.

4. A. W. Marshall, "Further Thoughts on Future Net Assessments," OSD/NA memorandum, May 9, 2000 (revised September 11, 2000), 2.

5. Marshall, "Further Thoughts on Future Net Assessments," 3.

6. Besides Marshall and Watts, the participants included: Aaron Friedberg (Princeton University), Karl Hasslinger (General Dynamics Electric Boat), Andrew Krepinevich (CSBA), Bob Martinage (CSBA), Andrew May (SAIC), Chip Pickett (Northrop Grumman), Steve Rosen (Harvard University) and Jan van Tol (OSD/NA). Invited but unable to attend were Eliot Cohen, Gene Durbin (who provided inputs via e-mail), and Jaymie Durnan (then Deputy Secretary of Defense Paul Wolfowitz's special assistant).

7. Barry Watts, transcript excerpts from the ONA workshop on the future role and focus of the Office of Net Assessment, March 11, 2003, 25.

8. A. W. Marshall, "Refocusing Net Assessment for the Future," OSD/NA memorandum for distribution, June 10, 2004, 2–3.

9. Ibid., 3–4.

10. Donald Rumsfeld, *Known and Unknown: A Memoir*, 293.

11. A. W. Marshall, "Defense Strategy Review (Short Outline)," February 23, 2001, 2.

12. Barry Watts, notes from a telephone conversation with Karl Hasslinger, March 22, 2001.

13. Ibid.

14. Marshall, "Defense Strategy Review (Short Outline)," 2.

15. Marshall and Roche, "Strategy for Competing with the Soviets in the Military Sector of the Continuing Political-Military Competition," 9–10.

16. C. K. Prahalad and Gary Hamel, "The Core Competence of the Corporation," *Harvard Business Review*, May–June 1990, 83.

17. Andrew May in Watts, "Transcript Excerpts from the OSD/NA Workshop on the Future Role and Focus of the Office of Net Assessment," March 11, 2003, 22.

18. Marshall, "Defense Strategy Review (Short Outline)," 2.

19. Barry Watts, notes from discussion with A. W. Marshall and Andrew May, March 18, 2003.

20. Barry D. Watts, "Barriers to Acting Strategically: Why Strategy Is So Difficult," in *Developing Competitive Strategies for the 21st Century: Theory, History, and Practice*, Thomas G. Mahnken, ed. (Stanford, CA: Stanford University Press, 2012), 50, 52–53.

21. Patrick E. Tyler, "U.S. Strategy Plan Calls for Insuring No Rivals Develop: A One-Superpower World," *New York Times*, March 8, 1992.

22. Eric Edelman, "The Strange Career of the 1992 Defense Planning Guidance," in *In Uncertain Times: American Foreign Policy after the Berlin Wall and 9/11*, by Melvyn P. Leffler and Jeffrey W. Legro (Ithaca, NY: Cornell University Press, 2011), 65.

23. Tyler, "U.S. Strategy Plan Calls for Insuring No Rivals Develop: A One-Superpower World."

24. Edelman, "The Strange Career of the 1992 Defense Planning Guidance," 64.

25. "Defense Planning Guidance, FY 1994–1999," draft March 20, 1992, declassified December 10, 2007, 3, 5.

26. DoD, "Quadrennial Defense Review Report," September 30, 2001, iv, 12. For more comprehensive account of dissuasion as a strategy, see Andrew F. Krepinevich and Robert C. Martinage, *Dissuasion Strategy* (Washington, DC: Center for Strategic and Budgetary Assessments, 2008), 1–6.

27. Aaron L. Friedberg, "The Struggle for Mastery in Asia," *Commentary*, November 2000, 26.

28. Andrew W. Marshall, "Near Term Actions to Begin Shift of Focus Towards Asia," OSD/NA memo for the secretary of defense, May 2, 2002, 1.

29. Ibid., 2.

30. US-China Economic and Security Review Commission, *2011 Report to Congress*, 112th Congress, First Session, November 2011, 182–93.

31. John A. Battilega, "Soviet Military Art: Some Major Asymmetries Important to Net Assessment," unpublished paper presented at the March 28–29, 2008, conference "Net Assessment: Past, Present, and Future."

32. Michael Pillsbury, ed., *Chinese Views of Future Warfare* (Washington, DC: National Defense University Press, rev. ed. 1998), xvii.

33. Ibid., xxxiv, xlii.

34. Ibid., 317.

35. Ibid., 326.

36. Yuan Wenxian, chief ed., 联合战役信息作战教程 [Lectures on Joint Campaign Information Operations] (Beijing: National Defense University Press, November 2009, 1–11; Bryan Krekel, Patton Adams, and George Bakos, *Occupying the Information High Ground: Chinese Capabilities for Computer Network Operations and Cyber Espionage* (Washington: Northrop Grumman Corporation, March 7, 2012), 14–20.

37. Information Office of the State Council, PRC, "The Diversified Employment of China's Armed Forces," April 2013, section 2, available at http://eng.mod.gov.cn/Database /WhitePapers/index.htm, accessed August 13, 2013.

38. Mark A. Stokes and Ian Easton, "The Chinese People's Liberation Army General Staff: Evolving Organization and Missions," unpublished draft November 26, 2012, 15, 19, 26.

39. Pillsbury, *China Debates the Future Security Environment* (Washington, DC: NDV Press, 2000), xv, 67–68.

40. Ibid., xxxv.

41. François Jullien, *A Treatise on Efficacy: Between Western and Chinese Thinking*, trans. by Janet Lloyd (Honolulu: University of Hawai'i Press, 2004), 15.

42. Ibid., 17.

43. Aaron L. Friedberg, "A History of the US Strategic Doctrine—1945–1980," *Journal of Strategic Studies*, December 1980, 37–71.

44. Aaron L. Friedberg, *The Weary Titan: Britain and the Experience of Relative Decline, 1895–1905* (Princeton and Oxford: Princeton University Press, 1988), 305.

45. Ibid., xv.

46. Aaron L. Friedberg, *A Contest for Supremacy: China, American, and the Struggle for Mastery in Asia* (New York: W. W. Norton, 2011), xii.

47. Ibid., xiii–xiv.

48. Ibid., xv; and Aaron L. Friedberg, "The Struggle for Mastery in Asia," 17.

49. Friedberg, *A Contest for Supremacy: China, American, and the Struggle for Mastery in Asia*, 144.

50. Timothy L. Thomas, *Three Faces of the Cyber Dragon: Cyber Peace Activist, Spook, Hacker* (Fort Leavenworth, KS: Foreign Military Studies Office, 2012), xiv, 66, 73, 89, 117, 119 223–35; Pillsbury, *China Debates the Future Security Environment*, xviii, 297, 299.

51. Admiral Jonathan Greenert and General Mark Welsh, "Breaking the Kill Chain: How to Keep American in the Game When Our Enemies Are Trying to Shut Us Out," *Foreign Policy*, May 16, 2013, available at http://www.foreignpolicy.com/articles/2013/05/16 /breaking_the_kill_chain_air_sea_battle?page=0,0, accessed February 18, 2014.

52. Donald Rumsfeld, *Quadrennial Defense Review Report*, February 6, 2006, 3, 9–10. 29–31, 32–33.

53. A. W. Marshall, handwritten notes for a dinner talk to the Chicago Council on Global Affairs, June 2, 2008, 1–2.

Conclusion

1. A. W. Marshall, "Net Assessment in the Department of Defense," ONA memo for record, September 21, 1976, 1.

2. A. W. Marshall, "1973–1980," interview by Kurt Guthe, April 9, 1994, 6–41, 6–42.

3. "The Man Who Showed Why Firms Exist," *The Economist*, September 7, 2013, 13–14.

4. Noel E. Firth and James H. Noren, *Soviet Defense Spending: A History of CIA Estimates, 1950–1990* (College Station, TX: Texas A&M University Press, 1998), 10.

5. A. W. Marshall, "Themes," interview by Kurt Guthe, September 24, 1993, 10–3.

6. "Soviet Death Rate Rising; Alcoholism, Influenza Blamed," *Gadsden Times*, August 31, 1982, 8.

7. James R. Schlesinger, "Uses and Abuses of Systems Analysis" in James R. Schlesinger, "Selected Papers on National Security 1964–1968," RAND P-5284, September 1974, 107.

8. Ibid., 116.

9. A. W. Marshall, "Early 1950s," interview by Kurt Guthe, September 16, 1993, 4–7.

10. Marshall, "Themes," interview by Guthe, 10–6.

11. Herbert Simon, "Rational Choice and the Structure of the Environment," (*Psychological Review* 63, no. 2, 1956): 129.

12. Lionel Tiger and Robin Fox, *The Imperial Animal* (New Brunswick and London, Transaction Publishers, 1998), 17 (originally published in 1971 by Holt, Rinehart and Winston).

13. Daniel Kahneman, "Maps of Bounded Rationality: A Perspective on Intuitive Judgment and Choice," Nobel Prize Lecture, December 8, 2002, in *Nobel Prizes 2002: Nobel Prizes, Presentations, Biographies, & Lectures*, ed. Tore Frängsmyr (Stockholm: Almquiest & Wiksell, 2003), 449.

14. Amos Tversky and Daniel Kahneman, "Judgment Under Uncertainty: Heuristics and Biases," *Science* 185, no. 4157, September 27, 1974, 1130.

15. Robin Fox, "Aggression Then and Now" in *Man and Beast Revisited*, ed. Michael H. Robinson and Lionel Tiger (Washington and London: Smithsonian Institution Press, 1991), 92.

16. Robin Fox, "Fatal Attraction: War and Human Nature," *National Interest*, Winter 1992/93, 20.

17. Douglass North, *Understanding the Process of Economic Change* (Princeton, NJ, and Oxford, UK: Princeton University Press, 2005), 19, 69.

18. Neil deGrasse Tyson, *Death by Black Holes and Other Cosmic Quandaries* (New York and London: W. W. Norton, 2007), 249–52.

19. Martin Shubik, "Terrorism, Technology, and the Socioeconomics of Death," *Comparative Strategy* 16, 1997, 406–8.

20. Pierre Wack, "Scenarios: Unchartered Waters Ahead," *Harvard Business Review*, September–October 1985, 73, 75; and Wack, "Scenarios: Shooting the Rapids," *Harvard Business Review*, November–December 1985, 10–11, 14. Kahn's 1965 *On Escalation:*

Metaphors and Scenarios is widely cited as the origins of scenario planning. In mid-1973 the price of a barrel of oil was $2.90; by December the Organization of Oil Exporting Countries (OPEC) was demanding $11.65. Daniel Yergin, *The Prize: The Epic Quest for Oil, Money & Power* (New York: The Free Press, 1991), 607.

21. Peter Schwartz, *The Art of the Long View: Planning for the Future in an Uncertain World* (New York: Doubleday Currency, 1991), 3.

22. Marshall, "Themes," interview by Guthe, 10–14, 15.

23. Firth and Noren, *Soviet Defense Spending: A History of CIA Estimates, 1950–1990*, 59.

24. CIA/DIA "Gorbachev's Modernization Program: A Status Report," DDB-1900–140–87, August 1987, 8.

25. A. W. Marshall, letter to Richard Kaufman, Joint Economic Committee, US Congress, September 10, 1975, 1.

26. Barry Watts, notes from a discussion with A. W. Marshall, April 4, 1988, 3.

27. Donald Rumsfeld, *Known and Unknown: A Memoir*, 224–25.

28. Donald H. Rumsfeld, *Annual Report to the President and the Congress*, 2002, 2.

29. A. W. Marshall, OSD/NA memorandum for Fred Iklé, September 21, 1987, 3.

30. "Secretary Rumsfeld Delivers Major Speech on Transformation," National Defense University, January 31, 2002, available at http://www.au.af.mil/au/awc/awcgate /dod/transformation-secdef-31jan02.htm, accessed January 27, 2014.

31. OSD, "Annual Report to Congress: Military and Security Developments Involving the People's Republic of China 2013," i, 32–33.

32. Michael Pillsbury, *China Debates the Future Security Environment*. See also, Michael Pillsbury, ed., *Chinese Views of Future Warfare* (Washington, DC: National Defense University Press, 1998).

33. See Air-Sea Battle Office, "Air-Sea Battle: Service Collaboration to Address Anti-Access & Area Denial Challenges," May 2013, available at http://navylive.dodlive.mil /files/2013/06/ASB-ConceptImplementation-Summary-May-2013.pdf, accessed June 7, 2013.

34. Barack Obama, "Sustaining US Global Leadership: Priorities for 21st Century Defense," January 2012, 2.

INDEX